C0-AVD-982

Pending Legislation Alert

As this book goes to press (June 1996), Congress is considering a number of changes in the laws affecting IRA and retirement plan distributions. Several of these proposals have been considered in prior years; nevertheless these -- or other changes -- could be enacted at any time. A summary of these proposals is provided here to alert readers to the necessity of checking on the current status of any tax rule before acting.

1.   The 15% excise tax on "excess distributions" (see Chapter 5) may be suspended temporarily (possibly for the three years 1996-1998). The effect of this change, if enacted, would be to enable participants to withdraw unlimited amounts from their retirement plans during the "window" period, without being subject to any tax other than the ordinary income tax on such withdrawals. Whether it is desirable to make large withdrawals to take advantage of this opportunity needs to be considered carefully in each case. See the *Valdez* and *Levine* case studies in Chapter 10. As currently written, the proposal would *not* suspend the 15% excise tax on "excess accumulations" that applies at death.

2.   "Five year forward averaging" (see Chapter 2) would be eliminated for distributions after 1998. "Ten year forward averaging" and "20% capital gain treatment" would be continued for those individuals who now qualify for it.

3.   The "minimum distribution rules" (see Chapter 1) would be modified by changing the definition of "required beginning date" for qualified retirement plans (but not IRAs). Under the proposal, a participant could postpone retirement distributions until actual retirement, even if that were later than age 70½. This option would not be available to participants who owned more than 5% of the sponsoring employer, or to IRA participants. Essentially this proposal would extend to all qualified plan participants (other than 5% owners) the option now allowed to certain "grandfathered" individuals (see "*The hardworking aged non-5% owners*" in Chapter 7). For planning implications of this change, see discussion in Chapter 7.

Life and Death Planning
for Retirement Benefits

The Essential Handbook for Estate Planners

Natalie B. Choate

Ataxplan Publications, Boston, Massachusetts

Second Edition, Completely Revised
First Paperback Edition

Life and Death Planning for Retirement Benefits

The Essential Handbook for Estate Planners

By Natalie B. Choate

Published by: Ataxplan Publications
Post Office Box 1093-W
Boston, Massachusetts 02103-1093

Library of Congress Cataloging-in-Publication Data
Choate, Natalie B.
Life and Death Planning for Retirement Benefits: The Essential Handbook for Estate Planners / Natalie B. Choate
      p.   cm.
Includes bibliographical references and index.

ISBN 0-9649440-0-6

1. Estate planning - United States. 2. Tax planning - United States. 3. Retirement income - Taxation - United States. 4. Inheritance and transfer tax - United States. I. Choate, Natalie B. II. Title

KF 6585 .C43 1996

To my mother

Jhan English Choate

who has had to put up with a lot

Warning and Disclaimer

The rules applicable to qualified retirement plan benefits and IRAs are among the most complex in the tax code. I have read few works on this subject that were, in my view, completely accurate; in fact most that I have seen, including, unfortunately, earlier incarnations of this work, contain errors. Furthermore, even accurate information can become outdated quickly as IRS or Congressional policy shifts. Despite my best efforts, it is likely that this book, too, contains errors. Citations are provided so that estate planning practitioners can check any statements made in this book and reach their own conclusions regarding what the law is. --*The author.*

This book is intended to provide general information regarding the tax and other laws applicable to retirement benefits, and to provide suggestions regarding appropriate estate planning actions for different situations. It is not intended as a substitute for the practitioner's own research, or for the advice of a qualified estate planning specialist. The author and publisher shall have neither liability nor responsibility to any person or entity with respect to any loss or damage caused, or alleged to be caused, directly or indirectly by the information contained in this book.

If you do not wish to be bound by the above, you may return this book to the publisher for a full refund.

Summary of Contents

Introduction 1

1   The Minimum Distribution Rules 9

2   Income Tax Issues 65

3   Marital Matters 103

4   Retirement Benefits and the Non-Citizen Spouse 138

5   The 15% Excise Tax 174

6   Life Insurance in the Retirement Plan 201

7   The Grandfathers 223

8   Disclaimers of Retirement Benefits 241

9   Other Topics 265

10 Case Studies 283

Appendix A - Tables 330
Appendix B - Forms 335
Appendix C - Checklists 391
Appendix D - Software Available 417

Bibliography 420

Glossary 426

Index 431

Table of Contents

INTRODUCTION 1

Are Retirement Plans the "Worst" Assets? 1
Limitations of this Book 2
Explanation of Terms Used 3
Other Hints for Using this Book 4
Abbreviations Used in this Book 6
Acknowledgments 7

CHAPTER 1 - THE MINIMUM DISTRIBUTION RULES . . . 9

Introduction 9

Death before the RBD: The Five Year Rule 10
The five year rule and its exceptions 11
The importance of having a "designated beneficiary" 12
Naming an individual as beneficiary 14
Naming the spouse as beneficiary 16
Naming more than one beneficiary 16
The pitfall of naming multiple beneficiaries 17
Naming a trust: how to 19
Naming a trust: benefits of 23
Naming an estate as beneficiary 24
Cleanup strategies -- death before the RBD 24

Lifetime Distribution Rules: The Required Beginning Date . . 26
The RBD (required beginning date) 26
Naming the spouse as beneficiary 28
Naming a non-spouse individual as beneficiary 29
Naming a trust as beneficiary 29
Four ways to deal with "irrevocable trust" rule 31
Naming an estate as beneficiary 34

Recalculating Life Expectancies: Participant and Spouse 35
How recalculation works 35
Which method is best? 36
Mechanics of making this election 38

Naming a Non-Spouse DB: The Incidental Benefit (MDIB) Rule 39
   Application during participant's life 39
   The "flip" at participant's death 40
   Whether to recalculate life expectancy: when a non-spouse is the DB 41

Changing the DB After 70½ 43
   Changing DBs after the RBD 43
   Changing DBs after age 70½ but before the RBD 47

How to Compute Life Expectancy and Installments 48
   Determining the participant's life expectancy 48
   Installments over P's LE -- term certain method 49
   Installments over P's LE -- recalculation method   51
   Determining the account balance the fraction applies to 53
   Installments over joint LE of P and S - fixed term method 53
   P and S -- both LEs recalculated annually 54
   P and S -- "split" method -- only one spouse's LE is recalculated 55
   Participant and non-spouse: the MDIB rule 56
   P dies before RBD: installments over DB's LE 58

From Which Plan Do Distributions Come? 59
   Notice 88-38 allows participants and beneficiaries to choose which IRA MRDs come out of 59
   What you can't do 61

Summary of Planning Principles 62

CHAPTER 2 - INCOME TAX ISSUES 65

Introduction 65

Income in Respect of a Decedent 65
   No stepped up basis 65
   The drawback of making IRD payable to a trust 66

Tax treatment of IRD paid to an estate 68
IRD payable to non-charitable trust 70
IRD payable to charity 70
Planning pitfall: "assignment" of IRD 71

Deduction for Estate Taxes Paid on IRD 76
How the deduction is calculated 76
Who gets the deduction 78
Do you "back out" the excess accumulations tax in computing the
S. 691(c) deduction? 78
S. 691(c) deduction for installment and annuity payouts 79
S. 691(c) deduction and charitable remainder trusts 81
S. 691(c) deduction on the income tax return 82

Lump Sum Distributions: The Requirements 83
Introduction 83
First hurdle: type of plan 84
Second hurdle: "reason" for distribution 85
Third hurdle: participant must be age 59½ or older 86
Fourth hurdle: only one use per customer 87
Fifth hurdle: distribution of entire balance in one taxable year . 87
Sixth hurdle: the five year requirement 91
Seventh hurdle: no prior rollovers 92
Eighth hurdle: type of recipient 93
Ninth hurdle: the election 93

Lump Sum Distributions: the Rewards 93
Introduction 93
Deduction from gross income 94
15% excise tax on excess distributions 95
Five year forward averaging 95
Ten year forward averaging 96
20% capital gain rate 96
Capital gain: what is an "active participant?" 97
Tax on OIP when there is a capital gain portion 99

Rollovers 99
In general 99
No rollover of minimum required distributions 101

Summary of Planning Principles 102

CHAPTER 3 - MARITAL MATTERS 103

Introduction 103
  Advantages of Leaving Benefits to the Surviving Spouse 104
  Estate tax 104
  15% excise tax 104
  Income tax 105

Spousal Rollovers 105
  Advantages of spousal rollover 105
  Drawbacks of spousal rollover 106
  Requirements for spousal rollover 108
  A minimum required distribution cannot be rolled over 110
  No time deadline for spousal rollover 111
  Rollover (or spousal election) for inherited IRA 112
  How does S elect to treat the deceased spouse's IRA as her
  own? 113
  What if S dies before rolling over? 114
  What if S is already over 70½ when she inherits the benefits? 115
  Rollover when S inherits benefits through an estate 116
  Rollover when S inherits benefits through a trust   117
  More on "pass-through" rollovers 118

The Spouse and S. 401(a)(9) 119
  Additional minimum distribution options available when S is
  the DB 119
  Which is better--rollover, or deferring distributions until P
  would have reached 70½? 120
  Benefits paid to a marital trust 121

Marital Deduction for Benefits Payable to QTIP Trust 122
  Non-tax reasons to name a QTIP trust 122
  How to qualify for the marital deduction when retirement
  benefits are payable to a QTIP trust 123
  "Income" requirement of marital trusts: general power trusts . 125
  "Income" requirement: QTIP trusts 127
  Practitioner response to Rev. Rul. 89-89 127

Income Tax Disadvantages When QTIP Trust is Beneficiary 129
    Loss of deferral during S's life: mandatory income
    distributions 129
    Loss of income tax deferral -- s. 401(a)(9) 131
    High trust tax rates 132
    Avoiding income tax on funding a marital trust 132

Simultaneous Death Clauses 132
    Uniform Simultaneous Death Law 132
    If P dies before age 70½ 133
    If P dies after the 70½ year 135
    Plan provisions 136

REA '84 and Spousal Consent 136

Summary of Planning Principles 137

**CHAPTER 4 - RETIREMENT BENEFITS AND THE
NON-CITIZEN SPOUSE** 138

Introduction 138

**Modified Marital Deduction for Transfers to a Non-Citizen
Spouse** 138
    How the "modified marital deduction" works 138
    "QDOTs" and other ways to qualify for the modified marital
    deduction 140

Distinguishing Features of a QDOT 141
    The five requirements 141
    Marital trust - QDOT created by decedent 142
    QDOT created by surviving spouse 143
    Payment of deferred estate tax by QDOT 144

Interplay of Income Tax and Deferred Estate Tax 144
    Income tax paid by S on plan distributions 145
    No 691(c) deduction for deferred estate tax 146
    Income taxes paid by the QDOT 147
    Income taxes on QDOT income taxable to S under s. 678, or
    DNI taxable to S 148

**Alternative 1: D Makes Benefits Payable to a
Marital Trust-QDOT** 149
   Mandatory income distributions 149
   Punitive trust income tax rates; use of general power marital
   trust to counteract 149
   Loss of income tax deferral after spouse's death 151

**Alternative 2: D Makes Benefits Payable to an
Estate Trust-QDOT** 151

Alternative 3: Spouse Rolls Over Benefits to QDOT-IRA ... 153
   When benefits are paid directly to S: the dilemma 153
   The combination QDOT-IRA 153
   No requirement that income be distributed annually 155
   Further deferral after spouse's death becomes possible 156
   Deferred estate tax payable on "principal distributions" 156
   What is "income?" 158
   Is a distribution from income or principal? 159
   Assets remaining in the QDOT at spouse's death 160
   Investment and distribution strategies 160
   Is an IRS ruling required? 162
   Choice of trustee 162

Alternative 4: Spouse Assigns IRA to a QDOT 163
   Assignment of inherited IRA to a QDOT 163
   Assignment of rollover IRA to a QDOT 164
   Advantages of assigning IRA to QDOT 165

**Alternative 5: Non-Assignable Annuities, and IRAs
Treated as Non-Assignable Annuities** 166
   Two alternatives for treatment of non-assignable assets 166
   How much of each annuity payment is "principal?" 167
   How does this formula apply to individual account plans? ... 168
   What is a non-assignable annuity? 169
   Election to treat inherited IRA as non-assignable 169

**Alternative 6: Non-Marital Deduction
Disposition Alternatives** 170
   Non-marital deduction disposition 170

Outright to spouse, not claiming marital deduction 170

Alternative 7: D Leaves Benefits to a
Charitable Remainder Trust 170

Summary of Planning Principles 171
Benefits that can be rolled over 171
Benefits that cannot be rolled over 173
Other comments 173

CHAPTER 5 - THE 15% EXCISE TAX 174

Introduction 174

The 15% Excise Tax on "Excess Distributions" 175
15% additional tax on distributions over $150,000 175
Certain distributions are excise tax-free 176
Special treatment for lump sum distributions: general rule . . . 176
Separate threshold for LSDs and other distributions: the
double exemption 177
Qualifying for the LSD exception 178
Planning implications of separate LSD threshold 178

Benefits "Grandfathered" from 15% Excise Tax 179
Electing to "grandfather" 8/1/86 plan balances 179
Drawbacks of electing grandfather treatment 180
How the grandfathered amount is recovered 180
Planning implications of grandfathered benefits 184

15% Estate Tax on Excess Accumulations 185
Additional estate tax applies to "excess" benefits 185
What annuity amount is used? 186
What annuity tables are used? 186
What interest rate is used? 186
Partial exception for insurance proceeds 188

Surviving Spouse's Option to Defer 15% Tax 188
S. 4980A(d)(5) election -- in general 188
Do not commingle benefits if no election made 190
Grandfathered status of benefits continues for spouse 190
All benefits must be payable to spouse 190

Benefits payable to marital trust, or to the estate 191
Life insurance proceeds 192
Simultaneous death; election by spouse's executor 193
Rollover distinguished 194

Other Excess Accumulations Tax Issues 194
Grandfathered benefits; the triple exemption 194
Who is responsible for payment of the tax? 195
Marital and charitable deductions, unified credit 196
Deduction for excess accumulations tax 197

Summary of Planning Principles 197

**CHAPTER 6 - LIFE INSURANCE IN THE RETIREMENT
PLAN** 201

Introduction 201

Income Tax Issues for the Insured Participant 202
Income tax consequences during employment 202
Income tax issues at retirement: the rollout 204
Distributing the policy to P 205
P buys policy from plan 206
Certain profit sharing plans 209

Income Tax Consequences to Beneficiaries 209

Estate Tax Issues 210
The life insurance "subtrust" 211
Can the three-year rule be avoided at rollout time? 212

15% Excise Tax Issues 214

Reasons To Buy Life Insurance Inside The Plan 216

Second-To-Die Insurance 217
Estate tax issues 217
15% excise tax 219
Income tax 220

Miscellaneous 220

Summary of Planning Principles 221

CHAPTER 7 - THE GRANDFATHERS 223

Introduction 223

Minimum Distribution Rule Grandfathers 223
    History of s. 401(a)(9) 224
    TEFRA 242(b) designations 226
    The hardworking aged non-5% owners 228

Pre-1987 403(b) Plan Balances 230
    403(b) plans partly grandfathered from minimum distribution
    rules.... 230
    ...But still subject to the MDIB rule 231
    What was the MDIB rule prior to 1986? 232
    Was there a separate MDIB rule for 403(b) plans? 233
    Distribution of pre-'87 balance can be postponed until actual
    retirement 235
    Consider naming credit shelter trust as beneficiary of 403(b)
    plans, if needed to bring funding up to $600,000 236
    Recommendations for 403(b) plans 237
    Once retirement occurs, what distributions must come out of
    the pre-'87 balance? 238

The Federal Estate Tax Exclusion Lives! 238

Rollover of Death Benefits by Non-Spouse Beneficiary 240

Summary of Planning Principles 240

**CHAPTER 8 - DISCLAIMERS OF RETIREMENT
BENEFITS** 241

Introduction 241

Disclaimers in Post Mortem Planning 243
    Funding credit shelter trust 243
    Salvaging spousal rollover 244

Planning in Anticipation Of Disclaimers 245

Disclaimers and the Plan Administrator 248

Effect of REA on Surviving Spouse's Ability to Disclaim 250
   The nine months requirement for qualified disclaimers 250
   Spousal rights in pension plans under REA 250
   The question presented 251
   Statute and G.C.M. 39858 252
   IRS position 253
   What to do: planning mode 254
   IRAs and profit sharing plans 255

**Are Disclaimers Effective to Change the "Designated
Beneficiary"?** 255
   Importance of having a "designated beneficiary" 255
   Statute 257
   Effect of GCM 39858 257
   Other rulings 258
   The way of the future? 260
   Summary 261
   What to do: planning mode 261
   Possible corrective legislation 263

Summary of Planning Principles 263

CHAPTER 9 - OTHER TOPICS 265

Charitable Dispositions 265
   Introduction: advantages of naming a charity as beneficiary . . 265
   Pitfall: naming a charity as one of several beneficiaries 267
   Pitfall: clearing a trust of charitable gift landmines 270
   Pitfall: naming a charity or CRT as beneficiary at 70½ 271
   Pitfall: charitable pledges and other debts 272
   Funding charitable gifts with plan benefits during life 273

Who are the "Beneficiaries" of a Trust? 275
   Introduction 275
   Disregarding "contingent" beneficiaries 275
   Are remaindermen beneficiaries? 276

When is a "trust for the spouse" the same as "the spouse?" . . 277

Probate Issues 279

Under Age 59½ -- Excise Tax on Premature Distributions . . 279

Planning for Disability 280
Designating a beneficiary for disability benefits 280
Power of attorney 281

Summary of Planning Principles 282

CHAPTER 10 - CASE STUDIES 283

**The Ables: When There Is No Other Asset Available to Fund the
Credit Shelter Trust (A Non-Excise Tax Case)** 283
The facts 283
Scenario 1: How to maximize income tax deferral and
eliminate estate taxes 284
Scenario 2: How to provide for Alice and achieve some
income tax deferral 285
Scenario 3: How to eliminate estate taxes and still protect
Alice 286
Estate tax savings of credit shelter trust 287
Higher income taxes on benefits paid to trust 287
How to name credit shelter trust as beneficiary 289
Looking ahead to the RBD 290

**The Bensons: A Second Marriage: Using Plan Benefits to Fund
a Marital Trust at the RBD** 290
The facts 290
Naming a QTIP trust as beneficiary 291
Variation: If Bob wants to maximize income tax deferral 292
Using a trust beneficiary as "DB" 293
Impact of trust income tax rates 294

Attorney Cavalho: The Rollover Decision 295
The facts 295
What would be the tax on various LSDs? 296
Aggregation issue 297
Other benefits of LSD 297

The Dingells: A Young Family; Life Insurance in the Retirement Plan 298
  The facts 298
  The solution 298

The Eatons: Pension Millionaires With Few Other Assets ... 300
  The facts 300
  Triggering 15% "excess accumulations" tax at Emily's death 301
  Advantage of paying 15% excise tax at Emily's death 302
  Other drawbacks of using IRA to fund credit shelter trust ... 303
  Other benefits of using IRA to fund credit shelter trust 304
  Should Emily withdraw sufficient money now to fund her credit shelter trust? 305
  Should Emily withdraw $150,000 a year? 306
  Should the contingent beneficiary be the children or the trust? 307

The Fallons: Pension Millionaires with Lots of Other Assets; Planning after the RBD (Married Couple); Generation Skipping; Naming Multiple Beneficiaries 309
  The facts 309
  It's too late to change Fred's "DB" 310
  Recalculation of life expectancy 310
  How do we assure Felicia "rolls over" Fred's IRA? 311
  Once Felicia survives Fred, what beneficiary designation is desirable for Felicia's (formerly Fred's) IRA? 312
  Need to divide the IRA before Fred's death 313
  Beneficiary designation for the "grandchildren" IRA 314
  Is it desirable to use the $1 million GST exemption on retirement benefits? 315
  What if Felicia predeceases Fred? 316

The Gregorios: A Childless Couple 316
  The facts 316
  Naming a charitable remainder trust as beneficiary 317

The Widow Heinrich: Planning after the RBD 320
  The facts 320
  Application of minimum distribution rules 321
  Ways to soften the blow 321

Dr. Vincent Valdez: Whether to Stop Funding a Large Retirement Plan 323
    The facts 323
    Review of alternative scenarios 323
    Conclusion 326

Sherman and Herman Levine: Planning When Death is Imminent 326
    The facts 326
    Review of alternatives 328
    Conclusion 329

APPENDIX A - TABLES 330
    1. IRC s. 4980A indexed "threshold amounts" for application of 15% Excise Tax 330
    2. MDIB Rule Divisor Table 331
    3. IRS "Table V": Single life expectancy. 332
    4. IRS "Table VI": Joint Life and Last Survivor Expectancy: Participant is Age 70 (or 71), Beneficiary is Age 35-74. ... 333
    5. Tax on various lump sum distributions 334

APPENDIX B - FORMS 335
    Table of Contents 335

APPENDIX C - CHECKLISTS 391
    1. Checklist For Meeting With Client 391
    2. Rollover Checklist 402
    3. Checklist of Required Distribution Results After RBD ("Permutations") 412

APPENDIX D - SOFTWARE AVAILABLE 417

BIBLIOGRAPHY 420

GLOSSARY 426

INDEX 431

Introduction

Are Retirement Plans the "Worst" Assets?

Everyone has heard it by now: retirement plans are the worst assets an estate planning client can hold. The beneficiaries must pay estate taxes *and* income taxes *and* excise taxes on these assets. The family is left with only 20% of the value of the retirement plan, or even less in some cases.

But what assets, exactly, are retirement benefits worse than? Most of the money contributed to retirement plans came from the pre-tax earnings of an employee or self-employed person. The only alternative to contributing that money to a retirement plan was to take it as taxable salary or self employment income. If the working person wants to build an estate from his earnings, then those earnings must sooner or later be subject to income taxes. If he contributes his earnings to a retirement plan, those earnings will be taxed later--perhaps much later, perhaps several decades later. If he does not contribute his earnings to a retirement plan, the earnings will be taxed sooner--to wit, immediately. With regard to income taxes, then, retirement plan assets are better than other assets.

What about estate taxes? Both retirement plan assets and non-retirement plan assets are subject to estate taxes at the same rate. Assets outside a plan can be given away during life, to reduce estate taxes; assets inside a plan cannot be given away (unless income tax is paid on them first). For the client who has sufficient non-plan assets to make all the lifetime gifts he cares to make, however, there is no estate tax difference, for the assets he intends to keep, between plan and non-plan assets.

The 15% excise tax? While it is true that this tax applies only to retirement plan assets, this unique negative feature must be weighed against the unique positive feature of such assets: the participant's option to defer income taxes on earnings from labor, and on investment income, for a potentially very long time. As case studies later in this book demonstrate, the economic benefits of income tax deferral often, perhaps even usually, outweigh the cost of the 15% excise tax.

In short, retirement benefits are not necessarily the "worst" asset in the estate plan. These assets have a unique tax feature (the potential for multi-decade income tax deferral) which in fact makes retirement benefits "better" than other assets. For the working person, retirement plans still offer the best tax shelter available, and one which he may be able to pass on to his family.

An important goal of estate planning for retirement benefits is to preserve the option of continued income tax deferral for the client's retirement plans for the longest period possible. The potential for continued income tax deferral after the death of the surviving spouse, over the multi-decade life expectancy of their children, is a valuable asset to be preserved. This goal will be attained only if estate planners and their clients understand, and use to advantage, the rules governing plan distributions. Those rules are the subject of this book.

Limitations of this Book

This book does not cover, or covers only briefly, the following topics: Annuity payouts generally; s. 457 plans; qualified domestic relations orders (QDROs); stock options and other non-qualified forms of deferred compensation; distributions of employer stock; ESOPs; REA consent requirements; pre-nuptial agreements; creditors' rights with respect to retirement benefits; state taxation of retirement benefits; and community property.   Other sources for information on some of these topics are mentioned in the Bibliography.

This book is designed to be used by estate and financial planners. It does not cover plan distribution issues which are of concern to plan administrators, but which do not have a significant impact on planning decisions, such as income tax withholding, rollover technicalities and distribution notice requirements. This book deals with estate planning and tax issues only. Investment and financial planning issues are of vital importance in decisions relating to retirement and retirement plans, but are not the subject of this book.

This book is far from the perfect product originally envisioned. Several important topics are covered only briefly or not at all. A planned appendix presenting various IRA providers' policies on permitted beneficiary designations never materialized. Several additional case studies would have been useful. Some parts of the book will be understandable only to experienced estate planning lawyers, while other parts present basic information in a manner easily accessible to non-professionals and probably "too elementary" for the experts. More and better editing would have improved the text.

I decided to publish the book anyway because I believe that, despite its many shortcomings, it will nevertheless be useful to the estate planners and participants who need the information it contains, most of which cannot be found in any other publicly distributed work. Readers who find errors, or who have suggestions for improvements in future editions, are invited to contact the author, in care of the publisher.

Explanation of Terms Used

Section numbers refer to the Internal Revenue Code of 1986 unless otherwise specified.

As used in this book, the terms "retirement plan" and "tax-favored retirement plan" refer to corporate and self-employed ("Keogh") pension, profit sharing and stock bonus plans that are "qualified" under s. 401(a), as well as simplified employee plans (SEPs) under s. 408(k), individual retirement accounts (IRAs) under s. 408(a), and tax-sheltered annuity (or mutual fund) arrangements established under s. 403(b). The narrower term "qualified plans" or "qualified retirement plans" includes only 401(a) plans.

The "participant" is the person whose benefits we are dealing with: the employee who has benefits in a pension or profit sharing plan, or for whom a tax-sheltered annuity was purchased; or the account-holder in the case of an IRA. For ease of understanding, throughout this book, except in some specific examples and case studies, the "participant" (P) is male and the feminine pronoun refers to the participant's spouse. Of course any statement would apply equally to a female participant and her male spouse.

Other Hints for Using this Book

There are many "gray areas" in the tax treatment of retirement benefits--questions the regulations simply do not answer; points of law subject to several totally different interpretations; or regulatory positions that seem contrary to law or for some other reason likely to be changed in the future. When a practitioner encounters one of these in practice, the response may differ depending on whether he is doing advance planning for a client, or is dealing with a *fait accompli*. For this reason, from time to time in this book, in suggesting ways to deal with an issue, I distinguish between "planning mode" and "cleanup mode."

"Planning mode" deals with advance planning, and suggests a "safe harbor" course of action--the steps that should produce a predictable result and offer peace of mind. "Cleanup mode" deals with the *fait accompli* situation: when it is too late for advance planning, usually because the participant has already died or passed his "required beginning date." In "cleanup mode," a more aggressive position may be appropriate on the issue, since there is often nothing to lose. Here, we want to consider every possible argument which may enhance or preserve the value of the retirement benefits for the client and his family.

Case studies in Chapter 10 illustrate the planning principles and real life issues created by the labyrinth of rules discussed in the earlier chapters. Throughout the book, the text contains cross references to related case studies in Chapter 10.

At the end of each chapter, there is a summary of the planning principles developed in that chapter. Bear in mind that most of these are general guidelines which do not apply to every case. The more detailed discussion in the chapter provides the basis for these "principles," and points out limitations and exceptions.

Appendix B provides beneficiary designation forms for a number of common situations, along with related trust provisions in certain instances and some other miscellaneous forms suggested in the text. Whenever a drafting suggestion or planning idea in the text is illustrated by a form in Appendix B, that form is cross-referenced. If there is no form reference, you can assume no form is provided.

This book deals with the *federal* tax law applicable to retirement benefits, but in a few instances state law has a bearing on the subject. When state law has a significant impact, this book will describe the applicable law of Massachusetts (my home state). Planners in other states will need to determine the law applicable to their clients.

Abbreviations Used in this Book

5YFA	Five Year Forward Averaging -- s. 402(d)(1)
10YFA	Ten Year Forward Averaging -- s. 1122(h) of TRA '86, as amended by TAMRA '88 (transition rules affecting individuals born before 1936)
CRT	Charitable Remainder Trust - s. 664
DB	Designated Beneficiary -- s. 401(a)(9)
DNI	Distributable Net Income -- s. 643(a)
GST tax	Generation Skipping Transfer tax --IRC ch. 13
IRA	Individual Retirement Account -- s. 408(a)
IRC	Internal Revenue Code of 1986
IRD	Income in Respect of a Decedent -- s. 691
IRS	Internal Revenue Service
IRT	Individual Retirement Trust -- s. 408
LE	Life Expectancy
LSD	Lump Sum Distribution -- s. 402(d) (until 1992 it was s. 402(e))
MRD	Minimum Required Distribution (see Chapter 1)
P	Participant
Prop. Reg.	Proposed Treasury Regulation; 1.401(a)(9)-1 unless otherwise indicated
QDRO	Qualified Domestic Relations Order -- s. 414(p)
QJSA	Qualified Joint and Survivor Annuity -- s. 417(b)
QPSA	Qualified Pre-retirement Survivor Annuity -- s. 417(c)
QRP	Qualified Retirement Plan -- s. 401(a)
REA	Retirement Equity Act of 1984, Pub. L. No. 98-397, 98 Stat. 1426 (codified in scattered sections of 26 and 29 U.S.C.)
S	Spouse
TAMRA '88	The Technical and Miscellaneous Revenue Act of 1988 (P.L. 100-647)
TEFRA '82	The Tax Equity and Fiscal Responsibility Act of 1982 (P.L. 97-248)
TRA '84	The Tax Reform Act of 1984 (P.L. 98-369)
TRA '86	The Tax Reform Act of 1986 (P.L. 99-514)
TSA	Tax Sheltered Annuity -- s. 403(b)
UCA '92	Unemployment Compensation Amendments of 1992 (P.L. 102-318)

Acknowledgments

I gratefully acknowledge, and thank, the following estate and retirement planning experts who took the time to review chapters of this book and give me their comments. Most of these comments led directly to changes and improvements in the work, although I retain responsibility for all deficiencies in the finished product: Ronald T. Martin, Esq., of the University of Miami Law School; Paul Frimmer, Esq., of Irell & Manella, Los Angeles; Randall J. Gingiss, Esq., of Katten, Muchin & Zavis, Chicago; Zoe M. Hicks, Esq., of Hicks & Montgomery, Atlanta; James H. Landon, Esq., of Jones, Day, Reavis & Pogue, Atlanta; George Mair, Esq., of Bingham, Dana & Gould, Boston; Michael G. Riley, Esq., of McDonald, Hopkins, Burke & Haber, Cleveland; and Lee Slavutin, M.D., C.P.C., of Stern Slavutin 2, Inc., New York.

I used to wonder why authors thanked their typists. Now having had first hand experience with the fantastic dedication and skill of the principal "word processor" of this book, Maureen Cash, I know. I relied heavily on her problem-solving ability and perfectionism, as well as the skills, professionalism and hard work of the others who worked on the production of the manuscript: in chronological order, Jeri Arbo, Sheila Irvine, Pat Longo and Joan Breen.

I am grateful also to those who shared information, provided inspiration or otherwise contributed to the process of producing this book, including Pat Annino, Alex Bove, Alfreda Russell, Rick Solano, cite-checker Mary Catherine McGurrin, and, most of all, my long-suffering husband, the incomparable Ian M. Starr.

In over twenty years of consciously or unknowingly gathering material for this book, I have talked with, listened to, or read the work of hundreds of estate planners, actuaries, accountants, lawyers, financial planners, retirees, trust officers, mutual fund personnel, plan administrators, IRS and DOL staffers, plan participants and writers who have studied the subject matter. Since almost everyone who spends time thinking about these issues or working with the actual problems of real life employers and employees has some interesting and new insight into the subject, I have learned from almost every encounter. I gratefully acknowledge the contributions of all of those from whom, or with whom, or because of whom, I learned the material in this book, including: Deborah Bailin, Ken Bergen, Carol Brown, Jeffrey M. Brown, Virginia Coleman, Steve Crispigna, George Cushing, James S. Davis, Andrew Fair, David Fine, Bob Freedman, Jack Green, Gabriel Heiser, Marcia Chadwick Holt, Arnold Hunnewell, Patricia Hurley, Russell Isaia, Judy Jarashow, Raymond E. Johnson, Bill Kirchick, Harry F. Lee, Dick Marcil, Colin Marshall, Ronald Martin, Tom McCord, Lou Mezzullo, Clint Monts de Oca, Guy Moss, Tim Nay, Jeffrey Pennell, Joan Politi, Charles Rosebrock, Mary Rowland, Donald O. Smith, Anne Q. Spaulding, Lawrence O. Spaulding, Jr., Bob Starr, Harvey B. Wallace II, Mervin Wilf, Mark W. Worthington, John Yagjian and William P. Young.

Special thanks to Bruce Temkin

1

The Minimum Distribution Rules

*The minimum distribution rules
of s. 401(a)(9) dictate how
quickly (or slowly) benefits come
out of retirement plans.
Understanding these rules is the
key to successful tax planning
for retirement benefits.*

Introduction

Congress wants tax-favored retirement plans to be
retirement plans -- not estate-building, wealth transfer vehicles.
To promote its favored result, Congress enacted Internal
Revenue Code s. 401(a)(9), which compels certain annual
minimum distributions from plans beginning at age 70½ or (if
earlier) at death. Failure to distribute the required minimum
results in a 50% excise tax on amounts that should have been
distributed but were not. S. 4974.

In addition to telling us how much the participant must
take out of the plan each year, the minimum distribution rules
contain substantial material dealing with designating a
beneficiary for retirement plan death benefits. If you want to
take advantage of a beneficiary's life expectancy in calculating
minimum distribution amounts, you must comply with these
rules.

There are really two sets of "minimum distribution
rules," dealing with two totally distinct situations: one set of
rules applies when the plan participant (P) dies before his
"required beginning date." The other deals with distributions

required *during life*, *i.e.*, distribution of "retirement benefits," when P reaches his "required beginning date."

From the estate planner's point of view, the minimum distribution rules generate two concerns. First, the planner must make sure that the participant or beneficiary complies with the minimum distribution rules by withdrawing each year at least the amount required by these rules, to avoid the 50% excise tax. Second, the designation of a beneficiary for death benefits needs to satisfy various rules if the client wants the option of postponing income taxation of the benefits for the longest possible time.

On July 27, 1987 the IRS issued proposed regulations ss. 1.401(a)(9)-1 & 2, 1.403(b)-2, 1.408-8 and 54.4974-2, interpreting and implementing the minimum distribution rules. To date, final regs. have not been issued, so these proposed regs. are *the* source material for understanding the minimum distribution rules. References in this chapter to "proposed regulations" refer to Prop. reg. 1.401(a)(9)-1 unless otherwise specified.

Warning: while the following discussion of the minimum distribution rules applies to most qualified retirement plans and IRAs, there are grandfather rules and exceptions which exempt some individuals and plans from some or all of the requirements. See Chapter 7, "The Grandfathers."

Note also: The 50% excise tax can be waived by the IRS if the failure to distribute the required minimum was due to "reasonable error." S. 4974(d).

Death before the RBD: The Five Year Rule

One part of the minimum distribution rules tells us what distributions are required if a participant (P) dies before his "required beginning date" (RBD), that is to say, before April 1 of the calendar year following the calendar year in which he reached or would have reached age 70½. S. 401(a)(9)(C). These rules are sometimes said to apply when death occurs "before age 70½." Strictly speaking, this should be "before the RBD."

The five year rule and its exceptions

Upon the death of a P before his RBD, the general rule is that all benefits must be distributed from the plan within five years after the date of death (the "five year rule"). S. 401(a)(9)(B)(ii). Although the Code says "within five years after the death" of P, the proposed regs. are a little more liberal, requiring that the distribution must occur by "December 31 of the calendar year which contains the fifth anniversary" of the date of death. Prop. reg. C-2.

An exception to this rule permits payments to be made over the life expectancy of P's "designated beneficiary" (DB) if certain requirements are met. S. 401(a)(9)(B)(iii). There are even more liberal exceptions to the five year rule if P's surviving spouse ("S") is the DB. S. 401(a)(9)(B)(iv). Here is an overview of the five year rule and its exceptions:

If P dies before April 1 of the calendar year following the year in which he reaches age 70½, all benefits from all his retirement plans must be distributed:

(a)   by 12/31 of the year which contains the fifth anniversary of P's death;

OR

(b)   if payable to S, in annual installments over S's life or life expectancy, beginning no later than 12/31 of the year after the year in which P died, or (if later) 12/31 of the year in which P would have reached age 70½;

OR

(c)   if payable to some other DB, in annual installments over the life or life expectancy of the DB beginning no later than 12/31 of the year after the year in which P died.

The importance of having a "designated beneficiary"

The option to defer income taxes can be extremely valuable. The financial effect on the family of being forced to take out all benefits *within five years after P's death,* versus being permitted to take them out gradually *over the life expectancy of a beneficiary,* can be dramatic.

Example: Lena and Tina. Two brothers died. Each brother left his entire estate, including a $500,000 IRA, to his daughter. Both daughters, Lena and Tina, were 38 years old. Each of the daughters, after taking a round-the-world cruise, buying a new house, and paying the estate taxes on her father's estate, was left with just one asset: the $500,000 IRA. Each daughter decided to regard the inherited IRA as her own retirement nest egg, and resolved to: withdraw from the IRA only the minimum amount required by law; invest the after-tax proceeds of the withdrawal; and accumulate the earnings (after taxes) as her retirement fund.

Each daughter kept her resolve, investing both in-plan and out-of-plan assets in 8% bonds, and paying income taxes on all plan withdrawals and bond interest at the rate of 36%, but there was one difference: Tina's father had named Tina as his "designated beneficiary" (DB), so Tina was entitled to withdraw her father's IRA in installments over her 44.4 year life expectancy. Lena's father had named no beneficiary; he never got around to filling out a designation of beneficiary form.

Under the terms of the account agreement governing his IRA, since he had not named any beneficiary, his "beneficiary" was his estate. In minimum distribution rule jargon, he "had no DB." Lena, the sole beneficiary of the estate, had to withdraw all money from her father's IRA within five years after his death.

After 30 years, Lena has a $1.5 million investment portfolio, all outside of any IRA. Tina has an investment portfolio of $1.4 million outside the IRA; and also has $1.5 million still *inside* the IRA she inherited from her father. Tina still has 14.4 years left in her "life expectancy" over which to withdraw the remaining IRA balance. After 30 years, the daughter who used the "installments over life expectancy" payout method has almost twice as much money as the daughter who withdrew benefits under the "five year rule."

Clearly, it is vital for the planner to understand how to go about naming a "DB." If the participant has a DB, then, on the participant's death, the DB will have the luxury of choosing to spread out the distributions from the IRA over his life expectancy. (Remember, these distributions are just the *minimum* the beneficiary must take. The beneficiary can always take out more than the minimum--in fact the IRS would be delighted to have him do so.) But if there "is no DB," then the recipient who inherits the benefits will have no choice--benefits will have to come out of the plan, and be taxed, within five years after P's death.

DB   is a term of art; it does not mean whatever beneficiary the participant happens to have named. A DB must be an individual or a group of individuals; but, if some tricky rules are complied with, the participant can name a trust as recipient of his death benefits and the *beneficiaries of the trust* will be treated as the participant's DB.

The DB might be a beneficiary designated by the participant on forms provided for that purpose by the plan; or the plan itself may dictate who is the participant's beneficiary.

Assuming an individual (or group of individuals) has been designated (either by the participant or by the terms of the plan), that individual (or group) will be his DB.

If the beneficiary of the participant's death benefits is "my spouse," or "my children," or "my issue" -- or any named human being -- everything is fine: the participant has a "DB," *i.e.,* an individual or group of individuals whose life expectancy(ies) can be used to measure minimum required distributions. If P's estate or a corporation is named as the beneficiary, or if a trust has been named but the technical requirements are not met, then for purposes of the minimum distribution rules, P is said to have "no DB" and therefore the benefits must be distributed within five years after his death.

Naming an individual as beneficiary

If one person (such as the participant's spouse or a child) is the DB, then, under the exception to the five year rule, the beneficiary can withdraw the benefits "in accordance with regulations" over a period of time that does not exceed his life expectancy.

The proposed regulations provide that, to use this method, the beneficiary's life expectancy is first determined according to the IRS's actuarial table. The table gives a fixed measuring period, a number of years, which is the maximum number of years over which benefits can come out. Then, each year, the benefits remaining in the plan are valued, and the beneficiary must withdraw at least a certain fractional portion of those benefits. The first year, the fraction will be [one] divided by [the beneficiary's life expectancy]. In the second year, it will be [one] divided by [the beneficiary's original life expectancy reduced by one year], and so on.

For example, if the beneficiary has a life expectancy of 27 years as of his birthday in the first year after the date of P's death, he must withdraw 1/27th of the benefits in that year; in the second year, he must withdraw 1/26th and so forth. For specific instructions on calculating minimum withdrawals, see the "How to Compute Installments" section of this chapter.

Each year, the benefits remaining in the plan are valued, and that year's new fraction is applied to the new plan value to determine that year's required *minimum* distribution. The beneficiary is, of course, free to withdraw more than the minimum in any year.

This fractional method of calculating minimum withdrawals tends to produce gradually increasing installments over the years, so long as the plan has a positive investment return. As long as the beneficiary's remaining life expectancy is greater than [100] divided by [the plan's annual growth rate], the plan balance will be growing faster than the beneficiary is withdrawing it. For example, if the plan is growing at 8% per year, and the beneficiary's life expectancy is 20 years, the required minimum distribution (1/20, or 5%) is less than the plan's earnings for the year (1/12.5, or 8%). Eventually the beneficiary's life expectancy is reduced to the point that he is withdrawing more than the year's investment return. If the plan is growing at 8% per year, this crossover point would be reached at 12.5 years before the end of the payout period. Even after this crossover point, however, the annual required minimum distributions tend to keep getting larger, because the fraction applied to them is greater, even though the plan balance is now shrinking.

If the DB is taking out the benefits in installments over his life expectancy, the Code says such distributions must begin "no later than one year after the date" of death, "or such later date" as the IRS may prescribe by regulations. The proposed regulations require that the installments "commence on or before December 31 of the calendar year immediately following the calendar year in which" P died. Prop. reg. C-3(a).

This feature of the installment method contrasts with the "five year rule." Under the five year rule, there is no requirement that distributions be made annually, or that any money come out of the plan at all until the last day of the period.

Naming the spouse as beneficiary

The minimum distribution rules, as well as other parts of the tax code, provide special breaks when the surviving spouse is named as the beneficiary of retirement benefits. Chapter 3, "Marital Matters," deals with all aspects of naming the spouse (or a trust for the spouse) as beneficiary.

Naming more than one beneficiary

If there are several people collectively who are the DB (such as "my surviving children"), then, according to the proposed regulations, the payout period is computed using the life expectancy of the beneficiary with the shortest life expectancy, *i.e.*, the oldest member of the group.

The proposed regulations provide that each of the beneficiaries may use his or her own life expectancy for his or her share of the benefits, *if* the retirement plan is divided into separate accounts which are separately accounted for. Prop. reg. H-2. Thus, if P has four children, he could have four separate accounts, one payable to each of the children, within the IRA or retirement plan, and each "account" would have its minimum distribution amount calculated separately each year based on the life expectancy of the individual who was the beneficiary of that segregated portion.

Under the proposed regulations, these "separate accounts" must be established "as of" the date of the participant's death. Does this mean "prior to" the participant's death? At least one letter ruling appears to support this conclusion. See Ltr. Rul. 9305025 (11/12/92), in which the IRS "blessed" dividing up an IRA into six separate but equal IRAs for the six children after the death of the parents, *provided* that annual distributions continued to be made from *all six* of the accounts based on the life expectancy of the *oldest* of the six children. If separate accounts "as of" the date of death did not mean "prior to" the date of death, each of the six beneficiaries could have used his or her own life expectancy for his or her own separate account.

On the other hand, many practitioners interpret "as of" the date of death to mean that a fractional division of the account that occurs *effective on* the date of death qualifies for "separate account" treatment, even if the accounts are not actually separated until after the date of death. The Code seems to support this conclusion, since the Code says a payout over the life expectancy of the beneficiary is available for "the portion" of the account that is payable to that beneficiary. S. 401(a)(9)(B)(iii).

The pitfall of naming multiple beneficiaries

The rules in the proposed regs. regarding what happens when there is more than one beneficiary can have unexpected consequences in some situations.

One requirement in the proposed regs. is that, when a participant has named more than one beneficiary, all members of the group must be individuals in order for the exception to the five year rule to be available. If even $1 of the benefit is paid to a non-individual, the participant is deemed to have "no DB," and the five year rule applies. See Prop. reg. E-5, "if a person other than an individual is designated as a beneficiary, the employee will be treated as not having any designated beneficiaries for purposes of Section 401(a)(9) even if there are also individuals designated as beneficiaries."

For example, suppose Wilma has $1 million in her pension plan. In her designation of beneficiary form, she directs the plan to pay $1,000 to her church and all the remaining balance to her son, Egbert. Her intent is that $1,000 would be distributed promptly on her death to her church and the balance could be distributed to Egbert over his life expectancy. Unfortunately, the minimum distribution rules don't work that way, according to the proposed regs. She has named more than one beneficiary (her church and her son), and one of those beneficiaries is not an individual. Therefore she is deemed to have "no DB," and the entire $1 million benefit must come out within five years after her death.

The "separate account rule" discussed above may not help in this situation, regardless of whether "as of the date of death" means "prior to the date of death" or "effective as of the date of death," because Wilma's charitable gift is pecuniary (a fixed dollar amount). Under the proposed regs., a "separate account" would be one with separate accounting for profits and losses. A fixed dollar amount established as of the date of death may not meet that definition. For more discussion of how to name a charity as beneficiary see Chapter 9.

The proposed regulations' rule that, if there are multiple beneficiaries, and any one of them is not an individual, there is no designated beneficiary at all, as well as the regulations' position that, if there are multiple beneficiaries, the life expectancy of the oldest must be used, seem flatly to contradict the Code's statement that, if "*any portion*" of the benefit is payable to a designated beneficiary, that portion can be distributed over the life expectancy of that beneficiary.

The IRS can reach a happy medium between the extreme position in its proposed regulations and the far more liberal position in the Code by treating fractional bequests of an account (such as "in equal shares to all my children," or "50% to charity and 50% to my children") as "separate accounts established as of the date of death," so long as the fractional division is applied to the date of death value of the account and the accounts are separated within a reasonable time thereafter.

Planning mode: There is a tendency to want to pay charitable bequests from the retirement plan, because a charitable recipient will pay no income tax on the benefits. While that planning idea is basically sound (see Chapter 9), a charitable gift should not be made from a retirement plan if the rest of the plan is expected to be distributed over the life expectancy of an individual, unless the "separate account" procedure of Prop. reg. H-2 is followed.

Cleanup mode: On the other hand, if you have a client who has already died, prior to his required beginning date, and who has left a charitable bequest to be paid out of retirement benefits, and you want the rest of the retirement benefits to be paid out over the life expectancy of an individual, do not despair. You may be able to win a ruling or a court decision in your favor based on the language of the Code quoted above, to the effect that the individual beneficiaries are entitled to a life expectancy payout as to the "portion" of the benefits payable to them, regardless of what other beneficiaries may be receiving some other "portion" of the retirement plan.

Naming a trust: how to

This section deals with the minimum distribution rules that apply when benefits are payable to a trust and the participant dies before his required beginning date (RBD). See the "Lifetime Distribution Rules" section of this chapter for the minimum distribution rules dealing with benefits payable to a trust when the participant does not die before the RBD.

Although the general rule is that the DB must be an

individual, the proposed regulations permit you to "look through" a trust instrument, and compute the measuring period as if the *trust beneficiary* were the DB, if five requirements are met. These five requirements (which must be complied with "as of the date of the employee's death," if the participant dies before his RBD) (Prop. reg. D-5, D-6) are:

1.   The trust must be valid under state law.
2.   The trust must be irrevocable.
3.   All beneficiaries of the trust must be individuals (no estates, corporations or charities).
4.   The beneficiaries must be "identifiable from the trust instrument."
5.   "A copy of the trust instrument is provided to the plan."

If these "trust rules" are complied with, the trust beneficiaries will be "treated" as DBs for purposes of s. 401(a)(9). The rules are generally not difficult to comply with. The two obstacles to success are, first, that most people are unaware of these rules and, second, that the people enforcing these rules are retirement plan administrators and members of the IRS's retirement plan staff, not people who are necessarily familiar with estate planning concepts.

The first requirement, that the trust be valid under state law, is certainly no obstacle. The requirement that the trust be "irrevocable" as of the date of death is likewise no obstacle since even a revocable trust becomes irrevocable at death. (Reminder: this section deals with the minimum distribution rules that apply when a participant dies before his "required beginning date." Once the participant reaches the all-important "RBD" the rules, including the rules for naming a trust as beneficiary, change. See "Lifetime Distribution Rules," below.)

(a)   Beneficiary identifiable

The requirement that the beneficiary of the trust be "identifiable" poses some issues. A beneficiary "need not be specified by name" so long as he is "identifiable." Prop. reg. D-2. What the regulation requires is that there be an ascertainable "oldest" beneficiary whose life expectancy can be the measuring period under the minimum distribution rules.

"The members of a class of beneficiaries capable of expansion or contraction will be treated as being identifiable if it is possible at the applicable time to identify the class member with the shortest life expectancy." Prop. reg. D-2. Thus, if the trust beneficiaries are "all my issue living from time to time," the beneficiaries are "identifiable" even though the class is not closed as of the date of death, since no member with a shorter life expectancy can be added later, *i.e.*, the oldest member of the class can be determined with certainty on the date of death.

(Actually, unless the trust instrument precludes the legal adoption of adults, it *is* technically possible for the class of the participant's "issue" to be expanded, after his death, to include a person who is older than the oldest member of the class living at the participant's death. Hopefully the IRS will not raise this "issue" in reviewing standard trust provisions for the benefit of "issue." See form 7.3 in Appendix B for a suggested trust provision covering this point.)

On the other hand, if the trustee has discretion to distribute "to such persons as the trustee shall select from the class consisting of my children, their spouses and their issue living from time to time," the beneficiaries are presumably *not* "identifiable," since we do not know whom the children may marry in the future and they might marry people with shorter life expectancies than they have.

(b)   Are remaindermen "beneficiaries?"

It appears that the IRS regards both income beneficiaries and remainder beneficiaries as "beneficiaries" for purposes of this rule. Under this view, a trust providing "income to spouse for life, principal to charity at spouse's death" would "flunk" the trust rules, because not all beneficiaries are individuals. This important question is discussed in detail in the "Who are the 'Beneficiaries' of a Trust?" section of Chapter 9.

(c)   Copy of trust to plan "as of" the date of death

The final requirement is that a copy of the trust must be provided to the plan "as of" the date of death. Prop. reg. D-6. Many people assume this means that the plan must have a copy of the trust in its files when death occurs -- in other words, a copy of the trust must be given to the plan *before* the date of death, otherwise "the plan" will not have a copy of the trust "as of" the date of death.

There are indications that the IRS will not be that strict in interpreting this rule. Giving a copy of the trust to the plan within a reasonable time after the date of death (before the first post-death distribution is required), *may* be sufficient to satisfy the "as of" the date of death requirement.

What does it mean to give a copy of the trust to "the plan?" Presumably, the trust copy must go to the person or company who is responsible for making sure benefits are paid to the right beneficiary, and for complying with the minimum distribution rules. That would be, in the case of QRPs, the "plan administrator." In the case of an IRA, it's not so clear who is supposed to get the copy of the trust.

Planning mode: If the estate plan calls for using the life expectancy of a trust beneficiary as the measuring period for the payout of benefits after death, it is advisable to give a copy of the trust to the plan administrator (or IRA trustee or custodian) right along with the designation of beneficiary form that designates the trust. If this is done, you are 100% sure that this requirement has been satisfied. Remember, the penalty for failure to comply with any of the trust requirements is draconian: the benefits must all be withdrawn from the plan within five years after the date of death.

The main obstacle to compliance with this requirement is the plan administrator. Some plan administrators refuse to accept copies of trust instruments. Either they don't have room in their files, or they don't want to be involved in their employees' personal estate planning matters, or they flat out say that it is unnecessary to give them a copy of the trust prior to the date of death. On the other hand, there are other plan administrators who, once the participant has died, refuse to recognize the trust beneficiary as the "DB" because they didn't have a copy of the trust prior to the date of death!

Cleanup mode: If your client has died, naming a trust as his beneficiary, without giving a copy of the trust to "the plan," do not give up on using the life expectancy payout method. The IRS may rule favorably if a copy of the trust is furnished to the plan within a reasonable time after the date of death. Also, since there really is no "plan administrator" for an IRA, it may be that if the account holder (participant) has a copy of his own trust (which he obviously does) the "copy of the trust" requirement is satisfied. See also "Cleanup Strategies" section, below.

Naming a trust: benefits of

If you comply with the trust rules, you can treat the oldest trust beneficiary for all purposes as the DB. The advantage of this is that you can use the oldest trust beneficiary's life expectancy as the measuring period for determining minimum distributions from the retirement plan to the trust. Also, some of the special tax breaks available to a surviving spouse may be available when the benefits are payable to a trust, if the spouse is the "sole" beneficiary of the trust. See Chapters 3 and 9.

Naming an estate as beneficiary

When benefits are payable to the participant's "estate," the participant is deemed to have "no DB," and the five year rule applies. This result seems harsh if all beneficiaries of the estate are individuals, or trusts which comply with the "trust rules," but it is clearly what the proposed regs. provide.

Cleanup strategies -- death before the RBD

When the participant dies before his RBD, and you discover that the beneficiary designation is not ideal, there are several strategies for correcting the situation and avoiding the five year rule.

1.   **Spousal rollover**. The IRS, in its rulings, has been liberal in permitting the spouse (S) to roll over benefits even when S was not named directly as DB, so long as S had the absolute right (as beneficiary of an estate or trust) to receive the benefits. See Chapter 3, "Spousal Rollover" section. By rolling over the benefits to her own IRA, S can comply with the "five year rule" but still defer income taxes on the benefits.

2.   **Disclaimers**. If S is not directly or indirectly named as beneficiary, consider whether qualified disclaimers can be used to shift the benefits over to S. See Chapter 8.

3.   **IRS Ruling**. Perhaps you believe there is a "designated beneficiary" (DB) entitled to use the life expectancy (LE) method, but the proposed regs. indicate otherwise. For example, perhaps P's beneficiary designation form said "pay $10,000 of my benefits to the Red Cross and the balance to my child." You reasonably believe that, under Code s. 401(a)(9), child is entitled to take his share of the benefits over his LE, but s. E-5 of the proposed regs. indicates that, since one of the named beneficiaries is not an individual, there "is no DB" and the five year rule applies. Consider applying for a ruling. The people on the IRS ruling staff, who are not the same people as the regulation-writing staff, may have a different interpretation of the law; they have issued rulings which in some cases appear contrary to the regulations. See, *e.g.*, Ltr. Rul. 9037048 (6/20/90), in which the beneficiary of a testamentary trust was treated as a "DB" despite the fact that the trust was clearly not irrevocable on the RBD as required by the proposed regs.

4.   **Wait and see**. If the client does not want to pay for a private letter ruling, use a "wait and see" approach. Begin distributions based on the assumption that there is a DB, and that the installments-over-life-expectancy method is available. This means making annual installment distributions, beginning within one year after the date of death, based on the LE of the person you believe is the DB. Once four years have elapsed, review the situation again. By then there may be final regulations, cases or other legal guidance providing a definitive answer one way or the other; or the client may have decided that it is worth seeking a private letter ruling. If the question has been answered unfavorably to your client, or if it still is ambiguous and your client still does not want to get a ruling, you can comply with the five year rule and distribute all benefits by December 31 of the year which contains the fifth anniversary of P's death.

Note, if using this approach, the importance of taking the first MRD by 12/31 of the year which contains the first anniversary of P's death. If this first deadline is missed, the DB will be stuck with the "five year rule." There is no known way of "restoring" the right to use the life expectancy method if the first year's installment is missed.

Lifetime Distribution Rules: The Required Beginning Date

Once a participant reaches age 70½, s. 401(a)(9) forces him to start taking money out of his retirement plans.

The RBD (required beginning date)

Money must start coming out of the retirement plan no later than the "required beginning date" (RBD), which is April 1 following the year in which the participant reaches age 70½. The *slowest* rate it can come out is, installments over the participant's life expectancy; or the joint life expectancy of the participant and his spouse; or the joint life expectancy of the participant and some other designated beneficiary -- who for this purpose will be deemed to be no more than 10 years younger than the participant, regardless of the beneficiary's actual age. (See "Incidental Benefit/MDIB" section, below.) A participant who has "no DB" as of his RBD must withdraw all plan benefits over only *one* life expectancy period -- his own. At age 70½, the "life expectancy" under IRS tables is either 15.3 or 16 years (see "How to Compute Installments" section).

Naming a DB at age 70½ is similar to naming a DB for pre-RBD death benefits with several *extremely important* differences:

(a)   The existence or non-existence of a DB on the

RBD, and the identity of the DB if there is one, freeze the payout period *permanently*. The participant can later change his DB, but can never do so in a way that lengthens the maximum payout period beyond what was established at the RBD. (The only "exception" to this rule is that, if the participant names his spouse as beneficiary, either before, at, or after his RBD, and she survives him, a spousal rollover can start a new payout period after the participant's death. See Chapter 3.)

(b)   Trust beneficiaries can be used as the DB -- but the trust must be IRREVOCABLE on the RBD. See trust rules, below.

(c)   The participant must make an irrevocable election whether or not to recalculate his (and his spouse's, if the spouse is the DB) life expectancy annually.

Traditionally, estate planners "planned" for only one event -- death. Later, planners added disability planning to their repertoire. Now planners must add a third focus to their efforts: the RBD. When a participant names a beneficiary *prior* to the RBD, it is similar to writing a will -- the participant can change his mind later and write a new will (or name another beneficiary). Estate planners are familiar with this mode and often do not realize that naming a beneficiary *on* the RBD has a quite different effect: the beneficiary designation on the RBD is not merely a will-like designation of who will receive the benefits after the participant's death (although it is that -- and to that extent is changeable); it is *also* an election as to how the participant's minimum distributions will be calculated each year, and on this point it is irrevocable.

The RBD is the continental divide. Planning should begin early for this event. If a trust is to be named as beneficiary, EXTREME CARE must be taken to comply with the trust rules discussed below.

The good news is that most people have a "DB" whether

they know it or not. A "DB," for purposes of the rules, is simply "an individual who is entitled to a portion of an employee's benefit, contingent on the employee's death or another specified event." Prop. reg. D-2(a)(1). The DB can be named in the plan itself, or (if the plan permits) by the participant on a beneficiary designation form.

Under many employer-sponsored plans, if the participant does nothing, his spouse is automatically his DB. Under many IRA arrangements, if the participant has not designated a beneficiary all benefits are payable to the participant's estate, and thus he is deemed to have "no DB." A participant who "has no DB" on his RBD will be required to withdraw all his plan benefits over the 15.3 or 16 years of his own life expectancy.

Naming the spouse as beneficiary

If the spouse is the DB, the participant can take his benefits out in installments over the joint life expectancy of the participant and the spouse -- whatever it may be. If the spouses are close in age, this will probably not be the longest possible payout period; for example, the joint life expectancy of two individuals age 70 and 68 is only 21.5 years. However, naming S as DB offers other tax and estate planning advantages (see Chapter 3), and it is what most people want anyway.

Naming the spouse as DB will almost always lengthen the payout period somewhat, compared to using just the participant's own life expectancy ("LE"), even if the spouse is the same age -- or even if the spouse is older. The LE of an individual age 70 is 16 years; but the LE of two individuals both of whom are age 70 is 20.6 years. Even if the spouse is age 80 (*i.e.* 10 years older than the participant) adding her extends the payout period to 17.6 years.

Naming a non-spouse individual as beneficiary

Naming a child or other younger generation beneficiary often produces the longest payout period, despite the limits imposed by the MDIB rule. See "Naming a Non-Spouse DB" section later in this chapter.

Naming a trust as beneficiary

Naming the client's revocable living trust as the beneficiary of retirement benefits is a perfectly normal and natural thing to do. Unfortunately, it is a trap for the unwary when the participant reaches his RBD. FAILURE TO COMPLY WITH THE FOLLOWING ALL IMPORTANT TRUST RULES WILL RESULT IN "HAVING NO DB," and all benefits will be required to be paid out over no more than the 15.3 or 16 years of the participant's own life expectancy. On the other hand, if you comply with these rules, the trust beneficiaries will be treated as the participant's "DB," and the oldest trust beneficiary's life expectancy will be combined with the participant's to determine the maximum payout period.

The trust rules are the same five examined earlier, but with a difference: the requirements must now be met *as of the RBD* (or, if later, as of the date the trust is named as beneficiary) and at all times thereafter. So, as of April 1 following the year the participant turns 70½:

(a)   *The trust must be irrevocable.*

(b)   All trust beneficiaries must be individuals.

(c)   The beneficiaries must be "identifiable from the trust instrument."

(d)   *"A copy of the trust instrument is provided to the plan."*

(e)   The trust must be valid under state law.

Requirement (e) again does not pose any problem, and for requirements (b) and (c) the issues are the same as when a trust is named as DB for pre-RBD death benefits. See "Death Before the RBD" section, above. Requirements (a) and (d) create problems at the RBD.

Copy of trust to the plan

You must give a copy of the trust to the "plan" *on or before the RBD.* As noted above, it is not clear how you comply with this requirement in the case of an IRA. The safest thing to do is to give a copy of the trust to the custodian or trustee of the IRA.

Trust must be irrevocable

If the client wants to name a trust as the recipient of his death benefits, and use the oldest trust beneficiary's life expectancy together with his own to calculate his minimum distributions, he cannot use his revocable living trust. He must use an irrevocable trust.

This is a pain in the neck but not an insuperable obstacle. Remember, the participant can always change his DB later -- daily if he wants to, as far as the IRS is concerned. He can even change it to a different trust -- as long as the trust is irrevocable. So naming an irrevocable trust as DB does NOT mean the client cannot later change the beneficiary of his death benefits.

Four ways to deal with "irrevocable trust" rule

How does the client who wants to use a funded revocable living trust to avoid probate, but also wants to name the same trust as beneficiary of his retirement benefits, deal with this problem?

Approach 1: One approach is to create a wholly separate, irrevocable, but otherwise identical, *un*funded trust to be the named beneficiary of retirement benefits. By using an unfunded irrevocable trust as beneficiary of his retirement benefits, plus a funded revocable trust for all his other assets, he maintains total flexibility to change his estate plan as he sees fit in the future. As to his retirement benefits, he can change the beneficiary at any later time, to an individual, or to another trust, as he prefers. As to his other assets, they are in a revocable amendable trust, so he can revoke it or amend it if he wishes.

The estate plan could be set up to have the revocable trust pour into the irrevocable trust at the participant's death if it is desired to have only one trust for simplicity of administration at that time. It should *not* be set up so that the irrevocable trust will pour into the revocable trust. That would cause the revocable trust to be the beneficiary and thus the participant would "have no DB" on his RBD.

Approach 2: Another approach is to use a funded, irrevocable trust to hold all of the client's assets (to avoid probate) and simply reserve, in the irrevocable trust, the power to compel the trustee to distribute all assets back to the donor-client. See form 7.1 in Appendix B. So long as the client reserves the right to withdraw all assets of the trust, the client's flexibility to later change the terms of his estate plan is preserved. If he later changes his mind about the terms of his estate plan, he can (i) withdraw all assets from the existing irrevocable trust and transfer them to a new irrevocable trust he likes better and (ii) name the new irrevocable trust as his new DB. This approach is less cumbersome to start with than approach no. 1 (because it requires only one trust, not two), but can be more cumbersome later, if any changes are to be made, because any amendment requires transferring all assets from the old trust, out to client and thence into the new trust.

Approach 3: Some practitioners, when planning for clients who are under age 70½, suggest using a typical revocable living trust as beneficiary, but providing that the trust will automatically become irrevocable on the client's RBD. Is this a good idea?

In the author's opinion, this approach should be strongly considered when planning for a client who is approaching his RBD -- perhaps age 65 or older. At this stage, the planner should discuss with the client the alternatives for beginning withdrawal of his benefits at age 70½. If, based on this discussion, the client concludes that this particular trust disposition is best both for purposes of post-death distributions and lifetime required distributions after 70½, it makes sense to adopt a plan which will not necessarily have to be altered in a few short years when a now-perfectly-foreseeable event (client's RBD) occurs. This approach does not eliminate the advisability of a "second look" at age 70, but may mean that the second look will be less costly and time consuming.

On the other hand, there are drawbacks to using this approach, namely:

1.   If a living trust will automatically become irrevocable at age 70½, the drafter must take extra precautions. For example, the planner would want to preserve the client's power to withdraw all assets from the trust to avoid a completed gift.

2.   The proposed regulations (issued in 1987) may be replaced at any time by final regulations, which may or may not resemble the proposed regs. with regard to this requirement. Thus, the extra legal time spent preparing an "automatically irrevocable" trust may be wasted.

This is a question on which professional opinions vary. Many planners are starting to include, in their standard form revocable trusts, a provision that the trust becomes irrevocable on the RBD. See form 7.1 in Appendix B.

Approach 4: Designate a trust as beneficiary if client dies before RBD, but individuals if death occurs on or after the RBD.

A client in his 40s or 50s who wants to leave benefits to his children as primary or contingent beneficiary often chooses to leave the benefits in trust for the children because of their youth. Typically such a trust will provide that the children's shares will be distributed to them outright at some suitable age such as 35 or 40. The trust instrument under which assets are to be held is the client's revocable "living" trust, which fulfills other functions such as avoiding probate. The client would prefer not to have this trust become automatically irrevocable at age 70½. It is reasonable to anticipate that, by the time this client reaches age 70½, his children will all have reached the age specified in the trust instrument for outright distribution of their shares, so leaving the benefits to a trust for them will no longer be necessary.

In this case, consider having a "split" designation of beneficiary (or contingent beneficiary) to avoid the risk of having a revocable trust as beneficiary on the RBD. The beneficiary designation form specifies the revocable trust as a beneficiary only if the client dies before his RBD. If the client lives past his RBD, the children individually become the beneficiary instead of the trust. See form 4.2 in Appendix B.

Clients who live in states where "avoiding probate" is a non-problem do not have to worry about these issues. They can simply name an irrevocable trust as DB and keep all their assets in their own names, outside of a trust.

Naming an estate as beneficiary

The IRS's position that an "estate" cannot be a DB (even if all beneficiaries of the estate are individuals) while a trust can be, can produce apparently arbitrary results. For example, if the beneficiary of Sylvia's IRA is a trust for the life benefit of Mickey, Sylvia can withdraw from her IRA over the joint LE of herself and Mickey. But if the IRA is payable to her estate, of which the same trust is the sole beneficiary (or even of which Mickey himself is the sole beneficiary) there "is no DB" and the joint life expectancy method cannot be used. See, *e.g.*, Ltr. Rul. 9501044 (10/14/94).

There is a reason for this distinction, however. A plan administrator can read the names of individual beneficiaries and determine their birthdates. A plan administrator can even, with a little more effort, read a trust instrument and determine who are the beneficiaries and what are their life expectancies. But when benefits are payable to "my estate," and the still-living participant reaches age 70½, the plan administrator can not determine who is the participant's beneficiary for purposes of computing minimum distributions. Even if the participant says "here's a copy of my will," the plan administrator can't be sure the will won't be contested or revoked.

Recalculating Life Expectancies: Participant and Spouse

A major question facing the participant who names his spouse as DB is whether the life expectancies of the participant, of the spouse, or of both should be recalculated annually.

How recalculation works

Absent "recalculation," the "life expectancy" period over which benefits may be paid out is established as a fixed number of years (or "term certain" or "period certain") on the RBD. Then each year the minimum distribution is calculated by multiplying the current account balance by a fraction: one divided by the remaining number of years in the term certain (see "How to Compute Installments" section below).

When life expectancy is being recalculated annually, on the other hand, you go back to the actuarial table each year, and determine an entirely new life expectancy based on the participant's new age. Under this method, life expectancy does not automatically go down by one full year each year -- it goes down by something less than a full year. For example, the life expectancy of a 70-year-old is 16 years, while the life expectancy of a 71-year-old is 15.3 years. Thus, for a participant who is using only his own life expectancy to calculate minimum distributions, the second year's fraction will be 1/15.3 if he is redetermining his life expectancy annually, compared to 1/15 if he is using a "term certain" and not recalculating. Redetermining life expectancy stretches out the distribution of benefits during the participant's lifetime.

The advantage of annual recalculation is that the participant or couple will never "outlive" the retirement benefits. The IRS tables provide a life expectancy of more than one year all the way up to age 110. The disadvantage is that, in the calendar year following the death of a person whose life expectancy is being recalculated annually, that life expectancy is reduced to zero. If the participant's spouse dies, and her life expectancy was being recalculated, for example, the participant's remaining benefits will have to be paid out to him over only his own life expectancy. If both spouses' life expectancies are being recalculated, and both spouses die prematurely, the children (or whoever is the next succeeding beneficiary) will not get the benefit of a longer payout period-- all remaining benefits will have to be distributed within *one year* after the surviving spouse's death.

In contrast, if life expectancies are NOT recalculated, the death of the participant or spouse makes no difference to the payout. The contingent beneficiaries, or the participant's estate, or whoever is next in line, simply continues to withdraw over the balance of the term certain.

Which method is best?

There is no simple answer to the question of whether it is desirable to recalculate annually. For a married couple whose principal goal is to enhance their own retirement security and maximize their tax deferred income from this plan, and whose health and genetic background indicate that they have an above-average life expectancy, recalculation of both life expectancies annually will *probably* provide the most extended payout term. However, if one or both spouses die prematurely, "recalculate both" is the worst method to use, because it would result in acceleration of distributions on the first death and immediate distribution of the entire balance within a year after the second death.

If the spouses appear to have below average life expectancies due to severe illness or other condition, then recalculation annually would probably not be advisable, and use of their fixed joint life expectancy period, determined as of the RBD, will probably produce a longer payout period and more tax deferral. (If both spouses clearly have shortened life expectancies, consider naming a child or grandchild as DB instead of the spouse, to gain greater income tax deferral, if this would not jeopardize the surviving spouse's financial security; see "Incidental Benefit (MDIB)" rule, below.)

Under any method, if the participant dies first, the benefits can be paid to the spouse at that point and rolled over by her to her own IRA, where she can start the process all over again by naming a new DB and choosing a payout period based on the joint life expectancy of, say, herself and the children. See Chapter 3.

A compromise position is to have the participant's life expectancy recalculated annually, but not the spouse's. (Prop. reg. E-7 permits the participant to recalculate the life expectancy of either spouse, neither, or both.) This hedges the bets. If the spouse dies first, then the participant will at least have assured that the minimum payout period over which the participant (and children if they succeed him) can take out the benefits is the spouse's original life expectancy. Thus there is a guaranteed minimum payout period, and no sudden acceleration of benefits if both spouses die prematurely. The payout period may be even more extended if the participant lives beyond his life expectancy.

This "split" method has three drawbacks. First, calculating the annual distribution is more complicated (see "How to Compute Installments" section of this chapter), although software can easily solve that problem. Second, it tends to produce slightly *larger* minimum required distributions than either of the other two methods (recalculate both, recalculate neither) in the early years, due to the IRS's prescribed formula which requires some rounding upwards of the spouse's age. Third, on the participant's death, it creates greater time pressures for the spouse to complete an immediate rollover, due to the acceleration of minimum distributions that occurs in the year following the death. See "Spousal Rollovers" section of Chapter 3.

Another "hedging the bets" approach is for the participant to have several plans (*e.g.*, divide one big IRA into three smaller IRAs) and elect a different method for each. See IRS Notice 88-38, discussed under "From Which Plan Do Distributions Come?" at the end of this chapter.

Mechanics of making this election

The recalculation issue is benign if the spouses are aware of it and make a knowledgeable election. Unfortunately, that does not always happen. The proposed regs. permit a plan to allow participants to elect one way or another but also permit plans to allow no choice -- and some plans and IRA account agreements require annual recalculation for both spouses. Furthermore, the proposed regs. say that if the plan (or IRA account agreement) is silent on this subject recalculation is mandatory! Prop. reg. E-7.

The election to recalculate or not must be made *irrevocably* as of the date of the first required distribution (Prop. reg. E-7(c)). This seems harsh since the election has no effect on the amount of the distribution until the second required distribution.

Normally, the election is made on the plan or IRA sponsor's account agreement or beneficiary designation form. Strangely, however, despite the importance of this election, some plans and IRAs do not have any particular form for making the election (and the IRS does not have any form on which participants can tell the IRS what election they have made). If the plan or IRA sponsor's forms do not cover this question, notify the administrator by (for example) a letter attached to the beneficiary designation form. See form 6.1 in

Appendix B. Be sure to get an acknowledgment of receipt from the administrator, and to save the receipted copy "forever"; it will be needed, potentially, for several decades as evidence that minimum distributions are being calculated correctly.

Naming a Non-Spouse DB:
The Incidental Benefit (MDIB) Rule

When a participant names someone other than his spouse as his DB, a special rule comes into play when determining the "joint life expectancy" of the participant and DB. The so-called "Minimum Distribution Incidental Benefit" (MDIB) Rule, is designed to prevent a participant from unduly postponing distribution of his retirement benefits. This rule was created by the Internal Revenue Service. It is not contained in the Code, though it is cryptically referred to in s. 401(a)(9)(G), s. 408(a)(6) and elsewhere. For details, see Prop. reg. s. 1.401(a)(9)-2, which this section summarizes.

Application during participant's life

Under the MDIB rule, P's minimum required distribution ("MRD") for each year is, as usual, determined by applying a fraction or "divisor" to the prior year end value of the account. However, when the MDIB rule applies, the fraction the participant is required to use is whichever of the following produces a *larger* MRD: the actual joint life expectancy of P and the DB; or the divisor specified in the "MDIB rule" table.

The "MDIB rule table" is contained in the proposed regs. at s. 1.401(a)(9)-2; and in IRS publication 590; and in Appendix A of this book. The MDIB rule table contains divisors based, in each year, on the joint LE of P and someone 10 years younger than P. *E.g.*, in the year P is 70, the MDIB rule divisor is 26.2, which is the joint LE of two people ages 70 and 60.

When P is age 81, the MDIB rule divisor is 16.8, which happens to be the joint LE of two people ages 81 and 71. The effect of the MDIB rule, approximately, is to "deem" the DB to be only 10 years younger than P every year. If the DB is less than 10 years younger than P, the MDIB rule has no effect because the real joint LE will always produce a larger fraction (smaller divisor) than the MDIB table.

For example, suppose P is age 71 in his "first distribution calendar year" and his non-spouse DB is age 47. The fraction determined using their actual initial joint LE is 1/36.5, but the fraction under the MDIB table is 1/25.3. The larger fraction, 1/25.3, must be used to determine the MRD for the first year.

Obviously, the MDIB rule forces distributions out of the plan at a faster rate than would use of the actual joint life expectancy of P and his DB. However, it still provides a means to stretch out payments substantially during P's lifetime. In effect it gives the advantages of recalculating life expectancies (P never "outlives" benefits) without the drawbacks (because there is no acceleration of payments at P's death).

The "flip" at participant's death

Furthermore, if P dies before all his benefits have been paid out, the MRD calculations after his death will be based on the *actual* original joint life expectancy period of P and DB. The MDIB rule simply does not apply to distributions after the date of death. Prop. reg. 1.401(a)(9)-2, Q-3. Thus, if P dies before all benefits have been paid out, the beneficiary can get an extremely long payout period for what remains in the plan at P's death.

This "flip" which occurs at P's death, from MRDs based on the MDIB table to MRDs based on the real joint LE of P and the DB, is extremely confusing because it is an exception to the normal rule that, once a participant dies, payments must continue to come out to the beneficiary "at least as rapidly" as

they were coming out before P died. (S. 401(a)(9)(B)(i).)
Under the MDIB rule, and the "flip" that occurs at P's death,
payments dramatically slow down upon P's death.

*Whether to recalculate life expectancy: when a non-spouse is
the DB*

The Code does not permit annual recalculation of life
expectancy for anyone other than the participant and the
participant's spouse. Therefore, the only election that needs to
be made when a non-spouse is the DB is whether to recalculate
the participant's life expectancy. The non-spouse DB's life
expectancy is fixed on the RBD and cannot be recalculated.

Should P's LE be recalculated when there is a non-
spouse DB? There is no simple "one-size-fits-all" answer to this
question. Remember, what happens each year with a non-spouse
DB while P is living is that you must determine *two* possible
MRDs: the MRD based on the *actual* joint LE of P and DB, and
the MRD based on the "MDIB divisor table." If the actual joint
LE (such as "46 years") is a larger number than the MDIB
divisor table number (such as "25.3") then you must use the
smaller number (25.3) because that produces a larger MRD.
Once P dies, you use the remaining *actual* LE, and no longer
need to bother with comparing the actual LE number with the
MDIB table number.

If you elect to recalculate P's LE, then, when P dies, his
LE will go to zero, meaning you are left with only the remaining
LE of the DB to measure payouts. If P's LE was not
recalculated, on the other hand, his LE would not "disappear"
at his death, so the remaining *joint* LE of *both* P and DB would
be available to measure payouts after P's death. Since the joint
LE of P and DB would necessarily be longer than the single LE
of DB, using the fixed term method will produce a longer
payout period (smaller MRDs) *after P dies.*

Does this mean a P who names a non-spouse DB should always elect the "fixed term" method? Not necessarily, because while P is still *living*, using the "recalculate" method may produce smaller MRDs, if the DB is not very much younger than P and P lives a long time. For example, suppose P is 70 and DB is 57. In the first year of the payout, their true joint LE (28.4) is ignored because the MDIB rule divisor (26.2) produces a larger distribution. However, when P gets older, the MRD could be quite different depending on which method P elected:

		Divisor when P is:		
		<u>Age 80</u>	<u>Age 85</u>	<u>Age 90</u>
1.	MDIB rule	17.6	13.8	10.5
2.	Actual remaining joint LE, fixed term method	18.4	13.4	8.4
3.	Actual joint LE, recalculated method	19.5	15.6	12.1

In this example, once P reaches his mid 80s, if he elected the fixed term method, the "actual joint LE" starts producing larger MRDs than the MDIB rule. That would never happen during P's lifetime if he had elected to recalculate.

Conclusion: although the differences are not dramatic, here are some guidelines on this decision:

1.   If the DB is *substantially* younger than P (*e.g.*, a child or grandchild) it will probably make *no difference*, as long as P is living, whether P's LE is being recalculated or not. This is because the MDIB rule will always "override" the actual joint

LE, that is to say, the MDIB rule will always produce a larger MRD. After P's death, the no-recalculation (fixed term) method will produce *slightly* smaller MRDs than the recalculation method. Therefore, if the DB is much younger than P, P should probably elect "fixed term" because that will produce slightly better results after P's death and will make no difference during P's life.

2.   If the DB is not much more than 10 years younger than P (*e.g.*, DB is in his late 50s), then the question is more difficult. Which method is "better" depends on when P dies. If P dies before the end of the original joint LE of P and the DB, the DB will be better off if the "term certain" method was used -- because the DB can withdraw over the balance of that joint LE and will not be forced to withdraw over only his or her own LE. But if P lives a long time, recalculation produces a better result, because smaller MRDs will be required during P's later life.

Changing the DB After 70½

Changing DBs after the RBD

This section deals with P's *naming* a new beneficiary after the RBD, not the death of the original DB. The death of a beneficiary after the RBD is NOT treated as a "change" of beneficiaries. Prop. reg. E-5(e)(2). For what happens if the DB *dies* after P's RBD, see "Checklist of Minimum Distribution Results" ("Permutations") in Appendix C.

The participant can change his DB after his RBD. There are limits to what can be done, but there is more flexibility than many people realize.

The limitations are: if the participant "had no DB" on his RBD, nothing he does later will change that fact. The participant can change the identity of the beneficiary who will receive the benefits after his death, but he cannot, after the RBD, create a DB for purposes of calculating a joint life expectancy payout period if there was no DB on the RBD. (The only "escape hatch" in this situation is this: if P "had no DB" on his RBD, but later names his spouse as beneficiary, and the spouse survives him, the spouse can then roll the benefits to a new IRA in her own name and properly name a DB for it. See Chapter 3.)

The other primary limitation is similar: you cannot, by changing to a younger DB after the RBD, lengthen the maximum payout period, but changing to an *older* DB will shorten it. Here are the rules that apply if the beneficiary is changed *after* the RBD:

(a)   If the new beneficiary has a longer life expectancy than the original "DB," the change has no effect on the minimum distributions. The MRDs continue to be measured by the joint LE of P and the original DB.

(b)   If the new beneficiary has a *shorter* LE than the original DB, then subsequent payouts will be measured by the new shorter joint LE of P and the new DB.

(c)   If P changes, after his RBD, from "having a DB" to "having no DB" (for example, by changing his beneficiary designation from "pay all to my child" to "pay all to my estate"), then subsequent MRDs will be measured by P's LE only.

(d)   If (b) or (c) applies, the change of DB affects the size of distributions beginning with the year *after* the year of the change. Prop. reg. E-5(c)(3).

Example 1: Changing to an older DB. If the original DB (as of the RBD) is P's brother (eight years younger than P) P can change and name his sister (six years younger than P) as his new DB. This will shorten the "joint LE" for purposes of calculating subsequent minimum distributions because the new DB has a shorter life expectancy than the original DB.

Example 2: Changing to a younger DB. If the DB on the RBD is P's six-years-younger sister, P can change and name his eight-years-younger brother as his new DB. However, because the RBD has already passed, this will not lengthen the maximum payout period, which will continue to be measured by the joint LE of P and the original DB, his sister.

Example 3: Changing away from the MDIB rule. If the DB is P's child, P can change the DB to P's spouse (S). The new maximum payout period will be, the joint life expectancy of P and S, or the joint life expectancy of P and the prior DB, whichever is shorter.

If the payouts prior to the change of DB were being measured under the MDIB rule limitation, does this artificially shortened "joint LE" continue if S is named as the new DB? Possibly not. Under the proposed regs., if "a new designated beneficiary with a life expectancy shorter than the life expectancy of the designated beneficiary whose life expectancy is being used to determine the distributions period...replaces a designated beneficiary, the new designated beneficiary is treated as the designated beneficiary for purposes of determining the distribution period." Prop. reg. E-5(c)(1). Thus, a P who named a child as his DB, and is taking distributions over the joint life expectancy of himself and the child as limited by the MDIB rule, can reduce the distributions payable during his life, even after his RBD, by marrying someone who is more than 10 years younger than he but older than the child and naming her as his new DB.

(Or, if he is already married to someone more than 10 years younger than he but older than his child, by naming his spouse as his DB instead of his child.)

Example 4: Changing from an individual to a trust. P can change his DB from any individual to a trust of which that individual or other individuals are the beneficiaries. The new trust must be irrevocable on the date it is named as beneficiary, and a copy of it must be simultaneously delivered to the plan. Of course, if the LE of the oldest trust beneficiary is shorter than the LE of the original DB, the change will shorten P's payout period.

A stumper: on his RBD, Grandpa names Lolita, his 25-year-old "significant other," as his DB. Payouts begin to Grandpa based on the joint LE of himself and Lolita, as limited by the MDIB rule. At age 73, Grandpa marries Lolita. Does the MDIB rule go away now that the DB has become the spouse? The answer to this is not clear.

The proposed regs. are very clear on what happens if (i) S is the DB on the RBD and (ii) S ceases to be the spouse due to divorce or death. In that case, the MDIB rule does *not* kick in. A change of status from "spouse" (on the RBD) to "no longer spouse" (sometime after the RBD) has no effect, and P can continue to withdraw over the joint LE of P and S. Prop. reg. 1.401(a)(9)-2, Q-7(d). The regs. are silent on a change of status in the other direction--from non-spouse on the RBD to, later, spouse.

The biggest problem with changing the DB after the RBD is often the fact that you cannot change the election regarding recalculation of life expectancy. For more discussion of the issues and solutions, see the *Fallon* and *Heinrich* case studies.

Changing DBs after age 70½ but before the RBD

A final emphasis: the key date is the RBD, April 1 following the year the participant turns 70½. The wise participant begins planning early for this event, and may file a beneficiary designation and elections regarding the form of benefits well before his RBD. As far as the minimum distribution rules are concerned, these are completely amendable and changeable at any time prior to the RBD. This may work favorably or unfavorably. Also, the plan may limit the options for later change even when the tax law does not.

Example 5: On June 1 of the year he turned 70½, Charlie filed an election form naming his estate as beneficiary, in effect electing to take his benefits in installments over his LE only, and by December 31 withdraws the first year's installment. The next year, BEFORE APRIL 1, he changes his mind and names his grandson Arthur as his beneficiary. Because he changed his beneficiary designation before April 1 (his RBD), he can use the joint LE of himself and Arthur (as limited by the MDIB rule) to measure his MRDs.

Example 6: In the year she turns 70½, Louise names her grandson Waldo as her "designated beneficiary," and her husband Ralph as her contingent beneficiary. Unfortunately, Waldo dies in an accident, just before Louise's RBD. Because he died before Louise's RBD, he was not her DB "on" her RBD. Ralph, the former contingent beneficiary, becomes the DB "on" the RBD and Louise must measure MRDs using the joint LE of herself and Ralph, not herself and Waldo.

Example 7: Roger retires at age 68 and elects to take his pension benefits in the form of a joint and survivor annuity with his wife Imelda. Later, he decides that an installment payout over the joint LE of Roger and his daughter Emily would be more advantageous. Unfortunately his employer's pension plan does not allow him to change his election even though the minimum distribution rules would. There is nothing he can do about this. Within certain limits, plans are allowed to be more restrictive than the Code.

Example 8: Brenda names her husband Amnon as the DB of her IRA. When Brenda reaches her RBD she files a form with the IRA administrator, directing that the account be distributed to her over her LE only. However, she does have a DB: husband Amnon. As far as the minimum distribution rules are concerned, her MRDs are based on the joint LE of Brenda and Amnon, and she is simply choosing to take out larger distributions (based solely on her own LE) than she has to. As far as the minimum distribution rules are concerned, she can switch any time to taking smaller distributions, based on the joint LE of herself and Amnon.

How to Compute Life Expectancy and Installments

Determining the participant's life expectancy

Prop. reg. s. 1.401(a)(9)-1(E) gives the method of determining P's "life expectancy" (LE) as of his RBD.

First, you determine the calendar year in which P will attain age 70½.

Second, you determine P's attained age as of his birthday which falls within that calendar year. If his birthday falls in the first half of the calendar year the attained age will be 70. If his birthday falls in the second half of the calendar year, then his attained age on the birthday which falls within the calendar year in which he attains age 70½ will be 71.

Finally, you compute the LE using Table V of regulation s. 1.72-9. (This table is also partially reproduced in IRS Publication 590 and in Appendix A of this book.) The column entitled "multiple" (or divisor) in Table V is the LE for the applicable attained age. For age 70 it is 16.0 years. For age 71 it is 15.3 years. The IRS tables are "unisex," so the LE for men and women is the same.

Installments over P's LE -- term certain method

Once you have determined the applicable LE, here is how you compute the required minimum annual distributions, according to Prop. reg. 1.401(a)(9)-1, if you are using the term certain method (no recalculation).

Assume Whit's 70th birthday was 8/1/95. He accordingly turns 70½ on 2/1/96, so his "Required Beginning Date" (RBD) is April 1, 1997. Since his age on his 1996 birthday (8/1/96) will be 71, his LE in his "age 70½ year" for purposes of the minimum distribution rules is 15.3 years. He does not elect to redetermine his LE annually. Table 1.1 shows how much the plan must distribute to him, when, to avoid the 50% excise tax.

Note the following with regard to Table 1.1: There are two distributions required in the first year (1997). Whit can avoid this doubling of required distributions by taking his first required distribution in the year he turns 70½, rather than waiting until April 1 of the next year.

The participant can always take out *more* than 401(a)(9) requires; 401(a)(9) simply dictates the minimum. Taking out more than the minimum in a particular year does not give the participant any "credit" that can be carried forward and applied to a later year's minimum distribution; each year stands on its own. So even if Whit withdraws 50% of his entire account balance in 1998 (way in excess of the 1/13.3 he is required to

Table 1.1

No later than this date	Distribute at least this much of his plan balance	Valued as of the last plan valuation date in
4/1/97	1/15.3	1995
12/31/97	1/14.3	1996
12/31/98	1/13.3	1997
12/31/99	1/12.3	1998
12/31/2000	1/11.3	1999
12/31/2001	1/10.3	2000
12/31/2002	1/9.3	2001
12/31/2003	1/8.3	2002
12/31/2004	1/7.3	2003
12/31/2005	1/6.3	2004
12/31/2006	1/5.3	2005
12/31/2007	1/4.3	2006
12/31/2008	1/3.3	2007
12/31/2009	1/2.3	2008
12/31/2010	1/1.3	2009
12/31/2011	100%	

withdraw), he will still be required, in calendar 1999, to withdraw 1/12.3 of whatever the remaining account balance was as of 12/31/98. (Of course, a larger-than-required withdrawal indirectly reduces the required distributions for later years, by reducing the year-end account balance on which the subsequent year's minimum is calculated.)

The minimum distribution requirements are independent of the 15% excise tax on "excess distributions" (see Chapter 5). If s. 401(a)(9) compels the participant to withdraw more than $150,000 in a particular year -- that's tough. He can make the withdrawal, and pay 15% excise tax on everything over $150,000; or not make it, and pay 50% excise tax on the money that should have been withdrawn but was not.

Installments over P's LE -- recalculation method

If payments are being made over Whit's LE solely, and he has elected to recalculate his LE annually, then each year's distribution during his life and for the year of death is calculated using a fraction, the denominator of which is Whit's LE as of his attained age on his birthday in that year. Table 1.2 shows the required distributions under this method.

Under the recalculation method, distributions continue until 2035 when Whit is age 110 and must withdraw 100% of the plan balance as of 12/31/2034. If Whit dies before reaching age 110, his beneficiaries will have to withdraw 100% of the benefits by 12/31 of the year following his death. To illustrate, suppose that as of 12/31/95 Whit's IRA balance was $1,000,000, growing annually at 8%. Whit turned 70½ in 1996, and his RBD is 4/1/97. Each year he withdraws the required minimum on the last possible date. He dies in the year 2000 at age 75. Table 1.3 shows the required distributions.

Table 1.2

No later than this date	Participant's Attained Age	Distribute at least this much of his plan balance	Valued as of the last plan valuation date in
4/1/97	71	1/15.3	1995
12/31/97	72	1/14.6	1996
12/31/98	73	1/13.9	1997
12/31/99	74	1/13.2	1998
12/31/00	75	1/12.5	1999
...etc.			

Table 1.3

Date	Withdrawal	Plan Balance
12/31/95	0	1,000,000
12/31/96	0	1,080,000
4/1/97	65,359	N/A
12/31/97	73,973	1,021,839
12/31/98	73,514	1,030,072
12/31/99	78,036	1,034,442
12/31/00	82,755	1,034,442
12/31/01	1,034,442	0

Determining the account balance the fraction applies to

The account value "as of the last valuation date" in the preceding plan year must be increased by certain plan contributions. See Prop. reg. F-5. For IRAs, the applicable valuation date is December 31st of the preceding year.

If all or part of the MRD for the age 70½ year is postponed until January, February or March of the following year (*i.e.*, the "age 71½" year), then the MRD for the "age 71½ year" is calculated in a special way. The appropriate fraction for the "71½ year" is applied to an "adjusted" preceding-year-end balance. The preceding-year-end balance is reduced by [the MRD for the age 70½ year] minus [amounts actually distributed in the age 70½ year]. Prop. reg. F-5(c)(2).

Example: David was born 1/1/25 and reached age 70½ in 1995. His wife Judith, who turned 74 in 1995, is named as his DB, and their joint LE is 18.6 years. David elects not to recalculate either LE. David has an IRA which had a value on 12/31/94 of $300,000. The MRD for 1995 is 1/18.6 x $300,000, or $16,130. David withdraws only $5,000 from the IRA in 1995. On 12/31/95, the IRA value is $325,500. In January of 1996, he withdraws the rest of the 1995 MRD ($11,130). The 1996 MRD will be 1/17.6 x ($325,500 - [$16,130-$5,000]), or $17,578.

Installments over joint LE of P and S - fixed term method

To determine the joint LE of P and spouse (S), use Table VI of reg. 1.72-9, using their attained ages as of their birthdays in the year P turns 70½. (Part of this table is reproduced in IRS Publication 590 and in Appendix A.)

For example, assume P turns 70½ on 2/1/93. His age on his 1993 birthday (8/1/93) is 71. S's date of birth was 4/15/25, so she will be 68 on her 1993 birthday. Table VI tells us that the joint LE of two people ages 71 and 68 is 21.2 years.

If neither spouse's LE is recalculated, then P will take distributions over the following schedule: 1/21.2 the first year; 1/20.2 the second year, 1/19.2 the third year, and so on. If either one or both die before the 21 years are up, the surviving spouse (or the contingent beneficiary) will continue to take installments over the remainder of the 21 years.

P and S -- both LEs recalculated annually

If both spouses' LEs are being redetermined annually, you start off the same as in the preceding example: the first year's (1993) installment would be (in the above example) 1/21.2 times the prior year end account balance, because 21.2 years is the joint and survivor LE of two people ages 71 and 68 under Table VI. Then in each subsequent year you look at the couple's joint LE under Table VI for their attained ages *in that year*; so the second year's (1994) required distribution would be 1/20.3 times applicable account balance, since 20.3 years is the joint LE of two people ages 72 and 69. This continues until one of them dies.

The distribution in the year one spouse dies will still be calculated based on their joint LE as of their birthdays in the year of death -- but in the *following* year, the decedent's LE is zero, so you switch to Table V and calculate further distributions based solely on the LE of the survivor.

So in this example suppose S dies in the second distribution year, 1994. The 1994 distribution is not changed -- it is still 1/20.3 as calculated above. But in the next year, 1995, we look solely at P's LE. He will attain age 73 in 1995. The LE of a 73-year-old under Table V is 13.9 years, so the minimum distribution will be 1/13.9 -- a substantial increase over the prior year's 1/20.3 distribution.

And of course when the surviving spouse dies, his or her LE also goes to zero and 100% of the plan benefits will have to be distributed by December 31 of the year after the year of death of the surviving spouse. (Note: if the *participant* died first, the surviving spouse could roll over the benefits to his/her own IRA and start a new distribution schedule going.)

P and S -- "split" method -- only one spouse's LE is recalculated

This is very tricky. To calculate the joint and survivor LE of two people, when one LE is being recalculated annually and the other is not, you must go through the following routine prescribed by the proposed regs. Alternatively, you can use a software program to do the calculations for you--see Appendix D.

In the following example, assume P turned age 71 in 1993, his first required distribution year, and S turned 68. His LE is to be recalculated, hers is not. Say it is now the fourth distribution year, 1996. Prop. reg. E-8(b) says you still use the joint and survivor LE from Table VI but you use P's *real age*, and an "adjusted age" for S. P's real attained age in year four is 74. S's real age is 71, but her "adjusted age" is determined as follows:

(a)   Determine her real LE, separately, for the year in which P reached age 70½. Her attained age in that year was 68. Her LE at age 68 under Table V was 17.6 years.

(b)   Now reduce her LE as determined under (a) above by one year for each year since that year. It has been three years, so her "adjusted" LE, in year four, is 17.6 minus 3, or 14.6.

(c)   Now determine the age in Table V which corresponds to a 14.6 year LE. That would be age 72. (If it came out in between two ages you would round up to the higher age). So her "adjusted age" is 72.

(d)   The joint and survivor LE of two individuals age 74 and 72 under Table VI is 18.2 years, so this year's required minimum is 1/18.2.

If S in this example dies, future installments would nevertheless continue to be calculated as before based on the "adjusted age" of the DB (ignoring the fact that she died, since P did not elect to recalculate her LE) and P's *actual* age. If P dies before S, future installments to S will be calculated based on the number of years remaining in her original LE (17.6 years). (Alternatively, she may elect to roll over the benefits to her own IRA and start a new minimum distribution game going.)

Participant and non-spouse: the MDIB rule

If P elects to take installments over the joint LE of himself and a non-spouse DB, the calculation of the annual required distribution during their joint lives will essentially be the same as when the spouse is the DB, *except* for one additional step required to comply with the MDIB rule: the actual joint LE must be compared with the "applicable divisor" shown in the MDIB table at prop. reg. 1.401(a)(9)-2, Q & A 4(a) (reproduced in Appendix A). The LE used must be the *smaller* of those two numbers.

If P's attained age in the year he turns 70½ is 70, the

divisor in the first distribution year under the MDIB rule is 26.2. If it is 71, it will be 25.3 years. This comparison is made annually.

Then, when P dies, the MDIB rule disappears, and the denominator now "flips" to being based on the true joint LE of the DB and P, because "the MDIB requirement does not apply to distributions after the employee's death." Prop. reg. 1.401(a)(9)-2, Q & A 3.

For example, suppose Mimi commences taking installments at her RBD (4/1/94) over the LE of herself and her daughter Grizelda. In 1993, Mimi turns 70½ (on November 1); her attained age on her 1993 birthday (5/1/93) is 70, and Grizelda's age on her 1993 birthday is 40. Their joint LE from Table VI is 42.9 years. But the maximum "applicable divisor" permitted for Mimi's first distribution year under the MDIB rule is 26.2. The distribution schedule during Mimi's life is shown in Table 1.4.

Table 1.4		
Latest Withdrawal Date	This Fraction	Applied to Plan Balance on
4/1/94	1/26.2	12/31/92
12/31/94	1/25.3	12/31/93
12/31/95	1/24.4	12/31/94
....etc.		

Now suppose Mimi dies at age 86 in 2009. In the following year, 2010, distributions will "flip" to being calculated on the *original* joint LE of Mimi and Grizelda, without regard to the MDIB rule. The joint LE of Mimi and Grizelda back in 1993 (ages 70 and 40) was 42.9 years. 17 years have passed since then, so the remaining period certain is 25.9 years (42.9 minus 17). (This assumes Mimi elected not to recalculate her LE annually.) So distributions will from now on be as shown in Table 1.5.

A tougher question is: what happens in the year of death? The MDIB rule does not apply to post-death distributions. Suppose Mimi had not yet, by the time she died, taken out the minimum distribution for the year of death, 2009, which was 1/10.2 of the account balance as of 12/31/08. Can Grizelda take out the 2009 minimum distribution based on the remaining actual joint LE, without regard to the MDIB rule? The answer to this is not known.

Table 1.5		
By This Date	**Take Out This Fraction:**	**Of Plan Balance on:**
12/31/10	1/25.9	12/31/09
12/31/11	1/24.9	12/31/10
... and so on until 2036		

P dies before RBD: installments over DB's LE

Upon the death of P before his RBD, if distributions are to be made over the LE of the DB, the required annual distributions to the DB are calculated as follows. If there is one DB, determine his LE from Table V based on his attained age as of his birthday in the year distributions are required to commence, *i.e.* (in the case of a non-spouse DB) the year after the year in which P died, or (if the DB is the S) the year in which P would have reached age 70½, if later.

If there are several DBs, determine which of them is the oldest. Distributions will be based on the oldest one's LE calculated as above, unless "separate accounts" were established for the DBs "as of" the date of death.

If S is the DB, the Code gives her the option to recalculate her LE annually, if the plan permits it. As with lifetime distributions, the plan may require or forbid recalculation; if the plan says nothing, recalculation is mandatory; and whatever method is "in effect" for the first required distribution must be used for all distributions. Prop. reg. E-7(c).

From Which Plan Do Distributions Come?

Notice 88-38 allows participants and beneficiaries to choose which IRA MRDs come out of

If the over-70½ client participates in more than one retirement plan, the MRD must be calculated separately for each plan, and each plan must distribute the MRD calculated for that plan. Thus if the client is a participant in two pension plans, a 401(k) plan and a 403(b) plan, he will receive four separate MRDs, one for each of these plans.

A different rule applies for IRAs. The MRD must be calculated separately for each IRA, but the participant does not have to take each IRA's calculated amount from that IRA. He can total up the MRDs required from all of the IRAs, and then take the total amount all from one of the IRAs, or from any combination of them. Notice 88-38, 1988-1 C.B. 524.

Since each IRA may have a different "designated beneficiary," or different method of computing the participant's (or spouse's) life expectancy, the Notice offers great planning flexibility.

Example 1: Anthony establishes two equal IRAs at his RBD, naming his wife Bernice as DB of one and their son Stacey as DB of the other. Because Bernice is the same age as Anthony, and Stacey is much younger, the annual MRD for each IRA will be different. Assuming Anthony wants to keep the bequests to his wife and son more or less equal, Anthony can (1) determine the MRD separately for each IRA, (2) determine the total MRD for the year (the sum of the MRDs from each IRA) and (3) take half of the total MRD from each IRA.

Example 2: At her RBD, Marcia established three equal IRAs, naming one of her three children as DB of each. Investment results differ in the three accounts, causing them to become unequal in value. Marcia wants each child to receive an equal amount, so each year she takes her MRD from the IRA which has grown the fastest, to bring it down in value to be equal to the others.

Example 3: Jo Claire established two IRAs at her RBD. Her spouse is DB of both, but on one account she elected to recalculate both spouses' life expectancies annually, and on the other she elected the fixed term method. Now she regrets the election to recalculate and wishes she had elected the fixed term method for both. By taking the MRD for both IRAs only from the "recalculate" IRA, she can gradually deplete that one and allow the "fixed term" IRA to grow.

Example 4: Burton, age 72, is the beneficiary of his late mother's IRA. In addition, he has an IRA of his own. Both generate MRDs each year. He can take the total MRD for each year from either account.

Example 5: Jeffrey dies, leaving two IRAs. One is payable to a marital deduction trust, the other to a credit shelter trust. The "trust rules" are complied with, so the beneficiaries of the respective trusts are treated as Jeffrey's DB, and the life expectancy of the oldest is used to measure the post-death MRDs. Assume the credit shelter trust permits accumulation of income. If the family's goal is to maximize income tax deferral and minimize estate taxes, then perhaps, although Notice 88-38 does not specifically mention this situation, each year's MRD could be taken entirely from the IRA payable to the marital trust. The credit shelter trust would get the maximum available income tax deferral and what income taxes had to be paid would be paid by the marital trust, where at least they could reduce the spouse's future taxable estate.

What you can't do

Notice 88-38 applies only to IRAs. MRDs from qualified plans and 403(b) plans cannot be combined. If a client is a participant in a 401(k) plan, a pension plan, a 403(b) plan, and two IRAs, he must calculate the MRD separately for *each* of his five plans; then he must take the 401(k) plan MRD from the 401(k) plan, the pension plan MRD from the pension plan and the 403(b) MRD from the 403(b) plan. Only the two IRAs can be mixed and matched, taking the combined required MRD from either IRA or both.

Also, it is *not* possible to modify MRD results by moving assets from one IRA to another.

Example 6: Lullie has two IRAs, with her husband as DB of one and their child as DB of the other. Having decided that her husband is well provided for by his own assets, Lullie would like to shift some assets from the "spouse IRA" to the "child IRA." If the transferred assets could then be distributed over the joint life expectancy of Lullie and her child rather than Lullie and her husband, this move would result in smaller MRDs and longer deferral. However, although the assets can be transferred, it won't accomplish anything as far as the minimum distribution rules are concerned. If assets in one IRA are moved to another IRA with a different designated beneficiary, the proposed regulations require the "new" and "old" assets in the transferee IRA to be accounted for separately, and the MRD to be computed separately for each "pool." Prop. reg. G-2(b). In other words, not only does transferring assets between IRAs after the required beginning date not improve the MRD status, it creates a major accounting headache.

Summary of Planning Principles

1.   The opportunity for continued income tax deferral on earnings and investment income is the most valuable feature of qualified retirement plans and IRAs. Preserving the option of continued tax deferral is an important goal of estate planning for retirement benefits. The minimum distribution rules set the outer limits on deferral and establish the requirements for reaching those limits. Planning for retirement benefits therefore requires familiarity with these rules.

2.   Naming a beneficiary for retirement benefits does more than determine who will receive the benefits after the participant's death; it also determines the maximum period of income tax deferral that will be available for those benefits.

3.   Once the participant reaches his "required beginning date," the maximum deferral period for his benefits, as dictated by his choice of beneficiary, becomes substantially irrevocable. He can later change his choice of beneficiary, but cannot extend the payout period.

4.   Naming the participant's "estate" as beneficiary,

generally speaking, substantially reduces the opportunities for continued income tax deferral compared with naming an individual beneficiary.

5.   Naming a trust as beneficiary has the same effect as naming an estate, unless the five "trust rules" are complied with.

6.   When the participant reaches age 70½, he must start withdrawing benefits. Naming a younger generation beneficiary at the "required beginning date" will produce the longest possible income tax deferral, both during the participant's life and after his death. Naming any designated beneficiary will almost always produce more potential income tax deferral than having "no DB."

7.   If the participant is naming more than one beneficiary, consider dividing the benefits into separate "accounts" before the RBD, especially if the beneficiaries are substantially apart in age, to enable each individual beneficiary to use his/her own life expectancy to measure payouts after P's death.

8.   Do not mix charities and individuals in a beneficiary designation if you want the individuals to be able to use the life expectancy method for payout of their share of the benefits, unless you comply with the "separate share" procedure. This issue is discussed in more detail in Chapter 9.

9.   When the participant reaches age 70½, consider carefully not only the choice of "DB" but also the decision whether to recalculate life expectancies.

10.   Carefully document the identity of the DB, and the choices regarding "recalculation," at the RBD and save these records "forever."

11.   If P is not certain about whom to name as DB at his RBD, or how to determine life expectancies, consider establishing separate IRAs, with different beneficiaries, or different methods of determining life expectancy, for each.

2

Income Tax Issues

*The impact of income taxes on
planning for retirement benefits,
and how to mitigate it*

Introduction

This chapter examines three aspects of the income tax treatment of retirement benefits: how benefits are taxed after the participant's death ("income in respect of a decedent" or "IRD"); the special tax treatment given to certain lump sum distributions; and deferring income taxes with "rollovers." The discussion of IRD emphasizes the income tax effects of leaving retirement benefits to trusts.

Income in Respect of a Decedent

No stepped up basis

"Income in respect of a decedent" (IRD) is income generated by an individual that is not realized until after his death. Unlike other assets, IRD does not get a "stepped up basis" upon the death of the individual who earned it. S. 1014. It remains taxable income in the hands of the beneficiary just as it would have been in the hands of the decedent. S. 691.

Death benefits under qualified plans, 403(b) plans, and IRAs are "IRD," and thus will be subject to income tax when distributed to the beneficiary. There are only two exceptions to this rule: the employee's after-tax contributions (or other "investment in the contract" or "basis"), and the pure death benefit portion of life insurance, are not subject to income tax. The recovery of the employee's "basis" or "investment in the contract" normally has little impact on planning decisions and so is not discussed in this book, except in connection with plan-held life insurance; this and all other aspects of plan-held life insurance are discussed in Chapter 6.

Thus, retirement plan benefits are generally subject to *both* estate taxes and income taxes. This creates numerous planning considerations. The primary planning consideration is the desirability of deferring the imposition of income taxes as long as possible; how to attain that goal was the subject of Chapter 1.

If an IRD item is paid out to the named beneficiary (for example, if a profit sharing benefit is paid directly to an individual who is the designated beneficiary), then that beneficiary pays income tax on that money as it is distributed to him or her. The rest of this section deals with the treatment of IRD payable to a *trust or estate*, including the planning pitfall known as "transferring" or "assignment of" IRD.

The drawback of making IRD payable to a trust

IRD paid to a trust is subject to the punitive trust income tax rates. A trust reaches the highest federal income tax bracket (39.6%) at $7,650 of taxable income (1995 rates). An individual taxpayer does not hit that bracket until he or she has more than $256,500 of taxable income. Thus, making retirement benefits payable to a marital, credit shelter or other trust will generally result (except in the richest families) in the benefits' being taxed more heavily than if the benefits were paid to individual family members.

Example: Grover dies, leaving his $200,000 401(k) plan to a trust for his wife, Ginger. The trust provides that the income of the trust is to be paid to Ginger; at her death the principal is paid to their children. Under the terms of the 401(k) plan, the only form of benefit permitted is a lump sum. Assume that "forward averaging" (discussed later in this chapter) is not available, and that this $200,000 is the only taxable income of the trust. The result? The trust receives the $200,000 distribution and pays $78,332 of federal income tax on it (1995 rates).

Now assume the lump sum had instead been paid to Ginger outright, and that she had other income exactly equal to her deductions and exemptions. She would have paid only $61,370.50 of income taxes on the distribution, almost $17,000 less than the trust had to pay. Thus if the benefits had been paid to the spouse individually rather than to a trust, she would have had substantially more money available to invest.

Note that the distribution, when it comes in to the trust, is "principal" for trust accounting purposes. However, for *income tax purposes*, it is "income."

A not-very-useful rule: generally speaking, a trust gets an income tax deduction for distributing income to trust beneficiaries. The beneficiaries then have to include that income on their individual tax returns. The calculation of what items of taxable income get passed out to the beneficiaries is based on a concept called "distributable net income" or "DNI." Distributions of "DNI" transfer the income tax burden from the trust to the beneficiary. The income will then be taxed at the beneficiary's personal rate rather than the trust's rate. Ss. 661, 662. This method of shifting the tax liability is not very useful because the purpose of paying benefits to a trust in the first place will generally be defeated if the benefits are immediately distributed to the beneficiary.

Example: Colin names his credit shelter trust as beneficiary of his $600,000 IRA. The goal is to keep the benefits out of the taxable estate of his wife Chandler. Colin dies. The trustee of the credit shelter trust withdraws the income of the IRA annually and also withdraws the $600,000 "principal" of the benefits in five annual installments of $120,000. Under the terms of Colin's credit shelter trust, all income is paid to Chandler, so the trustee distributes the IRA income to her and it is taxed at her personal income tax rate (31%). The annual withdrawals of $120,000 of "principal," however, stay in the credit shelter trust and are taxed at trust rates.

If the terms of Colin's credit shelter trust permit the trustee to distribute principal to Chandler, the trustee could reduce the income taxes by distributing to Chandler all the principal he is withdrawing from the IRA each year. This would cause the "principal" to be taxed at Chandler's rate rather than the trust's -- but it would also defeat the entire purpose of the credit shelter trust, which is to keep this asset out of Chandler's estate. Once five years had passed since Colin's death, the trustee would have withdrawn all benefits from the IRA and distributed them to Chandler and the credit shelter trust would be left with nothing.

Note: this is an extremely simplified description of a complex subject, namely, the income tax treatment of retirement benefits paid to and from trusts, a more thorough explanation of which is outside the scope of this book.

Tax treatment of IRD paid to an estate

IRD items will be taxed to the estate if paid to the estate. However, if the estate, before actually receiving the income, distributes the *right* to receive the income, then:

(a)   the distributee will be taxable on the income, if he/she acquired it by specific bequest or as residuary legatee of the estate; Reg. s. 1.691(a)-2(b), examples (1) and (2); 1.691(a)-4(b).

(b)   If the distribution is treated as a "sale," however, the estate is taxable. Reg. s. 1.691(a)-4(a). See "Planning pitfall: assignment of IRD," below.

If the will "bequeaths" retirement benefits to a particular beneficiary, but the benefits are paid to the estate before the estate gets a chance to assign the "right-to-receive" the benefits to the beneficiary, distributing the benefits to the beneficiary upon receipt should carry out DNI to the beneficiary. Although normally all items of income are pro-rated proportionately among beneficiaries who receive distributions, a different allocation specified in the governing instrument is respected. Reg. s. 1.661(b)-1. The following examples illustrate these rules.

Example 1: Larry names Liz as beneficiary of his pension plan. Liz is taxable on the plan distributions she receives after Larry's death.

Example 2: Mike names his estate as beneficiary of his IRA. His will provides that any IRA benefits are specifically bequeathed to Liz. After Mike's death, the estate assigns the IRA to Liz. Liz pays the tax on the IRA distributions. If the estate actually received distributions from the IRA, and passed those distributions out to Liz, Liz would pay the tax on the distributions.

Example 3: Eddie names his estate as beneficiary of his profit sharing plan. His will leaves $1 million to Liz. The executor assigns the profit sharing plan to Liz in partial fulfillment of the

$1 million bequest. The estate may have to pay income tax on the assignment; see "Planning pitfall: assignment of IRD."

IRD payable to non-charitable trust

If the right-to-receive IRD is distributed as a specific "bequest" from a trust, the same principles apply as apply to an estate. For example, if Rosie's 403(b) annuity is payable to her trust as beneficiary, and the trust says "the Trustee shall distribute all 403(b) annuity contracts to my spouse," Rosie's spouse will receive the 403(b) annuity contract, and will be taxed on distributions from it only as they are paid out of the 403(b) plan and into his hands.

If the right-to-receive the IRD is distributed to trust beneficiaries under a discretionary power to distribute principal, the beneficiaries presumably pay the income tax. Yet the regs. provide only that if a trust *terminates* and distributes the right-to-receive to the beneficiaries, the beneficiaries pay the tax. S. 1.691(a)-4(b)(3).

IRD payable to charity

If the right-to-receive IRD is specifically "bequeathed" to a charity by the decedent's will, or payable directly to the charity under a beneficiary designation form, s. 691 would impose the income tax on the charity. Since the recipient is tax exempt, there would be no income tax on the IRD.

If the right-to-receive IRD is bequeathed to a charity, but the IRD is actually paid to the estate before the estate has a chance to distribute the "right-to-receive," the tax treatment is trickier. There is no DNI deduction for distributions to a charitable beneficiary. S. 663(a)(2). Therefore, the only way to "transfer" the income tax liability to the charity is by means of a charitable deduction under s. 642.

S. 642 allows the income tax charitable deduction to an estate or trust for charitable gifts which are required by the governing instrument to be paid out of income. A specific bequest of retirement benefits to charity meets this requirement. A deduction is also allowed to an estate (but *not* a trust) for amounts "permanently set aside" for charity "pursuant to the terms of the governing instrument." S. 642(c)(2). This provision can eliminate income tax on retirement benefits paid to an estate which is passing to a charitable residuary beneficiary, even if the benefits are not distributed to the charity in the year received.

Planning pitfall: "assignment" of IRD

The major planning pitfall of IRD has to do with "assignments" of such income. The problem of "assignment" of IRD does not exist when IRD assets are divided up to fulfill fractional bequests; see, *e.g.*, Ltr. Rul. 9537005 (6/13/95), Ruling 7. The pitfall comes when IRD is used to satisfy a *pecuniary* bequest. It is generally assumed that a distribution of IRD in fulfillment of a pecuniary bequest would trigger immediate realization of the income by the estate or other funding entity. Yet, as the following discussion indicates, it is not clear under the Code that this would happen, especially if there is no other asset available to fund the bequest.

There are three rules under which the IRS can impose income tax on a trust or estate upon the funding of a bequest:

A.   The longstanding IRS position is that satisfying a pecuniary bequest (and certain other types of bequests) with property in kind is treated the same as satisfaction of a debt with appreciated property, *i.e.*, it triggers realization of gain under s. 663. However, retirement benefits, being IRD, are governed by s. 691. Therefore, this general IRS principle under s. 663 should not apply.

B.   Cancellation of an installment obligation after the obligee's death, or transferring it after the obligee's death to the obligor, generates realization (to the obligee's estate) of the deferred gain. This is due to a specific Code provision, s. 691(a)(5), which is clearly not applicable to retirement benefits.

C.   The only relevant Code section, therefore, is 691(a)(2), which taxes the "sale, exchange or other disposition" of IRD if made by the estate or by the "person who received such right by reason of the death of the decedent." But the transfer of IRD to "a person pursuant to the right of such person to receive such amount by . . . bequest, devise or inheritance" is NOT a taxable transfer under this section.

Now consider the following situation. Ron dies, leaving his $1 million IRA payable to his living trust as beneficiary. The trust contains a pecuniary marital formula bequest, under which the marital trust is entitled to $400,000. The trust holds no other assets except the IRA. Ron's trustee transfers $400,000 of the IRA to the marital trust and keeps the rest for the residuary credit shelter trust.

In this example, surely the IRA is transferred to the marital trust "by bequest from the decedent." The funding trust is not "selling" or "exchanging" the IRA -- it is fulfilling the pecuniary marital bequest, and a transfer in fulfillment of a bequest is not taxable under s. 691(a)(2). The trust has no choice regarding which asset to use to fund the marital trust -- the IRA is the only asset available.

The IRS, unfortunately, however, may not agree with this conclusion. The IRS, in its regs., does not come right out and say that fulfilling a pecuniary bequest with IRD is treated as a "sale or exchange" of the IRD, but strongly implies it. Reg. s. 1.691(a)-4(b)(2) says that, if IRD is transferred to "a specific or residuary legatee," only the legatee includes the IRD in income.

The negative implication is that fulfilling a pecuniary bequest with IRD does *not* carry out the taxable income to the legatee. In other words, satisfying a pecuniary bequest with IRD should be treated as a "sale," just the same as satisfying a pecuniary bequest with appreciated property. Furthermore, the IRS has indicated in at least one private letter ruling that it considers s. 663 applicable to funding a pecuniary bequest with IRD. Ltr. Rul. 9123036 (3/12/91) (using an installment obligation to fund a pecuniary credit shelter gift would trigger realization of gain).

Despite the IRS' apparent position, however, the Code treats these two events (funding a pecuniary bequest with appreciated property versus "assigning" IRD) differently, as the following discussion shows.

Although generally distributions to beneficiaries from an estate or trust "carry out" the trust's taxable income to the beneficiary (see ss. 661, 662), the recipient of a pecuniary bequest ("a specific sum of money") generally does not have to pay income tax on it, s. 663(a)(1), nor does he take over the trust's basis if the bequest is fulfilled by a transfer of property in kind. S. 643(e)(4). These provisions read together more or less force the conclusion that fulfillment of a pecuniary bequest with appreciated property causes the funding entity to realize income. Otherwise the income inherent in the appreciated property would just "disappear" and never be taxed.

IRD, however, is different. It is taxed under s. 691, not ss. 661-663. It is not "appreciated property." It is taxed only when s. 691 says it is taxed. S. 691's standards for carrying out the income tax burden to the beneficiaries are not the same as the "DNI" rules of ss. 661-663. Thus, it is quite logical, under the Code, that a pecuniary bequest funded with IRD could carry the income tax burden to the beneficiary when funding the same bequest with appreciated property would not.

The IRS MAY have recognized this; see Ltr. Rul. 9524020 (3/21/95), in which a funding trust was allowed to transfer an IRA directly to a surviving spouse in fulfillment of a pecuniary spousal share. The ruling did not say that the transfer generated current tax to the funding entity. On the other hand, the IRS did not mention the subject of IRD at all, so perhaps the issue was overlooked.

Planning mode: Because of the IRS' apparent position that funding a pecuniary bequest with IRD is a taxable transfer, planners are strongly advised to avoid having retirement benefits pass through a pecuniary funding formula. The best methods of avoidance are: if possible under all the circumstances, make retirement benefits payable to an individual rather than a trust; if the benefits are paid to a trust, make them payable to a trust that is not going to have to be divided up; if the benefits are going to be paid to a typical pourover trust which is divided between a marital and a family share, or between a generation skipping and a non-generation skipping share, either specify clearly (in both the designation of beneficiary form and in the trust instrument) which trust share these retirement benefits are supposed to go to (so that the benefits pass to the chosen trust directly, rather than through the funding formula), or use a fractional formula (fulfillment of which does not trigger immediate realization of IRD) rather than a pecuniary formula (which may).

Cleanup mode: Although it is highly advisable to steer clear of funding a pecuniary bequest with qualified plan or IRA benefits, inevitably some participants will leave their benefits payable to a trust which contains a pecuniary funding formula. This can happen when the benefits are paid directly to such a trust as beneficiary, or when the benefits are payable to the participant's estate and pass to such a trust under the residuary clause. In these circumstances, first look into the possibility of using disclaimers to get the benefits payable to the "right" beneficiary (see Chapter 8). If that course is not available, and the retirement benefit must pass through the pecuniary funding formula, there are still possibilities for avoiding current tax:

(a)   If benefits are used to fund a pecuniary bequest to a marital trust, and the surviving spouse has the unfettered right to withdraw all assets of the marital trust, see Ltr. Rul. 9524020 (3/21/95), where the direct transfer of QRP benefits to S's IRA in partial satisfaction of her statutory elective share was treated as a rollover avoiding current tax. Although the statutory share was apparently a pecuniary amount, the ruling did not discuss s. 691.

(b)   If the benefits are the only assets available to fund the bequest, consider the arguments above, based on the s. 691 language, that the beneficiary is entitled to the asset and therefore there is no taxable transfer.

(c)   If options (a) and (b) do not do the job, consider this argument. The Code provides that the income represented by qualified plans and IRAs is included in gross income only when it is "actually distributed" (s. 402(a)(1)) or "paid or distributed" (s. 408(d)(1)). These provisions override other normal income tax rules such as the doctrine of constructive receipt. Perhaps they also override s. 691(a)(2).

(d)   If these approaches fail, and the funding trust is required to recognize income upon transferring retirement benefits in fulfillment of a pecuniary bequest, the result is obviously unfavorable compared to the possibility of the continued deferral of income tax that might otherwise have been available, but not all hope is lost. If IRD is used to fund a pecuniary formula marital gift, so the distribution is treated as a "sale," the distribution will nevertheless carry out "distributable net income" (DNI) so that the marital share will still end up bearing some if not all of the income tax, if the amount of the marital gift cannot be determined as of the date of death from the governing instrument. S. 661(a)(2); Reg. s. 1.663(a)-1(b). The test of whether a bequest is of a "fixed and definite amount at the time of distribution" (which determines whether distributions in satisfaction of the bequest will give rise to gain or loss) is not the same as the test for whether the dollar amount of a bequest is "ascertainable at the date of the decedent's death" (which determines whether distributions in satisfaction of the bequest will carry out DNI). Rev. Rul. 60-87, 1960-1 C.B. 286. If funding the marital trust carries out DNI, it may be possible to use a spousal rollover to eliminate current tax liability. See Chapter 3. At the very least, the income tax burden is shifted to the marital deduction share, which is a better place for it to be.

(e)   If none of the foregoing works, and the estate or funding trust is required to recognize income but is not able to pass that income out to the recipient of the pecuniary bequest, the recipient should have a "basis" in the retirement benefits and be able to reduce the taxable income attributable to future plan distributions by the amount of that basis.

Deduction for Estate Taxes Paid on IRD

How the deduction is calculated

The federal estate tax paid on IRD is deductible for income tax purposes. To determine the amount of the deduction, first determine the estate tax on the entire estate. Next, determine the net value of all items of IRD that were includable in the estate. For definition of net value see s. 691(c)(2)(B). The estate tax attributable to the IRD is the difference between the actual federal estate tax due on the estate, and the federal estate tax that would have been due had all the IRD had been excluded from the estate. This amount is deductible by the beneficiaries who *received* the IRD, regardless of who actually *paid* the estate tax. If there are several beneficiaries who received IRD, the deduction is apportioned among them in proportion to the amounts of IRD each received.

Example: Harvey dies with a $2 million taxable estate that includes a $1 million pension plan. The federal estate tax on a $2 million taxable estate, after deducting the unified credit and the maximum credit for state death taxes, is $488,400. If the $1 million IRA were excluded from the taxable estate, the taxable estate would be only $1 million, and the estate tax would be $119,800. Thus the amount of federal estate tax attributable to the IRA is $488,400 minus $119,800, or $368,600. Thus, Harvey's beneficiary will be entitled to an income tax deduction of $368,600 and will pay income tax on only $631,400 of the $1 million. Note that, even though the IRA constituted 50% of the taxable estate, it accounted for 75% of the estate tax.

Note also the following:

(a)   The deductible portion of the estate tax is computed at the marginal rate, not the average rate; this is favorable to the taxpayer.

(b)   State estate taxes are *not* deductible; this is unfavorable.

(c)   The 15% excise tax on "excess accumulations" (see Chapter 5) is not part of the "federal estate tax paid" on the IRD for purposes of this deduction.

Who gets the deduction

The person who pays the estate tax is not necessarily the person who gets the deduction for the estate taxes paid. *E.g.*, suppose Jack dies with an estate of $3 million. He leaves $1 million of it (consisting entirely of IRD) to his daughter Jill as named beneficiary of his IRA. He leaves his $2 million probate estate (which is not IRD) to his son Alex. Alex pays the entire federal estate tax of $916,000. The s. 691(c) deduction ($427,600) goes to Jill because she received the IRD.

Do you "back out" the excess accumulations tax in computing the s. 691(c) deduction?

The IRS takes the position in its regulations that, when you recalculate the tax as it would have been without including the IRD item, you must also recalculate any deductions that are dependent on the size of the gross estate, such as a formula marital deduction. See regulation s. 1.691(c)-1(2). It is not clear whether you must also "back out" any deduction taken for the 15% excise tax on excess accumulations.

Example: Suppose Harvey's estate paid an "excess accumulations" tax of $45,000 on his $1 million pension plan death benefit. This 15% excise tax was deducted in arriving at the taxable estate of $2 million. When calculating the estate tax "as if" the pension benefit had not been an asset of the estate, if you have to add back in the excise tax of $45,000 (which would not have been paid if the pension benefit had not been in the estate) you get a smaller income tax deduction. See Table 2.1.

Table 2.1

	A Actual Estate	B Hypothetical Estate without Pension	C Hypothetical Estate without Pension and without Excise
Gross estate	2,045,000	2,045,000	2,045,000
Less: 15% excise tax	-45,000	-45,000	N/A
Less: pension	N/A	-1,000,000	-1,000,000
Taxable estate	2,000,000	1,000,000	1,045,000
Federal estate tax	488,400	119,800	135,730
IRD Deduction	N/A	368,600	352,670

S. 691(c) deduction for installment and annuity payouts

Calculating the s. 691(c) deduction is fairly easy when the beneficiary receives a distribution of the entire benefit all at once. What if the retirement benefit is not distributed as a lump sum but rather in installments over the life expectancy of the beneficiary? Clearly the deduction will also be spread out; but how much of the deduction is allocated to each payment? How much of each distribution represents "IRD" that was included in the gross estate, and how much represents income earned by the retirement plan after the date of death? The author is aware of no regulations, cases or rulings on point.

There appear to be three possible methods for allocating the s. 691(c) deduction to instalment payments received from the retirement plan:

1.   *Annuity method.* When IRD is in the form of a joint and survivor annuity, the Code and regulations require that the s. 691(c) deduction be amortized over the surviving annuitant's life expectancy and apportioned equally to the annuity payments received by the survivor. S. 691(d). To date, the IRS has not to the author's knowledge applied this method to installment payments that are payable for a fixed term.

2.   *"Mortgage" method.* Another method would be to treat the date-of-death value as a lump sum value which will be paid, with interest, to the beneficiary over the term. Each payment will consist partly of "interest" and partly of "principal," similar to the payments of principal and interest on a self-amortizing home mortgage. Under this method, the earlier payments would be weighted more heavily towards "interest"; the "principal" (which is actually the IRD) would make up a larger portion of the later payments. Under this approach, the s. 691(c) deduction would be substantially postponed compared to the other two methods. The author has not encountered anyone who has advocated or used this method.

3.   *"Dollar for dollar until it's gone" method.* This is the only method the author has ever heard of anyone's actually using. The 691(c) deduction is applied, dollar for dollar, to each distribution received until the 691(c) deduction has been entirely used up. The deduction is entirely "front end loaded."

Example: In the case of retirement benefits that are being paid to grandchildren in installments over the life expectancy of the oldest grandchild, a case could be made that no actual "principal" is distributed until the last five to ten years of what may be a 50 or 60-year payout. The IRS could argue that the deduction for estate taxes may not be taken until the final five to ten years of the payout.

S. 691(c) deduction and charitable remainder trusts

Suppose P leaves his $200,000 IRA payment to a charitable remainder annuity trust (CRUT). The CRUT holds no other assets and receives no other assets. The CRUT is to pay a 10% unitrust payment each year to P's child (C), and on P's death whatever is left in the CRUT is paid to the Red Cross. C is 48 years old at P's death. Assume the value of C's unitrust interest is $180,000 for estate tax purposes. Assume the federal estate tax attributable to this interest is $83,000.

The first year after P's death the unitrust earns 7% ($14,000) but pays out 10% ($20,000) to C. Clearly, $6,000 of the C's payment is coming from the "principal" of the unitrust, and just as clearly this payment is coming out of "IRD" that the CRUT received. If the IRD character of this distribution were recognized, C would get a 691(c) deduction of $83,000/$180,000 X $6,000 = $2,766. However, there is no mechanism by which a CRT can pass out such a deduction.

A special "tiered" system of tax accounting applies to CRTs (see s. 664). It appears that the 691(c) deduction would reduce the "taxable income" of the trust. S. 1.664-1(d)(2). All the distributions to C would be deemed to come entirely out of the "net taxable income" of the CRT until it had all been used up. The income of the CRT that was "sheltered" by the 691(c) deduction would effectively become "principal" that could be distributed to C tax-free. However, the tax-free principal of the CRT is not deemed to be distributed to C until all net *taxable* income has been previously distributed. This point would never be reached in most CRTs, unless the unitrust payout rate substantially exceeds the anticipated income. In this example, if the trust continues to earn 7%, the 10% unitrust payments will not be coming out of the non-taxable funds until approximately year 26. Thus, some part of the unitrust payments C receives after age 74 will be tax free "return of principal" because of the s. 691(c) deduction, but he gets no benefit from it for the first 26 years.

S. 691(c) deduction on the income tax return

The 691(c) deduction is reported as an "other miscellaneous deduction" on the beneficiary's income tax return (line 27 of Schedule A in 1995). As such, it is not subject to the 2% floor. S. 67(b)(8); see line instructions to IRS form 1040, Schedule A. However, the 691(c) deduction is an itemized deduction subject to the reduction of 3% of AGI in excess of $114,700 (as of 1995), if paid to an individual. S. 68.

Example: In 1995, Joyce receives a $500,000 distribution from her deceased mother's IRA. Assume the 691(c) deduction allocable to this distribution is $200,000. Assume Joyce's other AGI is $114,700, she is single, and she has no other itemized deductions. Her $200,000 itemized deduction for the estate tax paid on the IRD she has received will be reduced by 3% of her "excess" AGI. Her excess AGI in this example is $500,000 so the itemized deduction is reduced by $15,000.

The impact of the 3% reduction rule will vary from beneficiary to beneficiary depending on the size of the distribution and the amount of the beneficiary's other income and deductions. In the case of a very high income taxpayer, with few itemized deductions, the benefit of the 691(c) deduction could be substantially reduced by the s. 68 adjustment.

Example: same facts as in the preceding example, except now Joyce has $2 million of other income in excess of $114,700 and no other itemized deductions. If she did not receive the $500,000 IRA distribution, her taxable income would be:

Taxable income: 2,114,700

With the distribution, her income is:

Gross:		2,614,700
Less: itemized deduction	200,000	
Reduced by (3% x $2,500,000)	-75,000	
	125,000	-125,000
Taxable income		2,489,700

The 691(c) deduction is effectively chopped from $200,000 to $125,000.

The fact that the 3% reduction rule does not apply to trusts may offset somewhat the higher income tax bracket generally applicable to IRD paid to trusts.

Lump Sum Distributions: The Requirements

Introduction

Through the years, s. 402(d) (called 402(e) until 1992) has provided a special gentle treatment for "lump sum distributions" (LSD) from qualified plans. A person who wishes to obtain this special treatment is confronted with some of the most convoluted requirements known to post-ERISA man.

Congress has changed the rules on LSD treatment so often that the IRS has been utterly unable to keep pace with regulations. There are only assorted proposed and temporary regulations issued from 1975 through 1979 (under old Code s. 402(e)), which became obsolete before they could be finalized.

The instructions to IRS forms 4972 and 1099R are often the most up-to-date indication of the IRS's interpretation of s. 402(d).

This section first, in summary fashion, goes through the obstacle course of requirements which must be met to gain this special treatment, to identify the issues the planner must deal with. Other sources (see Bibliography) can provide more detail on the particular requirements that may apply to your client's situation. The next section then discusses the benefits of LSD treatment, including how to calculate the tax under the potentially very favorable "ten year forward averaging," "five year forward averaging," and "20% capital gains tax" methods available for qualifying LSDs.

This chapter does not exhaust the intricacies of s. 402(d). The following aspects of LSDs are not treated here: LSDs under QDROs; interplay with the $5,000 death benefit exclusion or s. 691(c) deduction; an LSD paid to multiple recipients; distribution of employer securities or annuity contracts as part of an LSD.

To achieve the favorable tax treatment, the taxpayer must clear nine requirement "hurdles," many of which are surrounded by hidden issue "landmines."

First hurdle: type of plan

Only distributions from s. 401(a) "qualified plans" (pension, profit sharing or stock bonus) can qualify as LSDs. Both corporate plans and self-employed ("Keogh") plans can give rise to LSDs, but a distribution from an IRA, SEP-IRA or 403(b) plan can never qualify for LSD treatment. S. 402(d)(4)(A).

Second hurdle: "reason" for distribution

The distribution must be made either:

(i)   On account of the employee's death; or
(ii)   After the employee attains age 59½; or
(iii)   On account of the employee's "separation from service." S. 402(d)(4)(i-iii).

However, since a *separate* requirement of LSD treatment is that the distribution must be received "on or after the date on which the employee has attained the age of 59½" (see "Third hurdle"), the foregoing requirements are of significance primarily for determining whether a separate "LSD triggering event" has occurred (see "Fifth hurdle") and, in planning (prior to 1996) for people who were born before 1936. (These individuals did not reach age 59½ until 1994 or 1995, but were grandfathered from the age 59½ requirement because they were born before 1/1/36. TRA '86 s. 1122(h)(3)).

Furthermore, reason (iii) is not available to the self-employed person; a distribution to a self-employed person is eligible for LSD treatment only under reasons (i) or (ii), or if he is "disabled," which for this purpose means "unable to engage in any substantial gainful activity by reason of any medically determined physical or mental impairment which can be expected to result in death or to be of long continued and indefinite duration." S. 72(m)(7).

(a)   Landmine: separation from service

A treatise could be written on the subject of what constitutes "separation from service." If the employee in question was fired, moved to another state and is now working for a competing company while engaged in bitter litigation with his former company, he has probably "separated from service." On the other hand, if he merely changed from full time work to part time; or if the "old" employer sold all its assets to a new company, which rehired the employee the next day to do the same job at the same desk; then further research is required to determine whether there has been a "separation from service." Defining separation from service is beyond the scope of this book; see Bibliography.

(b)   Landmine: "on account of"

Occasionally taxpayers have had problems asserting that a particular LSD was made "on account of" an LSD triggering event. For example, if an employee receives a distribution upon separation from service, but at the same time the plan is terminating and *everyone* is receiving a full distribution whether or not he separated from service, the IRS may say the distribution is "on account of" the plan termination (which is not an "LSD triggering event") and *not* "on account of" the separation from service. Now that LSD treatment can be elected only after age 59½, and only once per employee, and now that any LSD after age 59½ can qualify for the special tax treatment (regardless of whether disability, separation from service, etc. has occurred) the issues which surrounded the "Second hurdle" should fade in importance, but they still matter for purposes of the "Fifth hurdle" discussed below.

Third hurdle: participant must be age 59½ or older

Only distributions received "on or after the date on which the employee has attained age 59½" can qualify for five year forward averaging (5YFA). S. 402(d)(4)(B)(i). This requirement is *not* waived for death benefits. The beneficiaries of an employee who died before reaching age 59½ cannot use

5YFA for any of the death benefits. *Cebula v. Comm'r*, 101 T.C. No. 5 (7/21/93).

Note that it is the *participant's* age at death which matters, not the beneficiary's age. An under-age-59½ beneficiary is eligible for LSD treatment as long as the deceased participant was over age 59½ at death.

The over-age-59½ requirement does not apply to individuals born before 1936 (all of whom reached age 59½ before July 1, 1995). TRA '86 s. 1122(h)(3).

Fourth hurdle: only one use per customer

The special 402(d) treatment is available only once "with respect to an employee" after 1986. S. 402(d)(4)(B). So if Reggie left General Motors at age 60, elected LSD treatment for his pension plan distribution, and went to work for Ford, he will not be able to use 402(d) again when he ultimately retires from Ford, nor would his survivors be able to use it for distributions of death benefits from the Ford plan.

Fifth hurdle: distribution of entire balance in one taxable year

The distribution, to qualify, must be a "distribution within one taxable year... of the balance to the credit of [the] employee... from the plan." S. 402(d)(4)(A). This hurdle is surrounded by landmines. The general guiding principle is that the employee's entire balance in all "aggregated plans" must be distributed to him within one calendar year.

Exception: "Accumulated deductible employee contributions" can be ignored in determining whether the employee has received a distribution of his entire plan balance. S. 402(d)(4)(A). This type of contribution, which was permitted under s. 72(o) only for the years 1982 to 1986, is rarely encountered.

Clearly, if an employee takes out, say, one-third of his plan balance in 1995 and leaves two-thirds in the plan, the distribution of the one-third portion in 1995 does not qualify for LSD treatment because it is not a distribution of the entire balance. Now suppose the employee takes out the remaining two-thirds of his balance in 1996. He has taken out 100% of his (remaining) plan balance in 1996. Is the 1996 distribution an LSD? It is a distribution of 100% of the balance to his credit in one calendar year if the "balance to his credit" simply means the entire balance as of the date of distribution. The question is whether the IRS would look back at the *1995* distribution, and say in effect that the employee's plan balance was distributed over *two* years.

The IRS' position is that, in order to qualify for LSD treatment, there can be distributions in only one taxable year following the most recent LSD "triggering event" (see "Second hurdle"). See Prop. Reg. 1.402(e)-2(d)(1)(ii); Rev. Rul. 69-495, 1969-2 C.B. 100. The "balance to the credit" of the employee is determined as of the first distribution following the "LSD triggering event." This is the "balance" that must be distributed "in one taxable year." Notice 89-25, 1989-1 C.B. 662, Q&A 6.

Example: Elaine retired from Acme Widget in 1995 at age 64. She withdrew $60,000 from her $800,000 Acme Widget Profit Sharing Plan account in order to fulfill her lifelong dream of traveling around the world in a submarine. Returning to the U.S. in 1996, paler but wiser, she wants to cash in the rest of her profit sharing account. This final distribution would not qualify for LSD treatment because the entire balance that existed on the most recent "LSD triggering event" (separation from service) was not distributed all in one calendar year.

In contrast to this, suppose that Elaine, upon returning from her cruise, was tragically killed in a car accident on her way to the Acme benefits office. Now there is a new "LSD triggering event," the death of the participant. Her beneficiary can elect LSD treatment for her remaining profit sharing balance even though Elaine, had she lived, could not have done so.

Another alternative: suppose Elaine had withdrawn the $60,000 for her cruise before she retired (some profit sharing plans permit in-service withdrawals; pension plans never can). Then her later "separation-from-service" would have been a new LSD triggering event and, apparently, the final distribution would qualify for LSD treatment.

The IRS instructions to form 4972 (1995) make no reference to this requirement. Prior distributions from the same plan are referred to only in connection with the rule that if any previous distribution from the same plan was rolled over, subsequent distributions cannot receive LSD treatment (see "Seventh hurdle"). These instructions refer to the "triggering events" (death, separation from service, etc.) only in connection with individuals born before 1936.

These instructions give the erroneous impression that the IRS regards the "LSD triggering events" as relevant only for certain "grandfathered" individuals, and otherwise obsolete. However, unless the IRS has had an unpublicized change of heart, Notice 89-25 is still in effect. The Code's definition of LSD still includes the requirement that the distribution be of the "balance to the credit" of the employee which becomes payable "after the employee attains age 59½," or "on account of" the employee's death, separation from service or disability.

Here are other landmines surrounding this hurdle:

(a)   Landmine: post year-end vesting and other
        adjustments

If you THINK you have withdrawn 100% of your plan balance, then after the end of the year you receive a little extra due to a previous bookkeeping error, you have probably lost your LSD eligibility. S. 402(d)(6)(B). If the post-year-end increase comes about because the employee is rehired, and prior forfeited amounts are reinstated, there is a "recapture" provision so the benefits received from LSD treatment must be "paid back" to the IRS. If the post-year-end increased vesting did not occur because of a rehire, but rather due to a plan termination (which sometimes causes 100% vesting of everyone retroactively), the status of the prior LSD treatment is unknown.

(b)   Landmine: aggregation of plans

In determining whether the entire "balance to the credit" of an employee has been distributed, certain plans must be aggregated. Specifically all profit sharing plans of the same employer are considered to be one "plan" for this purpose; all pension plans of the employer are treated as one plan; and all "stock bonus plans" are treated as one. S. 402(d)(4)(C).

Unfortunately it is not always easy to determine what "type" a particular retirement plan is. The plan name is not always revealing:

The Mega Corp. Employees Retirement Plan?

The Sanford & Sons, Ltd., Employees' Trust?

The employee is entitled to a summary plan description for each plan; that should tell what type it is. If not, you could request the answer in writing from the company benefits office; or request a copy of the complete plan or of the most recent IRS annual report (form 5500 series) from the employer.

It may be impossible to obtain distribution of 100% of all similar plans. *E.g.*, the employer may have two pension plans (a defined benefit and a money purchase), but permit lump sum distributions from only one of them.

Furthermore, dissimilar "types" of plans may nevertheless have to be aggregated if they have interrelated benefit formulas. If the participant's employer maintains more than one plan, and it is proposed to have an LSD from only one of them, it may require a legal opinion of an ERISA lawyer, or the employer's counsel, to be sure that this requirement is met for the proposed distribution.

(c)   Landmine: employers under common control

When aggregating "plans of a similar type" of the "employer," who is the "employer"? Must we aggregate separate "employers," too, if they are under common control?

When two employers are under "common control" (*e.g.*, a proprietorship and a corporation owned by the same person) s. 414 says the two entities will be treated as one "employer" for purposes of certain Code sections relating to retirement plans. S. 414(b),(c). S. 402 is not among the listed sections. This would seem to imply that employers are not aggregated for purposes of s. 402. However, the author is not aware of any authority one way or the other on this question.

If your client is taking an LSD from an employer's plan, while he still has a balance in a plan of "similar type" maintained by a different employer that is under common control, this question should be checked thoroughly.

Sixth hurdle: the five year requirement

To get LSD treatment, a living employee must have been a "participant" in the plan for at least five taxable years prior to the year of the distribution. S. 402(d)(4)(F). To determine whether a   client meets this requirement, one must first determine what it means to be a "participant" and what time period constitutes a "year" of participation. Prop. reg. 1.402(e)-2(e)(3) adds no enlightenment, simply paraphrasing the statute.

In determining what constitutes "participation" for purposes of the five-year requirement, the IRS apparently will

use the "active participation" definition of s. 1.219-2(d)(1) --
i.e., only a year in which a contribution is actually made (or
required to be made) to the employee's account will count. See
Ltr. Rul. 8749081 (9/14/87). See sources cited in the
Bibliography for more detail on this requirement, including what
constitutes a "year."

This requirement does not apply to death benefits. It
applies only to distributions "to" the employee.

Seventh hurdle: no prior rollovers

This hurdle is especially tricky because it is not found (or
even referred to) in s. 402(d). IRC s. 402(c)(10), added by UCA
'92, provides that, "If paragraph (1) [of 402(c)] applies to any
distribution paid to any employee," then 402(d) treatment will
not be available for any subsequent distribution from the same
plan (or from any other plan required to be aggregated with the
distributing plan).

The "paragraph (1)" referred to (402(c)(1)) says that
properly rolled over distributions will not be included in income.
S. 402(c)(10) therefore denies LSD treatment to subsequent
distributions if a prior distribution from the same plan was rolled
over and excluded from gross income.

Notice 92-48, 1992-2 C.B. 377, explains: "If you have
previously rolled over a payment from the Plan (or certain other
similar plans of the employer), you cannot use [LSD] tax
treatment for later payments from the Plan." See also the
instructions to IRS form 4972 (1995), providing that a
distribution is not eligible for LSD treatment if "the participant
or his or her surviving spouse received an eligible rollover
distribution from the same plan... and the proceeds of the
previous distribution were rolled over..."

Eighth hurdle: type of recipient

Only individuals, estates and trusts can elect LSD treatment. A distribution to a partnership or corporation will not qualify for the special treatment. S. 402(d)(4)(B).

Ninth hurdle: the election

If you meet all the requirements described above, LSD treatment is not automatic; it is elected by filing form 4972.

Landmine: The election, to be valid, must be made for all distributions in the same year which qualify for LSD treatment.

Example: Thalia is a participant in both the Great Northern Skateboard Company Pension Plan (balance $200,000) and Profit Sharing Plan (balance $300,000). She is retiring in 1995 and wants to cash in her pension plan balance, and get LSD treatment for it, but roll over her profit sharing plan balance to an IRA. If she receives total distributions from both plans in one year, she must elect LSD treatment for both or neither; she cannot elect LSD treatment for one and roll over the other. S. 402(d)(4)(B)(ii). This problem can be avoided either by taking the rollover distribution and the LSD distribution in separate taxable years; or by taking out the "rollover plan" balance over two years, so it does not qualify for LSD treatment.

Lump Sum Distributions: the Rewards

Introduction

An LSD for which a proper election is made is excluded from the recipient's adjusted gross income. S. 402(d)(3); s.

62(a)(8). The distribution is taxed separately, under one of the methods nicknamed "ten year forward averaging," "five year forward averaging," or 20% capital gain tax method, or some combination of these. A table in Appendix A shows income tax payable on various sizes of LSDs under the special averaging methods.

See the *Cavalho* case study for discussion of the impact of LSD treatment on planning decisions.

Deduction from gross income

Even if the special tax rates for LSDs produced no tax benefit in themselves (see discussion below), the fact that this special treatment keeps 100% of the retirement plan proceeds out of adjusted gross income (AGI) can be beneficial. It means the distribution will not be included in AGI for purposes of --

--the threshold for deducting medical expenses (7.5% of AGI) (s. 213(a)).

--the threshold for reduction of itemized deductions (s. 68) ($114,700 in 1995).

--the threshold for reducing personal exemptions (s. 151(d)(3)) ($172,050 for a married couple in 1995).

--determining how much of the recipient's Social Security benefits for that year will be subject to income tax under s. 86.

Ironically, although the LSD is not included in AGI for purposes of reducing itemized deductions by 3% of AGI in excess of the applicable threshold, in the case of an LSD payable to a beneficiary the s. 691(c) deduction for estate taxes paid on that very same LSD *is* counted as one of the itemized deductions subject to the s. 68 adjustment.

15% excise tax on excess distributions

The 15% excise tax is applied separately to LSDs (tax-free threshold amount $750,000) and to all other plan distributions (taxable if over $150,000), even if received in the same year. See Chapter 5.

Five year forward averaging

Under the special method for taxing LSDs (popularly known as "five year forward averaging," although these words do not appear in the Code), the distribution is taxed as follows:

(i)   Take 20% of the distribution.
(ii)   Determine the tax on the amount so determined using the tax tables "Schedule X" (single individuals) (reproduced in form 4972 instructions).
(iii)   Multiply the result by five.

Exceptions:
--   There is a "minimum distribution allowance" which produces an even lower tax for distributions under $70,000.
--   No tax is paid currently on the value of certain annuity contracts included in the distribution, though it is still counted as part of the LSD.
--   The above method determines the tax on the "ordinary income" portion of the LSD. See below for possible capital gain treatment.

Because the "single individual" tax rate hits 39.6% at $256,500 of taxable income (1995), 5YFA means that an LSD does not hit that marginal bracket until it exceeds $1,282,500 (five times $256,500). Also, because the LSD is not added to the taxpayer's other income, it gets the benefit of the lower brackets (five times) before hitting the top marginal rate. An LSD of $750,000 would pay income tax of only $216,853 -- less than 29% -- and no 15% excise tax (see Chapter 5).

From 1987 to 1991, when the top income tax bracket was 28% (reached at $29,750 for single individuals) "income averaging" seemed obsolete. The 1993 tax law changes brought it back to life. For a taxpayer in the 39.6% bracket, a 29% tax can look very attractive. For smaller distributions, the bargain is even more irresistible; a LSD of $70,000 to $116,750, for example, would be taxed at only 15%.

Ten year forward averaging

Ten year forward averaging (10YFA) is available only to individuals born before 1936. TRA '86 s. 1122(h) as amended by TAMRA '88, s. 1011A(b)(11), (13)-(15). 10YFA is the same as 5YFA, except that:

(i)   You determine the tax on 10% of the LSD and multiply it by 10 (rather than 20% multiplied by five).

(ii)   The tax is determined using 1986 rates (conveniently reproduced in the instructions to form 4972).

Top rates were higher in 1986 than now. 10YFA produces a lower tax than 5YFA only for distributions of less than (approximately) $375,000.

20% capital gain rate

If the employee was a participant in the plan prior to 1974, part of the LSD is eligible to be treated as a "capital gain" taxed at the 20% rate that once upon a time applied to long term capital gain. Prop. reg. 1.402(e)-2(d) provides that the "capital gain" portion of the distribution is determined by deducting the "ordinary income portion" (OIP) from the "total taxable amount" (TTA). The OIP is determined by multiplying the TTA by the following fraction:

> Numerator: Calendar years of active participation after 1973.
>
> Denominator: Total calendar years of active participation.

In the case of pre-1974 years, the employee gets twelve months' "credit" for each calendar year or partial calendar year of participation. For post-1973 years a different rule applies -- he gets one *month's* credit for each calendar month or part of a month in which he is an active participant.

If the capital gain method results in a higher tax, the participant can elect to have his capital gain portion treated as ordinary income; or rather, technically, to "treat pre-1974 participation as post-1973 participation." See s. 402(e)(4)(L) (including its various requirements) as it existed prior to repeal by TAMRA '88 s. 1011A(b)(8)(G).

Capital gain: what is an "active participant?"

What is an "active participant" for purposes of the fraction described above? The regs. under s. 219(g) (which limits the IRA contribution deduction for those who are "active participants" in various types of retirement plans) gives a very specific definition. Under Reg. s. 1.219-2 (8/7/80) a person is an "active participant" in a money purchase pension plan in a particular year *only* if some of the employer contribution was required to be allocated to his account for that year; or in a profit sharing plan *only* if any forfeiture or employer contribution was added to his account in that year. This s. 1.219-2 definition would seem to indicate that the OIP/TTA fraction is "frozen" when a plan permanently discontinues contributions, since "active participation" (in the s. 219 sense) ends then.

But the IRS apparently does not apply the s. 219 definition of "active participation" to s. 402 for this purpose. Although this is not 100% clear, it appears that the IRS uses, for purposes of determining the "capital gain" portion of an LSD, a definition which makes no distinction between "participation" and "active participation," thus rendering nugatory the word "active" in the Code's phrase *"active* participation." The IRS definition is in a 1975 proposed regulation, s. 1.402(e)-2; and is repeated in the instructions to form 1099-R, which is the tax form used (by the employer) to report how much of each distribution is ordinary income and how much is capital gain. From the 1995 "Instructions for Forms 1099, 1098, 5498, and W-2G," p. 24: "Active participation begins with the first month in which the employee became a participant under the plan and ends with the earliest of --"

(i)   The month the employee receives the LSD.

(ii)   The month the employee dies.

(iii)   In the case of a common law employee, the month of separation from service.

(iv)   In the case of a self-employed person who receives the LSD on account of disability, the month in which he becomes disabled.

The effect of this definition is to gradually and inexorably reduce the capital gain portion of the distribution, even if the plan has been "frozen solid" since 1974, since the fraction keeps changing until events (i) - (iv) occur.

This definition appears arbitrary and capricious, first, because it ignores the word "active" in the Code, and second, because the IRS uses the s. 219 definition intact for another part of s. 402 (the "five years of participation" requirement) (see "Sixth hurdle" in the preceding section of this chapter) when to do so favors the Treasury.

Tax on OIP when there is a capital gain portion

Once you have determined how much of the total taxable amount (TTA) is the "ordinary income portion" (OIP) (to be taxed under 5YFA or 10YFA), and how much is capital gain (to be taxed at a flat 20%), how do you calculate the tax on the OIP? There are two possible methods:

> (i)   Calculate the 5YFA (or 10YFA) tax on the TTA then multiply the result by the fraction OIP/TTA; or
> (ii)   Calculate the 5YFA (or 10YFA) tax on the OIP only.

Method (i) was required by Code s. 402(e)(1)(B) before it was repealed by TRA '86. However, the grandfather rule which continues 20% capital gain treatment for those born before 1936 appears to adopt method (ii): see s. 1122(h)(3)(b) of TRA '86 as amended by TAMRA '88 s. 1101A(b)(11), (13)-(15). IRS form 4972 for 1995 clearly uses method (ii) (see part III of form). Method (ii) produces a lower tax than method (i). Thus, the treatment of "grandfathered" individuals is more favorable than the treatment they would have received prior to the change in the law.

Rollovers

In general

Under s. 402, certain retirement plan distributions are not taxed in the year received if they are "rolled over" to a different retirement plan or IRA.

Of course there are various requirements that must be met to obtain tax-free rollover treatment. Until 1992, the requirements for a valid rollover were almost as difficult and perilous as the lump sum distribution rules, but the "Unemployment Compensation Amendments of 1992" (P.L. 102-318) ("UCA") (applicable to distributions after 1992) vastly liberalized the rules, and now rollovers are much easier. Now, ANY distribution from a qualified plan, IRA or TSA can be rolled over, with only the following exceptions:

(a)   A required distribution under s. 401(a)(9) cannot be rolled over (see further discussion below).

(b)   A payment which is one of a series of "substantially equal payments" over the life expectancy of the participant, the joint life expectancy of the participant and designated beneficiary, or any period of 10 years or more cannot be rolled over. Reg. s. 1.402(c)-2, Q&A-5, explains how to determine whether a distribution is part of a series of "substantially equal installments" over 10 or more years.

(c)   Certain corrective or "deemed" distributions cannot be rolled over (for example, the P.S. 58 cost of insurance in a plan, or a plan loan that is foreclosed, or the return of an excess 401(k) contribution).

(d)   Death benefits cannot be rolled over by any beneficiary other than the surviving spouse. (But see Chapter 7 for "grandfather" rule). For more detail on spousal rollovers, see Chapter 3.

(e)   Non-taxable distributions (return of after-tax contributions) cannot be rolled over.

No rollover of minimum required distributions

The rule that a minimum required distribution (MRD) cannot be rolled over can take participants by surprise.

For example, the first distribution received in any year for which a distribution is required will be applied first to the MRD for that year, and thus can be rolled over only to the extent it exceeds the MRD. The first year for which a distribution is required is the year the participant reaches age 70½. Even though the first MRD does not have to be taken until April 1 of the *following* year, any distribution received on or after January 1 of the 70½ year will be first applied to MRD for that year, which cannot be rolled over. Reg. s. 1.402(c)-2, A-7. This can create problems since the *amount* of the first year's MRD will not actually be known until the RBD.

Example: Leonard turns 70½ in 1996. On 1/1/96 he retires from his job at Consolidated Cattle Corp. and asks the plan administrator of the CCC retirement plans to distribute all his benefits to his IRA in a "direct rollover." CCC replies that it cannot roll over the MRD for 1996. Leonard replies, fine, he will take the 1996 MRD as a taxable distribution and roll over the rest. Since he has named his 40-year-old wife Louise as his designated beneficiary (DB) (see Chapter 1), he says, the MRD should be 1/42.9th of the account balance, based on their 42.9 year joint life expectancy. The plan administrator says, "Louise is your wife and DB now, but the MRD is based on who is your beneficiary on your RBD, which does not occur until 4/1/97. Between now and then, Louise could die, or you could get divorced, or you could simply change your mind and designate your estate and therefore have 'no DB.' Accordingly, we will distribute to you the MRD calculated based solely on your own LE -- which is 1/16th of the account, not 1/42.9th."

For similar problems facing the surviving spouse, see

Chapter 3. The "Rollover Checklist" in Appendix C lists issues to consider before rolling over retirement plan benefits.

Summary of Planning Principles

1.   If possible, consistent with the client's estate planning goals, leave retirement plan death benefits to individual beneficiaries rather than trusts, because of the higher income tax rates generally applicable to trusts.

2.   Do not use retirement benefits to fund a pecuniary bequest. Do not arrange retirement benefits so that they will have to pass through a pecuniary formula in a will or trust.

3.   As between the "marital share" and the "credit shelter" share, it is generally better to use IRD to fund the marital share, so no part of the "credit shelter" is "wasted" paying income taxes. Income taxes paid out of the marital share will reduce the future taxable estate of the spouse. Exception: the advantages of long term income tax deferral that are available for certain "credit shelter" type dispositions can sometimes outweigh the drawbacks of funding a credit shelter gift with IRD.

4.   When determining what benefits each beneficiary will receive, consider the impact of the s. 691(c) deduction for estate taxes paid on IRD. This deduction benefits the person who receives the IRD, not the person who pays the estate tax.

5.   Always determine whether a plan the client participates in is potentially eligible for favorable "lump sum distribution" income tax treatment, and whether such treatment would be beneficial. Do not take steps (such as a rollover) which would eliminate eligibility for beneficial LSD treatment without carefully considering the alternatives.

3

Marital Matters

*Rules and planning concerns
when leaving retirement benefits
to the surviving spouse or a
marital trust*

Introduction

This chapter first summarizes the incentives offered by the tax laws for naming the spouse as beneficiary of retirement benefits, then examines two of these "special breaks" (rollovers, s. 401(a)(9) provisions) in detail. Naming a marital trust is more complicated and less advantageous tax-wise than naming the spouse individually; why this is so is explained in "Marital Deduction for Benefits Payable to QTIP Trust" and "Income Tax Disadvantages When QTIP Trust is Beneficiary." The next sections look at other topics involving husband, wife and retirement benefits: simultaneous death clauses; and "REA" rights. The final section of the chapter summarizes the planning considerations. If the participant's spouse is not a U.S. citizen, this Chapter 3 is just the introduction; Chapter 4 is the main course.

Advantages of Leaving Benefits to the Surviving Spouse

The estate, excise, and income tax laws often favor naming the spouse (S) as the beneficiary of retirement benefits.

Estate tax

If there is a choice of assets, generally speaking it is preferable to make the retirement benefits payable to the spouse, and use other assets to fund the "credit shelter" amount. If retirement benefits are made payable to a credit shelter trust, the income taxes the trust must pay on those benefits (see "Income in Respect of a Decedent" in Chapter 2) will come out of the "credit shelter" amount. In effect, some of the participant's (P's) exemption is "wasted" paying income taxes.

If S is the beneficiary, she too will have to pay income taxes, but at least the income taxes she pays will reduce her future taxable estate. The decedent's credit shelter will not have been partially "wasted" paying income taxes. See the *Able* and *Dingell* case studies. The same estate tax "benefit" can be achieved by naming either S individually or a marital trust as beneficiary, but excise and income tax considerations favor naming S individually rather than a marital trust.

Note: this is not a hard and fast rule. The income tax deferral advantages of making benefits payable directly to children or grandchildren, rather than to the spouse, can outweigh the estate tax disadvantage of using such benefits to fund the "credit shelter amount."

15% excise tax

If S is the beneficiary of all or almost all of P's retirement benefits, she has the option to defer imposition of the

15% excise tax at P's death, and instead elect that (for purposes of the 15% excise tax) she herself will be treated as the owner of the benefits. No other beneficiary has this option. In order for this option to be available, other beneficiaries must be entitled to no more than a "de minimis" share of the benefits. See Chapter 5 for a detailed discussion of this election.

Income tax

S has more options than other beneficiaries do for deferring income taxes on inherited retirement benefits. See "Spousal Rollovers" and "The Spouse and S. 401(a)(9)," below.

Spousal Rollovers

Advantages of spousal rollover

The surviving spouse's ability to "roll over" inherited benefits to her own IRA gives her a powerful option to defer income taxes that is not available to other beneficiaries. By rolling over benefits to her own IRA, the surviving spouse becomes the "participant" with regard to those benefits under the minimum distribution rules (see Chapter 1). She can then name her own "designated beneficiary" (DB) for the account, and commence distributions at *her* "required beginning date" over the joint life expectancy of herself and the new DB. Whatever minimum distribution requirements were in effect prior to the decedent's death "disappear" once the benefits have been rolled over by the surviving spouse (although of course they remain in effect until then).

This does not mean that naming the spouse as beneficiary is necessarily the way to achieve the longest income tax deferral on benefits; in fact it often is not. Nevertheless, the spousal rollover is still an extremely valuable deferral tool for two reasons: first, most participants want to name their spouses as beneficiaries, despite the longer income tax deferral that may be available if children or grandchildren are named, so the rollover becomes a way to revive the option of longer deferral if S survives P; second, once P has died or passed his "required beginning date" (RBD), the rollover shines as a way to correct problems that may exist with P's beneficiary designation.

The spousal rollover is so valuable that it is frequently the object of *post mortem* planning efforts. Chapter 8 discusses the use of qualified disclaimers to redirect to the surviving spouse retirement benefits that were left payable to the "wrong" beneficiary, so the spousal rollover can be used.

Drawbacks of spousal rollover

The principal drawback of a spousal rollover is its effect on the 10% pre-age 59½ distribution penalty (s. 72(t)). If the surviving spouse is younger than age 59½, she is entitled to withdraw from the deceased spouse's plan or IRA without penalty, because the penalty does not apply to death benefits. Once she rolls over the benefits to her own IRA, however, they lose their character as "death benefits" and she will not be able to withdraw them until she reaches age 59½ unless she either pays a 10% penalty or qualifies for one of the exceptions. (See Chapter 9).

Because of this situation, most if not all planners consulted by young widows have advised their clients either not to roll over any benefits until after reaching age 59½, or to roll over only funds they are certain they will not need until after that age; and in the meantime to withdraw from the deceased spouse's plan as much as they need, without penalty, to pay living expenses.

Bulletin: As this book went to press, the IRS had just issued a private letter ruling, Ltr. Rul. 9608042 (12/1/95), indicating a totally new, and highly disadvantageous, rule applicable to spousal withdrawals from IRAs. In this ruling, P died while S was under age 59½. The ruling confirmed that S could withdraw death benefits from P's IRA with no 10% penalty (s. 72(t)), despite S's being under age 59½, because death benefits are not subject to that penalty. However, the ruling went on to say that by withdrawing any benefits penalty-free before age 70½ S would be making an "irrevocable election" not to treat P's IRA as her own IRA. According to this ruling, by taking even $1 from the plan before reaching age 59½, S would be forever precluded from rolling over the balance of this IRA. There is no basis for this statement in the Code or regulations. Is this statement a mistake? Or is it a new IRS policy? Whatever else it may be, it is a trap for the unwary. Its consequences can presumably be avoided by having S do a partial rollover (of funds she does not expect to need pre-age 59½) to her own IRA, *before* she starts withdrawing penalty-free money, pre-59½, from P's IRA. If this ruling represents an IRS policy shift, it's a strange one. It singles out (a) young widows (b) who inherited IRAs from their deceased spouses and (c) who need some of the inherited IRA money to live on. Unaffected are (a) widows over 59½ (who can roll over benefits, then withdraw from the rollover IRA without penalty) (b) widows who inherit qualified plans (the ruling terms apply only to inherited IRAs) and (c) widows who are wealthy enough not to need the inheritance for current living expenses.

Requirements for spousal rollover

S. 402(c)(a) allows the participant in a qualified retirement plan (QRP) to "roll over" certain plan distributions to another QRP, or to an individual retirement account (IRA), provided various requirements are met. If death benefits are paid to the participant's surviving spouse, the rollover rules "apply to such distribution in the same manner as if the spouse were" the participant, with only one exception: the surviving spouse may roll over only to an IRA, not to another QRP.

The tests for determining whether a distribution is an "eligible rollover distribution," and the other rollover rules, are the same for the surviving spouse as they would have been for the decedent; see Chapter 2. The most significant rules for planning purposes are:

1.   A minimum required distribution (MRD) (see Chapter 1) cannot be rolled over. S. 402(c)(4)(B). See further discussion below.

2.   "Any distribution which is one of a series of substantially equal periodic payments" made annually or more often (a) over the life or life expectancy of P, (b) over the joint life or life expectancy of P and a designated beneficiary, or (c) over a "specified period of 10 years or more" may not be rolled over. S. 402(c)(4)(A).

3.   If any distribution from a QRP has been rolled over (by either P or S), no subsequent distribution from that plan (to either P or S) will be eligible for "lump sum distribution" treatment under s. 402(d) (see Chapter 2). S. 402(c)(10).

4.   Non-taxable distributions (such as return of after-tax contributions, or the pure death benefit portion of insurance

proceeds) may not be rolled over. Reg. s. 1.402(c)-2, Q&A3(b).

Note the following:

1. The spouse can roll benefits to a pre-existing IRA or to a new IRA established just to receive this rollover. If the spouse has not made a 4980A(d)(5) election (see Chapter 5), however, it is extremely important NOT to roll the benefits to a pre-existing IRA; a new IRA should be established to keep the inherited benefits (which are exempt from 15% excise tax if no 4980A(d)(5) election was made) separate from any IRA funded with the spouse's own contributions (or contributions made on her behalf to a "spousal IRA" established by the deceased spouse).

2. There is no time deadline, as such, for a spousal rollover; see further discussion below.

3. The distribution does not need to be a total distribution of the entire account balance. Partial distributions are eligible for rollover, unless they are part of a series of substantially equal payments (see Chapter 2).

4. The IRS has permitted the spouse to roll over benefits from decedent's plan and IRA into another IRA *still in the name of the decedent*. Ltr. Rul. 9418034 (2/10/94). This approach may be more attractive than a rollover to an IRA in the spouse's own name when the surviving spouse wants to have the benefits in a particular IRA (due to investment or distribution alternatives, or because of preference for a particular custodian), but wants the benefits to retain their status as "death benefits" exempt from the penalty on premature distributions. (But see the "Bulletin" above.)

A minimum required distribution cannot be rolled over

The spousal rollover is not available for any minimum required distribution (MRD). For example, suppose P dies in February 1996 at age 72. At the time of death, he had not yet withdrawn the MRD for 1996. S is named as P's "DB." She can receive a distribution of P's benefits in 1996 and roll over everything except the 1996 MRD.

The prohibition against rolling over MRDs could have a harsh result in certain circumstances.

Example: Melvin and Minnie: On his required beginning date (RBD), Melvin had named his estate as beneficiary of his profit sharing plan, and commenced taking MRDs based on his life expectancy, recalculated annually (see Chapter 1 for explanation of these terms). As explained in Chapter 1, when a person whose life expectancy is being redetermined annually dies, his life expectancy becomes "zero" in the year following the death. After his RBD, Melvin changed his beneficiary designation and named his wife Minnie as beneficiary of the account. However, it was too late for her to become a "designated beneficiary," so he still had to continue withdrawals over only his single life expectancy. Suppose Melvin's "age 70½ year" was 1995 and his life expectancy in that year was 16 years. Accordingly, he withdrew his MRD of 1/16 of the account for 1995. In 1996, he properly withdrew 1/15.3 of the account balance, then died.

Clearly, Minnie can roll over the balance of Melvin's profit sharing plan account *provided* it is all distributed to her (or distributed directly to her IRA) by the end of 1996. Once December 31, 1996 has passed, a new calendar year begins for purposes of the minimum distribution rules applicable to Melvin's account. The MRD for 1997 will be 100% of the account, since Melvin's life expectancy is now zero. Accordingly, Minnie would presumably not be able to roll over any portion of the account that is distributed after 1996.

Despite the clear rule in s. 402(c)(4)(B), however, the IRS has allowed a surviving spouse to roll over the entire account in this situation in at least one case. Ltr. Rul. 9005071 (11/13/89) involved exactly the "Melvin and Minnie" facts discussed above. The IRS stated that the surviving spouse could receive and roll over, in the year following the participant's death, 100% of the plan balance, so long as the deceased participant had withdrawn, prior to his death, the MRD for the year of death.

No time deadline for spousal rollover

There is no deadline, as such, for making a spousal rollover. Of course, once any benefits are actually distributed to S, they must be rolled over within 60 days or not at all. But there is no time limit based on the decedent's death after which it becomes "too late" to roll over distributions. The only rule is that a distribution can be rolled over by S if the deceased participant could have rolled it over had it been paid to him (but see the "Bulletin" earlier in this chapter).

Nevertheless, it is normally advisable to complete the rollover quickly, for the following reasons:

1.   If S happens to die before completing the rollover, a rollover by S's executor will probably not be allowed.

2.   If P was already past his RBD when his death occurred, minimum distributions must continue to be made until the rollover occurs; thus a long delay wastes deferral opportunities.

3.   If P was already past his RBD when he died, and was recalculating his life expectancy, the MRDs will jump in the year

following his death, even to the point of eliminating the possibility of a rollover (if his was the only remaining life expectancy) (see "Melvin and Minnie" example earlier in this chapter). In this situation the rollover should take place in the same year as the first spouse's death.

4.   If P died before December 31 of the year he reached (or would have reached) age 70½, there may be less urgency to complete the rollover as far as the minimum distribution rules are concerned (see "The Spouse and S. 401(a)(9)" below). However, the failure of most plan and IRA documents to specify who gets the benefits if the primary beneficiary dies after P but before withdrawing the benefits can cause substantial problems, and result in loss of deferral, again indicating that prompt rollover action is beneficial.

Rollover (or spousal election) for inherited IRA

S. 408(d), in a backhanded way, permits a surviving spouse to treat an inherited IRA as if it were S's *own* IRA. Specifically, the Code provides that distributions from an "inherited IRA" may not be treated as tax-free rollovers; but then it goes on to say that an "inherited IRA" means an IRA acquired by reason of the death of another individual, if the person who inherited the account is not the spouse of the decedent. S. 408(d)(3)(C). Thus an IRA inherited by the spouse is not subject to the restrictions applicable to an "inherited IRA," and by negative implication S may roll over distributions to her from the deceased P's IRA as if it were S's own IRA.

The option to treat the IRA as S's own IRA is not available if benefits are paid to a marital trust. Ltr. Rul. 9321032 (2/24/93).

How does S elect to treat the deceased spouse's IRA as her own?

S. 408(a)(6) does not provide specific payout rules for IRAs. Rather, it simply provides that the minimum distribution rules for IRAs shall be similar to the s. 401(a)(9) minimum distribution rules for qualified plans, but the actual rules shall be contained in future regulations to be issued by the IRS.

All we have by way of regulations at this time are the proposed regs. issued in 1987 that have never been finalized. Prop. reg. s. 1.408-8, Q and A-4(b) provides that S "may elect" to treat her interest in an IRA inherited from the deceased spouse as her own account. The proposed regulation provides as follows: "an election will be considered to have been made by S if either of the following occurs." Then two "occurrences" are described. These two "occurrences" are not positive "elections"; rather they are simply events that are consistent with the idea that the IRA now belongs to S, and inconsistent with the idea that the IRA still "belongs" to the decedent. The first "occurrence" is: an amount required to be distributed under the minimum distribution rules has not been distributed within the required time after the death of the first spouse. The second "occurrence" is: S makes a contribution to the account. "The result of such an election is that S shall then be considered the individual for whose benefit the [IRA] is maintained."

The proposed regulation does not specify any other method of "converting" the deceased spouse's IRA into S's IRA. What if S, although not having made any contribution to the account, and not having reached the point at which the first distribution would be required to come out if she did not make the election, files a written election with the IRA administrator that she elects to treat it as her own IRA? Presumably a positive written election such as this would be sufficient, and the two "occurrences" listed in the regulation are not meant to be the exclusive method by which S can convert the decedent's IRA into her own IRA.

The IRS has recognized in at least one private letter ruling that a direction to transfer funds from an IRA in the name of the decedent to an IRA in the name of the spouse "constitutes a sufficient election" to treat the decedent's IRA as the spouse's IRA; Ltr. Rul. 9534027 (6/1/95). However, a rollover "in and of itself need not constitute" such an election if the benefits are rolled into an IRA still in the name of the decedent. Ltr. Rul. 9418034 (2/10/94).

What if S dies before rolling over?

The IRS will not allow the executor of S's estate to exercise S's personal right to treat the deceased spouse's IRA as S's own IRA, Ltr. Rul. 9237038 (6/16/92). Compare this ruling with other IRS holdings:

--An executor may not make a $2,000 IRA contribution on a decedent's behalf. Ltr. Rul. 8439066.

--Where a participant had received a distribution but then died before rolling it over, his executor can roll over the distribution to an IRA in the decedent's name, provided the rollover is completed within 60 days after the distribution was received by the participant. *Gunther v. U.S.*, 573 F. Supp. 126, 127 (1982) (USDC MI, 51 AFTR 2d 83-1314). Temp. reg. s. 54.4981A-1T (d-5)(c).

It is very important to make sure that there is an appropriate contingent beneficiary named in the *first* spouse's beneficiary designation form, *and* that it is clear that the benefits will pass to this contingent beneficiary if S does not get around to naming her own DB before she dies. This way, if P dies, and then S also dies before getting a chance to do the rollover, there will at least be a "DB" in place, so that (if S's death occurs before December 31 of P's "70½ year") the DB's life expectancy can be used for the payout after S's death. (In Ltr. Rul. 9237038, S's estate was the contingent beneficiary.) See "The Spouse and S. 401(a)(9)" in this chapter, and forms 1.1, 2.1 and 2.2 in Appendix B.

If P is already past his RBD, the question of whether it is possible to get the benefits of a rollover in case of simultaneous or close-in-time deaths may be even more critical. See the *Fallon* case study in Chapter 10 and form 4.1 in Appendix B; and discussion in "Simultaneous Death Clauses" section of this chapter.

What if S is already over 70½ when she inherits the benefits?

What if S is already beyond age 70½ on the date she "rolls over" to her own IRA? Clearly she could schedule withdrawals over her own remaining life expectancy; but is it too late for her to name a new DB and get two life expectancies? And is it too late to elect into or out of recalculation of her life expectancy? The proposed regs. do not discuss this question. The definition of "required beginning date" is strictly April 1 following the year in which the participant turns 70½ -- regardless of whether the participant (in this case, the surviving spouse who has inherited plan benefits after her RBD) even had an IRA or plan benefit of any kind on that date.

This issue was squarely presented in Ltr. Rul. 9311037 (12/22/92). A and B were married to each other. Both were past age 70½ when A died. B was the DB of A's IRA. B rolled over A's IRA to a new IRA in B's name, but B's RBD had already passed when B established this IRA. B named C and D as the primary beneficiaries to receive the balance in this new rollover IRA at B's death. B requested and received a ruling that C and D would be treated as B's "designated beneficiaries" for purposes of the minimum distribution rules applicable to B's

IRA established by a rollover from A's IRA.

From the ruling: "While the proposed regulations do not specifically answer [this question], in the absence of final regulations, issues may be resolved by a reasonable interpretation of the proposed regulations and statutory provisions. Accordingly, it is a reasonable interpretation of the minimum distribution requirements... that [C and D] may be treated as [DBs] since they were designated before your first required distribution date."

Ltr. Rul. 9534027 (6/1/95), also involving spouses who were both past age 70½ when the first one died, reached the same conclusion. This ruling held that, if the spousal rollover occurred in 1995, the spouse's "required beginning date" for the newly created rollover IRA would be December 31 of the following year (1996), and the "designated beneficiary" would be determined as of that date.

Of course, letter rulings cannot be relied upon as precedent. Thus, a surviving spouse confronted with this situation will have to either apply for her own letter ruling, or take the risk of acting without one, or be conservative and not try to use the joint life expectancy of herself and the new designated beneficiary.

Rollover when S inherits benefits through an estate

The IRS, in private letter rulings, has permitted a spousal rollover where the spouse was not named as the "DB," but the benefits were payable to P's estate and S was the sole beneficiary of the estate. See, *e.g.*, Ltr. Rul. 8911006 (12/12/88); 9402023 (10/18/93) (S was sole beneficiary and executrix).

In two other rulings, S was not the sole beneficiary, but was the residuary beneficiary and also was the executrix. As executrix, she distributed the right to receive P's retirement benefits (which were payable to the estate) to herself in partial fulfillment of the residuary bequest. The IRS allowed her to then roll the benefits over. Ltr. Rul. 9351041 (9/30/93); 9545010 (8/14/95). Query whether the result would be the same if S had not been the executrix.

In still another ruling, S claimed a statutory share of the estate. Under applicable state law, a surviving spouse who elected the statutory share could also specify which assets would be used to fund that share. S exercised this right by directing the trustee of the decedent's qualified retirement plan (which was payable to the estate) to transfer assets of the plan directly into an IRA in S's own name. This was held to be a valid "direct rollover." Ltr. Rul. 9524020 (3/21/95).

Rollover when S inherits benefits through a trust

There have been letter rulings permitting a spousal rollover where benefits were payable to a marital trust under which S had an unlimited right to withdraw the principal. S exercised her power to withdraw the funds from the IRA into the marital trust, then out to herself and into her own IRA. Ltr. Ruls. 9302022 (10/19/92); 9426049 (4/12/94); 9427035 (4/29/94).

Ltr. Rul. 9426049 is probably the most "extreme" of these favorable rulings. The decedent's benefits were payable to a trust that was to be divided into two subtrusts at his death. S and a bank were co-trustees, but S had the right to remove the bank, and become sole trustee, one year after P's death. After the expiration of the one-year period, the trustees allocated the retirement benefits to one of the subtrusts, and caused them to be distributed to S under a discretionary power to pay her principal "in her best interest." This was held to be a valid rollover because of the spouse's power to remove the co-trustee and distribute principal to herself, even though for the first year after P's death she had no such power.

These rulings can be useful in "cleanup mode." The approach could also be useful for planning purposes. A client who wants to divide benefits between the spouse and a "credit shelter trust" by a formula could leave the benefits to a trust, have the trustee apply the formula to determine how much the spouse is entitled to, and then have the trustee direct the plan administrator to pay the "marital" portion of the benefits directly to the spouse. See form 3.2 in Appendix B.

At least two rulings have denied rollover status for an IRA payable to a QTIP trust where S's power to withdraw principal was not immediate and unlimited. Ltr. Ruls. 9322005 (2/24/93) (S could receive principal only in discretion of a third party trustee); 9321032 (2/24/93).

More on "pass-through" rollovers

While the IRS has been generous in permitting spousal rollovers even when benefits pass through an estate or trust, a word of caution is in order. First, the IRS's liberality has been expressed only in private letter rulings, which cannot be relied upon as precedent. Second, in the more recent rulings (*e.g.,* 9426049, 9427034, 9427035, 9524020) the IRS has started including the following recital, which did not appear in the earlier rulings (compare, *e.g.,* Ltr. Ruls. 8911006 and 9302022):

> Generally, if a decedent's qualified retirement plan proceeds pass through a third party, e.g., an estate, and then are distributed to the decedent's surviving spouse, the spouse will be treated as acquiring them from the third party and not from the decedent. Thus, generally, the surviving spouse will not be eligible to roll over the qualified plan proceeds into his or her own IRA.

This new statement may indicate that the IRS wants to put the brakes on "indirect" spousal rollovers.

In the author's view, this purported limitation on the spousal rollover is not justified. The requirement that assets must pass "from the decedent" to the spouse is a requirement of the estate tax marital deduction. S. 2056(a). It has nothing to do with rollovers or any other income tax concept. The spousal rollover provisions of the Code apply "if any distribution attributable to an employee is paid to the spouse." The Code does not limit rollover treatment to distributions which are "acquired" from the decedent.

The Rollover Checklist, in Appendix C, should be helpful in considering a prospective spousal rollover.

The Spouse and S. 401(a)(9)

Additional minimum distribution options available when S is the DB

The minimum distribution rules under s. 401(a)(9) (see Chapter 1) give several special breaks when the spouse is named as beneficiary. While the spousal rollover is by far the most powerful and universally beneficial income tax deferral tool available to S, the special spousal provisions of s. 401(a)(9) can be significant in particular situations. Here are the three special breaks s. 401(a)(9) allows when S is named as beneficiary:

(a)   When P reaches his RBD, he must start taking out benefits over the joint life expectancy ("LE") of himself and his "designated beneficiary" (DB). If his DB is his spouse (S), he can use their actual joint LE to measure minimum required distributions ("MRDs"). If P's DB is someone other than his spouse, he can use the actual joint LE only if the DB is not more than 10 years younger than P. If the non-spouse DB is more than 10 years younger than P, P must use a special table to measure MRDs, which essentially treats the DB as being 10 years younger than P. See "Incidental Benefit/MDIB Rule" section of Chapter 1. The ability to use the actual joint LE of P and S provides improved deferral opportunities for a participant whose spouse is more than 10 years younger than he -- in other words, not too many people.

(b)   S's LE can be redetermined annually. This option is available both during P's life (if the joint LE of P and S is being used to measure P's MRDs), and after his death if S is P's DB. See Chapter 1 for detail and planning considerations involved in this option.

(c)   If P dies before his RBD, P's non-spouse beneficiaries must begin withdrawing their benefits from the plan within one year after the date of death (or else withdraw all the benefits within five years after P's death). If S is the beneficiary, on the other hand, she does not have to start withdrawing benefits until the end of the calendar year in which P would have reached age 70½. If S dies before December 31 of the year in which P would have reached age 70½, her death will start a new "five year rule" period running. S. 401(a)(9)(B)(iv)(II); prop. reg. 1.401(a)(9)-1, C-5.

Which is better--rollover, or deferring distributions until P would have reached 70½?

At first it might appear that, if P died before reaching age 70½, and P were younger than S, option (c) would produce longer income tax deferral for S than a rollover. If she rolls over the benefits to her own IRA, she will have to start withdrawing from the plan when *she* reaches age 70½; if she leaves the benefits in P's plan she can postpone the start of distributions for a longer period, until *P* would have reached age 70½. This conclusion is correct -- *provided* S withdraws all the benefits and rolls them over to her own IRA no later than December 31 of the year P would have reached age 69½. If she does not complete her rollover by that date she will have to start, in the following year, to take out benefits over only her own LE; and if she dies after December 31 of the year P would have reached age 70½, still without having done the rollover, the contingent beneficiaries will have to take the benefits over the remainder of S's LE, rather than over their own LE.

Once P would have reached age 69½, the spousal rollover will produce much longer income tax deferral both during S's life (because she can use two LEs instead of just one to measure her minimum required distributions) (MRDs) and after S's death (because the next beneficiaries can use their own LE to measure MRDs rather than being stuck with only the remainder of S's LE).

However, there are other factors to consider besides federal income tax deferral in deciding whether S should roll over the decedent's retirement benefits. See the "Rollover Checklist" in Appendix C.

Benefits paid to a marital trust

If benefits are paid to a marital trust or other trust for the life benefit of S, are these special spousal options under s. 401(a)(9) available? This question is discussed in the "Who are the Beneficiaries of a Trust?" section of Chapter 9.

Marital Deduction for Benefits Payable to QTIP Trust

Non-tax reasons to name a QTIP trust

P may not want to leave benefits outright to S for any number of reasons: fear of S's remarriage; fear, in a second marriage, that S may divert assets away from P's children by the first marriage; S may be mentally ill, a spendthrift or an alcoholic; or S may simply be inexperienced in investing or a "soft touch" for requests for loans or gifts from needy relatives. In all these cases, P may prefer to leave money in trust for S, rather than outright to her, and this usually means naming a "qualified terminable interest property" (QTIP) trust as beneficiary. Unfortunately, the price of protecting the benefits from these various risks is high in most cases: higher income taxes, and substantial loss of income tax deferral, as compared with leaving the benefits to S outright.

The client who wants to make his benefits payable to a QTIP trust faces several hurdles: qualifying for the marital deduction (discussed in this chapter); complying with the proposed regulations' "trust rules" so S can be treated as a "designated beneficiary" for purposes of the minimum distribution rules (see Chapter 1); and avoiding triggering an income tax when funding the QTIP (see Chapter 2).

The IRS's "test" for determining whether S is the beneficiary for purposes of the spousal rollover is different from its test for determining whether S is the beneficiary for purposes of s. 401(a)(9); which is in turn different from its test for determining whether the interest qualifies for the marital deduction.

Although some practitioners believe that a marital deduction trust should be treated exactly the same as a spouse for purposes of the many rules applicable to retirement benefits, that is *not* what the law provides. Table 3.2 provides a quick reference comparison of the different tax treatments that apply when benefits are left to a "QTIP" marital deduction trust rather than outright to S. In this chart, it is assumed that the QTIP trust provides all income to S for life, and otherwise complies

Table 3.2

Recap of differences between naming spouse vs. naming a marital trust as beneficiary.		
	Outright to Spouse	**QTIP Marital Trust**
Marital deduction available?	yes	yes
Maximum payout period is over life expectancy of . . .	S and her DB, if rollover is used or if both spouses die before 70½	S's LE only
Can S defer start of distributions until P would have reached age 70½?	yes	probably not
Can S elect to defer 15% excise tax, under 4980A(d)(5)?	yes	no

with all marital deduction requirements, but does not give S the unlimited right to withdraw principal.

How to qualify for the marital deduction when retirement benefits are payable to a QTIP trust

Benefits paid directly to S outright in a lump sum should qualify for the marital deduction, provided S is a U.S. citizen and it is clear that S is entitled to withdraw all the benefits. See, *e.g.*, Ltr. Rul. 8843033 (8/2/88).

If it were not for the rulings discussed below, most

practitioners would conclude that they could simply name a QTIP trust as beneficiary of the client's IRA and leave it at that. "Obviously" the IRA would qualify for the marital deduction since the QTIP trustee could withdraw the benefits from the IRA at any time and reinvest them inside the QTIP trust. S would be fully protected by her right to receive all income of the trust and her power to require the trustee to invest in income producing property.

However, the IRS, in Technical Advice Memorandum (TAM) 9220007, took a different view. This TAM held that the IRA *itself* was to be considered "terminable interest property." The IRA agreement in question (which was quite standard) did not contain any statement about when benefits would be paid out, other than the statement required by the minimum distribution rules to the effect that "benefits must be distributed no later than, etc." The IRA agreement did not explicitly state that the account holder could withdraw all benefits from the IRA at any time.

The TAM writer looked for a provision that would require the QTIP trustee to withdraw all income annually from the IRA and found no such provision. The TAM went on to conclude that the QTIP trustee's ability to opt for some "settlement option" that would pay out all the income annually was not sufficient; since the mandatory income provision was not included as of the date of death, some discretionary act of the QTIP trustee *post mortem* could not cure it.

Rev. Rul. 89-89, 1989-2 C.B. 231, discussed a designation of a marital trust as beneficiary for an IRA that did work. In this ruling, the IRA beneficiary designation form itself contained all the required marital deduction trust provisions. Rather than simply naming the QTIP trustee as the beneficiary of the IRA, the beneficiary designation form also stated how benefits had to be withdrawn. Specifically, it required the QTIP trustee to withdraw from the IRA each year, and place into the

QTIP trust, all the income earned by the IRA that year.

Thus the IRS has given us a road map of what will definitely "work" in order for an IRA (or other retirement plan death benefit) payable to a QTIP trust to qualify for the marital deduction: having the IRA custodian (or plan administrator) be required to pay out to the QTIP trust all the income earned on the benefit every year. This is an awkward requirement in the case of IRAs since most IRA custodians are not equipped to deal with, and do not charge for, fiduciary responsibilities such as determining what is "income" and what is "principal." Since few planners want to take the risk that the marital deduction will be disallowed, many planners choose to use the Rev. Rul. 89-89 language (as subsequently refined; see examples in forms 3.3, 3.4 and 3.5 in Appendix B).

This series of IRS rulings appears to be erroneous to the extent it implies that the only way an IRA or other retirement benefit payable to a marital trust can qualify for the marital deduction is if the plan document (or IRA agreement) contains language requiring annual distribution of all income. The following paragraphs analyze the question by reference to the IRS's own regulations.

"Income" requirement of marital trusts: general power trusts

Under s. 2056(b)(5), a trust qualifies for the marital deduction if the spouse is entitled to all income of the trust for life, payable at least annually, and has the power, exercisable by her alone and in all events, to appoint the principal to herself or her estate, with no power in any other person to appoint any of the property to someone other than the spouse ("general power marital trust").

Although generally this type of marital trust must provide that S is "entitled for life to all the income" of the trust, long-standing IRS regulations make it clear that this does not mean that income must actually be distributed to S every year; rather, there are several ways S's interest can be arranged and still meet the "entitled to all the income" requirement. For example:

1.   A power in the trustee to hold unproductive property will not disqualify the trust if S has the right to require the trustee to either make any such property productive or convert it to productive property within a reasonable time. S. 20.2056(b)-5(f)(4).

2.   If the corpus of a trust consists substantially of non-income producing property, and S does not have the power to compel the trustee to make it income producing, the trust will still qualify for the marital deduction if S can "require that the trustee provide the required beneficial enjoyment, such as by payments to the Spouse out of other assets of the trust." - 5(f)(5).

3.   An interest qualifies if the income may be accumulated in the sole discretion of S. - 5(f)(7).

4.   An interest qualifies if S has "the right exercisable annually (or more frequently) to require distribution to herself of the trust income, and otherwise [*i.e.*, if she does not require such distribution in any year] the trust income [for such year] is to be accumulated." -5(f)(8).

Thus, contrary to the implication of Rev. Rul. 89-89, an IRA (for example) payable to a marital trust should qualify for the marital deduction so long as the spouse has the power to *require* that the IRA income be distributed to her (no. 4 above), or to require the trustee to distribute other assets to her (no. 2 above) to make up for the IRA income's being accumulated.

"Income" requirement: QTIP trusts

The regulation quoted above deals with "general power" marital trusts. There are other kinds of marital trusts. Under s. 2056(b)(7), a trust qualifies for the estate tax marital deduction if the spouse is entitled to all income for life, payable at least annually, and no person has the power to appoint any of the principal to someone other than the spouse during her lifetime, provided the executor files a special election with the estate tax return. This type of trust is called a "qualified terminable interest property" ("QTIP") marital trust.

The final QTIP regulations specify that the same principles apply to "qualified terminable interest property" (in trust or otherwise) as apply to general power marital trusts in determining whether S is "entitled for life to all of the income." Reg. s. 20.2056(b)-7(d)(2). Thus, the same alternative methods for meeting the "entitled to all income" requirement are available for QTIP trusts as for general power trusts.

Practitioner response to Rev. Rul. 89-89

To summarize, if you want retirement benefits paid to any marital trust to qualify for the marital deduction, one approach is to include language such as that used in Rev. Rul. 89-89 in your IRA beneficiary designation. You may also choose to include language requiring the trustee to withdraw at least enough from the IRA annually to comply with the minimum distribution rules, which Rev. Rul. 89-89 ignored. This approach is apparently being adopted by many practitioners. See, *e.g.*, Ltr. Ruls. 9321035 (2/24/93); 9321059 (2/26/93); 9418026 (2/7/94); 9348025 (9/2/93).

However, as the preceding discussion shows, there are several other methods that estate planning lawyers can use to qualify retirement benefits payable to a marital trust for the marital deduction. Although the forms in this book use the "safe harbor" approach of Rev. Rul. 89-89, practitioners may well choose to use some other approach in the instruments they draft.

Certain forms that have been approved in letter rulings also specifically address trust accounting issues. See, *e.g.*, Ltr. Rul. 8728011 (language detailing allocation of administration expenses between income and corpus).

Note: Despite some statements to the contrary that have appeared in print, the Rev. Rul. 89-89 language requires only that the income earned by the retirement plan be distributed to the spouse annually. The plan (or IRA) must distribute to the QTIP trust the greater of the net income for the year or the MRD for the year; but the QTIP trustee is not required to distribute the greater of these two amounts out to the spouse. The QTIP trustee is required to distribute only the "income" of the trust. If the MRD for the year is greater than the income, the excess is considered to be, for trust accounting (and marital deduction) purposes, "corpus" of the QTIP trust. See discussion of IRD in Chapter 2. The Code does not require that "corpus" be distributed to S as a condition of obtaining the marital deduction.

If relying on Rev. Rul. 89-89, it is also advisable to have, as a backup, matching language in the QTIP trust itself requiring the trustee to withdraw those amounts from the IRA or plan every year. This provides some protection in case the client, having dutifully signed the designation of beneficiary forms his lawyer so carefully prepared, with all the elaborate language, later signs some new substituted form that might be given to him when (for example) he transfers to a different investment, or when the plan sponsor simply issues new forms periodically. See forms 3.5 and 7.4 in Appendix B.

Finally, when retirement benefits are payable to a QTIP trust, the executor needs to elect QTIP treatment for the benefits themselves as well as for the trust, according to Ltr.

Rul. 9442032 (7/27/94).

Another alternative to avoid this issue, in the case of an IRA, is to structure the IRA *itself* as a QTIP: use a "trust IRA" rather than a "custodial IRA," include all required and desirable marital trust provisions, and have the IRA trustee pay the annual income directly to S. The major drawback of this approach is that eventually the minimum distribution rules will start requiring distributions of principal as well as income, and if the principal is all dribbled out to S it will not be "protected" for the children (as it would be if it were payable to a QTIP trust). Thus this alternative is normally attractive only to someone whose only goal in QTIPing the benefits is to protect S from mishandling a lump sum, rather than someone whose goal is (*e.g.)* to preserve principal for children of a first marriage.

Income Tax Disadvantages When QTIP Trust is Beneficiary

Loss of deferral during S's life: mandatory income distributions

The language used in Rev. Rul. 89-89 may involve a significant loss of potential income tax deferral. The minimum distribution rules would normally require S, as P's "DB," to withdraw *less* than the income every year until near the end of the "life expectancy" payout period.

For this reason, if the client's retirement benefits total less than $600,000, and the client is determined not to leave any assets outright to S, consider making the retirement benefits payable to the credit shelter trust, and using other assets to fund the QTIP trust. Although this is contrary to the usual "rule of thumb" ("don't waste your credit shelter paying income taxes"), it will increase the potential income tax deferral, because the credit shelter trust is not subject to the mandatory income payout requirement.

If S is not a beneficiary of the credit shelter gift, only the children are, the income tax deferral may be further enhanced, assuming the children are younger than S, because the payout will be spread out over a longer "life expectancy" period.

The loss of potential deferral of income taxes caused by following Rev. Rul. 89-89 is not a concern, of course, if it is expected that S will want to withdraw all income of the benefits in any case, for her living needs.

It may be that, with careful planning and proper timing, the annual income distribution problem can be mitigated by spousal rollovers. The trustee of the marital trust could withdraw the retirement plan's "income" once a year, as Rev. Rul. 89-89 apparently requires, and then immediately distribute it to S. S could then roll over to her own IRA the excess of the total distribution over that year's required "minimum distribution." (The required annual minimum distribution is not eligible for rollover. S. 408(d)(3)(E).) The annual required minimum distribution would normally be less than the plan's "income" for the year until the final years of S's life expectancy, depending on the plan's rate of return.

If S is relatively young, this technique of rolling over the "excess" income distribution every year can provide substantial additional tax deferral. As long as her rollover occurred within 60 days after the income was distributed from P's plan to the marital trust, and provided she received and rolled over no more than one distribution in any 12 month period, this may qualify as a proper spousal rollover. The IRS has ruled (albeit only in private letter rulings) that a plan distribution that passes through a marital trust on its way to S is eligible for a spousal rollover, provided that S had an absolute right to receive it, *i.e.*, the distribution of the retirement benefit to her from the marital trust was not subject to a third party's discretion. See rulings cited in "Spousal Rollovers" section of this chapter.

The annual distribution of plan income to the marital trust and thence to S would be mandatory under the Rev. Rul. 89-89 language.

Loss of income tax deferral -- s. 401(a)(9)

Even if the problem of mandatory income distributions can be tempered by means of the spousal rollover, it will still be true in many cases that making retirement benefits payable to a marital trust will result in much less income tax deferral during S's life than would be available if the benefits were payable to S personally and she rolled them over to her own IRA. With the rollover IRA, she can defer distributions altogether until she reaches age 70½, at which time she could begin withdrawing them over the joint life expectancy of herself and a younger beneficiary.

When she is receiving the benefits as beneficiary of a marital trust, in contrast, the minimum distribution rules will probably require annual non-rollable distributions to the trust beginning the year after P's death, and only S's own life expectancy can be used to measure the payout. (This conclusion is based on the assumption that S is the oldest beneficiary of the trust; and that she is not considered the "sole" beneficiary of the trust because there are remainder beneficiaries. See "Who are the Beneficiaries of a Trust?" in Chapter 9.)

When benefits are payable to S individually, she can roll them over to her own IRA, name the children as beneficiaries and thus achieve a long period of deferral (over the children's life expectancies) for any benefits remaining in the IRA at her death. When the benefits are paid to a marital trust, in contrast, the minimum distribution rules will continue to operate based on the life expectancy of S solely (assuming she is the oldest beneficiary of the trust, and the other requirements for naming a trust as beneficiary are met. See Chapter 1).

Making benefits payable to a marital trust, as opposed to S individually, often results in sacrificing decades of potential additional income tax deferral -- all benefits will have to be distributed by the time S reaches age 86, approximately, whereas some deferral until the oldest child reaches that age is usually achievable when benefits are paid to S individually.

High trust tax rates

The 1993 tax law changes further battered retirement benefits payable to a QTIP trust (or to any other trust where the benefits are expected to be retained by the trust, rather than immediately distributed to the beneficiaries), by imposing high tax rates on trust income. See Chapter 2.

Avoiding income tax on funding a marital trust

Do not leave benefits to any trust under which the benefits would have to pass as part of a pecuniary gift--for example, a typical "pourover" trust with a pecuniary marital deduction formula. Instead, leave the benefits directly to the marital trust itself, or else use a fractional funding formula, to avoid a possible realization of taxable income to the estate or to the funding trust. See "Income in Respect of a Decedent" in Chapter 2, and form 3.4 in Appendix B.

Simultaneous Death Clauses

Uniform Simultaneous Death Law

If the participant (P) names his spouse (S) as his beneficiary, and they die simultaneously, it will be presumed under the Uniform Simultaneous Death Law that S predeceased.

A presumption that S survives, if contained in P's will or pourover trust, will NOT govern retirement plan death benefits payable directly to S. Thus, in order to have a presumption that S survives in this situation, the presumption must be contained in the designation of beneficiary form itself. Such a presumption is often used, if S's estate is smaller than P's, to equalize the estates for estate tax purposes. What is the effect of such a survivorship presumption under the minimum distribution rules?

If P dies before age 70½

If P and S die simultaneously before December 31 of the year in which P reached (or would have reached) age 70½, there appears to be no disadvantage to presuming S survives, from the point of view of s. 401(a)(9), if S is personally named as the "DB," regardless of whether the presumption is recognized by the IRS for s. 401(a)(9) purposes. This is so because under these circumstances, even if S survived P, the "five year rule" is applied as if S were the participant. Prop. reg. s. 1.401(a)(9)-1, C-5. Therefore, the benefits will have to be distributed within five years after S's death, unless there is a DB succeeding S, in which case the benefits can be distributed over the LE of the DB. Assuming the children are named as P's contingent beneficiaries, and the benefits are payable to them if S dies before having withdrawn all P's benefits or named a new beneficiary, the children would be treated as S's "DBs" and the benefits could be paid over their LE.

Thus, there is no disadvantage under s. 401(a)(9) to presuming S survives if that presumption is desirable for estate tax purposes (or for s. 4980A(d)(5) purposes -- see below), *provided* a proper contingent "DB" is in place.

What if not S individually, but a marital trust is named as beneficiary? Here the result may be very different. Suppose P designates a QTIP trust as his primary beneficiary and his five children as contingent beneficiaries. The "trust rules" are complied with. The beneficiary designation form presumes S survives P in case of simultaneous death.

Assume the QTIP trust is to be distributed outright to the children on S's death, so the children get the benefits outright either as remainder beneficiaries of the QTIP trust or as contingent beneficiaries under P's beneficiary designation form. P and S both die, simultaneously, prior to December 31 of the year in which P reached (or would have reached) age 70½. There are three conceivable outcomes under s. 401(a)(9):

(a)   One possibility is that prop. reg. s. 1.401(a)(9)-1, C-5 applies, and the five year rule applies "as if" S were the participant. This good outcome would occur if S is regarded as the "sole beneficiary" of the QTIP trust. Unfortunately it seems unlikely that this result will obtain. See "Who are the Beneficiaries of a Trust?" in Chapter 9.

(b)   A second possibility is that the IRS would disregard the presumption of survivorship for purposes of s. 401(a)(9) and would treat the children as P's "DB." There is no reason to believe this would be the outcome.

(c)   The third possibility, which now seems the most likely outcome, is that the benefits would have to be distributed to the QTIP trust over the LE of S as it existed on P's death. Unless the beneficiary designation form and/or plan document clearly establish that S's LE is NOT to be redetermined annually, the IRS presumption that it is redetermined will apply and all benefits will have to be distributed within a year after S's death.

The moral of the story is this: until December 31 of the year P reaches age 70½ --

(i)   if S is named personally as the DB, and the right "contingent" DBs would take on her death after P's, there is no disadvantage to presuming S survives P in case of simultaneous death. Therefore if estate-equalizing considerations favor presuming S survives P there is no reason not to do so.

(ii)   if a marital trust is named as DB, there is probably a major disadvantage to presuming S survives. Therefore, the s. 401(a)(9) reasons for presuming S predeceases P need to be weighed against the estate tax reasons (if there are any) for presuming S survives.

If P dies after the 70½ year

Once the RBD has passed, the payout period of P's benefits is "carved in stone," and the only way it could be varied would be if S survived P and rolled over the benefits (or, in the case of an IRA, elected to treat P's IRA as her own). Presuming S survives P in case of simultaneous deaths would theoretically enable S's executor to roll over the benefits or, in the case of an IRA, elect to treat the IRA as S's own IRA. Unfortunately it does not appear that the IRS will allow a surviving spouse's executor to take these actions. (See discussion in "Spousal Rollovers" section of this Chapter.)

Nevertheless, because of the tremendous potential value of these rights S has, it is worth trying to preserve those options in case of simultaneous death, especially if P's elections on the RBD now seem regrettable. One approach which has yet to be tested is this: If IRA death benefits are being made payable to S to take advantage of the spousal rollover or 4980A(d)(5) election (see Chapter 5), specify in the beneficiary designation form that S is presumed to survive in case of simultaneous death. Then have S elect in writing, *while P is still living*, to treat the IRA as her own (in the event she survives P), and name her own DB. The IRS has not yet ruled one way or the other on whether the spouse can make the election, before P's death, to treat P's IRA as S's IRA if she survives. See the *Fallon* case study and form 4.1 in Appendix B.

Plan provisions

Before attempting to create a presumption of spousal survival in a designation of beneficiary form, check the plan to make sure it does not create an irrebuttable presumption that P survives beneficiary in case of simultaneous deaths.

REA '84 and Spousal Consent

The Retirement Equity Act of 1984 requires spousal consent in order for a participant to withdraw benefits from certain kinds of retirement plans in other than "qualified joint and survivor annuity" form, or to make death benefits payable to a beneficiary other than the spouse. These requirements apply to all pension plans, and some profit sharing plans. They do not apply to IRAs or 403(b) plans.

Needless to say the spousal consent requirement creates serious obstacles when the spouses are separated, divorcing or otherwise hostile. It can also create very serious and sad problems when the spouse is mentally ill or disabled to such an extent that he or she is unable to consent.

Practitioners who have carefully studied REA and its requirements are bedeviled by such problems as precisely when (relative to the distribution date) spousal consent must be obtained in order to be valid under REA; whether a new spousal consent is required for every distribution if installments are being paid out prior to the required beginning date; whether the REA consent requirements limit the ability of a participant and spouse to change the form of benefits after the RBD; and whether a waiver contained in a prenuptial agreement can meet (or beat) the spousal waiver requirements of REA.

This book does not cover these extensive problems. For other sources of information, see the Bibliography. See also discussion of REA issues in connection with disclaimers in Chapter 8.

Summary of Planning Principles

1.   The tax laws generally, though not always, favor naming the spouse, personally, as DB of retirement benefits and using other, non-IRD assets to fund a credit shelter trust.

2.   The IRS has issued rulings which provide clear instructions for qualifying retirement benefits payable to QTIP trusts for the estate tax marital deduction. Although the method specified in these rulings is not the only way to obtain the marital deduction for benefits payable to a QTIP trust, many practitioners are choosing to use it.

3.   Making benefits payable to a QTIP trust often results in a substantial loss of potential income tax deferral compared with leaving benefits to S outright.

4.   Review the issues discussed in the "Simultaneous Deaths" section of this chapter before inserting a "presumption of survivorship" clause in a beneficiary designation.

5.   Upon P's death it is extremely important for S to immediately consider her options, and to roll over the benefits if that is the chosen option, since her executor probably cannot exercise these options on her behalf.

4

Retirement Benefits
and the Non-Citizen Spouse

If the participant's spouse is not a U.S. citizen, the usual marital deduction is not available. A "modified" marital deduction is available if certain requirements are met. A long menu of planning alternatives offers a few practical solutions.

Introduction

This chapter explains the tax issues involved when the participant's spouse is not a U.S. citizen, then examines each of the alternative methods for disposing of retirement benefits in this situation, with emphasis on those most likely to be used.

Modified Marital Deduction for Transfers to a Non-Citizen Spouse

How the "modified marital deduction" works

For the estates of decedents dying after November 10, 1988, property passing to a surviving spouse (S) who is not a United States citizen will not qualify for the "normal" estate tax marital deduction. S. 2056(d). However, if the property is placed in a certain kind of trust, called a qualified domestic trust ("QDOT"), either by the decedent (D) himself or by S, it will qualify for a *modified* version of the marital deduction.

Under this modified marital deduction, the property is deducted on Schedule M of D's estate tax return; but then, if principal is ever distributed to S from the QDOT, the principal distribution is subject to an estate tax at that time, computed at D's rate. If the estate tax is paid from the QDOT, the tax payment itself is treated as a further distribution subject to estate tax. Principal remaining in the QDOT at S's death is subject to the deferred estate tax at that time. S. 2056A(b).

(Note: an important exception to the general rule is that lifetime principal distributions to S on account of "hardship" are not subject to the deferred estate tax. The final regs.' generous definition of "hardship" will make this exception a useful planning tool in many situations. Since the implications of this hardship exception are the same for retirement benefits as for other QDOT assets, the subject is not further discussed here. The rest of the chapter refers to QDOT principal distributions as if they were always taxable; the reader should bear in mind that the hardship exception may of course be available for any such distribution.)

In other words, under the modified form of marital deduction available when S is not a U.S. citizen, the property is not deducted from D's estate and then added to S's estate, as normally occurs when the marital deduction is taken. Rather, the property remains permanently taxable as part of D's estate. The tax is merely deferred, either until the property is distributed to S out of the QDOT, or until S's death. The QDOT property will *also* be subject to U.S. estate tax as part of S's estate, under normal estate tax principles, although her estate will receive a credit for the deferred estate tax paid on the property by the QDOT. S. 2056(d)(3). In other words, if the non-citizen spouse dies a U.S. resident, the estate tax payable on the QDOT at S's death is essentially going to be at D's marginal rate, or at S's marginal rate, whichever is higher.

(Note: If the non-citizen spouse is or becomes a non-U.S.-*resident*, different considerations may apply. That situation is beyond the scope of this book.)

"QDOTs" and other ways to qualify for the modified marital deduction

In order to qualify for even this modified version of the marital deduction, it is essential that the property in question be placed in a QDOT. This can happen in a number of ways. One is for D to have arranged his estate plan so that property for which the marital deduction is sought will pass automatically on his death to a QDOT. If D's estate plan failed to do this, the modified marital deduction is still available if S herself transfers the property to a QDOT prior to the filing of the estate tax return and no later than one year after the due date of the return. Reg. s. 20.2056A-1(a)(iii).

Still a third method of qualifying for the modified marital deduction is available for "non-assignable property" -- property which passes to S outright, but which cannot legally be transferred by S to a QDOT, or for an "individual retirement account" (IRA) which S elects to treat as non-assignable. Treasury regulations allow S to get QDOT treatment for "non-assignable property" by agreeing to transfer the property to a QDOT later, as she actually receives it; or, alternatively, by agreeing with the IRS that she will pay the deferred estate tax on the property when she actually receives the property.

The special problems of leaving benefits to a non-citizen spouse can also be eliminated by having the spouse become a U.S. citizen prior to the filing of the estate tax return, if she was a U.S. resident at all applicable times; s. 2056(d)(4). Under those circumstances the "regular" marital deduction becomes available. This is often the simplest solution to the problem if S intends to remain permanently in the U.S. anyway. This approach should be explored at the planning stage if possible or, if not then, as soon as possible after D's death, since becoming a citizen takes time and should not be left to the last minute.

The rest of this chapter does not discuss that approach but rather assumes S will remain a non-U.S. citizen.

Distinguishing Features of a QDOT

The five requirements

The distinguishing characteristics of a qualified domestic trust are set forth in s. 2056A(a):

(a)   At least one trustee of the QDOT must be an individual citizen of the United States or a United States domestic corporation.

(b)   The trust must be "maintained" under, and the administration of the trust must be governed by, the laws of a particular state or the District of Columbia. Reg. s. 20.2056A-2(a).

(c)   No principal distribution may be made from the trust unless the U.S. trustee has the right to withhold from the distribution the deferred estate tax discussed above.

(d)   The trust must meet any additional requirements imposed by the Secretary of the Treasury by regulations to insure collection of the tax. In proposed regulations 20.2056A-1 *et seq.*, issued December 31, 1992, the Service proposed some such additional requirements, such as bonding for non-bank trustees and limits on non-U.S. real estate investments. The proposed regs. on this particular subject were modified and reissued as Temporary and Proposed Regs. in August 1995.

Temp. reg. s. 20.2056A-2(d).

The regulations also provide various requirements for agreements and elections by the executor and surviving spouse; these requirements are not discussed in this chapter.

Note that there is no requirement that all of the QDOT income be distributable annually to S, or even that S be the sole beneficiary of the QDOT. The QDOT requirements are concerned only with the identity of the trustee, necessary elections, and security for collection of the deferred estate tax.

In summary, in order to obtain the modified version of the marital deduction for property when S is not a U.S. citizen, the property must be placed in a trust which meets the above requirements; and *in addition* the property must pass from D to S (or to a trust for S's benefit) in a way that qualifies for the marital deduction (aside from the QDOT requirements). A QDOT established by S (which needs to meet only the QDOT requirements) may look very different from a QDOT established by D (which must meet both the QDOT requirements and the "regular" marital deduction requirements). The difference is significant when planning for retirement benefits.

Marital trust - QDOT created by decedent

Regardless of whether the surviving spouse is a U.S. citizen, the marital deduction is not allowed for property passing in trust for a spouse unless the trust meets certain requirements familiar to all estate planners: a "marital deduction trust" will be a non-deductible "terminable interest" unless it fits into one of three categories. Two of these categories are the common forms of marital deduction trust, which are statutory exceptions to the "terminable interest rule": the "general power marital trust" and the "QTIP marital trust" (see Chapter 3).

Thus a QDOT created by transfer from D must generally

be either a "general power marital trust" or a "QTIP marital trust," meeting all the usual requirements of a marital trust, including, most significantly with regard to retirement benefits, the requirement that all income be distributed annually. A third category of trust gift that qualifies for the marital deduction is the rarely-used "estate trust." Estate trusts are discussed in a separate section of this chapter.

QDOT created by surviving spouse

If property passes from D to S *outright*, it qualifies for the marital deduction under s. 2056(a). An outright bequest is not a "terminable interest," and accordingly does not have to comply with the marital deduction trust rules. Those rules apply only to trust-gifts that would otherwise be non-deductible "terminable interests." Therefore, when S receives an outright bequest, and then transfers the inherited property into a QDOT she creates, there is no requirement that the terms of the QDOT be similar to those of a "normal" marital deduction trust, provided that the trust contains only property transferred to it by S. Only the QDOT requirements need be met.

Thus, S could, if she wanted to for some reason, name others as beneficiaries of the QDOT besides herself, or provide for the accumulation of income. Of course, her transfer of assets into the QDOT will be subject to gift tax to the extent it puts the property irrevocably beyond her control; and even if the initial transfer to the trust is structured so as not to trigger gift tax, distributions to someone other than S during her lifetime would constitute completed gifts, resulting in a gift tax payable by her. See reg. s. 20.2056A-4(d), ex.5.

Note: if the trust to which S transfers property also contains any property transferred directly to it by D then the *entire trust* must qualify for the "regular" marital deduction under s. 2056. Reg. s. 20.2056A-4(b)(1). In this chapter, a

"QDOT funded by S" means a QDOT exclusively so funded.

Payment of deferred estate tax by QDOT

Once the property is in a QDOT (whether transferred there by D or by S), all distributions from the QDOT will trigger the deferred estate tax, with just the following exceptions:

(a)   Distributions of *income* to S will not trigger the tax.

(b)   A distribution to S "on account of hardship" is exempt from the tax.

(c)   Distributions to S to reimburse her for certain income taxes are not subject to the tax.

Any other distribution to S, and any distribution to anybody else, would trigger the deferred estate tax.

There are two other events, besides distributions, that cause the deferred estate tax to be due:

(a)   If the trust ceases to qualify as a QDOT, the tax is imposed at that time.

(b)   In any case, the tax is payable upon the death of S.

Interplay of Income Tax
and Deferred Estate Tax

Retirement benefits generally are subject both to income tax as "income in respect of a decedent" ("IRD") (see Chapter

2) and estate tax. In most situations, the beneficiary can deduct the federal estate taxes paid on retirement benefits in determining the income tax payable on those benefits. When the benefits are paid to a non-citizen spouse or a QDOT, however, it is much less clear how the income tax and the deferred estate tax relate to each other.

Under the statute, it appears possible that S could be required to pay *both* income tax *and* deferred estate tax on the full amount of inherited retirement benefits, with neither tax deductible in determining the other. The regs. make it clear in a couple of situations that amounts used to pay income tax on IRD will not *also* be subject to the deferred estate tax; in other situations we are left to hope that this result is allowed, without specific authority.

Income tax paid by S on plan distributions

The Code exempts from the deferred estate tax, distributions to S from a QDOT made to reimburse S for *federal* income taxes imposed on S on any item of income of the QDOT "to which the surviving spouse is not entitled under the terms of the trust." The IRS in its regs. has expanded this inadequate and incomprehensible Code provision in such a way as to alleviate the double taxation effect in some specific situations.

Under the regs.' scheme, if S receives a distribution from D's retirement plan and then "assigns" that distribution to the QDOT, the QDOT can reimburse S for the federal income tax on the distribution, free of deferred estate tax.

Note the following:

(a)   Suppose the Acme Widget Profit Sharing Plan distributes $100,000 to S as a death benefit from D's account in the plan, S immediately takes the $100,000 check and deposits it in the QDOT, and S then has to pay (say) $40,000 of federal income tax on the distribution. The QDOT can reimburse her for the $40,000 without having to pay deferred estate tax on the distribution.

(b)   This estate-tax-free reimbursement is available only for taxes imposed by subtitle A, federal income taxes. It is not permitted for state income taxes, or the 15% excise tax (in subtitle D).

(c)   The reimbursable tax is calculated at the marginal rate -- the difference between S's actual income tax for the year and S's tax if the distribution had not been included.

(d)   Suppose when the profit sharing plan makes its distribution to S, the plan *withholds* $40,000 of income tax from the distribution. The withheld taxes are paid directly to the IRS. S contributes to the QDOT only the net check she receives ($60,000). Because a profit sharing plan is "non-assignable" (see separate discussion of "non-assignable benefits" later in this chapter), if there is tax withheld from the distribution, or if S pays the tax before she transfers the benefits to the QDOT, S is permitted to transfer the net after-tax amount to the QDOT, without being liable for the deferred estate tax on the portion of the distribution used to pay federal income taxes. Reg. s. 20.2056A-5(c)(3)(iv).

No 691(c) deduction for deferred estate tax

Suppose S cashes in D's retirement benefits and pays the entire amount (net of income taxes) to a QDOT. Since the QDOT eventually will have to pay a deferred estate tax on the benefits, is S entitled to a deduction, in determining her income tax on the benefits, for the estate taxes payable on the benefits? Any other beneficiary of IRD would be entitled to such a deduction, under s. 691(c). (See Chapter 2.)

The answer appears to be no. S. 691(c)(2)(A) allows an income tax deduction for estate taxes imposed on IRD "under section 2001 or 2101." The deferred estate tax is imposed by s. 2056A. The regs. overcome the double tax effect, at least in some situations, by deducting the income taxes from the amount on which the deferred estate tax is paid. S is not allowed to get a double deduction by also removing the estate tax from the amount on which income taxes are paid.

Income taxes paid by the QDOT

Assume D left his retirement benefits to a QTIP-QDOT which provides "all income to S for life, remainder to my issue." Because S is only the income beneficiary, she is not treated as the "owner" of the trust principal for income tax purposes under s. 678. Accordingly, income taxes on distributions of IRD to the trust are imposed directly on the trust.

In this situation, all income taxes on the benefits (both federal and state, apparently) are exempt from the deferred estate tax. "Payments to applicable governmental authorities for income tax or any other applicable tax imposed on the QDOT" (other than the deferred estate tax itself) are exempt from the deferred estate tax. Reg. s. 20.2056-5(c)(3)(ii).

In contrast, when benefits are payable to S personally and then transferred by S to the QDOT, only the *federal* income taxes paid by S can be reimbursed by the QDOT free of deferred estate tax.

This slight discrepancy in treatment of state income taxes argues in favor of D's leaving his benefits to a QTIP-QDOT, rather than outright to S. The downside of leaving the benefits to a life income QTIP-QDOT, however, is that the benefits will be taxed at trust rates, whereas income taxes might be lower if paid at S's personal rate.

Income taxes on QDOT income taxable to S under s. 678, or DNI taxable to S

As noted, the regs. provide that if retirement benefits are distributed to, and taxable to, a QDOT, the income taxes paid by the QDOT are not subject to the deferred estate tax. What if, under s. 678, S, not the trust, is taxable on a plan distribution received by the trust, because she has the power to withdraw the distribution from the trust? The regs. do not explicitly give relief here. The regs. explicitly exempt from the deferred estate tax only income taxes "imposed on the QDOT," or paid by S on a plan distribution received by S and assigned to the QDOT.

However, the regs. do state that the non-taxable reimbursement of S for income tax is "not limited to" the specific situations mentioned. S. 20.2056A-5(c)(3)(iv). Presumably, to be consistent, reimbursement of S by the QDOT for income tax paid by S on trust income she *is* entitled to receive would also be allowed free of deferred estate tax, despite the fact that the Code allows tax-free reimbursement of S only for taxes on trust income she is *not* entitled to receive.

The result should be the same when a "principal" distribution of IRD is made from the plan to the QDOT, and S is not deemed the owner of the QDOT principal under s. 678, but the trustee distributes the principal to S under a discretionary power to distribute principal. The principal distribution carries out "distributable net income" (DNI) to S. Under ss. 661 and 662, a distribution of DNI is taxable to S rather than to the trust. The portion of such a principal distribution which S is required to pay to the IRS as income taxes should not be subject to the deferred estate tax.

With this background on the requirements for a QDOT, and the income tax treatment of benefits payable to or transferred to a QDOT, we next look at the pros and cons of specific alternatives for disposing of retirement benefits in the estate plan when the surviving spouse is not a U.S. citizen.

Alternative 1: D Makes Benefits Payable to a Marital Trust-QDOT

Mandatory income distributions

One disadvantage of making retirement benefits payable to a marital trust is the IRS's apparent position, as evidenced in a series of rulings, that the benefits will not qualify for the marital deduction unless all income of *the plan* is required to be distributed annually out to the marital trust. Such mandatory income distributions would be disadvantageous if, but for the IRS's apparent position on the issue, the marital trust as beneficiary of the benefits would draw out, and pay income tax on, some amount less than all of the income of the plan for the year. This issue is discussed in detail in Chapter 3. The considerations on this point are the same for a non-citizen spouse as for a citizen spouse.

Punitive trust income tax rates; use of general power marital trust to counteract

Another disadvantage of making retirement benefits payable to a marital deduction trust is that "principal" distributed from the retirement plan to the marital trust will be subject to income tax at trust income tax rates. This can be a major drawback. If the marital trust has more than $7,650 of taxable income (1995 rates), the excess over that amount will be taxed at 39.6%, the highest marginal rate. S, as an individual, does not reach the highest tax bracket until she has more than $256,500 of taxable income. Thus, in all but the wealthiest families, S will be in a much lower income tax bracket than the trust. The high trust income tax rates are not a drawback, however, if (a) S is already in the top income tax bracket anyway or (b) the trust can arrange its withdrawals of principal from the retirement plan so as to keep its taxable income under $7,650 a year and thus out of the highest bracket.

A marital trust for the benefit of a *citizen* spouse would have another way of minimizing income taxes on a principal distribution from the retirement plan to the trust, namely, passing some or all of the distribution out to the spouse-beneficiary, if the trust permitted this. This safety valve is not helpful in the case of a marital trust-QDOT, however, because distributions of principal from the QDOT to S will attract the deferred estate tax (except in cases of hardship).

This problem of a discrepancy between income tax brackets of S (low) and trust (high) is not a problem in a marital trust over which S has a lifetime power to invade principal. An unrestricted power to withdraw principal would cause S to be treated as the owner or "grantor" of the trust under s. 678, and thus to be personally taxable on the trust's income. Of course, she is unlikely to exercise the withdrawal power under a QDOT because exercise would trigger the deferred estate tax.

The risk of using this approach in the case of a marital trust-QDOT, at the moment, is that, as yet, the regulations do not explicitly permit the QDOT to reimburse S for income tax she is required to pay on the trust's income under s. 678, without paying the deferred estate tax on the reimbursement, although it appears *likely* that this is permitted; see income tax discussion, above.

Loss of income tax deferral after spouse's death

The third drawback of making benefits payable to a marital deduction trust is the loss of potential income tax deferral after the death of S. See Chapter 3.

Alternative 2: D Makes Benefits Payable to an Estate Trust-QDOT

The "estate trust" is an obscure and rarely used method of obtaining the marital deduction. Under an "estate trust," the trustee is not required to distribute all income to the surviving spouse -- income may be accumulated. On the death of S, all assets of the trust are distributed to S's estate. Because no part of the trust is ever distributed to anyone other than S or S's estate, the trust does not violate the "terminable interest rule" and accordingly does not need to meet the requirements of S.2056(b)(5) ("general power marital trust") or 2056(b)(7) ("qualified terminable interest property" or "QTIP") in order to qualify for the marital deduction.

The "estate trust" is rarely used in estate planning because of its requirement that all trust property be distributed to S's estate upon her death. The client who seeks to tie up his spouse's inheritance in trust during her life normally does not then want the entire trust to become subject to her power of disposition (or claims of her creditors) at her death.

However, this obscure device may have some utility in planning for retirement benefits, if the IRS continues to hold its apparent ruling posture requiring, as a condition of obtaining the marital deduction for retirement benefits payable to a marital trust, that the income of the plan (or IRA) must be distributed out of the plan (or IRA) annually. This requirement can be avoided, without sacrificing the marital deduction, by using an "estate trust."

Example: Gordon would like to leave his retirement benefits outright to his spouse, Gina, and would do so but for the fact that Gina is not a U.S. citizen and Gordon wants the benefits to qualify for the marital deduction. Instead, he leaves the benefits to an "estate trust" that is also a QDOT, with the following dispositive provisions:

1.   The trustee is required to withdraw from the retirement arrangement each year at least the amount required to be distributed under the minimum distribution rules.

2.   The trustee must withdraw from the retirement such additional amounts as Gina requests it to, (optional) and may withdraw more in its discretion.

3.   (Optional) Gina can withdraw income and principal from the trust at will (subject to the trustee's power to withhold deferred estate tax).

4.   The trustee can pay income or principal to Gina in the trustee's discretion.

5.   On Gina's death the trust terminates and all assets are distributed to Gina's estate.

This scheme, compared with a "traditional" marital trust, offers the following additional opportunities for income tax deferral. First, during Gina's life, there is no requirement that income be distributed to her annually, so the income can be retained inside the retirement plan or IRA (subject to the minimum distribution rules), thus allowing ongoing deferral of tax on the income. Second, under the minimum distribution rules, an "estate trust" might possibly be regarded as a trust of which Gina is the sole beneficiary, meaning that minimum distributions to the trust would not have to begin until Gordon would have reached age 70½ (see Chapter 3). However, if Gina also dies before 12/31 of the year Gordon would have reached age 70½, the five-year rule would be applied as if Gina were the "participant." Since Gina's "estate" would then own the IRA, that could mean the benefits would have to be entirely distributed within five years after her death. If Gina dies after 12/31 of the year Gordon would have reached age 70½, her estate becomes the owner of the benefits by virtue of termination of the estate trust and the beneficiaries of her estate can withdraw the remaining benefits over the remainder of her life expectancy.

Alternative 3: Spouse Rolls Over Benefits to QDOT-IRA

As noted, if property passes outright to S, the modified marital deduction can still be obtained if S transfers the property to a QDOT. This option poses special problems in the case of retirement benefits that are paid to S individually.

When benefits are paid directly to S: the dilemma

If S personally is named as the beneficiary, and she leaves the benefits in D's plan, the benefits will not qualify for the marital deduction because the retirement plan is not a QDOT. If she withdraws the benefits from the plan or IRA, with the idea of transferring them to a QDOT, she will have to pay income tax on the benefits.

The combination QDOT-IRA

One way out of this dilemma is for S to take the benefits out of D's retirement plan and roll them over to a QDOT that is also an "individual retirement account" (IRA) under s. 408. This will not merely salvage the marital deduction; it will provide income tax deferral opportunities that are superior, both during S's life and after her death, to those available if D had made his benefits payable directly to a traditional marital trust-QDOT.

The following discussion compares, on the one hand, leaving benefits outright to S which she then rolls over to a combination IRA-QDOT, with, on the other hand, leaving benefits to a marital trust-QDOT established by D. In fact, it is possible to have benefits payable to a marital trust-QDOT established by D and *also* have the benefits be rolled over by S to a QDOT-IRA, if D's marital trust-QDOT gives S the absolute and unrestricted right to withdraw the benefits from the marital trust (under recent IRS ruling policy; see Chapter 3). In *this* section, it is assumed for the sake of comparison that benefits left by D to a marital trust-QDOT established by D in fact remain in the marital trust, either because S does not have the right to withdraw them or because S does not choose to withdraw them.

There is no tax or legal obstacle in the way of combining an IRA and a QDOT. There is only the practical difficulty of drafting the document and finding a U.S. bank willing to serve as trustee. Unfortunately, this may not be easy to do, especially in the case of a smaller retirement benefit. Larger banks' fee schedules make them good choices only for accounts worth $500,000, $1 million or more. Smaller bank trust operations accept smaller trusts and IRAs, but in the author's experience smaller banks refuse to accept an *IRA* in the form of a trust because their IRAs are administered by an outside provider which furnishes all the forms and monitors compliance. Since the bank does not have true in-house IRA capability, it is not willing to take on something as unique as a QDOT-IRA.

S. 408(a) defines an "individual retirement account" as "a *trust* [emphasis added] created or organized in the United States for the exclusive benefit of an individual or his beneficiaries," provided that the governing instrument creating the trust meets the various requirements of s. 408, such as limiting contributions to $2,000 per year plus rollovers, prohibiting investment in life insurance, etc. S. 408(h) permits a custodial account to be treated as a trust for purposes of s. 408 if various requirements are met, and most IRAs are in fact set up as custodial accounts. If the amount involved is large enough to justify a professional trustee's fee, there is no reason why the neighborhood bank and trust company should not be willing to serve as trustee. It is probably already serving as trustee of a few QDOTs, and as custodian of numerous IRAs, and should have no problem combining both responsibilities for one entity for its customary fee.

No requirement that income be distributed annually

The requirement that income be distributed at least annually to S as a condition of obtaining the marital deduction applies only when property is left by D to a marital trust. When property is left outright to S, the gift qualifies for the marital deduction under 2056(a) and the special trust rules of s. 2056(b) *et seq.*, designed to cure marital bequests of "terminable interests," do not apply. A QDOT established by S therefore does not have to require annual distribution of income.

Reg. s. 20.2056A-4(d), example 5, in discussing gift and generation skipping transfer (GST) tax aspects of S's transfer to the QDOT, confirms that, for all purposes of gift, income, estate and GST taxes *other than* s. 2056(d)(2)(A), S is treated as the transferor of the QDOT when S receives an outright bequest and transfers it to a QDOT. This reg. confirms that, when S is the transferor to the QDOT, "a QTIP election cannot be made for the QDOT. This is so because the marital deduction is allowed under Section 2056(a) for the outright bequest to" S.

Note: the QDOT regs. specify that the marital deduction trust requirements, such as annual distribution of income, *do* apply to a trust which contains *any* property contributed by D. Thus it is essential, if S rolls over benefits to a QDOT-IRA, that the trust not contain any benefits transferred directly to it by D.

Accordingly, if S is named as beneficiary of retirement benefits, and can roll them over to her own IRA, the family will be able to obtain greater income tax deferral on those benefits than would be available if the benefits are paid to a QDOT established by D. The only restrictions on S's ability to defer will be the minimum distribution rules, applied as if *she* were the participant. She can defer the commencement of distributions until her own required beginning date (April 1 following the year in which she reaches age 70½). She can then take distributions over the joint life expectancy of herself and a younger beneficiary (say a child or grandchild), subject to the MDIB rule (see Chapter 1), which would give her an initial projected withdrawal period of about 26 years commencing at age 70½.

Despite the attractiveness of not having to distribute all income to S annually, it may still be desirable (for reasons discussed below) for all income to be transferred annually in a plan to plan transfer, treated for trust accounting purposes as an income distribution, to a non-QDOT IRA maintained by S.

Further deferral after spouse's death becomes possible

After S's death, if S has named a younger "designated beneficiary," the remaining plan benefits will be paid out over the life expectancy of the designated beneficiary, again resulting in substantial additional deferral compared to the marital trust-QDOT. When retirement benefits are paid to a marital trust-QDOT, there can be no income tax deferral beyond the original life expectancy of S.

Deferred estate tax payable on "principal distributions"

There is a price to be paid for the greater income tax deferral that can be obtained with a QDOT-IRA. The price is paid when "principal" for which the marital deduction was taken in D's estate is distributed from the QDOT-IRA to S. At that time, the deferred estate tax, as well as income taxes, will have to be paid on the principal distribution. Of course, deferred estate tax is due whenever principal is distributed to S from *any* QDOT; but with a "regular" QDOT, it is possible for the trust to exist for S's entire lifetime without ever distributing principal. With a combination QDOT-IRA, the minimum distribution rules of s. 401(a)(9) require certain amounts to be distributed every year after age 70½. See Chapter 1. "Principal" will have to be distributed out to S when the minimum required distributions from the IRA exceed the "income" of the IRA.

If S has named a child or grandchild as designated beneficiary of her QDOT-IRA, and (after age 70½) is taking out required minimum distributions under the MDIB rule, the distributions to S will not be coming out of "principal" until very late in S's life, or perhaps never. The minimum required distributions will be less than the annual income so long as the MDIB rule divisor, expressed as a percentage, is less than the rate of return, so for many years after S's required beginning date the IRA will actually be accumulating some of its income. Even after the crossover point (where the current year's required distribution exceeds the current year's income), the "excess" distributions can be taken from accumulated income until that account is exhausted, before reaching the initial "principal" of the IRA.

If D died when S was age 70, and the IRA consistently earns an 8% return, and distributes only the minimum required each year, the first distribution that would necessarily include principal (and therefore be subject to deferred estate tax) would not occur until S was age 97. If S dies before age 97, the deferred estate tax will obviously be due at the time of her death -- but that is true under any QDOT disposition. The point of this discussion is that rolling benefits over to a combination QDOT-

IRA can be effective, despite the minimum distribution rules of s. 401(a)(9), to defer the "deferred estate tax" on the retirement benefits until S reaches a very advanced age.

What is "income?"

Distributions of "income" are not subject to the deferred estate tax. It may not be easy to determine what is income and what is principal unless careful trust accounting procedures are followed from the moment of D's death, especially if income is accumulated and re-invested over many years.

Whatever was in the retirement plan at D's death is the initial "principal" of the QDOT-IRA. Reg. s. 20.2056A-5(c)(2) states that "income" of the QDOT will mean income as it is defined in s. 643(b), "except that income does not include capital gains ... [or] other item that would be allocated to corpus under applicable local law."

Note: The statement that "income does not include capital gains" is unfortunate. If the trust has capital gains in its principal account, those are indeed part of the principal. However, if income is reinvested, and the reinvestment produces capital gain in the "income" account, that should be considered "income" for purposes of s. 2056A, even if it is taxable as capital gain. To avoid unnecessary taxes due to this point, either income should be distributed annually to S (or, preferably, if permissible under the rollover rules, to a non-QDOT IRA maintained by S), or the income account should be invested to produce only "income," not "growth."

S. 643(b) defines "income" as "the amount of income of the estate or trust for the taxable year determined under the terms of the governing instrument and applicable local law."

A standard form IRA account agreement, generally speaking, has nothing to say on the subject of distinguishing income from principal. If the IRA is administered as a trust, then normal trust accounting procedures should apply and accumulated income would not be considered part of the "principal" even if it were reinvested in a capital-gain-producing asset. However, all capital gains accruing in the IRA assets that existed on the date of death, or from the reinvestment of the sale proceeds of those assets, would be considered "principal."

The regs. are quite clear that attempts to artificially pump up "income" and depress principal will be frowned upon. For example, all IRD will be treated as "principal" unless otherwise provided in future administrative guidance. However, the allocation of annuity payments between "corpus" and "income" by the method prescribed in the regs. (discussed later in this chapter) will be respected. S. 20.2056A-5(c)(2).

Is a distribution from income or principal?

When a distribution is made to S, how does the trustee (and how does the IRS) determine whether it is coming out of "income" earned after D's death (not subject to the deferred estate tax), or is a distribution of "principal" (taxable)? The suggested approach would be to specify in the QDOT-IRA instrument that all distributions will be deemed to come first out of income until the income account is exhausted. Alternatively, the instrument could give the trustee the power to designate each distribution as being made from income or principal; while this would give the trustee more flexibility (which could be desirable if there is to be a "hardship" distribution of principal), it also imposes more responsibility.

Or combine these approaches to get the benefits of both: have the instrument state that "all distributions to Spouse shall be deemed distributions of income unless charged to principal by the trustee."

Assets remaining in the QDOT at spouse's death

On S's death, the deferred estate tax can no longer be deferred. The deferred estate tax is imposed on "the value of the property remaining in a qualified domestic trust on the date of death of the surviving spouse." S. 2056(A)(b). It is not entirely clear from this phrase that undistributed income would be excluded from the tax base. The proposed regulations issued in 1992, s. 20.2056A-5, specified that "the amount subject to tax is the value of the trust *corpus* on the date of S's death" (emphasis added). However, the final regs. issued in August 1995 deleted this statement, retaining the ambiguity of the statute.

This situation leads to the following conclusions: distribute all income to S, so that it is not still in the trust at S's death or the IRS might try to impose deferred estate tax on it; emphasize income investing rather than "growth" investing; and maintain, forever, meticulous trust accounting records.

Investment and distribution strategies

There are two ways that the deferred estate tax problem can grow worse over the duration of the rollover QDOT-IRA.

(a)   Capital growth

One is from capital gains resulting from the initial investments of the IRA assets (and reinvestment of proceeds of those original assets). If there are capital gains in the original investments, the deferred estate tax will grow larger and larger. The structure of the deferred estate tax encourages investing for income only and discourages investing for "growth" or capital gain.

(b) Income growth

The second problem area is growth coming from the reinvestment of income, if the reinvestment of income produces capital gain; see "What is Income?" above.

(c) Strategy

One possible solution to this situation may be for S to establish a *second* IRA which is not a QDOT. Then, once a year, the trustee of the QDOT-IRA can distribute all income of the QDOT-IRA to S, thus cleaning all income out of the QDOT. The distribution of income to S from the QDOT-IRA is not subject to the deferred estate tax. She can then roll it over (to the extent the distribution exceeds the required minimum distribution for the year) to the other, non-QDOT-IRA. The non-QDOT-IRA can be invested without concern for the deferred estate tax. (Note: before undertaking this strategy, it is essential to verify that the annual distributions of income to S would not be considered "a series of substantially equal periodic payments" and as such not eligible for rollover. S. 402(c)(4)(A); see Chapter 2.)

Furthermore, if S has withdrawn all income of the QDOT-IRA each year, and rolled it over to another, non-QDOT, IRA, she can elect to satisfy the minimum distribution requirement each year, once she reaches age 70½, by using a combination of distributions from both IRAs. Notice 88-38, 1988-1 C.B. 524. See Chapter 1. She could make her annual required withdrawals in this order:

1. Withdraw the minimum required distribution (MRD) amount from that year's QDOT-IRA income.

2. If the income of the QDOT-IRA exceeds the MRD, transfer the excess income to the non-QDOT IRA.

3. If the MRD for that year exceeds the QDOT-

IRA's income for that year, withdraw the balance of the MRD from the non-QDOT-IRA.

4. Withdraw MRD amounts from the "principal" of the QDOT- IRA (the part subject to deferred estate tax) only after the non-QDOT-IRA has been exhausted.

Is an IRS ruling required?

"Receipt of a favorable opinion letter on an IRA ... is not required as a condition of receiving favorable tax treatment." Rev. Proc. 87-50, section 2.08. In fact, although it will issue opinion letters on prototype IRAs, "The Service will not issue rulings or determination letters to individuals with respect to the status of their" IRAs. *Id.*, s. 4.03. There is unlikely to be any "approved prototype" IRA agreement that is also a QDOT in the foreseeable future.

Fortunately, the IRS has supplied a "Model Trust Account" form for an IRA, known as Form 5305. "Individuals who adopt the Model Trust ... Account will be treated as having an arrangement that meets the requirements of section 408(a)." *Id.*, s. 5.01. By adopting form 5305, and adding to it the provisions required for a QDOT (and other provisions deemed desirable for proper trust administration), S has a QDOT-IRA.

Choice of trustee

As a practical matter, the trustee of a QDOT-IRA must be a U.S. bank or other financial institution; it is unlikely that an individual will be able to qualify.

In order for the trust to be an IRA, the trustee must be a bank or such "other person who demonstrates to the satisfaction" of the IRS that "such other person will administer" the IRA in the required manner. S. 408(a)(2). The procedure for a non-bank to seek IRS approval to serve as trustee of IRAs involves a $3,000 filing fee, as well as demonstrating institutional soundness and continuity to the IRS. It is generally undertaken only by a firm which has plans to serve as trustee for many customers. It is hard to see how an individual could demonstrate the required "permanence." Therefore, even though an individual can serve as trustee of a QDOT, an individual will not be able to be trustee of a QDOT-IRA.

Furthermore, in order to qualify as a QDOT, there must be at least one U.S. trustee. This leads to the conclusion that the trustee of a QDOT-IRA must be a U.S. bank.

Alternative 4: Spouse Assigns IRA to a QDOT

Assignment of inherited IRA to a QDOT

Another approach to obtaining the modified marital deduction is for S to assign ownership of an inherited IRA to a QDOT she creates. The QDOT becomes the "owner" (account holder) of the IRA. The Code does not prohibit the assignment of an IRA.

The QDOT should be in the form of a revocable trust under which the grantor (the surviving non-citizen spouse) reserves the right to withdraw all principal and income (subject only to the trustee's right to withhold the deferred estate tax from principal distributions). This will cause the QDOT to be a "grantor trust" under s. 676 as to both income and principal. The assignment of an IRA to such a trust should not be treated as an "assignment" under the Code since the trust and grantor are effectively deemed "one taxpayer" and you cannot "assign" something to yourself. The spouse-grantor would still be the "participant" in the IRA for purposes of the minimum distribution rules.

The IRS in its final QDOT regs. recognizes the

assignment of an inherited IRA to a "grantor trust" QDOT as acceptable. The following is from the preamble to the regs., s. E: "In general, individual retirement accounts under s. 408(a) are assignable . . . . However, if an [IRA] is assigned to a trust with respect to which [S] is *not* treated as the owner under section 671 *et seq*. . . . then the entire account balance is treated as a distribution . . . includible in [S's] gross income" in the year of the assignment. (Emphasis added.)

The final regs. also eliminate another possible problem with this approach, namely, the possible difference between irrevocably "assigning" an IRA to a QDOT and actually "transferring" the IRA property to the QDOT. Generally, property inherited outright by S must be actually transferred to a QDOT by a certain deadline to qualify for the modified marital deduction. The regs. provide that the "assignment" of an IRA to a QDOT (provided the various technical details are complied with) "is treated as a transfer of such property to the QDOT, regardless of the method of payment actually elected." S. 20.2056A-4(b)(7).

Assignment of rollover IRA to a QDOT

The final regs. mention the assignment approach only in connection with an IRA owned by D of which S is named beneficiary and which S then "assigns" to a QDOT she has created, with no rollover involved. The regs. do not specifically "bless" a rollover of D's benefits by S to her *own* IRA, followed by assignment of the rollover IRA to a QDOT. It is hard to see how (or why) the IRS would make any distinction between these two situations. Yet the IRS makes just such a distinction in a closely related question; see "Election to treat inherited IRA as non-assignable," below.

Despite the apparent simplicity of rolling over D's benefits to a new IRA created by S, then assigning ownership of the new IRA to S's revocable living trust-QDOT, however, there are still a number of unanswered questions and cautious drafting is required.

On the death of S, would the IRA be distributed to the QDOT, or to some other beneficiary? If to the QDOT, is the QDOT then the "designated beneficiary" for purposes of the minimum distribution rules? If so, then in order to preserve the option of income tax deferral as long as possible, the QDOT presumably must be made "irrevocable" when the grantor-spouse reaches her required beginning date (April 1 following the year in which she reaches age 70½), and comply with all of the other "trust rules" of prop. reg. s. 1.401 (a)(9)-1, D-2, although, in order for it still to be a grantor trust, the grantor would still reserve the right to withdraw all principal and income from it including the right to take back the IRA. See Chapter 1.

The spouse-grantor then will be faced with this dilemma: the IRA is "owned" by an irrevocable trust. If she wants to alter the disposition of the assets after her death, she can withdraw the IRA from the QDOT, but only if she pays a whopping deferred estate tax.

If, on the death of the grantor-spouse, the IRA is distributable to some other beneficiary, not to the QDOT, the IRA agreement itself would presumably have to contain QDOT language giving the QDOT trustee the right to withhold the deferred estate tax from the IRA before the assets pass out to the other beneficiaries. Essentially you would be right back in the situation of "alternative 3" discussed above, drafting a hybrid QDOT-IRA.

Advantages of assigning IRA to QDOT

The "IRA assigned to a QDOT" has one definite advantage over the "combination QDOT-IRA," namely this: principal distributions from the IRA at some point during S's life are unavoidable under the minimum distribution rules if she lives long enough. With an "IRA assigned to a QDOT," the inevitable principal distributions come out of the IRA but go into the QDOT, and accordingly the deferred estate tax continues to be deferred. Principal distributions from a QDOT-IRA to S individually will trigger the deferred estate tax.

Alternative 5: Non-Assignable Annuities, and IRAs Treated as Non-Assignable Annuities

Two alternatives for treatment of non-assignable assets

The Code directs the IRS, by regulations, to permit the surviving non-citizen spouse to obtain QDOT treatment for assets, such as a life annuity, which S cannot readily transfer to a QDOT before the estate tax return is filed. S. 2056A(e). The regulations provide a method of obtaining QDOT-type marital deduction treatment for such annuities and for any "plan, annuity or other arrangement" that cannot be transferred to a QDOT (whether because of applicable federal or state law, or because of the terms of the "plan or arrangement"). S. 20.2056A-4(c)(1). For these assets, S is given a choice of two methods in lieu of immediately transferring the asset to a QDOT:

1.   S can agree to pay, each year, the deferred estate tax on all non-hardship corpus distributions S receives from the arrangement in that year. This right is granted in s. 20.2056A-4(c)(2) and accordingly such an agreement is referred to in this chapter as a "(c)(2) agreement."

2.   Alternatively, S can agree that she will transfer to a QDOT all non-hardship corpus distributions she receives from the arrangement, as she receives them. This type of

agreement is described in s. 20.2056A-4(c)(3) and is referred to in this chapter as a "(c)(3) agreement."

The advantage of the (c)(3) agreement compared with a (c)(2) agreement is that, under a (c)(3) agreement, S can continue to defer estate taxes until her death (or other triggering event), whereas under a (c)(2) agreement deferred estate taxes must be paid whenever principal is received. So why would anyone ever use a (c)(2) agreement? Its only advantage appears to be that it does not require drafting a QDOT. Perhaps if the asset in question is relatively small, and there is no QDOT already in existence created to receive other assets, the (c)(2) agreement would appear attractive.

The (c)(2) and (c)(3) agreement scheme applies to a genuinely nonassignable benefit payable to S, which she does not (or can not) take out of the plan and roll over to an IRA; or to an IRA established by D and inherited by S, which S elects to treat as a nonassignable benefit.

How much of each annuity payment is "principal?"

Under a (c)(2) or (c)(3) agreement, S is agreeing to do something whenever she receives a "corpus" (principal) distribution from the non-assignable annuity -- either to pay deferred estate tax on the "corpus" distribution, or to assign the "corpus" to a QDOT. The regs. dictate the method for determining how much of each distribution is considered "corpus."

Under the formula, the "total present value of the annuity or other payment" is divided by the "expected annuity term." The result is the "corpus amount" of the annual payment.

The total present value is "the present value of the nonassignable annuity ... as of the date of [D's] death, determined in accordance with interest rates and mortality data prescribed by s. 7520." The "expected annuity term" is "the number of years that would be required for the scheduled payments to exhaust a hypothetical fund equal to the present value of the scheduled payments."

S. 20.2056A-4(c)(4) provides "for purposes of this paragraph (c) the corpus portion of each nonassignable annuity or other payment is the corpus amount of the annual payment divided by the total annual payment." Thus it appears that this fraction and formula for determining "corpus" is the only method which may be used to determine the corpus portion of plan distributions when the plan distributions are subject to a (c)(2) or a (c)(3) agreement.

How does this formula apply to individual account plans?

Unfortunately, the formula is written solely with the true annuity model in mind. How it would apply to an individual account plan is not clear. It may produce the very undesirable result of requiring some portion of every distribution from the retirement plan to be treated as corpus.

The regs. give no guidance as to how this annuity scheme is to be applied to an individual account plan. For example, the executor is required to furnish to the IRS the "total amount payable annually under the nonassignable annuity or other arrangement, and including a description of whether the annuity is payable monthly, quarterly or at some other interval," as well as "description of the term of the nonassignable annuity" based on either a term certain or a measuring life concept. These concepts are virtually meaningless as applied to a typical IRA, profit sharing plan or money purchase plan.

In the case of non-assignable annuities, the regs. allow the income taxes payable on the "corpus portion" to reduce the amount S is required to remit to the QDOT. Reg. s. 20.2056A-

5(c)(3)(iv). The regs. specify that the amount of this income tax would be determined on a marginal basis.

What is a non-assignable annuity?

The regulatory relief is for "non-assignable" annuities and "arrangements," and for IRAs which S elects to treat as non-assignable. The final regs. make clear that all qualified plan benefits are considered "non-assignable." Under s. 401(a)(13), qualified retirement benefits cannot be assigned, as a matter of federal law. A qualified plan benefit, therefore, is automatically a non-assignable annuity for purposes of section 2056A, even if S has the option to take a lump sum.

Election to treat inherited IRA as non-assignable

The final regs. issued in August 1995 contain a new permitted approach, not mentioned in the proposed regs: the surviving non-citizen spouse may elect to treat an inherited IRA as a non-assignable annuity. S. 20.2056A-4(c)(1). Unfortunately, this new alternative does not appear useful, since the accounting treatment of IRA distributions is at best unclear and at worst very unfavorable, as discussed above.

The option to treat an IRA as non-assignable may or may not be available for a rollover (as opposed to an inherited) IRA: "The Commissioner will prescribe by administrative guidance the extent, if any, to which" the election may be made for plan or IRA benefits which were distributed to S and rolled over by her after D's death. S. 20.2056A-4(c)(1).

Alternative 6: Non-Marital Deduction Disposition Alternatives

Non-marital deduction disposition

D could leave his retirement benefits to his children or other non-spouse beneficiary, or to a trust which does not qualify for the marital deduction. S could be a beneficiary of the trust or not, as the client prefers. The advantages of a "non-marital deduction" disposition would be: avoidance of the "distribute all income annually" requirement that arguably applies to a marital trust; and avoiding the problems of collecting deferred estate taxes on an income-taxable asset. The disadvantages are those that exist whenever retirement benefits are paid in a non-marital deduction disposition, *e.g.*, some of the unified credit is "wasted" paying income taxes.

Outright to spouse, not claiming marital deduction

Another alternative is to make the benefits payable to S but not claim the marital deduction, even if this means paying estate tax on the benefits. The complications of the QDOT are avoided; and S will get the benefit of the s. 691(c) deduction for the estate taxes paid. This may be attractive if S will probably return to her country of origin. If S is likely to remain a U.S. resident, this approach would be unattractive because the benefits, already reduced by income taxes and by estate taxes at D's death, would be subject to estate tax again at S's death.

Alternative 7: D Leaves Benefits to a Charitable Remainder Trust

Another intriguing alternative is to make the benefits

payable to a charitable remainder trust (CRT) of which the non-citizen spouse is the only non-charitable beneficiary. This could be done in either of two ways under the regs. (although the Code itself does not permit either of them): a combination charitable remainder trust-QDOT; or a "non-assignable" life unitrust (or annuity) interest in a charitable remainder spendthrift trust. For reasons of space, a detailed discussion of these possibilities is omitted.

Summary of Planning Principles

As the discussion in this chapter indicates, there is no problem-free way to dispose of retirement benefits when the participant's spouse is not a U.S. citizen. An estate planner advising a client who has a non-citizen spouse, and who also has significant retirement plan assets, should weigh carefully the alternatives for disposition of this tax-sensitive property.

Benefits that can be rolled over

1.   There are only two ways to get both the income tax benefits of the spousal rollover and the estate tax "benefits" of the modified marital deduction: either S rolls over D's benefits to a combination QDOT-IRA, or S rolls over the benefits to a non-QDOT IRA that S then "assigns" to a grantor-trust-type QDOT she establishes. Typically, if the participant has already died, leaving his benefits outright to S, S will choose one of these two alternatives.

2.   In the planning stage, while the client is still alive, however, the choice is more complicated. The marital trust-QDOT will appeal to the client who wants to control the ultimate disposition of the asset, or who simply wants his estate plan to be "self executing," without requiring his spouse to

undertake additional steps after his death. Making benefits payable outright to S, "rollable" to a QDOT-IRA, will appeal to the client who has no objection to giving his spouse control, desires maximum income tax deferral and is willing to adopt a plan which requires post-death action by his spouse in order to succeed.

3.   The client may be attracted to the income tax deferral possibilities of the rollover, but reluctant to leave the subject of qualifying for the marital deduction entirely up to *post mortem* action. If benefits are left outright to S, the benefits will not qualify for the marital deduction unless S takes all the actions necessary to transfer them to a QDOT after D's death. What this client might want, ideally, would be a plan which would have all the elements in place to automatically qualify for the modified marital deduction, without foreclosing the option of the spousal rollover.

One way to achieve this result would be for D to leave the benefits to a marital trust-QDOT, naming S as the contingent beneficiary. If D dies, and S does nothing, the trust will still qualify as a QDOT. If S wants to roll over the benefits to a QDOT-IRA (or IRA assigned to a QDOT), the trustee of the QDOT could disclaim the benefits and allow them to pass to S as contingent beneficiary.   See Chapter 8 regarding the problems of creating an estate plan that is contingent upon a disclaimer.

Benefits that cannot be rolled over

4.   If the benefits are non-assignable, and S cannot roll them over, the best alternative is probably for S to agree to deposit the benefits into a QDOT as they are paid to her ("(c)(3) agreement"). Agreeing to pay the deferred estate tax on non-assignable benefits as they are received ("(c)(2) agreement"),

and electing to treat an inherited IRA as a non-assignable benefit, appear to be unattractive alternatives.

Other comments

5.   If the marital trust-QDOT option is selected, consider using a general power marital trust so that "principal distributions" will be taxed at S's income tax rate, if that is going to be lower than the trust's income tax rate, and if the double tax dilemma is resolved by future administrative guidance from the IRS. Once the client has chosen to make the benefits payable either to S or to a marital trust, consider making them "disclaimable" to the other (trust or spouse) in case that option appears more attractive when death occurs. (See Chapter 8.)

6.   Finally, in administering any QDOT, the trustee should take advantage of the "hardship" distribution exception whenever possible; and should manage investments and distributions so as to minimize growth of the original "principal," while maximizing "income." All income should be distributed once a year to the surviving non-citizen spouse. It may be that, in the case of a QDOT-IRA, the excess of this income distribution over the required minimum distribution for the year can be rolled over by S to her own non-QDOT-IRA.

5

The 15% Excise Tax

A special excise tax is imposed on plan participants who "take out too much" from their retirement plans in any year, or who "have too much" in their plans at death.

Introduction

The 15% excise tax on "excess distributions" and "excess accumulations" was added to the Code by the Tax Reform Act of 1986. It applies to distributions (or deaths) occurring after 1986. S. 4980A (formerly called S. 4981A).

This is probably not the biggest tax your client faces, but it may be the most easily avoidable. In most cases, payment of this tax is completely optional. However, avoiding this tax comes only at the price of sacrificing further income tax deferral (*i.e.* by ceasing to contribute to plans, or withdrawing money early from plans). Since the value of long term income tax deferral often outweighs the cost of the 15% excise tax, it is true for many clients that the more excise tax they pay, the better off they are financially.

The 15% Excise Tax
on "Excess Distributions"

15% additional tax on distributions over $150,000

If, in any calendar year, a participant receives distributions of more than a certain "threshold amount" from his retirement plans, the excess over the "threshold amount" is subject to an excise tax of 15%.

The annual "threshold amount" is the greater of:

1. $112,500, indexed for changes in the cost of living after 1987; or

2. $150,000 (not indexed).

The indexed threshold amount for each year since 1987 is shown in Appendix A, Table 1. The method of indexing this number was changed by Congress as part of the General Agreement on Tariffs and Trade (GATT). Under GATT, the IRS continues to figure out the "real" cost-of-living adjustment in the $112,500-indexed figure; but then the annual threshold amount, rather than being the actual adjusted number so arrived at, is rounded down to the nearest $5,000. In 1995, for example, but for GATT, the indexed threshold would have been about $152,000. Because of GATT, however, this number was rounded down to $150,000.

For 1996, the threshold is $155,000. Because the threshold number is a moving target, in this book the threshold is generally described as "$150,000 per year." Bear in mind that this is a shorthand reference to the actual threshold of "$112,500, indexed, or $150,000, whichever is greater."

Note that the annual threshold is not *per plan* -- it is per recipient. All distributions received by the individual in one year from *all* his plans are counted towards the annual threshold.

Certain distributions are excise tax-free

Certain distributions do not count toward the annual threshold. In determining what distributions a participant receives for purposes of determining whether his distributions exceed the threshold, exclude the following:

--Withdrawal of the participant's own after-tax (non-deductible) contributions to the plan. S. 4980A(c)(2)(C).

--Death benefits received by a beneficiary are not subject to the tax (but see the "15% Estate Tax" section of this chapter for an optional exception to this rule if all death benefits are paid to the surviving spouse). (c)(2)(A).

--Payments to an "alternate payee" under a "Qualified Domestic Relations Order" (QDRO) are counted toward the annual threshold of the alternate payee, and not of the participant, *if* the alternate payee is required to include the payments in his/her income (as would normally be the case if the alternate payee is the spouse). (c)(2)(B).

Special treatment for lump sum distributions: general rule

A major variation in the application of the 15% excise tax has to do with lump sum distributions ("LSD"). S. 4980A(c)(4). There are two ways in which LSDs are treated differently under the 15% excise tax:

--The threshold amount for an LSD is five times the normal threshold amount.

--The threshold amount for LSDs is applied independently of the threshold amount for other distributions.

Thus for an LSD the annual threshold amount is the greater of $750,000, or $562,500 indexed for cost of living increases after 1987. *E.g.*, for 1996 it is $775,000 (five times $155,000). This increased threshold amount is important for a person who wishes to cash out his plan entirely; as long as the withdrawal meets the requirements for an LSD, the person can withdraw well over $150,000 in one year without paying any excise tax.

Separate threshold for LSDs and other distributions: the double exemption

In what amounts to a significant loophole, the excise tax threshold is applied separately for "lump sum distributions" and "other" distributions. In other words, in one year, a person can receive *both* an LSD of $750,000 *and* an "other" distribution (from another plan) of $150,000, without paying the tax.

This result seems strange since Congress's intent in enacting the 15% excise tax was allegedly to recapture tax benefits inadvertently given to people who used multiple employers and multiple plans to pyramid their contribution/benefit limits. Since by definition the "double exemption" is available only to a taxpayer who has multiple plans, it seems that the favoritism for those with more than one retirement plan has been continued.

Compare these two examples:

1.   Alice, age 65, has $750,000 in a corporate profit sharing plan and $750,000 in her IRA. Assuming she qualifies for LSD/forward averaging treatment in her profit sharing plan, she can take a $750,000 LSD from that plan and pay the five-year forward averaging tax; *and* withdraw $150,000/year from her IRA; and pay no 15% tax.

2.   Ralph, also age 65, has the same size retirement benefit, $1,500,000, but it is all in an IRA. He can withdraw only $150,000/year without paying the 15% tax. If his IRA earns 10%/year, he will be

withdrawing only the income. At some point after he reaches age 70½ he will be forced to start withdrawing more and will be forced to pay the 15% tax excise tax (unless, perhaps, there are substantial increases in the cost of living so that the $112,500/indexed threshold rapidly rises above $150,000).

Qualifying for the LSD exception

In order to qualify for the benefits given to LSDs, the participant has to meet all the technical requirements of an LSD under section 402(d) of the Code, *and* must elect five year forward averaging ("5YFA") or ten year forward averaging ("10YFA") for the LSD. Unfortunately, it is not easy to qualify for this special treatment. See the "Lump Sum Distributions: the Requirements" section of Chapter 2.

The "forward averaging" methods, 5YFA and 10YFA, can produce substantial income tax savings in and of themselves, especially for smaller distributions; see table in Appendix A. Because forward averaging can also have a significant effect on the *excise tax* it may be attractive even if it does not save substantial income taxes. It is thus important to find out whether your client's plan balances potentially qualify for 5YFA or 10YFA treatment.

Planning implications of separate LSD threshold

The major planning implications of the special treatment afforded LSDs are:

--do not lightly give up potential LSD treatment

--if possible, preserve multiple plans for the client, so as to give the client flexibility to use the "double exemption." See "Grandfathered benefits: the triple exemption" in the "Other Excess Accumulations Tax Issues" section of this chapter.

These points are KEY HIDDEN ISSUES whenever your client is considering rolling over funds from a corporate or Keogh plan (potentially eligible for LSD/5YFA treatment) to an IRA (never eligible for such treatment). While a rollover may seem harmless, it can potentially cost your client $112,500 or more in excise taxes (15% tax on the $750,000 LSD threshold amount which is lost by rolling over to an IRA). At the very least the rollover locks the client in forever to the $150,000 (or $112,500/indexed) per year maximum withdrawal amount. See the "Rollover Checklist" in the Appendix for other issues to consider before rolling over benefits.

Benefits "Grandfathered" from 15% Excise Tax

Electing to "grandfather" 8/1/86 plan balances

A person whose "accrued benefits" (or account balances) under all plans and IRAs as of August 1, 1986, exceeded $562,500 was entitled to elect to "grandfather" his 8/1/86 benefits from the impact of the new tax by filing form 5329 with his 1987 or 1988 income tax return. S. 4980A(f).

An unexpected problem in applying the grandfather rule is that many clients are unable to remember whether they made this election. Since filing the form would not affect the rest of the return, the client's copy of his 1987 or 1988 return may not be the "last word": form 5329 could have been filed and a copy not saved. Thus, often, planning for these individuals begins with obtaining copies of the entire, as-filed, 1987 and 1988 returns from the IRS.

Certain people have succeeded in making the grandfather election several years after the deadline by complying with certain quite rigorous IRS procedures. See *e.g.* Ltr. Rul. 9241050. A number of these requests have been granted, and many have also been denied.

Drawbacks of electing grandfather treatment

Congress put a price tag on electing "grandfather" treatment. A person who elected to grandfather his benefits did not have the benefit, during the years 1987 through 1994, of the $150,000/$750,000 annual threshold amount. Rather, he could use only the $112,500 indexed threshold amount.

The potential maximum loss from electing to grandfather was never substantial. Now it is zero, since the $112,500 indexed amount has climbed past $150,000. In other words, the only drawback of electing grandfather treatment was that the annual distribution threshold for "grandfathers" was between $112,500 and $150,000 from 1987 to 1994, whereas for non-grandfathers it was $150,000.

The grandfathered amount is not applied over and above the regular tax-free threshold amount. Rather, the grandfathered participant is entitled to recover, free of the excise tax each year, the applicable annual threshold amount *or* the applicable grandfather amount for that year, whichever is greater. Accordingly, it is possible for a person to completely waste his grandfathered amount. For example, if the total amount paid out to the participant in, say, 1987, was $112,500, some of the payout was deemed a distribution of his "grandfathered" amount. The grandfathered amount to that extent was wasted because the $112,500 could have been pulled out free of excise tax *without* the grandfather clause.

How the grandfathered amount is recovered

There are a number of methods that Congress and the IRS could have selected to allow recovery of the grandfathered amount. In its proposed and temporary regulations, the IRS has selected two methods, one of which is itself subdivided into two more methods. Temp. reg. s. 54.4981A-1T(b)(12),(13). The methods are the "attained age method," the "discretionary method" and the "discretionary method-accelerated."

1.   Rules common to both methods

Under both methods, the computation of the initial grandfathered amount ("IGA") is the same. It is the total account balance or accrued benefit on August 1, 1986 minus any distributions between 8/1/86 and 12/31/86. The participant is not allowed to determine this himself; he must request the information from the plan administrator and thus provide plan-originated documentation that the amount calculated is right.

If there is an account balance determination on the right date because there was a valuation on July 31, 1986 or August 1, 1986, then computation of the IGA is easy. If there was no valuation on that date, then the regulations provide a method for a weighted average of the account balance (or accrued benefit) on the last preceding and next succeeding valuation dates to determine the IGA. There appears to be an error in the formula provided in the temporary regulations for determining the IGA when 8/1/86 fell between two plan valuation dates: the IRS formula for determining the weighted average seems to give greater weight to the valuation date *farthest* from 8/1/86, and lesser weight to the valuation date *nearest* 8/1/86.

In calculating the IGA, TAMRA '88 makes clear that you exclude amounts which would not have been subject to the excise tax had they been distributed on August 1, 1986 (such as amounts segregated to be paid to an alternate payee under a QDRO, or the participant's own after-tax contributions). S. 4980A(d)(4)(B).

The 8/1/86 IGA is then reduced dollar for dollar by the amount of any distributions occurring between 8/1/86 and

12/31/86. The grandfathered amount is then further reduced each year by grandfathered amounts distributed after 1986.

Thus, on 1/1/88, for example, the remaining grandfathered balance will be the participant's grandfathered amount on 1/1/87 minus any grandfathered amounts which he is deemed to have recovered in 1987, *regardless* of whether the alleged grandfathered distributions in 1987 resulted in any tax benefit. At the end of each year the participant will have a new balance in his account and (if he received any distributions during the year) will have a new reduced "remaining undistributed value of the grandfathered amount."

Ltr. Rul. 8927070 (4/13/89) indicates that a distribution that is rolled over tax-free to an IRA will not reduce the unrecovered grandfather amount. This ruling illustrates an important concept: a person's "grandfathered balance" is not attached to a particular plan. It is just a free-floating dollar amount. Thus distributions from *any* plan are wholly or partly charged against a person's grandfathered balance (see how to compute this, below), even if that particular plan was not in existence on 8/1/86. For example, a worker who had a $1 million grandfathered profit sharing account balance on 8/1/86, then lost 100% of his profit sharing plan investments in the stock market crash of October 1987, would not lose his "grandfathered balance." If he then rebuilt his retirement assets back to $1 million through participation in a new employer's pension plan, his "grandfathered balance" would still be there and could be applied to the new plan.

The grandfathered amount is not increased for changes in the cost of living since 8/1/86.

If a person who has elected grandfather treatment receives both an LSD and a non-LSD in the same year, he is required to apportion the year's grandfather recovery amount between the two distributions, even if one of the distributions is under the threshold amount. The Temp. regs. and instructions for IRS form 5329 tell how to do this.

Having determined the participant's "grandfathered balance," we next turn to the two methods for determining how much of each distribution is "grandfathered."

2.   Discretionary method

The method most or all "grandfathers" elected is the "discretionary method."

Under the discretionary method, 10% of the participant's distributions each year are treated as recovery of the grandfathered amount until the entire grandfathered amount is used up (or until the recovery is "accelerated"; see below).

For example, suppose a participant had a grandfathered balance of $3 million on 8/1/86. His plan balance is $4 million as of the beginning of 1989. He elected the discretionary method and he received no distributions between 8/1/86 and 1/1/89.

In 1989 he receives a distribution of $200,000. $20,000 of that (10% x $200,000) is deemed to be a distribution from his grandfathered balance; thus, the amount subject to excise tax in 1989 will be the total distribution minus the greater of (i) $122,580 (the 1989 indexed threshold amount), or (ii) $20,000. Obviously in this example the indexed amount provides a larger exemption so it is used as the threshold amount rather than the deemed grandfather distribution. The $20,000 grandfather distribution is "wasted." His remaining grandfather amount, available for distributions after 1989, is $2,980,000.

Under the discretionary method, a participant has the very valuable option, in any year, to accelerate the recovery of his grandfathered amount. This is called the discretionary method "accelerated." Once the accelerated method is elected, all plan distributions for the year of the election *and subsequent years* will be applied dollar-for-dollar to the grandfathered amount until the grandfathered amount is used up. Thus if the participant who took a withdrawal of $200,000 had elected to accelerate the recovery of his grandfathered amount, the total $200,000 distribution would be deemed to be recovery of grandfathered amounts, no excise tax would be due, and the remaining grandfathered balance would be reduced by $200,000 rather than just $20,000. All distributions thereafter would reduce the grandfathered balance dollar for dollar.

3.   Attained age method

The other method of calculating the "grandfathered" part of each year's distribution is the "attained age method." To date, no source known to the author has come up with a case in which the "attained age method" produces a better result for the client. Accordingly, everyone who elected to grandfather his benefits apparently elected the "discretionary method," and we need not discuss the attained age method.

Planning implications of grandfathered benefits

A person who elected "grandfather" treatment has more options for excise tax-free distribution of his benefits than others do.

A person who did not elect grandfather treatment (either because he wasn't eligible to or because he chose not to) has very narrow choices for his plan distributions if he wants to avoid the 15% excise tax. Generally, he is limited to taking out no more than $150,000 per year from all his plans. After 1995, he will be able to take out more each year as the $112,500/indexed amount increases beyond $150,000. *If* he is lucky enough to have a plan that would qualify for 402(d) LSD/5YFA or 10YFA treatment, and has a balance in that plan of less than five times the annual threshold amount, he can take a lump sum and elect forward averaging for it, and thus get a one-time larger-than-$150,000 distribution without paying excise tax. Those are his only choices.

In contrast, the person who *did* elect grandfather treatment has many more options:

1.   He can take out larger-than-$150,000 distributions whenever he wants to.

2.   He does not have to worry about the technical requirements of "lump sum distributions" under s. 402(d).

3.   His "lump sum distribution" dollar limit is his unrecovered grandfather balance, not $750,000.

4.   He can take out large distributions in several years, not just once.

5.   Theoretically he could get three "exemptions" from the 15% excise tax. See "Grandfathered benefits: the triple exemption" in the "Other Excess Accumulations Tax Issues" section of this chapter.

15% Estate Tax on Excess Accumulations

Additional estate tax applies to "excess" benefits

When a participant dies, a 15% additional estate tax applies to his "excess retirement accumulations." He has "excess" accumulations if the combined value of all of his plan benefits immediately before his death exceeds the at-death threshold. The at-death threshold is the value (determined under IRS tables) of an annuity equal to the annual threshold amount then in effect, for the life of a person who was the same age as the decedent's attained age at death. The "excess" is subject to a 15% excise tax over and above any other applicable estate tax. S. 4980A(d).

If the estate is subject to the excess accumulations tax,

an estate tax return must be filed even if the total estate is not otherwise taxable. S. 6018(a)(5) (as amended by TAMRA '88).

What annuity amount is used?

The "annual threshold amount" is the greater of the $112,500/indexed amount as of the date of death, or $150,000 not indexed. However, if the decedent had elected grandfather treatment, the threshold amount is only $112,500/indexed to the date of death. What the indexed amount will be when your client dies is something of a wild card.

What annuity tables are used?

The value of the hypothetical annuity is determined by reference to the IRS tables (Reg. s. 20.2031-7) used in valuing annuities for gift and estate tax purposes. The age used is the decedent's attained age in whole years as of the date of death. Temp. reg. s. 54.4981A-1T, d-7(b).

Until 1989, the only published IRS annuity tables assumed an interest rate of 10%. Using the 10% tables, the value of an annuity of $150,000 per year for someone age 70 would be $907,830. As the client gets older, the value of the hypothetical life annuity declines. By the time the client reaches age 80, the present value of a life annuity of $150,000 per year would be only $654,885.

What interest rate is used?

Effective April 1, 1989, as a result of Section 5031 of TAMRA '88, creating s.7520 of the Code, the IRS is required to update the s. 20.2031-7 tables monthly to reflect changes in interest rates. To accommodate this change in the law the IRS published Notice 89-24, 1989-1 C.B. 660, which provides that the new interest rate applicable to valuing annuities for purposes of s. 2031 (and by extension, under the temp. regs., s. 4980A) is 120% of the "applicable federal midterm rate," rounded to the nearest 2/10 of 1%. This rate is published monthly in an IRS news release. The only practical method to find out this rate is to subscribe to a private service which provides it. See Bibliography for details.

Once you have obtained the "s. 7520 rate" for the month in which death occurs, the factor for determining the value of the hypothetical annuity is obtained from IRS publication 1457 (8/89) "Actuarial Values, Alpha Volume." Turn to the page of "table S" ("Single Life _%, Based on Life Table 80 CNSMT") which corresponds to the particular interest rate you are using.

For example, if the relevant rate (120% of federal midterm rate etc.) for the month of your decedent's death was 9.6%, you turn to the page headed "Table S (9.6%)," and look down the column for "annuities" until you come to the line corresponding with your client's attained age at death. For a 70 year old decedent, at 9.6% interest, the annuity factor is 6.5580, so the value of the hypothetical $150,000/year annuity is 6.5580 X $150,000 = $983,700.

The IRS may by regulation make the monthly interest rate changes inapplicable in whatever instances it chooses, but so far has not chosen to exempt s. 4980A from the effects of fluctuating interest rates.

If interest rates rise to 15% or 20%, the threshold amount, based on the value of a hypothetical annuity, would drop, exposing many more clients to the excise tax on excess accumulations. If interest rates plunge, on the other hand, the cost of an annuity would climb, and fewer clients would have to worry about the excess accumulations tax.

Partial exception for insurance proceeds

Any increase in benefits at death which is represented by life insurance is not subject to the excess accumulations tax. For example, assume the participant's profit sharing plan account balance immediately before death consisted of:

$500,000	Side fund investments
$ 9,000	Cash value of $100,000 life insurance policy on participant's life
_____	
$509,000	Total account balance

The total death benefit is $600,000 ($500,000 side fund plus $100,000 life insurance proceeds). The amount "counted" in applying the excess accumulations tax is only the $509,000 pre-death account balance. The $91,000 "pure death benefit" portion of the insurance is not counted in determining whether the plan benefits exceed the at-death threshold.

Surviving Spouse's Option to Defer 15% Tax

S. 4980A(d)(5) election -- in general

TAMRA '88 added an exception to the excess accumulations tax, s. 4980A(d)(5). The exception allows the surviving spouse (S), if substantially all benefits are payable to her, to elect not to pay the excess accumulations tax on the decedent's death but instead to defer it. If she makes this election, the excise tax will be applied to the inherited benefits as if they were *her* benefits.

In other words, the 15% excise tax on excess

accumulations and distributions from now on will apply to the combined value of her own benefits plus the benefits she has inherited from the deceased spouse. When in the future she takes any distributions from either "pot" all such distributions in any one year will be combined for purposes of applying the $150,000/year threshold. At her subsequent death, her own benefits and the first spouse's benefits that she inherited (to the extent she has not taken distribution of them) will be combined for purposes of determining the excess accumulations tax.

Normally, once a plan participant has died, and his estate has either paid or not paid the excess accumulations tax (depending on whether the amount of his benefits was over or below the threshold amount), all post-death distributions would be totally free of the excise tax on excess distributions regardless of the amount. S. 4980A(c)(2)(A).

Note: if S does *not* make the 4980A(d)(5) election, the excess accumulations tax must be paid if the value of the decedent's benefits exceeded the threshold. If the benefits were under the threshold, there would be no reason to make the election. Even if the benefits are over the threshold, it might be advisable *not* to make the election, especially if S has some retirement plan assets of her own. It may be better to pay a small excise tax at the first spouse's death, and free up the first spouse's benefits forever from the threat of this tax, than to postpone it. Postponing the tax will limit S's distribution options to the usual $150,000/year, and perhaps result in a much larger excess accumulations tax at S's death.

The election is made by filing a statement, signed by S, with the federal estate tax return, form 706. See instructions to Schedule S of form 706.

Do not commingle benefits if no election made

It is *extremely important*, if S does not make the 4980A(d)(5) election, to keep the deceased spouse's retirement benefits separate from S's. Once the first spouse has died, his benefits become forever free of the 15% excise tax--*if* no 4980A(d)(5) election is made, and *if* the benefits are kept separate from retirement benefits originating from the surviving spouse. See, *e.g.*, Ltr. Rul. 9402022 (10/18/93). If the deceased spouse's benefits are rolled over to an IRA in which they are commingled with S's own contributions, the tax-free status is totally lost. Temp. reg. S. 54.4981A-1T, d-10. This result could be disastrous if the decedent's benefits were substantial. At the moment, there is no known way to recover from this mistake, *i.e.*, no way to separate the commingled benefits so as to restore the excise-tax-exempt nature of the inherited benefits.

Grandfathered status of benefits continues for spouse

If S makes the 4980(d)(5) election, and if the decedent had elected to grandfather his 8/1/86 plan balances, S will apparently continue to have the benefit of the decedent's unrecovered grandfather amount. See Ltr. Rul. 9450041 (9/22/94) (third ruling request).

All benefits must be payable to spouse

If S is to have the option of making the 4980A(d)(5) election, *all* of the decedent's retirement plan death benefits (under *all of his plans*) must be paid to S. If more than a *"de minimis"* amount is paid to other beneficiaries, the 4980A(d)(5) election is not available and the excise tax must be paid at the first spouse's death. S. 4980A(d)(5)(B). (The only exception to this pertains to certain insurance benefits -- see below.)

The Senate Committee report on TAMRA states that, "For purposes of this rule, an amount will not be considered de minimis if it exceeds 1 percent of the decedent's retirement accumulation." CCH Standard Fed. Tx. Reptr. 1996 para. 35,980. The IRS temporary reg. dealing with the 15% excise tax, s. 54.4981A-1T, was issued before the (d)(5) exception was added to the statute by TAMRA, and accordingly provides no further guidance on the spousal election.

Since there is no official guidance other than legislative history as to what "*de minimis*" means, planners are wise to use the 1% figure as the rule. In other words, in "planning mode," if you want to preserve for the spouse the option of making the 4980A(d)(5) election, make 99% (or more) of the participant's benefits payable to the spouse individually. See the *Eatons* case study for planning difficulties caused by this rule. In "cleanup mode," however, if the participant has already died, leaving almost all of his benefits (but less than 99%) to S, it may be worth trying to make the 4980A(d)(5) election, since "de minimis" is not defined in the statute, regulations or any other binding authority.

Benefits payable to marital trust, or to the estate

Nothing in TAMRA indicates that benefits payable to a marital trust count as benefits paid "to" the surviving spouse. Therefore, making benefits payable to a marital trust will apparently not satisfy s. 4980A(d)(5). However, the IRS has been generous, in rulings, in permitting 4980A(d)(5) elections, even when the spouse is not personally named as the beneficiary, under the following circumstances:

(i)	S "becomes" the beneficiary, by virtue of disclaimers made by the original beneficiaries; or

> (ii)   Benefits are payable to a trust or estate under the terms of which S has the unfettered right to, and does, withdraw the benefits.

See Ltr. Ruls. 9426049 (4/12/94); 9450041 (9/22/94); 9450042 (9/23/94).

Life insurance proceeds

Although the general rule is that S must be the beneficiary of all the benefits (or all but a "de minimis" amount) in order for her to be able to make this election, there is an exception for the pure death benefit portion of any plan benefits (for example, the excess of life insurance proceeds over the cash value of the policy immediately before death). S. 4980A (d)(5) requires only that the spouse be the beneficiary of all "interests described in paragraph (3)(A)." (3)(A), which is part of the definition of "excess retirement accumulation," refers to "the value of the individual's interest ... in qualified employer plans" and IRAs, but paragraph (4)(C) says that in calculating the "excess retirement accumulation" you exclude "the excess (if any) of - (i) any interests which are payable immediately after death, over (ii) the value of such interests immediately before death."

As to what is the value of a life insurance policy immediately prior to death, the IRS temporary regs adopt a bright line test: the pre-death cash surrender value. The portion not subject to the excess accumulations tax (and by implication not subject to the requirement that all benefits must be paid to S to get the (d)(5) election option) is the amount excludable from income under section 101(a). Thus, it apparently will not be necessary to determine the interpolated terminal reserve value of policies in plans, or factor in the decedent's actual state of health (see Chapter 6). Temp. reg. 54.4981A-lT(d), d-6(c).

It makes sense that the pure death benefit, which is not subject to the excess accumulations tax anyway, is not required to be paid to S as a condition of her electing to defer the 15% excise tax. However, this makes it a bit complicated to name a beneficiary for plan benefits. You may end up designating S as the beneficiary of the side fund, and the cash value of life insurance policies, and a trust or other beneficiary as the beneficiary of the rest of the life insurance proceeds. It is not clear that the IRS would recognize, for income tax purposes, the allocation of the cash value to one beneficiary and the pure death benefit to another.

Simultaneous death; election by spouse's executor

It is not yet known whether the IRS will permit the executor of a deceased surviving spouse to make the 4980A(d)(5) election. In cases where the surviving spouse was younger than the participant, and dies simultaneously or shortly after him, the surviving spouse's executor's ability to make the election -- if recognized by the IRS -- could reduce the excess accumulations tax.

Example: H is a 65-year-old plan participant (P) with a 55-year-old spouse, "S." He dies in 1995 with a $1,200,690 plan benefit. Assume the IRS "s. 7520 rate" in effect at his death was 10%. Based on the IRS 10% annuity tables, the cost of a life annuity of $150,000 for a 65-year-old is $1,019,550, meaning that he had an "excess accumulation" of $181,140 and his estates owes excise tax of $27,171. S dies shortly after P. She is his beneficiary. *If* she survives P (or is presumed to survive him), and *if* her executor is permitted to make the 4980A(d)(5) election to treat the benefits as hers, and *if* she has no other benefits, the excise tax is eliminated because the "hypothetical annuity cost" for a person age 55 is $1,200,690.

Rollover distinguished

One more note: the 4980A(d)(5) election is not dependent on S's "rolling over" benefits to her own IRA. If she makes the election, the benefits are treated as "hers" for purposes of s. 4980A *only*. She can still leave the benefits in the decedent's plan, or roll them to her own IRA if she wants to, or roll some and leave some. The minimum distribution rules will be applied to the benefits based on the decedent's age, S's age and whether the benefits are "rolled over" by S--*without regard* to whether S made a 4980A(d)(5) election.

Other Excess Accumulations Tax Issues

Grandfathered benefits; the triple exemption

If the decedent elected to grandfather his 8/1/86 plan balance by timely filing form 5329, then his excess accumulations tax threshold will be the greater of (a) his unrecovered grandfather amount as of the date of death or (b) the threshold computed under the usual value-of-annuity method, using the $112,500/indexed number as the annuity amount. It is possible for some clients in effect to get three "exemptions" from the 15% excise tax by careful scheduling of lifetime distributions. This possibility disappears at death, when only one "exemption" remains available.

Example: Patricia is a widow, age 75. She has $2 million in her IRA and $775,000 in a pension plan eligible for "five year forward averaging." She has a $900,000 remaining unrecovered "grandfather" balance. Assume that her "excess accumulations threshold" would be $1.1 million if she died today. Thus, if she died today, her estate would owe an excise tax of $251,250, computed as follows:

Total plan balances	2,775,000
Less: threshold	-1,100,000
"Excess accumulation"	1,675,000
Times tax rate	x 15%
Excess accumulations tax	$251,250

Now suppose, instead, Patricia had withdrawn $900,000 from her IRA in December 1995, and elected to "accelerate" the recovery of her grandfather balance so it was all applied to this distribution, and she paid no excise tax. Then, in January 1996, she takes a $775,000 lump sum distribution from the pension plan and elects "forward averaging" treatment for it, so that distribution is also excise tax-free. *Then* she dies. Her remaining plan balance is fully sheltered by the "regular" at-death threshold of $1.1 million. The excise tax has been reduced from $251,250 to zero.

Is it worthwhile to withdraw large sums prior to death to take advantage of the doubling or tripling of exemptions available to the client who has a remaining grandfathered balance and/or a plan balance eligible for "lump sum distribution" treatment? It very well may be; but, as always, the savings on 15% excise tax achievable by making early withdrawals must be weighed against the loss of future income tax deferral on the benefits. See the *Sherman and Herman Levine* case study.

Who is responsible for payment of the tax?

The excess accumulations tax is an addition to the federal estate tax. Thus it is reported on the estate tax return (form 706, Schedule S) and the executor is liable for it. Under the Massachusetts tax apportionment statute, ch. 65A s.5, the executor has the right to recover the tax from the recipient of the benefits, unless the decedent's will indicated otherwise.

In the author's view, a standard tax clause in the will, directing that "all estate taxes" or "all taxes arising by reason of my death" be paid from the residue of the estate, would be sufficient to make the estate bear the 4980A tax on retirement benefits; specific reference to s. 4980A is not needed. Of course, proper consideration should be given to the questions of (a) who should bear this tax -- the estate or the recipient of the retirement benefits -- and (b) where will the cash come from to pay the tax (which can be a severe problem if substantial retirement plan assets are tied up in restricted payout forms such as annuities); but these issues apply to *all* estate taxes imposed on the benefits, not just the 4980A tax.

At the planning stage, consider whether the tax should be paid by the recipient rather than the "residue" of the estate. For example, if all retirement benefits are payable to the surviving spouse, with the idea that she will elect to defer the excise tax, she has an incentive *not* to defer the tax if the excise tax is payable from the "residue" of the estate and she is not the beneficiary of that residue. See form 8.2 in Appendix B.

Marital and charitable deductions, unified credit

The unified credit is not available to reduce the tax; the charitable deduction is not available. The marital deduction also is not available, although the surviving spouse can elect to defer the excise tax if she is the beneficiary of substantially all the benefits (see discussion above). Thus, a person whose estate is not otherwise taxable (whether because it is fully sheltered by the federal exemption amount or because of the marital or charitable deduction) may nevertheless be subject to this tax.

Deduction for excess accumulations tax

The recipient of a decedent's retirement benefits must include such benefits in his gross income as "income in respect of a decedent" (IRD) under section 691 (see Chapter 2) but gets no 691(c) deduction for any excess accumulations excise tax paid. S. 691(c)(1)(C), added by TAMRA '88.

However, the decedent's estate apparently gets an estate tax deduction for the excess accumulations tax. S. 2053(c)(1)(B), as amended by TAMRA '88, provides that the prohibition in s. 2053(c)(1)(B) against deducting property taxes, income taxes and any "estate, succession, legacy or inheritance taxes" shall "not apply to any increase" in the estate tax by reason of s. 4980A. Apparently Congress intended that the excess accumulations tax would be deductible as an expense of administration.

This deduction has the following effects. First, the "true" excise tax rate on excess accumulations is not 15%, but rather 7%-9%, for a taxable estate, depending on the decedent's bracket for the "regular" federal estate tax (40% - 55%). Second, in a reduce-to-zero marital formula estate plan, the excise tax reduces the marital deduction share, not the "credit shelter trust," and the estate tax savings from the deduction will not be realized until the second death.

Summary of Planning Principles

1.   The 15% excise tax is a factor to be considered in all choices regarding retirement benefits; it may affect decisions regarding contributions, investments, distributions, and choice of beneficiary for death benefits. However, the 15% tax is not a bugbear, to be avoided at all costs; it is simply one of many factors to be weighed.

2.   To evaluate the impact of this tax at the planning stage, when deciding whether to continue contributing to a plan, or whether to withdraw benefits from a plan sooner than required, compare the cost of future excise taxes with the value of future income tax deferral. See the *Dr. Vincent Valdez* case study.

3.   For a client whose retirement benefits are primarily a wealth-accumulation vehicle, to be passed on to younger generations, the availability of continued income tax deferral over the life expectancy of the client, spouse and/or children will often outweigh the cost of increased 15% excise taxes, sometimes by a considerable margin.

4.   For a client whose retirement benefits are primarily retirement benefits, not a wealth-transfer vehicle, there may be a shorter time frame for potential income tax deferral, especially if the client wants to withdraw more than the annual threshold amount during his retirement years. For this client, the cost-benefit analysis may be a closer call. Is a retirement plan still the best way to accumulate savings for retirement, despite the fact that withdrawals during retirement will be subject to this tax? Ironically, the 15% excise tax has a more negative effect on those who are actually using retirement plans for their intended purpose -- saving for retirement -- than on those who don't need these dollars for retirement and just want to pass them on to younger generations.

5.   If the client has a retirement plan which is potentially eligible for lump sum distribution treatment (*i.e.*, if he is a member of a corporate pension, profit sharing or stock bonus plan or a Keogh plan), he should be made aware of the advantages of retaining that status, as opposed to, for example, rolling over benefits to an IRA.

6.   At the fact gathering stage, be sure to determine whether the client has a "grandfathered" balance and whether any of the client's retirement plans are potentially eligible for "lump sum distribution" treatment (see Chapter 2). The "Checklist for Meeting with Client" in Appendix C covers these points, which could have a major impact on the client's planning options with regard to the 15% excise tax.

7.   If the client participates in more than one plan, and two or more of these plans would be treated as separate plans for purposes of determining the "distribution of the entire balance to his account" requirement of the lump sum distribution tax, and at least one of the plans would be eligible for forward averaging, the client should consider keeping the plans separate to enhance his future "LSD" options.

8.   If the client's benefits are large enough to be subject to the excess accumulations tax:

   A.   Consider naming the spouse as beneficiary of all benefits so she will have the option to defer the 15% excise tax.

   B.   Make sure the tax clause in the client's will causes the burden of this tax to fall on the "right" person, and that funds are available to pay the tax.

   C.   Consider withdrawing some benefits prior to death -- see discussion at no. 11 below.

9.   A surviving spouse (S), when faced with the choice of making a "4980A(d)(5) election" to defer excise taxes on benefits inherited from a deceased spouse, should consider the following points:

A.   It may be less expensive to pay the tax at the first death than to defer it, especially if S has other benefits of her own, is not young, and/or may need to draw out more than the annual "threshold" amount from the decedent's benefits.

B.   If the "(d)(5) election" is not made, the inherited benefits will be forever free of the 15% excise tax, PROVIDED they are not commingled with S's own benefits.

C.   S should not confuse the (d)(5) election with the "rollover" decision.

10.   Benefits inherited by S from a deceased spouse must NEVER be commingled with S's own retirement benefits if no 4980A(d)(5) election was made at the first spouse's death. If the (d)(5) election *was* made, there is no drawback to commingling inherited benefits with S's own benefits.

11.   When death is imminent, and death will necessitate payment of the 15% excess accumulations tax, consider withdrawing the applicable annual "threshold" amount from retirement plans during life to reduce this tax. Also, when death is imminent, and perhaps even before, consider using lifetime withdrawals to take advantage of the "double" or "triple" exemptions available (during life *only*) to clients with LSD-eligible and/or "grandfathered" benefits. However, do not make withdrawals without weighing the cost in terms of lost potential future income tax deferral. See the *Sherman and Herman Levine* case study.

6

Life Insurance
in the Retirement Plan

*Life insurance in a retirement
plan behaves differently from
other retirement plan assets.
Planning for a retirement plan
that contains life insurance
differs accordingly.*

Introduction

This chapter explains the income, estate and 15% excise tax consequences, to the plan participant (P) and his beneficiaries, of buying and holding life insurance in a qualified plan. To enhance understanding, these consequences are contrasted with (a) the tax treatment of non-life insurance plan benefits and (b) the tax treatment of life insurance that is not held in a qualified plan. The chapter also discusses estate planning considerations involved when dealing with plan-owned life insurance.

There are limits on how much life insurance can be purchased in a qualified plan. Generally, the plan must comply with the "incidental benefit rule" in purchasing life insurance for participants, as well as ERISA fiduciary investment rules. These plan-level requirements are beyond the scope of this book. For other sources, see the Bibliography. Similarly, the analysis of insurance products is beyond the scope of this book.

Income Tax Issues
for the Insured Participant

Income tax consequences during employment

Generally, an employee pays no income tax on his employer's contributions to a retirement plan, or on plan earnings, until these are actually distributed to him. However, if the employer contributions (or plan earnings) are used to purchase *life insurance* on the employee's life, then the employee *does* become currently taxable on part of the retirement plan contributions or earnings.

S. 72(m)(3)(B) governs the tax treatment of life insurance contacts purchased by qualified plans when (a) the premium is paid with deductible employer contributions or with plan earnings and (b) the policy proceeds are payable to P or P's beneficiary. The amount "applied to purchase" such life insurance, as determined by IRS regulations, is includible currently in P's gross income.

The regulations provide that the amount of "life insurance protection" deemed purchased in any year is the difference between the death benefit payable under the policy and the cash surrender value of the policy at the end of the year. Reg. s. 1.72-16(b)(3). Once the "amount of life insurance" is thus determined, the IRS next tells us how much of the employer contribution and plan earnings are deemed to have been "applied to purchase" this life insurance. The IRS has issued the following pronouncements on this subject:

1.   **Term Insurance.** When a qualified plan buys term insurance on the life of a participant, the entire premium is includible in the participant's gross income. Rev. Rul. 54-52, 1954-1 C.B. 150.

2.   Other Insurance. If the policy provides more than "pure" death benefit protection, for example, if it also provides annuity benefits or if it has or will have a cash value, Rev. Rul. 55-747, 1955-2 C.B. 228 provided a table, called "P.S. 58," to be used to calculate the amount includible in the participant's gross income. This ruling was later modified by Rev. Ruls. 66-110, 1966 C.B. 12, and 67-154, 1967-1 C.B. 11, which provided that the insurer's lowest published rate for one-year term insurance available on an initial issue basis for "all standard risks" could be used if that rate was lower than the "P.S. 58 cost." Generally, the insurer's published term rates are considerably lower than the P.S. 58 Table rates.

Note: in the rest of this chapter, "P.S. 58 cost" is used as shorthand for "the amount the participant is required to include in gross income because of the plan-held life insurance." In any particular case, this may be the rate from Table P.S. 58 or the insurance company's actual term rates if lower. Note also that "Table P.S. 58" deals only with single life policies. The IRS has not issued any rulings or pronouncements regarding the amount includible in gross income on account of plan-owned second-to-die policies.

The amount of currently taxable income generated by a plan-owned policy rises as the employee gets older because term rates go up with age. This increase may be mitigated by an increase in the cash value, which reduces the "pure death benefit."

The employee must find the cash elsewhere to pay the income tax on the P.S. 58 cost. For example, an employee in the 45% tax bracket (considering federal, FICA, state and local income taxes) must earn $818 of taxable salary to pay the income tax on $1,000 of P.S. 58 cost. For this individual, the tax on $1,000 of P.S. 58 cost is $450. He must earn $818 of taxable salary in order to have, after income taxes, the $450 of cash he needs to pay the income tax on the P.S. 58 cost. This income tax obligation continues even if the employer stops paying premiums on the policy. This may happen if the policy becomes "self-financing," so the premiums are paid through policy dividends. If the only source of value in the policy is employer contributions and plan earnings, the annual P.S. 58 cost would continue to constitute gross income to the employee.

When a participant is considering purchasing insurance through a retirement plan, the insurance agent should provide a projection showing what the taxable income will be each year, for the full anticipated life of the policy, under the "guaranteed" as well as the "projected" scenario.

The amount included in the employee's gross income over the years on account of the P.S. 58 cost is considered his "investment in the contract" and in effect becomes his "basis" in the policy. The participant is entitled to recover this basis tax-free, but only if the policy itself is distributed to him. Reg. 1.72-16(b)(4). If the policy lapses, or is surrendered for its cash surrender value (CSV) at the plan level, the participant's "basis" disappears and cannot be offset against other plan distributions. In other words, the payment of income taxes over the years on the P.S. 58 cost generates a "basis" that may or may not be recouped later.

On the other hand, since the "P.S. 58 cost" is supposed to represent the annual cost of pure insurance protection, it is surprising the IRS allows it to be used as "basis" for any purpose; it is really an expense. An "owner employee" does not get to treat even the "P.S. 58 cost" as an investment in the contract. Reg. s. 1.72-16(b)(4).

Income tax issues at retirement: the rollout

At retirement, the participant will typically face some thorny issues regarding the life insurance policy.

A life insurance policy cannot be rolled over to an IRA. S. 408(a)(3). Also, with some possible exceptions (see "Certain Profit Sharing Plans," below), the IRS requires that policies be either converted to cash or distributed to the participant at retirement. This is one of the constellation of plan qualification requirements known as the "incidental benefit rule." See Rev. Rul. 54-51, 1954-1 C.B. 147, as modified by Rev. Ruls. 57-213, 1957-1 C.B. 157, and 60-84, 1960-1 C.B. 159. So, at retirement, if P wants to keep the policy in force, P must either take the policy out of the plan as a distribution, or buy the policy from the plan. A third alternative is to simply terminate the policy.

Distributing the policy to P

If the policy is distributed to P, P must include in gross income the "fair market value" of the policy. Reg. s. 1.402(a)-1(a)(1)(iii). The IRS has stated that the "fair market value" of a life insurance policy is its CSV *unless* "the total policy reserves [established by the insurer to cover the death benefit, advance premium payments, etc.] represent a much more accurate approximation of the fair market value of the policy." If the total reserves for the policy substantially exceed the policy's cash surrender value, the reserves represent a much "more accurate approximation of the fair market value of the policy," and P is required to include the amount of the policy reserves, not the CSV, in gross income. Notice 89-25, Q&A 10, 1989-1 C.B. 662.

This is hardly a bright line test. How much larger than the CSV must the reserves be before the reserves are deemed to "substantially exceed" the CSV? In the example given in the Notice, the reserves were 3.8 times greater than, and were held to "substantially exceed," the CSV. It would appear that, if the policy is to be distributed *or sold* to P, the following steps are required:

1.   Determine the policy's CSV.

2.   Obtain from the insurer a statement of the value of all policy reserves as of the proposed date of distribution of the policy.

3.   If (2) "substantially exceeds" (1), use (2) as the policy's value.

4.   If (2) does not "substantially exceed" (1), use (1) as the policy's value.

5.   If (2) exceeds (1), but it is unclear whether (2) "*substantially*" exceeds (1), obtain an IRS ruling regarding which figure to use.

In determining his taxable income from distribution of the policy, P is entitled to offset, against the "fair market value" of the policy, the amounts includible in his gross income over the years on account of the policy (P.S. 58 cost), which are considered to be "premiums or other consideration paid" by P. Reg. s. 1.72-16(b)(4).

A discrepancy between the CSV and the "policy value" may create problems at the *plan* level, possibly affecting the plan's qualification, according to Notice 89-25. Those issues are beyond the scope of this book.

P buys policy from plan

If the policy is distributed to P at retirement, then all further opportunity to defer income taxes on the amount represented by the policy value (and on the potential future earnings on that amount) is lost. For this reason, many retiring participants look at the possibility of purchasing the policy from the plan. Although this requires P to come up with some cash from other sources, it does allow him to continue deferring income tax on the policy value. P will own the policy (which he can transfer to an irrevocable trust, if he wants to remove the proceeds from his gross estate); and the plan will own cash, which can then be distributed to P and rolled over to an IRA for maximum continued deferral.

Buying the policy from the plan creates an ERISA problem. ERISA s. 406(a) prohibits the sale of plan assets to a "party in interest." The definition of "parties in interest" includes categories one would expect, such as plan fiduciaries, the employer, and officers, directors and 10% owners of the employer. It also includes, surprisingly, any *employee* of the employer. ERISA, s. 3(14). Thus, as an initial proposition, the sale of a life insurance policy from the plan to the insured employee is a "prohibited transaction."

The Department of Labor has issued a "Prohibited Transaction Class Exemption" (PTE 92-6, 2/12/92; reproduced at CCH Pension Plan Guide, Vol. 5, paragraph 16,637) which exempts such sales if certain requirements are met. Thus, if the desired approach is to have P buy the policy from the plan, there are two ways that this might be accomplished:

1.   Comply with PTE 92-6; or,

2.   If P does not have any connections with the employer or the plan except as an employee, it might be worth exploring the possibility that the sale is not a "prohibited transaction" once P retires and ceases to be an employee. Consult an ERISA specialist before deciding on this course.

To comply with PTE 92-6 when the insured employee

is buying the policy from the plan, the following two requirements must be met:

1.   The contract would, but for the sale, be surrendered by the plan. This requirement is not normally a problem when the participant is retiring, because, as noted, qualified plans are generally required to sell or surrender the policy at that point.

2.   The price must be "at least" the CSV.

To comply with PTE 92-6 *and* avoid any income tax inclusion to P, it would appear that the price should be the *greater* of:
(a)   The cash surrender value; or
(b)   The amount P would be required to include in gross income if the policy were simply distributed to him (see previous discussion).

If using (a), note that P is not allowed to offset his "basis" in the contract against the purchase price, because PTE 92-6 sets the CSV (with no offset) as the *minimum* purchase price to avoid a prohibited transaction.

The price under (b) would be used if the policy reserves "substantially exceed" the CSV *and* the value of the policy reserves, minus P's basis, exceeds the CSV.

Note also that the rollout problem may not wait until the client is age 65. It could crop up earlier if the client is laid off, chooses early retirement or becomes disabled. Some of these situations will be made even more difficult by the forced unraveling of the insurance-retirement plan marriage.

In contrast, if the employee buys his insurance *outside* of the retirement plan to begin with, these issues at retirement simply do not arise. All retirement benefits can be cleanly rolled over to an IRA and taken out when the employee feels like it (subject to the minimum distribution rules); and the cash value build-up of the insurance policy is not subject to income tax at retirement or death or any other time.

Certain profit sharing plans

Even if the participant is retiring, it may be possible that these unpleasant choices can be postponed *if* the plan is a profit sharing plan *and* the policy was purchased with money held in the plan for more than two years, because this type of money is not subject to the "incidental benefit rule." Rev. Rul. 60-83, 1960-1 C.B. 157. Under this circumstance, it may be possible for the participant to leave the policy in the plan along with his other plan benefits and withdraw it at some later time, subject only to the minimum distribution rules. Of course, the annual taxable income to him from the existence of the policy in the plan will continue.

The ability to keep the policy in the plan does not exist even for a profit sharing plan in the case of many small businesses, where the retirement plan is often terminated altogether when the owner retires. This would typically be true, for example, in the case of a small medical practice. If the plan is terminated, then the retiring business owner or doctor must either pay income tax on the value of the policy, cash it in at the plan level (terminating coverage), or buy it back from the plan with after-tax dollars accumulated outside the plan.

Income Tax Consequences to Beneficiaries

Life insurance proceeds paid out of a retirement plan to a beneficiary are subject to income tax, to the extent of the policy's CSV immediately prior to death. S. 72(m)(3)(C) dictates that, in the case of a life insurance policy purchased by a retirement plan, the distribution of the CSV is treated as a "payment under such plan," rather than as a distribution of life insurance proceeds. Thus, to the extent of the CSV immediately before P's death, life insurance proceeds are treated the same as any other distribution from a retirement plan, which are normally subject to income tax when paid out to the beneficiaries after the participant's death.

Despite the fact that P might have been taxable on *more* than the CSV if the policy had been distributed to him during life (see Notice 89-25 discussed above), the regulations clearly state that only the CSV is taxable to the beneficiaries after P's death. Also, the beneficiaries are entitled to offset the amount of P's "basis" in the policy (*i.e.*, the amount included in P's gross income over the years on account of the P.S. 58 cost) against the amount otherwise includible in their gross income. See Reg. s. 1.72-16(c)(3). The $5,000 death benefit exclusion may also be available; s. 101(b).

This treatment of plan-owned life insurance compares unfavorably with the treatment of insurance policies purchased outside of retirement plans, proceeds of which are received by the beneficiaries 100% income-tax-free. S. 101(a).

Estate Tax Issues

For most estate tax-conscious clients, an important consideration in buying life insurance is to keep the insurance out of the insured's estate and his spouse's estate, to increase the value of the benefits for their children. If the policy is purchased *outside* the retirement plan, it is easy to accomplish this goal. The parent creates an irrevocable trust for the benefit of the spouse and children; and the trustee buys the policy. The policy proceeds are never part of either spouse's estate.

The life insurance "subtrust"

If the policy is bought through a retirement plan, on the other hand, it is not clear how, if at all, the proceeds can be kept out of the participant's estate.

Generally, the estate tax includability of retirement plan benefits is governed by s. 2039. However, s. 2042, not s. 2039, governs life insurance even if the insurance is held inside a retirement plan. S. 2039(a). Life insurance is subject to estate tax if the insured owns any "incident of ownership." S. 2042. To keep plan-held life insurance out of the insured participant's estate, therefore, it would be necessary to deprive the participant of such "incidents of ownership" as the power to name the beneficiary of the policy, the power to surrender or borrow against the policy, and a reversionary interest (worth 5% or more) in the policy. S. 2042(2).

Some practitioners believe this goal can be accomplished by establishing a "subtrust," which is defined as "an irrevocable life insurance trust slotted within the trust otherwise used to fund the pension or profit sharing plan" (definition from "The Qualified Plan as an Estate Planning Tool," by Andrew J. Fair, Esq., published by Guardian Life Insurance Company of America, New York, NY, 1995) (Pub. No. 2449).

The merits of the subtrust have been debated in numerous articles. See the Bibliography. Some writers conclude that the subtrust "works" to keep policy proceeds out of the estate, without disqualifying the underlying retirement plan. Other writers state that either the existence of the "subtrust" disqualifies the plan, or, if the plan *is* qualified, it is impossible for the participant not to have estate-taxable "incidents of ownership" in the policy.

It remains to be seen whether the subtrust device works as a way of keeping the policy proceeds out of the estate. To date, there is no published ruling or case upholding (or denying) the estate tax exclusion for life insurance held in a retirement plan "subtrust." A loss on the estate tax issue would result in a tax of 40%-60% of the amount of the policy proceeds.

Furthermore, even if the subtrust concept "works" to keep the death benefit out of the gross estate if P dies prior to retirement, new problems arise once P reaches retirement. If he then either buys the policy out of the plan or receives it as a distribution (see discussion above), P is right back in the position of owning the policy. He will then have to contribute it to an irrevocable trust, and survive for three more years after the transfer, in order to get it out of his estate again. S. 2035.

Can the three-year rule be avoided at rollout time?

As discussed above, the normal course is for the retirement plan to sell or distribute the policy to P at retirement. P may wish at that point to transfer the policy to his children or to an irrevocable trust to get the proceeds out of his estate. Since gifting the policy would not remove the proceeds from P's estate until three years have elapsed, practitioners look for an alternative way to get the policy into the hands of the beneficiaries without the three year waiting period.

Since the plan cannot distribute benefits to anyone other than P during P's lifetime, the only way out is for the plan to *sell* the policy to the intended beneficiaries, or else distribute or sell the policy to P, and have P sell it to the beneficiaries. Such sales raise several issues.

The first problem is the "transfer for value" rule of s. 101(a)(2). Life insurance proceeds are taxable income to a recipient who acquired the policy in a "transfer for value," unless an exception applies. The purchase of the policy from P, or from the plan, by P's children (or a trust for their benefit) would be a "transfer for value," causing the eventual death benefit to be taxable income instead of tax exempt income.

However, the transfer for value rule does not apply if the policy is bought by the insured, a partner of the insured or a partnership in which the insured is a partner. Thus, the sale could be made to a partnership in which P and his children are the partners, to avoid the "transfer for value" problem.

The next question is, whether life insurance owned by a partnership in which P is a partner is in or out of P's gross estate. As a partner, does P have "incidents of ownership" in a policy owned by the partnership? A number of cases and IRS rulings have held that a partner does not have "incidents of ownership" in a policy on his life held by the partnership. It should be noted that these cases and rulings apparently involved arms' length, business partnerships, not family partnerships formed solely for the purchase of life insurance. Nevertheless, this is a promising route to explore when buying an insurance policy from a retirement plan. A discussion of partnership-owned life insurance is beyond the scope of this book.

Another alternative which has been suggested by a prominent estate planning attorney is for P to sell the policy, for fair market value, to a "defective grantor trust," i.e., a trust all of which is deemed to be "owned" by P under the "grantor trust rules" of ss. 671-677. The theory is that a transaction between P and his "grantor trust" is not treated as a sale (and therefore there is no "transfer for value") because P and the trust are regarded as "one taxpayer" for income tax purposes. The trust could be structured so it would not be included in P's estate. Exploration of this intriguing idea is also beyond the scope of this book.

The third problem is the prohibited transaction rules of ERISA, discussed above. The Department of Labor's class exemption, PTE 92-6, exempts the sale of a life insurance policy by the plan to the insured participant or his beneficiaries, if various requirements are met. If the sale is to someone other than the participant, and would be a prohibited transaction if not specially exempted, the following requirements must be met, in addition to those discussed elsewhere:

1.   The buyer must be a "relative" of the insured participant. "Relative" means either a relative as defined in s. 3(15) of ERISA or IRC s. 4975(e)(6) (spouse, ancestor, lineal descendant or spouse of a lineal descendant), or a sister or brother.

2.   The buyer must be the beneficiary of the policy.

3.   The policy must first be offered for sale to P, who must give a written refusal to purchase, and must consent to the proposed sale to the beneficiary.

Note that the PTE's definition of "relative" does not include partnerships or trusts.   If the strategy is to sell the policy from the plan directly to a partnership of P and P's children, the plan's ERISA counsel will have to determine whether (a) the transaction is a "prohibited transaction" and (b) if it is, whether the transaction is exempt under PTE 92-6. These issues can be avoided by having the plan sell or distribute the policy to P, and having P make the sale to the partnership or trust.
A final problem is, how the partnership (or trust) is going to get the money to buy the policy.

15% Excise Tax Issues

Over and above the income taxes that have to be paid on plan benefits when they are taken out of a plan, there is a 15% excise tax on so-called "excess withdrawals" and "excess accumulations." See Chapter 5. The tax on excess withdrawals applies if P takes out more than a specified "threshold" amount ($155,000 as of 1996) from the plan in any one year. Thus, if retirement comes, and P decides to have the policy simply distributed to him at that time, and the amount included in P's income by virtue of this distribution exceeds the "threshold" amount, P would have to pay the 15% excise tax on the excess.

Distributions that are considered a return of the employee's own after-tax contribution are not subject to the 15% tax. S. 4980A(c)(2)(C); s. 72(f). Thus, if the policy is distributed to P, the amount which is excluded from his income as being his "investment in the contract" should also be excluded in determining the amount of "excess distribution" for the year.

At death, the excess accumulations tax does not apply to the pure death benefit portion of insurance, that is to say, the excess of the death benefit over the "value" of P's benefits immediately prior to death. S. 4980A(d)(4)(c). What is the "value" of P's interest in plan-held life insurance immediately before death? Temporary regs. issued in 1987, which expired December 9, 1990, provided that "value" for this purpose meant "cash surrender value," Temp. Reg. s. 54.4981A-1T, d-6(c), not apparently the potentially greater "fair market value" of the policy as described in Notice 89-25.

It is sometimes suggested that a participant with a very substantial plan balance reduce the exposure of this account balance to the excise tax by using some of it to buy insurance. To the extent the otherwise taxable account balance is "spent" buying term insurance, excise taxes have been saved. Excise-taxable account dollars have been converted into non-excise-taxable term insurance premiums or proceeds. To the extent taxable account balance dollars are converted to the cash surrender value of a policy, the cash surrender value remains subject to the 15% excise tax; only the "pure death benefit" is exempt from the 15% excise tax.

The approach recommended, therefore, by those who advocate plan-owned life insurance as a way of reducing excise tax exposure, is this: A major policy is bought "inside" the retirement plan. For the first year or two or three of the policy's life, the cash value of a whole life insurance policy is less than the cumulative premiums invested, if a substantial commission is paid to the life insurance agent. This is so because the insurer does not start investing premium dollars and adding them to the "cash value" of the policy until the agent's commissions have been paid from the premium flow.

Then, before the cash value starts to grow substantially, the insured employee buys the policy from the plan for its (somewhat depressed) cash surrender value. Excise taxable-plan benefits have evaporated to the extent the premiums paid up to that point, plus income those dollars would have earned in some other form of investment, exceed the cash surrender value.

An alternative view is, if the participant has a large enough plan balance to be concerned about the excess accumulations tax, he should be even more concerned about the estate tax. By buying his insurance outside the plan, he can with little difficulty avoid the 50% estate tax. If he buys the insurance inside the plan, it will be difficult, at best, to avoid the estate tax on those benefits. Instead, this participant should withdraw funds from the retirement plan as needed to pay the insurance premiums, and buy the life insurance through an irrevocable insurance trust *outside* the retirement plan. This way he will save 15% excise taxes *and* estate taxes.

Reasons To Buy Life Insurance
Inside The Plan

There can be good reasons to buy life insurance inside a retirement plan. For example, this approach can be attractive if:

1.   The client is rated or uninsurable, but there is a group policy available inside the plan which the client can purchase without evidence of insurability. *This possibility should always be investigated in the case of a client with a severe health problem.*

2.   The purchase of insurance can increase permitted contributions to a defined benefit plan that is otherwise "maxed out."

3.   The client needs insurance but has no money to pay for it outside the retirement plan. In this case, however, it is still advisable to look at the possibility of taking some money out of the plan to buy the insurance. Unless there is some reason the client cannot conveniently get money out of the plan (unacceptable level of tax on plan distributions; creditor or marital problems; plan doesn't permit it), the purchase of insurance outside the plan may be more tax-effective.

Second-To-Die Insurance

Buying a second-to-die ("joint and survivor life") policy inside a retirement plan raises additional problems.

Estate tax issues

Trying to minimize estate taxes on a second-to-die insurance policy (insuring the lives of P and S) owned by a retirement plan involves considerable complexity. If the policy is purchased *outside* the plan, the following legal paperwork is required in order to avoid estate tax: Draft irrevocable trust to buy policy. In other words, complete estate tax exclusion involves one life insurance policy and one trust.

If the policy is bought *inside* a retirement plan, on the

other hand, one source recommends the following, substantially more complex steps to reduce (not eliminate) estate tax:

1.   Draft an irrevocable trust to receive the second-to-die policy from the plan if P dies before S.

2.   The irrevocable trust buys a single life insurance policy on P so the trust can pay income and estate taxes due on the second-to-die policy at P's death.

3.   P executes a special beneficiary designation, leaving the second-to-die policy to the irrevocable trust, with waiver of QPSA (see Chapter 3) by S, and containing a presumption of S's survivorship, in case of common accident, as to the policy.

4.   If S dies before P, then:

          A.   The second-to-die policy must be distributed to or purchased by P; if purchased, comply with DOL PTE 92-6;

          B.   P transfers the second-to-die policy to an irrevocable trust, which removes the policy from his estate *if he lives more than three years;*

          C.   The irrevocable trust buys additional insurance on P to pay the estate taxes that will be due if P dies within three years.

          D.   To avoid estate taxes altogether if S dies first, skip steps A-C, and instead of P's buying the policy from the plan, a family partnership of P and his children buys the policy.

5.   Buy a single life policy on S to finance step 4A or step 4D (as the case may be).

6.   If P retires, the policy is purchased from the plan by a family partnership of P, S, and the children. No mention of how this purchase is financed.

This scheme involves one trust, either three or four separate life insurance policies, and possibly a family partnership.

15% excise tax

With a second-to-die policy, a 15% excise tax problem will arise if P dies before his spouse. When a participant holds second-to-die insurance in his retirement plan, and then dies before his spouse, the disposition of the policy recommended by those who advocate buying this type of policy in a retirement plan is for P to leave the policy to a trust, to keep the policy out of the estate of the surviving spouse. Here's the problem:

The 15% "excess accumulations" tax generally applies at death. An escape hatch is available if the participant's spouse (S) survives him. S can elect to defer the excess accumulations tax. S. 4980A(d)(5); see Chapter 5. Under this election, S consents to be treated as the "owner" of the benefits for purposes of s. 4980A so there will be no 15% excise tax payable at P's death, but in subsequent years S will be subject to the 15% "excess distributions" tax on withdrawals in excess of the annual "threshold" amount and/or to the "excess accumulations" tax on amounts remaining in the plan at *her* death.

If P's retirement benefits are substantially in excess of the excess accumulations tax "threshold amount," this option could be extremely useful. But this option is available *only if* all of P's retirement benefits are paid to S *individually*. If one of the assets in the retirement plan account is a second-to-die life insurance policy, and that policy is left to a trust, bypassing S, the 15% excise tax cannot be deferred. It will have to be paid at the first death.

To avoid this, P could leave the policy (along with the rest of his benefits) outright to S *individually*. This would avoid the 15% excise tax, but then the policy will be in S's estate. She would then have to set up a new irrevocable trust for it, transfer the policy to the trust and hope to survive three years (to avoid a "gift in contemplation of death" problem under s. 2035), in order to get it out of her estate.

Income tax

An additional complexity with employer-provided second-to-die insurance is that there are no IRS rulings or regulations indicating how to calculate the amount to be included in P's gross income for this form of coverage.

Miscellaneous

Borrowing against the policy at the plan level may cause the plan to be subject to income tax on "unrelated business taxable income." See Ltr. Rul. 7918095 (1/31/79).

The "P.S. 58 cost" that the employee must report each year on his income tax return is not considered a "distribution" to the employee for purposes of the 10% penalty on premature distributions (see Chapter 9). IRS Notice 89-25.

Does the "P.S. 58 cost" income that the employee pays taxes on every year count towards the minimum distributions required under s. 401(a)(9)? Nothing in the proposed regs. says that it does.

Summary of Planning Principles

1.   If it is possible under the plan to designate a different death beneficiary for the life insurance policy proceeds, on the one hand, and any other plan death benefits, on the other, determine how much of the life insurance proceeds would be subject to income tax if the client died today, *i.e.*, the cash surrender value (CSV) of the policy. If the CSV is relatively small, and the client has insufficient other assets to fully fund a "credit shelter trust," consider naming the credit shelter trust as beneficiary of the plan-held policy. Since most of the proceeds would be income tax-free, the usual drawbacks of funding a credit shelter trust with plan benefits (see Chapter 2, and the *Allen Able* case study) would be minimized. The rest of the benefits, being fully income-taxable, could be left to the surviving spouse, who could roll them over to an IRA and continue to defer income taxes. See the *Dingells* case study, and form 3.8 in Appendix B.

2.   Is it possible to further fine-tune the beneficiary designation for the life insurance policy, to the extent of directing that the income-taxable portion (pre-death CSV, minus P's investment in the contract, minus $5,000 death benefit exclusion if applicable) will be paid to S, and the "pure death benefit" portion, return of basis and $5,000 exclusion amount would pass to, say, the credit shelter trust? It is not clear that such a beneficiary designation would be effective, as far as the IRS is concerned, to allocate the income-taxable portion to one beneficiary and the income-tax-free portion to the other. Although the author has found no IRS pronouncement on the subject one way or the other, the IRS might require the taxable and tax-free parts of the policy proceeds to be allocated among the recipients in proportion to what each receives from the contract. See form 3.9 in Appendix B.

3.   If a substantial portion of the death benefit under the life insurance contract will constitute taxable income to the beneficiary, consider making the life insurance proceeds payable to S, who can then roll over the taxable portion. S. 402(c)(2), (c)(9).

4.   In general, it is better to buy life insurance outside the retirement plan if estate taxes are a consideration. While the "subtrust" scheme may offer a chance of keeping plan-owned insurance out of P's estate, it is at best an unproven technique. Definite estate tax exclusion can be easily obtained for insurance owned outside the plan. With estate tax rates at 40%-60%, this factor will weigh heavily, especially for older and wealthier participants.

5.   If the client is not insurable at standard rates, always investigate the availability of group insurance through his retirement plan (and elsewhere).

6.   If life insurance is owned by the client's retirement plan, investigate the "subtrust" as a way of keeping the policy proceeds out of the gross estate.

7.   When the time comes to remove the policy from the plan, investigate ways to get/keep the policy out of the client's gross estate without triggering the "three year rule" of s. 2035, while avoiding a "transfer for value" or "prohibited transaction."

7

The Grandfathers

*There are exceptions, in the
form of "grandfather rules," to
almost every requirement in the
law governing tax treatment of
retirement benefits. Proper use
of these rules can save money
for your clients.*

Introduction

This chapter discusses the three "grandfather" rules
which are exceptions from the minimum distribution rules of s.
401(a)(9); and two other obscure grandfather rules, namely, the
continued availability of the estate tax exclusion for retirement
benefits of certain individuals, and the former ability of non-
spouse beneficiaries to roll over inherited benefits.

Other significant "grandfather" rules are discussed in
other chapters: The grandfathering of certain benefits from the
15% excise tax in Chapter 5; and "ten year forward averaging"
or "20% capital gains tax" income tax treatment for certain
lump sum distributions in Chapter 2.

Minimum Distribution Rule Grandfathers

Chapter 1 describes the "minimum distribution rules" of
s. 401(a)(9) as they are today, in 1996. Today's rules have
evolved through a number of mutations over the years. At
several stages of this evolution, "grandfather" exceptions were
created, so that today some individuals have benefits that are
wholly or partly exempt from the rules. The three types of

benefits grandfathered from the minimum distribution rules are: benefits covered by a TEFRA "242(b) designation"; benefits of unretired, born-before-6/30/17, non-5% owners; and pre-1987 403(b) plan account balances.

History of s. 401(a)(9)

Prior to TEFRA '82, the minimum distribution rules applied only to Keogh plans (see Glossary) and only to lifetime distributions. All benefits had to be distributed not later than the taxable year (a) in which the participant reached age 70½, or, (b) "in the case of an employee other than an owner employee... in which he retires," if later; or, beginning in that year, over the life or life expectancy of the employee (or of the employee and his spouse).

TEFRA significantly expanded the minimum distribution rules. For plan years beginning after 1983, 401(a)(9) would apply to all "qualified plans," corporate as well as Keogh. Effective for 1984 and later years, all benefits were required to be distributed not later than the year in which the participant attained age 70½, or, "in the case of an employee other than a key employee who is a participant in a top heavy plan, in which he retires," whichever was later (or, beginning in such year, over the life or life expectancy of the employee or employee and spouse). TEFRA '82, s. 242(a).

TEFRA also added the *after-death* minimum distribution requirement. After 1983, all qualified plans would have to provide that, if any employee died before his entire interest had been distributed, the balance of the interest would "be distributed within five years after his death (or the death of his surviving spouse)." An exception provided that, if distributions had already commenced, over a permitted term certain (such as the life expectancy of the employee and spouse), the balance of the employee's interest could continue to be paid out over the rest of the term certain. TEFRA '82, s. 242(a). TEFRA included a grandfather exception for this substantial extension of the minimum distribution rules. See "TEFRA 242(b) designations," below.

S. 401(a)(9) was amended again by the Tax Reform Act of 1984, s. 521(a). The wording of s. 401(a)(9) became substantially similar to what it is today. For the first time, the use of a "life expectancy" payout was extended to any "designated beneficiary," not just the spouse, for both retirement and death benefits.

TRA '84 added the requirement that, in the case of death benefits, if distribution had begun in accordance with the lifetime minimum distribution rules, and the employee died before his entire interest had been distributed, "the remaining portion of such interest will be distributed at least as rapidly as under the method of distributions being used... as of the date of his death." Finally, TRA '84 added the special rule that a surviving spouse beneficiary would not have to begin taking out death benefits until the year the employee would have reached age 70½, and the concept that the life expectancy of an employee and spouse could be redetermined annually.

As amended by TRA '84, s. 401(a)(9) retained the concept that distributions would have to begin in the year in which the employee attained age 70½, or in the year of retirement, whichever was later, except for *certain* employees. Certain employees would have to begin withdrawals at age 70½, and would not have the option of delaying distributions until actual retirement. However, TRA '84 slightly changed the definition of these "certain employees." The restricted participants under TRA '84 were "5% owners" rather than "key employees." S. 416(i)(1)(A)(iii).

The changes made by TRA '84 were regarded as "cleaning up" the changes made by TEFRA '82. Accordingly, TRA '84 said that these amendments were to take effect "as if" included in TEFRA, and the TEFRA grandfather rule was continued. Accordingly, the TRA '84 changes would not apply to "distributions under a designation (before January 1, 1984) by any employee in accordance with a designation described in section 242(b)(2) of [TEFRA] (as in effect before the amendments made by this Act)." TRA '84, s. 521(d)(2)-5.

The Tax Reform Act of 1986 brought more fine tuning. The minimum distribution rules were extended for the first time to 403(b) plans; and the exception permitting non-key or non-5% owner employees to postpone distributions until actual retirement was finally eliminated. Each of these changes created a new batch of "grandfathers."

TEFRA 242(b) designations

The famous TEFRA section 242(b)(2) provides that a plan will not be disqualified "by reason of distributions under a designation (before January 1, 1984) by any employee of a method of distribution...

"A.   which does not meet the requirements of [401(a)(9)], but

"B.   which would not have disqualified such [plan] under [401(a)(9)] as in effect before the amendment" made by TEFRA.

TEFRA affected many people. First, it affected all plan participants by adding the new minimum distribution requirement for death benefits. Second, it affected *corporate* qualified plan participants because it created stringent and specific minimum distribution requirements, where before there had been only the vague "incidental death benefit rule" (see discussion of 403(b) plans, below). Finally, it affected "key employees" in "top heavy plans" a little more than it affected non-key employees because, under the new rule, they would have to start taking minimum distributions in the year they reached age 70½ whether they had retired or not.

As a result, there was a flurry of activity among sophisticated plan participants trying to make a "designation" by December 31, 1983 that would enable them to continue to use the older, more liberal rules. The benefits of a participant who made a proper and timely "designation" would not be subject to the new minimum distribution rules.

Theoretically, participants with "242(b) designations" can postpone distributions until actual retirement, and their death benefits are not subject to the "five year rule" or the "at least as rapidly" rule. Unfortunately, TEFRA 242(b) designations have not proved as useful as originally expected for several reasons:

(a)   The requirements for a valid "designation" (as set forth in IRS Notice 83-23, 1983-2 C.B. 418, 11/15/83) are quite restrictive. "The designation must, in and of itself, provide sufficient information to fix the timing, and the formula for the definite determination, of plan payments. The designation must be complete and not allow further choice." P. 419. This does not mean the designation may not be amendable or revocable. Rather, the designation must be self-executing, requiring no further actions or designations by the participant to determine the size and date of distributions. Many purported TEFRA 242(b) designations do not meet this test.

(b)   Also, a participant generally cannot carry over a 242(b) designation from one plan to another. For example, by rolling over corporate plan benefits protected by a 242(b) designation into an IRA, the participant loses the 242(b) protection. However, grandfather protection is not lost if benefits are moved to another plan without any election on the part of the participant--*e.g.*, as a result of a plan merger--IF the transferee plan accounts for such benefits separately. Prop. reg. s. 1.401(a)(9)-1, J-2, J-3.

(c)   TEFRA 242(b) designations generally attempted to defer distributions for as long as possible. However, individuals grandfathered from the minimum distribution rules by a 242(b) election may want to make withdrawals sooner than their "designation" indicates for any number of reasons--*e.g.*, to avoid the 15% excise tax, or simply to pay living expenses. However, "any change in the designation will be considered to be a revocation of the designation." Notice 83-23, p. 420 (next to last sentence).

(d)   If the 242(b) designation is revoked or modified in any way, drastic results ensue. In effect the grandfathered status is revoked retroactively, and the participant is required to take "make-up distributions"--withdraw from the plan all the prior years' distributions he had skipped. Prop. reg. s. 1.401(a)(9)-1, J-4.

Thus, participants relying on a TEFRA 242(b) designation live in a perilous state. The longer they defer their distributions, the larger becomes the "make-up" distribution which will be required if they ever change their minds.

The hardworking aged non-5% owners

A person who attained age 70½ before January 1, 1988 (*i.e.* was born on or before June 30, 1917), and who was not a 5% owner (see s. 416(i)) at any time during a plan year ending during or after the calendar year in which he reached age 66½, is entitled to defer commencement of distributions until actual retirement. See s. 1121(d)(3)-(5) of TRA '86, as amended by TAMRA '88. These non-5% owners, would now (as of 1995) be at least 78 years old and since they are still working I refer to them as HANOs (Hardworking Aged Non-5% Owners).

These individuals are not subject to the same hazardous conditions as those relying on TEFRA 242(b) designations. The HANO can take money out of his plan any time he wants to without thereby losing his "grandfathered" status and without triggering any requirement of "make-up" distributions; and he can make or modify elections regarding the form of distribution of his benefits with no adverse effect on his protected status.

However, the effects of indefinitely postponing all distributions until retirement at some ancient age are not all benign. The plan balance grows larger and larger if it is not depleted by withdrawals; and the period over which it will have to be withdrawn will be much shorter, once the employee actually does retire, because his life expectancy will be that much shorter. Unless he also managed to qualify for grandfather status under s. 4980A (see Chapter 5), his exposure to the 15% excise tax may be increasing each year as he keeps deferring a larger and larger plan balance to be distributed over a shorter and shorter life expectancy.

Distribution planning for these individuals is a delicate balancing act. If they are determined to shoot for the longest possible income tax deferral, the best advice may be to either (a) make the benefits payable on death to grandchildren, then keep working until death (never "retire"), so the benefits can be distributed over the grandchildren's life expectancies; or (b) marry a very young spouse, retire and take out the benefits over the joint life expectancy of the participant and spouse.

Pre-1987 403(b) Plan Balances

403(b) plans partly grandfathered from minimum distribution rules....

At one time, 403(b) plans (see Glossary) were exempt from most of the "minimum distribution rules." The Tax Reform Act of 1986 made these plans subject to the minimum distribution rules on the same basis as other plans. TRA '86 s. 1852(a)(3)(A) added s. 403(b)(10) which provides that "under regulations prescribed by the Secretary" a 403(b) plan will lose its tax-favored qualities "unless requirements similar to Section 401(a)(9) are met (and requirements similar to the incidental death benefit requirements of Section 401(a) are met)." This amendment was to apply "as if" included in the Tax Reform Act of 1984 (see section 1881 of TRA '86), because it was considered a technical correction of TRA '84.

Prop. reg. s. 1.403(b)-2 (7/27/87) governs these distributions. These proposed regulations refer to 403(b) annuities and mutual fund-custodial accounts collectively as "403(b) contracts." The regs. say that 403(b) annuities and custodial accounts will be treated the same as individual retirement annuities under 408(b) and individual retirement accounts under 408(a), respectively, and accordingly the minimum distribution rules will be the same as for IRAs under proposed regulation 1.408-8. However, certain *plan participants* and *plan balances* are "grandfathered":

(a) <u>Transition rule for older participants still working</u>

There is a "transition rule" for 403(b) *plan participants* who turned age 70½ before 1988. These participants do not have to commence withdrawals from *any* part of their 403(b) plans until April 1 of the year following the year in which they retire. Notice 88-39, 1988-1 C.B. 525. These participants are in the same situation as the "hardworking aged non-5% owners" discussed in the previous section.

(b)   Grandfathering of pre-'87 balance

The grandfathering for certain *plan balances* is available regardless of the participant's age. The *amount* that is grandfathered is the account balance on December 31, 1986 -- *provided* that the plan sponsor/custodian keeps records that enable it "to identify the pre-'87 account balance and subsequent changes as set forth in" the regulations. (These regulations pertain to whether withdrawals made over the years from the 403(b) arrangement come out of the pre-'87 or post-'86 account balance). "If the issuer does not keep such records, the entire account balance" is subject to the full panoply of minimum distribution rules.

...But still subject to the MDIB rule

Even though pre-'87 balances are not subject to the so-called "minimum distribution rules" of s. 401(a)(9) of the Code, they are still subject to the "incidental death benefit" rule, which pre-dated the 1986 tax act.

Thus, any 403(b) plan, if the custodian keeps proper records, contains two portions: the December 31, 1986 account balance (as reduced by subsequent distributions); and the post-'86 account balance, which consists of post-'86 contributions, earnings on post-'86 contributions, and earnings on pre-'87 contributions (minus distributions therefrom). These two different portions are subject to two different sets of distribution rules. The post-'86 balance is subject to all the minimum distribution rules of 401(a)(9) and to the "minimum distribution incidental benefit" (MDIB) rule, which is the modern version of the "incidental death benefit" rule. The pre-'87 account balance is subject only to the MDIB rule.

The IRS tells us in proposed regulation 1.403(b)-2, Q & A-3, that the pre-'87 account balance "must satisfy the MDIB rule contained in Q & A-2 of s. 1.401(a)(9)-2." That Q & A, in turn, tells us that the distribution of benefits "must satisfy either the rules in effect as of 7/27/87 [the date the proposed regulation was issued] interpreting s. 1.401-1(b)(1)(i)," or "the rules in Q & A -3 through Q & A -7."

So, there are two ways to comply with the MDIB rule with respect to the pre-'87 balance in a 403(b) plan. One is to comply with the incidental death benefit rule as it existed prior to TRA '86. The other is to comply with the *new* minimum distribution rules, as tightened up by TRA '86. Use of the new rules would eliminate any benefit of being "grandfathered," but may appeal to some participants as being easier than trying to figure out what the "grandfather rule" allows.

What was the MDIB rule prior to 1986?

To discover what the older version of the MDIB rule was, we first look at the referenced regulation, s. 1.401-1(b)(1)(i). This old regulation is simply a general rule defining what a "pension plan" is. It is a plan maintained "primarily to provide systematically for the payment" of benefits to the employee after retirement; and it "may also provide for the payment of incidental death benefits." Commerce Clearing House interprets the old regulation as follows: "The IRS maintained that these definitions imposed a requirement that benefits payable to the beneficiary of an employee in a qualified pension or profit sharing plan be *incidental* to the primary purpose of distributing accumulated funds *to the employee*." CCH 1994 Standard Federal Tax Reports para. 17,726.04 [emphasis added].

Since the cited regulation is not particularly enlightening regarding any requirement for distributions *during life*, we must look at the "rules interpreting" that regulation at the time the proposed regulations were issued (7/27/87). These are contained in Rev. Ruls. 72-241 and 72-240, 1972-1 C.B. 108.

The incidental death benefit rule, pre-1987, was nowhere near as specific and stringent as today's minimum distribution rules. It did not require distribution at any particular age -- only that distributions must begin at the "normal retirement age" specified in the plan, or, if later, at actual retirement. Also, unlike today's rules, the rule had no application after the death of the participant. All the old rule required was that:

> (a)   Distributions must begin to the participant by "normal retirement age," or actual retirement if later.

> (b)   When distributions commenced, if any form of installment or annuity payout was elected, the actuarial value of the participant's expected lifetime distributions had to be at least 50% of the total value of the benefits; *i.e.*, the expected death benefits had to be less than 50% of the total value.

Was there a separate MDIB rule for 403(b) plans?

Under s. 403(b), the employer does not typically adopt any retirement "plan" *per se*; the employer simply buys annuity contracts (or contributes money to mutual fund custodial accounts) for individual employees. Thus, unlike a "qualified"

401(a) pension or profit sharing plan, a 403(b) arrangement would not necessarily have a formal definition of "normal retirement age." Thus, the required distribution date that applied to qualified retirement plans under the "incidental benefit rule" ("normal retirement age," or actual retirement if later) could not be applied to 403(b) arrangements without some modification. There is some evidence that "age 75" was used as a substitute for "normal retirement age" in applying the "incidental benefit rule" to 403(b) arrangements prior to TRA '86. See Ltr. Ruls. 7825010, 7913129.

A more recent ruling apparently indicates that, whatever the rule may really have been prior to 1986, the IRS's position now is that age 75 is and always has been the outer limit. Ltr. Rul. 9345044 (8/16/93) contains the statement, "In general, regarding pre-1987 account balances, the IRS has generally interpreted the requirement that benefits in retirement arrangements be used primarily for retirement purposes to mean that annuity payments from tax-sheltered arrangements will begin no later than age 75." Contrary to this statement, however, the two earlier rulings cited above made no reference to such a concept or to the "incidental benefit rule."

Furthermore, if letter rulings are to be our source of guidance, the IRS's requirement seems to have been that payments must commence at retirement *or age 75, whichever is later,* at least in some cases (Ltr. Rul. 7913129, 12/29/78). This interpretation is consistent with the only "official" pre-1987 statement of the rule, namely, that a pension plan's primary purpose is to provide benefits to the employee *after retirement.* Reg. s. 1.401-1(b)(1)(i). It is also consistent with the "grandfather rule" which allows 403(b) participants who turned age 70½ before 1988 to defer distributions until actual retirement; it would be unusual to give "grandfathered" individuals a better deal under the "grandfather" rule than they had prior to the new legislation they are "grandfathered" from.

(It is unusual but not unheard of -- see "Lump Sum Distributions: the Rewards" section of Chapter 2.)

So is age 75 (or actual retirement if later) the required beginning date for 403(b) plan pre-'87 balances? There is no authority for this conclusion other than private letter rulings. It is quite possible that some employers obtained IRS approval, pre-1987, for 403(b) arrangements with earlier or later ages for required commencement of benefits.   Nevertheless, this statement of the "incidental death benefit rule for pre-'87 account balances" seems to be now accepted. See Krass, Stephan J., Esq., *The Pension Answer Book* (10th ed., Panel Publishers 1995), Q29:40, p. 29-44.

This tortuous discussion of the incidental death benefit rule leads to the following tenuous conclusions.

Distribution of pre-'87 balance can be postponed until actual retirement

Until actual retirement, a 403(b) participant is not required to make ANY withdrawals from his grandfathered (pre-'87) balance.   Accordingly, the annual minimum distributions that begin at the participant's required beginning date (April 1 following the year the participant turns 70½) should be calculated using only the post-'86 balance. Furthermore, it is advisable to withdraw only the *minimum* required amount each year from a grandfathered 403(b) plan. If more money is needed in a particular year, it should be drawn out of some other plan, because any amounts taken out of a 403(b) plan in excess of the required minimum distribution are deemed to come out of the grandfathered balance.

*Consider naming credit shelter trust as beneficiary of 403(b)
plans, if needed to bring funding up to $600,000*

In general, it is preferable to fund a "credit shelter trust"
with assets other than retirement benefits. See Chapter 2. For
many working people, however, the only way to fully fund a
$600,000 credit shelter trust is to use some retirement benefits
for this purpose. In such a situation, it may be more favorable
to use a 403(b) plan which contains a "grandfathered" balance
than to use some other retirement plan that is fully subject to the
"minimum distribution rules."

If a plan that is fully subject to the minimum distribution
rules is made payable to the participant's credit shelter trust, the
trustee of the credit shelter trust will in most cases be required
to draw out from the plan, every year, an installment which
(after some years) will include plan "principal" as well as
"income." The principal that is taken out of the plan and placed
in the credit shelter trust will be subject to high trust income tax
rates (39.6% on taxable income above $7,650) (1995 rates).
(See discussion of trust income taxes in Chapter 2.)

If 403(b) benefits are made payable to the credit shelter
trust, by way of contrast, there would be no requirement for
distributing any particular amount at any particular time after the
participant's death from the pre-'87 account balance. See Ltr.
Rul. 7825010 (3/21/78). The trust would have to withdraw the
amounts required by the minimum distribution rules from the
post-'86 balance (which includes the earnings on the pre-'87
balance), but would never have to touch the principal of the pre-
'87 balance.

If the pre-'87 balance is preserved intact inside the plan
until the death of both spouses, it could then be distributed to
the children and taxed at their personal income tax brackets.
Thus, if a client must use retirement plan death benefits to "fill
up" a credit shelter trust, it is better to use a 403(b) plan with a

hefty pre-'87 balance for this purpose, and make *other* plans payable to the spouse personally.

An intriguing question is whether it is possible to make the pre-'87 balance payable to one beneficiary (*e.g.*, the credit shelter trust) and the post-'86 balance payable to another (*e.g.*, the spouse).

Recommendations for 403(b) plans

A 403(b) plan participant who has reached age 70½, but not yet retired, might adopt the following program:

(a)   From the custodian or administrator, obtain a statement verifying that it has a method for identifying the pre-'87 balance in accordance with regulations. If the custodian is complying with this requirement, the pre-'87 balance should be showing up as a separate item on all account statements.

(b)   Figure out how much retirement plan money (if any) must be paid to the client's credit shelter trust in order for it to use up the entire federal estate tax exemption amount, then figure out which 403(b) plans have the highest relative proportion of pre-'87 balance and use those to "fill up" the credit shelter trust in the following manner. Name the participant's credit shelter trust as "designated beneficiary" for the selected plans, give a copy of the credit shelter trust to the plan administrator, and begin withdrawals, from the post-'86 balance *only*, over the joint life expectancy of the client (participant) and the oldest beneficiary of the credit shelter trust.

(c)   Notify the custodian that the client does

not intend to make any withdrawals from the pre-'87 balance until actual retirement (or age 75, if later).

Once retirement occurs, what distributions must come out of the pre-'87 balance?

Either at the "normal retirement date" specified in the plan (if one is specified), or possibly at age 75 if no other "normal retirement age" is specified, or upon actual retirement if later, a 403(b) plan participant should set up a payment schedule from the pre-'87 balance which is designed to pay to him, during his life expectancy, more than 50% of the actuarial value of the pre-'87 balance. This is the "incidental benefit rule" as it existed pre-1987. For the possibility that the 50% requirement may not apply if the participant's spouse is the beneficiary, or if the payout period is limited to the lives/life expectancies of the participant and spouse, see Rev. Rul. 72-240, previously cited, and Ltr. Rul. 7825010.

The Federal Estate Tax Exclusion Lives!

Once upon a time IRC s. 2039 provided an unlimited federal estate tax exclusion for most kinds of retirement benefits. Then the exclusion was limited to $100,000 by TEFRA '82 and repealed by TRA '84.

However a retroactive grandfather clause was included in TRA '84 for both laws; and then the Tax Reform Act of 1986 made major substantive retroactive amendments to these grandfather clauses. The retroactive TRA '86 changes made it substantially easier to qualify for the exclusion than it was under the "original" grandfather provision in TRA '84.

However, the TRA '86 amendments are so obscure that they are not even mentioned in widely used estate tax reporting services. The casual researcher will find only the strict TRA '84 grandfather rules (as embodied in IRS Temp. Reg. S. 20.2039-1T, 1/29/86) under which only participants who were "in pay status" and had "irrevocably elected a form of benefits" by 1982 or 1984 still qualified for the exclusion. But TRA '86 simply *repealed* those two requirements and substituted others. Thus Temp. Reg. s. 20.2039-1T is nugatory.

The best explanation of this incredible tangle appears in Ltr. Rul. 9221030 (2/21/92). The current requirements for a decedent's estate to be eligible for a total (or $100,000) estate tax exclusion, as stated by the IRS in this ruling, are:

1.   A decedent who separated from service before 1983, and died after 1984, without having changed the "form of benefit" before his death, will be entitled to 100% exclusion of the benefit. A change of beneficiary is fine; it is a change of the *form of payment* of benefit that triggers loss of the exclusion.

2.   If the decedent separated from service after 1982 but prior to 1985, and did not change the form of benefit between the time of separation from service and the time of death, the estate is still entitled to the exclusion but it is limited to $100,000.

Both of these exclusions under the retroactive amended grandfather clause are available *regardless* of whether the election of form of benefits was irrevocable, and *regardless* of whether the benefits were "in pay status" on December 31, 1984 or any other particular date.

Under the ruling in question, "A" retired in 1979, selected a form of benefit and designated a beneficiary. He had the right to change the form of benefit but never did. The plan administrator made some minor administrative changes in the method to be used for calculating certain joint and survivor benefits, but this was not deemed to be a change of form of benefit by the participant. "A" also changed his beneficiary a couple of times, but never changed the form of benefit. (The particular form of benefit he had selected was equal annual installments payable annually over his and his spouse's joint life expectancy.) The IRS held that "A's" estate was entitled to a 100% exclusion of the benefits from the gross estate.

Rollover of Death Benefits by Non-Spouse Beneficiary

Under current law, no beneficiary other than the surviving spouse can elect to treat the decedent's IRA as his or her own IRA. However, *any* beneficiary (even a non-spouse) of an IRA participant who died *before 1984* could do just that. See Prop. Reg. s. 1.408-8, A-4.

Summary of Planning Principles

1.   Although the "grandfather rules" affect relatively few clients, significant tax savings can be achieved for some of those who are eligible for grandfather treatment. Accordingly, it is important to determine what if any "grandfathering" your client may be entitled to. Use of the "Checklist for Meeting with Client" in Appendix C can assure that you do not overlook "grandfather" benefits your client may qualify for.

2.   The planning principles, if any, for each "grandfather" rule appear at the end of the discussion of that rule.

8

Disclaimers of Retirement Benefits

Disclaimers have proven useful in post mortem planning for benefits. Nevertheless, questions remain regarding the use of qualified disclaimers of retirement benefits to solve estate planning problems.

Introduction

A disclaimer is the refusal to accept a gift or inheritance. The law recognizes disclaimers: the law recognizes that a person cannot be forced to accept a gift or inheritance. State laws dealing with disclaimers generally regulate what actions will be recognized as "disclaimers" and to whom a gift or inheritance will pass if it is "disclaimed" by the original beneficiary.

A "disclaimer" is not a "gift." Since the person making the disclaimer never "accepted" the property in the first place, the theory goes, he never owned it and therefore he could not have given it away. The disclaimed asset passes to the next beneficiary in line, usually as if the person making the disclaimer had predeceased the person from whom he inherited.

The tax code recognizes disclaimers if they meet certain requirements. If a disclaimer is "qualified," then it is not treated as a taxable gift. S. 2518.

Example: Mary dies, leaving her $100,000 IRA to Maureen as primary beneficiary. Maureen is already wealthy, and does not need the money. Maureen disclaims the IRA by means of a "qualified disclaimer" meeting the requirements of s. 2518 and applicable state law. As a result of the disclaimer, the IRA passes to the contingent beneficiary, Maureen's poor cousin Pat. Maureen has not made a taxable gift. By contrast, if Maureen had "accepted" the IRA (for example, by cashing it in and putting the proceeds in her bank account), and then written a check to Pat, she would have made a taxable gift.

The principal requirements for a "qualified" disclaimer under s. 2518, stated in a necessarily oversimplified fashion, are:

1.   The disclaimer must be made within nine months after the disclaimed property was "transferred" to the disclaimant.

2.   The disclaimant must not have accepted any benefits from the property disclaimed.

3.   The property must pass, as a result of the disclaimer, to someone other than the disclaimant. Exception: property can pass to the decedent's spouse as a result of the disclaimer, even if she is also the person making the disclaimer.

4.   The disclaimant must not have any power (as trustee or otherwise) to determine who gets (or benefits from) the property after the disclaimer.

5.   Generally speaking, the disclaimer must be effective under state law.

Disclaimers have proven their worth in *post mortem*

planning for retirement benefits, as examples in the following section show. *Post mortem* planning flexibility can be increased if the possibility of disclaimers is planned for in the drafting stage, although excessive reliance on possible future disclaimers should be discouraged.

Disclaimers in Post Mortem Planning

Disclaimers have proven to be of great value in "cleaning up" beneficiary designations where the deceased participant named the "wrong" beneficiary. Disclaimers have been used to redirect benefits to the surviving spouse (so she can roll them over), and to create funding for a credit shelter trust which would otherwise have no assets. The following rulings illustrate the range of possibilities, and the creativity of *post mortem* planners, in using disclaimers to correct *pre mortem* mistakes:

Funding credit shelter trust

Ltr. Rul. 9442032 (7/27/94): the plan participant (P) named his spouse (S) as primary beneficiary and his living trust as contingent beneficiary. The trust provided that all IRA benefits had to be allocated to the marital trust, over which S had a general power of appointment. Apparently, however, no assets at all passed to the credit shelter trust. "To enable [the] estate to fully utilize the available unified credit," S, as beneficiary of the IRA, disclaimed her interest in the IRA, and then, as beneficiary of the marital trust, disclaimed her general powers over the marital trust. As a result of these disclaimers, the IRA was now payable to a trust of which she was merely the life income beneficiary, with no general power of appointment. Then, as executor, she made a fractional QTIP election for the IRA and the trust. The non-elected portion of the IRA and marital trust became in effect the credit shelter trust.

Salvaging spousal rollover

Ltr. Rul. 9045050 (8/15/90): P named his living trust as his beneficiary. S was a trustee of the living trust. Upon P's death, S, as trustee, made a qualified disclaimer of the benefits. As a result of the disclaimer, all the benefits passed to S outright rather than to the trust, and she rolled them over.

Ltr. Rul. 9450041 (9/22/94): P's benefits were payable to a marital trust. Upon S's death, the marital trust was to pass to a family trust for P's children and their issue or (in default of issue) to nieces, nephews and a charity. S disclaimed all her interests under the marital trust, so the property passed to the family trust. Then every beneficiary of the family trust (the children and grandchildren, the nieces and nephews and the charity) disclaimed his, her or its interest. The benefits passed to S by intestacy and she rolled them over.

The most interesting aspect of this ruling was that S's disclaimer was not timely -- it was made more than nine months after P's death. Therefore, for federal transfer tax purposes, S's disclaimer was not a qualified disclaimer. However, under applicable state law, a non-timely disclaimer was effective to transfer title to those who would have received the property if the disclaimer had been properly made. Since S's non-qualified disclaimer was legally effective as a transfer under state law, it was treated for tax purposes as a "new" transfer -- essentially, as a gift by S to the beneficiaries of the family trust.

Because S's non-qualified disclaimer was treated as a "new" taxable transfer, the disclaimers by all the beneficiaries of the family trust were timely (and "qualified") under s. 2518 because they were made within nine months after the property was transferred to *them* by S's non-qualified disclaimer, even though made more than nine months after P's death.

Finally, since S's non-qualified disclaimer was a "new" transfer, it would normally have resulted in a taxable gift by her to the beneficiaries of the family trust. However, since they all disclaimed this "gift," the property went to S by intestacy, and S's "transfer" was a transfer to herself, which is not taxable! This ruling shows creative *post mortem* planning and a bit of luck in the terms of the state disclaimer statute.

Planning in Anticipation Of Disclaimers

It is wise, at the estate planning stage, to anticipate the possibility of disclaimers. For example, a participant (P) may be trying to choose between naming his spouse (S) as beneficiary, to achieve deferral of income taxes via a spousal rollover, on the one hand, and naming a credit shelter ("bypass") trust as beneficiary, on the other hand, to take full advantage of his unified credit. Each choice has its merits and a clear "winner" may not be apparent during the planning phase.

P may decide to make the benefits payable to S as primary beneficiary, because his main goal is to provide for S's financial security (for example), but provide that, if S disclaims the benefits, the benefits will pass to the credit shelter trust. If funding the credit shelter trust appears to be the more attractive alternative at the time of P's death, S can activate the credit shelter plan by disclaiming the benefits, which will then pass to the credit shelter trust as contingent beneficiary. Ltr. Rul. 9320015 (2/17/93) contains an example of this type of planning. See also the *Eaton* case study. A plan like this might name a *different* contingent beneficiary (such as P's children) if S *actually* predeceases P. See form 3.6 in Appendix B.

The apparent flexibility of disclaimers can tempt planners, in the author's view, to rely excessively on potential future disclaimers as a way of carrying out the estate plan. There are various reasons planners recommend plans reliant on disclaimers. One seems to be the requirement in the proposed minimum distribution regulations that a trust named as beneficiary must be irrevocable as of the "required beginning date" (RBD) (see Chapter 1). By naming the spouse as primary beneficiary at the RBD, and the credit shelter trust as merely contingent beneficiary, one can apparently avoid the irrevocability requirement. Then when the participant dies the spouse can disclaim the benefits and allow them to flow to the credit shelter trust. Since the trust has by that time become "irrevocable" (as a result of the participant's death) the minimum distribution "trust rules" are satisfied. See Ltr. Rul. 9537005 (6/13/95) for an example of this type of plan.

Another justification for this approach is that it avoids the need to spend time analyzing the choices at the planning stage. Thus, professional fees are lower. The estate plan relies on the fiduciaries and beneficiaries to make the actual decisions later, when a more informed choice can be made.

For most clients, the "credit shelter trust" estate plan offers substantial estate tax savings. Before making these substantial savings dependent on prospective disclaimers by beneficiaries or fiduciaries, the planner needs to weigh carefully the definite, substantial savings of a credit shelter trust against the risks and drawbacks of relying on disclaimers. For example:

1.   Disclaimers by fiduciaries pose several issues. Although such disclaimers are clearly permitted and recognized under s. 2518, there can be state law obstacles. Also, s. 2518 requires that the disclaimed property must pass either to the spouse, or to someone other than the disclaimant, without any direction on the part of the disclaimant; the implications of these requirements are unclear where it is proposed to have property pass by disclaimer from one discretionary trust to a second discretionary trust with the same trustees or beneficiaries.

2.   Another requirement of a qualified disclaimer is

that the disclaimant must not have accepted any benefits of the disclaimed property. Often a retired participant will have set up his IRA or other retirement arrangements so that payments are made, automatically, every month or every quarter. Such payments may continue to flow in after P's death, and be received and deposited by the beneficiary, before the disclaimer subject is even broached, and this may constitute "acceptance" of the benefits, making a qualified disclaimer impossible.

3.   Disclaimers have an inexorable deadline of nine months after the date of death. Thus, an estate plan which depends on disclaimers is extremely dependent on rapid action *post mortem*, especially if an IRS ruling is required.

4.   No matter how cooperative and disclaimer-friendly the proposed disclaimant may have been during the planning stage, the emotional turmoil caused by P's death, or other factors, could cause him or her to have a change of heart and not sign a disclaimer when the time comes.

5.   If the surviving spouse is to disclaim, she cannot thereafter retain any discretionary distribution powers over the disclaimed benefits (unless limited by an ascertainable standard). For example, if S is disclaiming benefits which will then pass to a credit shelter trust for issue, she cannot be a trustee of that trust if the trustee has, say, discretionary power to "spray" the trust among P's issue; nor can she have a power of appointment enabling her to, *e.g.*, decide which issue of P will receive the trust after her death. Thus, taking advantage of the flexibility of disclaimers may eliminate the use of other, even more flexible *post mortem* planning tools, such as a spousal power of appointment.

6.   Most plan administrators are unfamiliar with

disclaimers, and may even be hostile to the idea (see further discussion below). Using a disclaimer for retirement benefits will, at the least, necessitate spending some time educating and/or negotiating with the plan administrator.

7.   If the benefits are subject to REA, the planner needs to consider the effect of this law on the possibility of a qualified disclaimer by the surviving spouse. See discussion below.

8.   It is not clear to what extent, if any, the IRS will recognize a qualified disclaimer as effective to change the "designated beneficiary" for purposes of s. 401(a)(9). See discussion below.

Disclaimers and the Plan Administrator

Some practitioners are concerned that plan administrators may refuse to recognize disclaimers. The plan administrator may take the position that the plan requires the benefits to be paid to the beneficiary named by P, and the plan has no authority to pay the benefits to someone else if the named beneficiary is in fact living.

This should not be a concern. Retirement plan documents generally provide that the interpretation of the plan and administration of the trust are governed by state law to the extent not contrary to (or preempted by) ERISA. If the applicable state law permits disclaimers, the plan is required to give effect to them, in the author's view, unless the plan contains a specific provision to the contrary.

Most non-ERISA trust instruments say nothing one way or the other about disclaimers, but no one argues that trustees generally are entitled to ignore legally valid disclaimers. An ERISA trust is not different from any other trust except to the extent federal law requires it to be. In GCM 39858 (9/9/91), the IRS recognized that disclaimers do not violate ERISA (*i.e.*, a disclaimer is not an "assignment" of benefits).

In a similar vein, the IRS has recognized that a plan must conform to a state's "slayer" statute, and not pay benefits to the person who murdered the participant, even if that person is named as the beneficiary. See, *e.g.*, Ltr. Rul. 8908063 (11/30/88). There is no legal basis in ERISA or elsewhere for a plan administrator to disobey a state statute of general applicability.

On the other hand, qualified retirement plan administrators are justified in exercising caution when dealing with disclaimers. For example, in GCM 39858, while the IRS strongly endorsed the validity of disclaimers of qualified plan benefits, the Service limited its approval to disclaimers that are "qualified" under s. 2518. Only "qualified" disclaimers, that satisfy both the requirements of state law and of s. 2518(b), received the IRS's blessing as (1) not constituting an assignment of benefits prohibited by s. 401(a)(13) and (2) effective to shift the income tax burden to the next beneficiary in line.

Thus, the IRS has left open the possibility that a non-qualified disclaimer (even if valid under state law) would be a prohibited "assignment" of benefits -- which could, if allowed to occur, disqualify the plan. The plan administrator should consider when confronted with a purported disclaimer, obtaining an opinion of counsel that the disclaimer meets the requirements of applicable state law and of s. 2518.

On the other hand, despite the language of GCM 39858 limiting approval to "qualified" disclaimers, the IRS has approved a non-qualified disclaimer of qualified plan benefits at least once. See Ltr. Rul. 9450041 (9/22/94), previously discussed in this chapter. This ruling gave effect to the disclaimer for purposes of s. 402(c) (which determines who pays the income tax), and did not discuss the plan qualification issue or mention GCM 39858.

These issues are of less concern to IRA administrators, since IRAs are not subject to the prohibition against "assignment" of s. 401(a)(13).

Effect of REA on Surviving Spouse's Ability to Disclaim

The nine months requirement for qualified disclaimers

One of the requirements for a disclaimer to be "qualified" under s. 2518 is that the disclaimer must be made no later than "nine months after the ... date of the transfer creating the interest" being disclaimed.

The IRS's regulations under s. 2518 provide that, generally speaking, the nine months are measured "with reference to the taxable transfer creating the interest in the disclaimant." A "taxable transfer" does not mean a transfer that was taxed, but simply a "completed" transfer for gift and estate tax purposes. "When there is a completed gift for federal gift tax purposes" (regardless of whether any gift tax is imposed), the nine months begin on the date of the completed gift, regardless of whether the gift is brought back into the estate for estate tax purposes. Reg. s. 25.2518-2(c)(3).

Federal law gives married persons certain rights in each other's retirement benefits. If S acquired rights in P's benefits more than nine months before the date of death, is it "too late" for her to disclaim these benefits when P dies?

Spousal rights in pension plans under REA

The Internal Revenue Code and the Employee Retirement Income Security Act of 1974 (Pub. L. No. 93-406; 29 U.S.C. ss. 1001 *et seq.*) ("ERISA"), both as amended by the

Retirement Equity Act of 1984 (Pub. L. No. 98-397) ("REA"), give spouses certain rights in each other's retirement benefits. REA requires all qualified pension plans to pay a "qualified pre-retirement survivor annuity" ("QPSA") to the surviving spouse of any participant who dies prior to commencement of withdrawal of his plan benefits, with limited exceptions. REA also requires pension plans to distribute benefits to most married participants only in the form of a "qualified joint and survivor annuity" ("QJSA") (which is a life annuity to P and a survivorship annuity to S) unless S consents to some other benefit form. A spouse cannot be involuntarily divested of her QPSA and QJSA rights except by divorce.

The QPSA and QJSA requirements apply to both "defined benefit" and "money purchase" pension plans. S. 401(a)(11)(B). Thus, under a qualified pension plan, S acquires vested rights in P's benefits from the same moment P does (or upon their marriage, if the marriage occurred when P was already in the plan).

REA applies differently to most profit sharing plans, and does not apply at all to IRAs; see separate discussion of profit sharing plans and IRAs at the end of this section. The rest of this section deals with disclaimers of REA-guaranteed rights under pension plans.

The question presented

If P's participation in a plan is deemed to create a "transfer" of the survivor annuity rights to S, then the question is whether it will be too late, at P's death, for S to disclaim the survivorship annuity if more than nine months have passed since P joined the plan.

Example: Bill goes to work for Acme Widget Co. and becomes a participant in the Acme Pension Plan. Under the pension plan,

Bill's wife Isabelle is entitled to QJSA and QPSA benefits; in other words, whenever "accrued benefits" are credited to Bill under the pension plan, Isabelle automatically "accrues" some benefits at the same time. If Bill's working for Acme Widget is deemed to constitute a "transfer" of some of his pension benefits to Isabelle, then it would be too late, upon his death, for her to disclaim any benefits that "accrued" more than nine months prior to Bill's death. Therefore a purported "disclaimer" by Isabelle would be either completely ineffective or would be a taxable gift by her to the next beneficiaries.

Statute and G.C.M. 39858

S. 2503(f) provides that *certain* spousal waivers of retirement benefits are exempt from gift tax. Specifically, s. 2503(f) says that, "If any individual waives, *before the death of a participant,* any survivor benefit, or right to such benefit, *under s. 401(a)(11) or 417* [REA benefits, in other words], such waiver shall not be treated as a transfer of property by gift for purposes of this chapter" (emphasis added). Thus, the Code has a specific exemption from gift tax for *certain* spousal waivers, namely, waivers (1) of REA-guaranteed survivor benefits (2) that occur before the death of the participant. Does this mean that (1) waivers of *other* spousal plan benefits, (2) or waivers that occur *after* the participant's death, *are* taxable gifts?

1.   Many plans, for administrative reasons, give spouses more benefits than REA strictly requires. Although the statutory exemption is limited to REA-guaranteed benefits, presumably the IRS would not attempt, in the case of a spousal waiver, to assess gift tax on the "enhanced" value of any plan spousal benefits over the strict minimum guaranteed by REA. However, there is no authority specifically on this question, yet, one way or the other.

2.   The IRS has answered the second question. The Service announced in GCM 39858 (9/9/91) that s. 2503(f) does not imply Congressional intent to impose gift tax on spousal waivers that occur *after* P's death. The IRS stated that "no inference should be drawn from s. 2503(f) that a disclaimer of plan benefits *after* the participant's death should receive unfavorable tax treatment simply because Congress provided for favorable gift tax treatment if plan benefits are waived *before* the participant's death."

IRS position

GCM 39858 involved a spousal disclaimer of REA-guaranteed benefits. The IRS stated that: "There is no evidence that Congress intended to preclude a spouse from disclaiming or renouncing benefits under a qualified plan payable after the participant's death." In view of the IRS's strong policy statement in this GCM, it appears the IRS has answered, for now, any questions that might exist about the disclaimer of REA-guaranteed benefits: such benefits can be the object of a qualified disclaimer, according to GCM 39858.

Nevertheless, it should be noted that this language was mere "dictum," not essential to the "holding" of the GCM. The holding of the GCM was simply that a "qualified disclaimer" would not constitute a prohibited "assignment of benefits" under s. 401(a)(13) and would be effective to shift income tax liability to the next beneficiary. The ruling involved a spouse's disclaimer of a QPSA, but the fact that this disclaimer was "qualified" was stipulated by the parties, so no-one ever asked the IRS to rule that the disclaimer was in fact qualified. Thus it is conceivable that the IRS could, at some future date, decide that a spousal waiver of REA-guaranteed benefits, by disclaimer, after the participant's death, was not a "qualified disclaimer."

What to do: planning mode

REA permits a spouse to waive her QPSA rights if P is over age 35. The law contains elaborate requirements for such a waiver. Unless the QPSA is the only death benefit provided by the plan (which is the case in some defined benefit plans; but presumably there would be no reason to waive the QPSA in such a case), the effect of the waiver is to allow P to designate another beneficiary for the portion of the benefits represented by the QPSA, or to designate S as the beneficiary but change the form of benefits from a QPSA to something else.

If the plan permits S to give an unqualified waiver of her QPSA rights, and she does so, reserving no right whatsoever to veto P's future choice of beneficiary, and P names S as his beneficiary (but still has the right to designate someone else, without her consent), any possible questions about S's right to later disclaim should go away. Accordingly, such an unqualified waiver of QPSA rights would appear to be a recommended ingredient of an estate plan intended to be activated by means of a spousal disclaimer where there are REA - guaranteed benefits.

Another approach to this problem is, rather than making the benefits payable to S and "disclaimable" to the credit shelter trust, to make the benefits payable *to the trust* as primary beneficiary, and disclaimable to S (as secondary beneficiary), in addition to obtaining an unqualified spousal waiver of QPSA rights. This method works if the trust or applicable state law permits trustees to disclaim. This approach has been sanctioned in Letter Rulings 8838075 (7/1/88), 9045050 (8/15/90), and 9247026 (8/24/92) (trust disclaimed, benefit passed to S who rolled it over to an IRA). The nine months question is sidestepped.

IRAs and profit sharing plans

IRAs are not subject to REA at all. IRA beneficiary designations are normally completely revocable at will by the participant. Thus, even if S is named as beneficiary of P's IRA prior to P's death, there is no "transfer" to her until the actual date of death, so S has nine months from that date to execute the disclaimer. Reg. s. 25.2518-2(c)(3). See, *e.g.*, Ltr. Ruls. 9037048 (6/20/90); 9320015 (2/17/93).

Under a profit sharing plan, REA generally requires that P's spouse be named as beneficiary of his death benefits unless she consents to naming another beneficiary. However, REA permits profit sharing benefits to be distributed to P (solely) during life without S's consent. There is generally no QJSA requirement for lifetime distributions from profit sharing plans as there is for pension plans. If P is free to withdraw his benefits during life without spousal consent, the "transfer" of the benefits to her clearly does not occur until P's death and the "when do the nine months begin?" problem does not exist.

Unfortunately, this general rule does not apply to all profit sharing plans. Some profit sharing plans are subject to the same REA rules as pension plans -- for example, a profit sharing plan which was at one time a pension plan; or which contains assets resulting from a merger with or a transfer from a pension plan; or which offers certain annuity benefits.

Are Disclaimers Effective to Change the "Designated Beneficiary"?

Importance of having a "designated beneficiary"

S. 401(a)(9)(B) generally requires that retirement benefits payable on account of a P's death prior to age 70½ be entirely distributed within five years after the date of death. If the benefits are payable to a "designated beneficiary" (DB), however, the benefits may be distributed (beginning within one year after the death) in installments over the life expectancy of the DB. The IRS's proposed regulations issued in 1987 provide detailed requirements for determining *whether* a participant has a "DB" and *who* that DB is. See Chapter 1.

Suppose child, C, is named as the primary beneficiary of parent's (P's) retirement benefits, and grandchild (GC) is the contingent beneficiary. P dies at age 65. At that time, C is age 42, so his life expectancy is 40.6 years and GC is age 17, so his life expectancy is 64.8 years. (See reg. s. 1.72-9, Table V.) C disclaims all interests in the benefits by means of a qualified disclaimer under s. 2518. Accordingly, the benefits become payable to GC. But who is the "DB" for purposes of s. 401(a)(9)? More specifically, whose life expectancy is used as the measuring period for the annual required minimum distributions under s. 401(a)(9)(B)(iii): C's or GC's?

If C had *actually* predeceased P, then unquestionably GC would be entitled to withdraw the benefits in installments over his 64.8 year life expectancy. Prop. reg. 1.401(a)(9)-1, E-5(a)(1) and (e)(1). Where C is merely "deemed," for gift tax purposes, to have predeceased P, but is actually still alive, will the change of identity of the "DB" be recognized under s. 401(a)(9)?

The proposed minimum distribution regulations do not address this. The proposed regulations say only that (with certain exceptions not relevant) "the DB will be determined as of the employee's date of death." D-4. The question is, whether a qualified disclaimer will be given the same effect under s. 401(a)(9) as under s. 2518, and treated as effective retroactive to the date of death.

Statute

S. 2518 recognizes qualified disclaimers "for purposes of this subtitle." Section 2518 is part of Subtitle B of the Internal Revenue Code, "Estate and Gift Taxes." The minimum distribution rules under s. 401(a)(9) are part of Subtitle A, "Income Taxes." Therefore section 2518 does not govern the result under s. 401(a)(9).

The income tax rules applicable to trusts, in Subtitle A, contain their own section dealing with disclaimers, s. 678(d). S. 678(d) provides that a beneficiary will not be treated as having held or released a power over a trust if the power "has been renounced or disclaimed within a reasonable time after the holder of the power first became aware of its existence." There is no statutory provision other than s. 678(d) dealing with the effectiveness of disclaimers *for purposes of Subtitle A*.

Effect of GCM 39858

It is widely believed that, in General Counsel Memorandum 39858 (9/9/91), the IRS "blessed" disclaimers of retirement benefits for all purposes, but this is not the case. In this GCM, the IRS Chief Counsel's office recognized the effectiveness of a qualified disclaimer of retirement benefits for *certain purposes*: to wit, the GCM states that a disclaimer meeting all requirements of s. 2518 *and* applicable state law will not be deemed an "assignment or alienation" of plan benefits in violation of ERISA's anti-alienation provisions (s. 401(a)(13)) and will be effective to shift the income tax on the benefits from the disclaimant to the person who actually receives the benefits. The GCM did *not* address other issues, such as the effect of a disclaimer for s. 401(a)(9) purposes.

The IRS's recognition of qualified disclaimers for purposes of imposition of income tax is encouraging. Perhaps it means that the IRS will recognize qualified disclaimers for all subtitle A purposes, including 401(a)(9); but it is not determinative on this question. The IRS was probably more or less forced to recognize qualified disclaimers as effective to shift the income tax burden to the "new" beneficiary by the unique income tax treatment of retirement benefits. Taxation of retirement benefits is generally governed by s. 402, which taxes only "amounts actually distributed to any distributee." "Normal" income tax rules (such as the doctrine of constructive receipt) are suspended. When a disclaimer is clearly effective, under s. 2518, to shift ownership of the benefit to a new beneficiary, the IRS would find it difficult to impose income tax on the disclaimant, since the income tax falls only on "amounts actually distributed" and nothing is "actually distributed" to the disclaimant.

This type of statutory restraint does not apply to s. 401(a)(9), however. The IRS could ignore disclaimers for purposes of s. 401(a)(9) without violating the letter or spirit of s. 2518, or s. 401(a)(9) -- or GCM 39858.

Other rulings

There are as yet no revenue rulings or cases deciding this issue.

Several private letter rulings, while not precisely determining the question, do not support the conclusion that a qualified disclaimer by a beneficiary is treated the same as the death of that beneficiary for purposes of determining who is the "DB" under s. 401(a)(9).

In Ltr. Rul. 9320015 (2/17/93), the IRS refused to decide who were the "designated beneficiaries" for purposes of s. 401(a)(9) in a disclaimer situation. The basis for its refusal was that the question was hypothetical (P had not died yet).

In Ltr. Rul. 9037048 (6/20/90), P had reached age 70½

and elected to take benefits out of his IRA in installments over the joint life expectancy of himself and his spouse (S). When he later died, S disclaimed in favor of the contingent beneficiary, a trust for their child. The IRS ruled that, because the disclaimer met all the requirements of s. 2518, the disclaimed interests in the decedent's IRA passed to (and were taxable to) the contingent beneficiary.

Nothing in this ruling, however, turned on the issue of whether the disclaimer changed the "DB" for s. 401(a)(9) purposes. That aspect was moot because P was already past age 70½ when he died, so the question of whether he did or did not have a "DB" was settled at his "required beginning date." (See Chapter 1.) What prevailed at his later death was significant for s. 401(a)(9) purposes only insofar as the IRS did not rule that the disclaimer constituted a *change* of beneficiary; the IRS stated simply that distributions after the decedent's death would have to continue at least as rapidly as under the method in effect prior to his death, *i.e.*, installments over the life expectancy of decedent and spouse.

In Ltr. Rul. 9450040 (9/22/94), the IRS specifically refused to treat a qualified disclaimer as a "death" for the purpose of determining the DB under the minimum distribution rules. In this ruling, P (husband), was past age 70½, and was withdrawing his IRA benefits over the joint life expectancy of himself and his wife, with both life expectancies recalculated annually. Husband died. Wife proposed to execute a qualified disclaimer so that the benefits would pass to their children. If the IRS had treated the qualified disclaimer as a "death" for purposes of s. 401(a)(9), then all benefits would have had to be distributed within a year after husband's death. Since both spouses' life expectancies were being redetermined annually, the deaths of both would have resulted in both life expectancies going to zero in the year following the year of death (see Chapter 1).

Instead, the IRS said it would not be appropriate to treat the wife as dead, since she was not in fact dead, and therefore the children could continue to withdraw the benefits over the remaining life expectancy of the wife, recalculated annually, so long as she was actually alive. Although the ruling in this particular case was favorable to the taxpayers, it may have negative implications for use of disclaimers as a post-mortem planning device to shift benefits from an older generation to a younger in hopes of getting an extended payout period.

As Paul Frimmer of Los Angeles, a leading estate planning lawyer, teacher and writer, has pointed out, there are numerous instances under both state and federal law in which a disclaimant is not treated as "predeceasing" the transferor. For example, in determining a distribution "by right of representation," some state laws require *per capita* distribution at the level of the oldest generation which has any living member -- and a living person who disclaims the property is still treated as a "living member" for this purpose, even though he receives no benefits. Also, a child who disclaims in favor of his children is not treated as deceased for purposes of the "predeceased child" exception under the generation skipping transfer tax.

The way of the future?

In another ruling, the IRS analyzed a disclaimer as if it were a change of "designated beneficiary" made by P at the moment of death. This letter ruling may point the way to the future; it seems to adopt the most sensible approach to "integrating" qualified disclaimers and s. 401(a)(9). In Ltr. Rul. 9537005 (6/13/95), P was past his RBD and was taking minimum required distributions based on the joint life expectancy of P and his DB, S, recalculated annually. A revocable trust was named as P's contingent beneficiary. At P's death, S proposed to disclaim the benefits and allow them to pass to the trust, of which she was the life beneficiary.

The IRS made specific findings that the trust met the requirements of the "trust rules" of the proposed regulations, including the requirement that the trust be irrevocable as of the later of the required beginning date or the date the trust is named as beneficiary. Prop. Reg. 1.401(a)(9)-1, D-5. The IRS considered the date of death to be the date the trust was named as beneficiary, because "as a result of the proposed disclaimer, the residuary trust will be the beneficiary of the IRA as of the date of the decedent's death." Since the wife was the "DB" both before (individually) and after (as trust beneficiary) the date of death and disclaimer, the IRS was able to conclude that payments would continue to be made "at least as rapidly" after P's death as before, and therefore payments could continue to be made over the wife's life expectancy.

Summary

It is to be hoped that the IRS will give full effect to qualified disclaimers, retroactive to the date of death, for purposes of s. 401(a)(9); treating a qualified disclaimer as a change of "designated beneficiary" by the participant, as of the moment of death, would be a sensible outcome. The point of this discussion is that the IRS has not yet announced that it will do so, and planners must deal with the possibility that the IRS may *not* do so.

What to do: planning mode

This issue is not a problem for a disclaimer from S to any trust of which she is the oldest beneficiary. Either way, her life expectancy can be used; there is no attempt to lengthen the s. 401(a)(9) distribution period by means of the disclaimer.

On the other hand, if the goal is to permit shifting of the

benefits, by disclaimer, from an older beneficiary (*e.g.*, child) to a younger (*e.g.*, grandchild), so that, if it appears desirable at the time of P's death, the longer life expectancy of the younger beneficiary can be used, planners have the following choices:

The first would be to set up the benefits so they are payable to the older beneficiary, disclaimable to the younger, on the theory that, most likely, disclaimers will be recognized for 401(a)(9) purposes. Then, at P's death, if it is decided to do the disclaimer, the parties can apply for an IRS ruling at that time if the rules are still unclear. Unfortunately, since the nine month deadline for a qualified disclaimer is non-extendable, there will not be much time to get a ruling. Conditional disclaimers are not permitted.

Another alternative is to proceed without a ruling, which may be possible if the rules are clearer at the time of the client's death than they are now. If the rules are not any clearer then than now, however, it would be rather hazardous to proceed with a disclaimer, and a schedule of distributions based on the assumption that the disclaimer is effective to change the "DB" to a younger person with a longer life expectancy, in view of the 50% excise tax imposed on amounts that are not distributed when required. S. 4974.

The other choice is to arrange the plan benefits so the disclaimers will go in the *other* direction, *i.e.*, from the younger to the older generation, so the younger beneficiaries, with their long life expectancies, are clearly the "designated beneficiaries," and the parties can either do an installment payout to them over their life expectancy, or have the younger generation disclaim to the older. However, this choice may not be available if the younger generation beneficiaries are minors, since a disclaimer by a minor usually requires court proceedings and the consent of a guardian *ad litem*.

Possible corrective legislation

Legislation passed by Congress in late 1995 (but vetoed by President Clinton) would have eliminated this problem by amending s. 2518(a) to provide that qualified disclaimers are effective for purposes of "Subtitle A" (which contains s. 401(a)(9) among other things) as well as for purposes of Subtitle B (estate and gift taxes). See H.R. 2419, 104th Cong., 1st Sess. s. 14619(e) (1995). As written, this change would have been effective as to "transfers and disclaimers" occurring after the date of enactment.

Summary of Planning Principles

1. Upon the death of a client, all plan and IRA beneficiary designations should be reviewed as soon as possible. No benefits should be distributed to any beneficiary until this review is completed. If any beneficiary designation appears undesirable, consider the use of qualified disclaimers to redirect benefits to the "right" beneficiary.

2. When preparing beneficiary designations as part of the estate planning process, be sure to name a contingent as well as a primary beneficiary. Consider whether different contingent beneficiaries should be named in case of a disclaimer by, as opposed to the death of, the primary beneficiary.

3. When choosing among competing considerations in naming a primary beneficiary, the client should make the choice based on the relative priorities the client assigns to the choices (such as "financial security of spouse" versus "saving estate taxes for children"). To allow maximum flexibility after the client's death, name the second choice as contingent beneficiary.

4.   If it is proposed to make funding a credit shelter gift contingent on a surviving spouse's disclaimer, weigh carefully the substantial and irreplaceable estate tax savings of a credit shelter trust against whatever considerations are causing the plan to be structured this way. The inconvenience of adopting an irrevocable trust at age 70½, for example, may not be sufficient reason to risk the loss of $200,000 of estate taxes.

5.   If a proposed disclaimer involves a spouse's disclaimer of REA-guaranteed benefits, or a shift of benefits to a contingent beneficiary who has a longer life expectancy, consider the issues discussed earlier in this chapter in order to be sure the disclaimer will be effective to accomplish the goals.

6.   When the possibility of a qualified disclaimer is anticipated, take steps beforehand to facilitate that process, including: spousal waiver of REA rights, if needed; clear instructions to the beneficiaries regarding the choices that will be available to them and what considerations should be applied in making the choice; granting disclaimer authority to fiduciaries, along with guidelines for exercise of the power to disclaim; review the plan documents, s. 2518 requirements, and state law to make sure these pose no obstacles to the proposed disclaimers; and make sure that there are no instructions on file for "automatic" benefit distributions which could cause the beneficiary to receive and be deemed to have "accepted" benefits after P's death, and thus lose the right to disclaim.

9

Other Topics

*Funding charitable gifts with
retirement benefits; who are the
"beneficiaries" of a trust;
probate issues; premature
distributions; planning for
disability.*

Charitable Dispositions

Introduction: advantages of naming a charity as beneficiary

Because retirement plan death benefits are subject to income tax (see Chapter 2), it may be attractive to name a charity or charitable remainder trust as the beneficiary. Charities and charitable remainder trusts are both exempt from income taxes, and thus can collect the entire death benefit without paying income taxes.

This sort of disposition is attractive mainly to someone who has charitable intentions. For the individual who definitely wants to leave some assets to charity, using the retirement benefits for that purpose is often the most tax-effective way to fund the gift.

Example: Helen wants to leave half of her $1.2 million estate to her favorite charity, the Nature Conservancy, and half to her nephew Achilles. Her assets are: a $600,000 IRA and $600,000 of cash. Achilles is in the 40% income tax bracket. If Helen simply leaves half of each asset to Achilles and half to the charity, here is what each receives:

	Charity	Nephew
½ cash	300,000	300,000
½ IRA	300,000	300,000
Gross bequest	600,000	600,000
Less: income tax on ½ IRA	-_____0	-120,000
Net bequest	600,000	480,000

If, instead, she leaves the entire IRA to the charity and all the cash to nephew Achilles, her beneficiaries receive more, at the expense of the IRS:

	Charity	Nephew
IRA	600,000	0
Cash	_____0	600,000
Gross bequest	600,000	600,000
Less: income tax on IRA	-_____0	-_____0
Net bequest	600,000	600,000

The Shumaker and Riley article cited in the Bibliography provides a good numerical comparison of different methods of funding a charitable gift.

In addition to being a tax-efficient way to fund charitable bequests, leaving benefits to a charitable remainder trust can also help the not-particularly-charitably-inclined client achieve dispositive goals. For example, as explained in Chapter 1, when a participant is past his "required beginning date" (RBD), has no "designated beneficiary," has elected to recalculate his life expectancy, and has no spouse who can roll over the benefits after his death, the participant's beneficiaries are faced with the disastrous "one year rule" under the minimum distribution rules: all the benefits will have to be distributed within one year after the participant's death. While leaving the benefits to a charitable remainder trust can not change that fact, it can "soften the blow" by either eliminating the income taxes on the benefits, or deferring them in a manner that approximates a payout over the life expectancy of the family beneficiaries. See the *Widow Heinrich* case study.

The *Gregorio* case study gives another example of using a charitable remainder trust to help achieve non-charitable goals, in this case preservation of principal for the benefit of a surviving spouse. Chapter 2 discusses the income tax aspects of leaving "income in respect of a decedent" (IRD) to charity or a charitable remainder trust, including the impact of the s. 691(c) deduction (for estate taxes paid on IRD) when benefits are paid to a charitable remainder trust.

The rest of this section examines some pitfalls of charitable giving with retirement benefits. A perennial debate, not addressed here, is whether a charitable split gift of retirement benefits can be structured so that the family beneficiaries actually receive *more* value than they would have received if the benefits had been left directly to the family.

Pitfall: naming a charity as one of several beneficiaries

While the advantages of naming a charity directly as beneficiary of all retirement benefits is obvious, naming a charity as one of *several* beneficiaries may present a problem.

According to the IRS, in its proposed regulations interpreting the minimum distribution rules (Prop. reg. s. 1.401(a)(9)-1), ALL beneficiaries of a retirement plan death benefit must be individuals, if ANY of the benefits are to be paid out over the life expectancy of a beneficiary. See Chapter 1. Thus a $1 million IRA payable at death "$1,000 to XYZ charity and the balance to my children" would have to be entirely distributed within five years after the date of death of a participant who died before age 70½. The participant ("P") would be deemed to have "no designated beneficiary" because one of his beneficiaries is not an individual.

Is the IRS's position correct? The proposed regulation appears to be harsher than the Code. S. 401(a)(9) itself says that "*if any portion* of the employee's interest is payable to (or for the benefit of) a designated beneficiary, *such portion*" may be distributed over the life expectancy of the designated beneficiary. S. 401(a)(9)(B)(iii) (emphasis added). Thus, the Code appears to permit a life expectancy payout to an individual designated beneficiary even if some other portion of the benefit is payable to a non-individual.

Even under the proposed regs., it may be possible to have a life expectancy payout to an individual of part of the benefit, and distribute the rest of the benefit to a charity, if the respective shares of the individual and charity are defined as fractional or percentage shares. This possibility rests on the proposed regs.' allowing this result if the benefit is divided into "separate accounts" "as of" the date of death. Since a fractional bequest (such as "half to my children and half to the Red Cross") would in effect divide the account into equal shares as of the date of death, some commentators believe this form of gift would qualify under the separate account rule. However, a pecuniary gift to charity, followed by a "residuary" gift to family (or vice versa) may not qualify as establishing "separate accounts" as of the date of death.

What to do: Unfortunately, the penalty for not complying with the minimum distribution rules is draconian, and the value to the family of the life expectancy payout method can be enormous. Therefore the consequences of "being wrong" here are major. If the client wants to make part of his benefits payable to charity and part payable to an individual, and wants the individual beneficiary to be able to withdraw his share of the benefits over his life expectancy, the client has only the following choices:

Safest route: Divide the account into "separate accounts" during the client's life and name the charity as beneficiary of one "account" and the individual as beneficiary of the other. This method clearly complies with the proposed regs. and will achieve the objective.

Second safest: Name the individual and charity as beneficiaries based on a fractional or percentage method. This *probably* works to establish "separate accounts" "as of" the date of death, in view of the clear language of the Code permitting life expectancy payout of the "portion" payable to the individual beneficiary.

Riskiest: Name two beneficiaries, one with a fixed dollar share and the other with a residuary share. Again, the Code may support you but the proposed regs. may not.

After death: If you have anything other than a "safest route" split bequest between a charity and an individual, you need to be concerned that the IRS may challenge the individual's right to take over his life expectancy. See "Cleanup strategies -- death before the RBD" in Chapter 1.

These concerns do not arise when the benefit is made payable partly to charity and partly to the participant's spouse, if the spouse is over age 59½, because the spouse does not need to take an installment payout of the decedent's benefits. She can roll over her share of the benefits to her own IRA and get an installment payout that way. See Chapter 3. However, if the spouse is under age 59½, she may not want to roll over the benefits because then any distributions to her would be subject to the 10% penalty on "premature distributions." S. 72(t). Thus, if the spouse is under 59½, and may want to withdraw from the benefits prior to reaching age 59½, and the participant wants to make part of the benefits payable to charity, the participant is stuck with the same "planning choices" (described above) as for any other individual beneficiary.

Also, the above discussion applies only to a participant who dies before his required beginning date. Once the participant reaches the RBD, it does not appear possible to have multiple "designated beneficiaries," one or more of whom are not individuals, unless the plan or IRA is divided into "separate accounts." See Chapter 1.

Pitfall: clearing a trust of charitable gift landmines

Suppose a participant is under age 70½. He wants to designate his revocable living trust as beneficiary of his retirement plan. His children are the beneficiaries of his revocable living trust. He wants the plan benefits to be paid out in installments over the life expectancy of his oldest child.

To achieve the desired result, of course, the various "trust rules" must be complied with. See Chapter 1. One of these rules is that all beneficiaries of the trust must be individuals. Any charitable gift payable from the trust at death, no matter how small, would apparently cause the trust to flunk this requirement. Even the typical normally innocuous statement "this trust shall pay any bequests under my will, if my probate estate is not adequate to pay the same," could make the trust "flunk" if in fact the probate estate is not adequate and the will contains charitable bequests.

Thus, when drafting a trust which contains charitable gifts, or which may be used to fund charitable bequests under the will, it is advisable to determine whether any retirement benefits may be payable to that trust, and if so to draft appropriate language to either:

(1)   insulate the retirement benefits from the charitable gifts, if the intent is for the retirement benefits to be paid out over the life expectancy of individual trust beneficiaries (see form 7.2 Appendix B); or

(2)   match the retirement benefits to the charitable gifts, if the goal is to have the retirement benefits pass to the charity free of income taxes; and

(3)   if some retirement benefits are to go to charity and some are to be paid out over the life expectancies of individuals, such benefits should come from different plans (or "accounts").

Pitfall: naming a charity or CRT as beneficiary at 70½

Suppose your under-age-70½ client has named a charity or CRT as his beneficiary. What happens when this client reaches his "required beginning date" (RBD)?

On the RBD, the client must begin withdrawing his benefits over his life expectancy (LE), or over the joint LE of himself and a "designated beneficiary" (DB). If his beneficiary is a charity, he will be limited to using only his own life expectancy, since a "DB" must be an individual and a charity is not an individual.

If the beneficiary of his death benefits is a trust, that trust must comply with the "trust rules" (see Chapter 1) if the LE of the *trust beneficiary* is to be used as part of a measuring joint LE for the payout of the participant's benefits. One of these rules is that "all beneficiaries of the trust must be individuals."

While it is not 100% clear that remainder beneficiaries are considered "beneficiaries" for this purpose (see "Who Are the Beneficiaries of a Trust?" in this chapter), it appears that a trust with a charitable remainder does not satisfy this requirement. Thus, if P's beneficiary is a CRT, apparently P "has no DB" and must use only his own LE to measure required payouts.

A solution sometimes suggested to this problem is to name the spouse (S) as "designated beneficiary," so P can use the joint LE of P and S to calculate distributions during his lifetime, and name the charity or CRT as contingent beneficiary. S can then disclaim the benefits at P's death, allowing them to flow to the charity or into the CRT. See Chapter 8 regarding disclaimers of retirement benefits.

However, relying on a primary beneficiary to disclaim is not very appealing to a client who definitely wants the benefits to go to charity at his death. A more straightforward way to achieve the objective is for the client simply to name the charity as beneficiary, and then start withdrawing the benefits over the client's single life expectancy, recalculated annually. This will provide an initial payout period of 15.3 to 16 years (see Chapter 1), which is a somewhat faster payout than if the client had named an individual "DB," but still perhaps "not bad." By recalculating LE annually, the client assures there will always be something left in the plan at his death to pass to the charity income tax-free. In the meantime, if the client is being forced by the minimum distribution rules to withdraw benefits from the plan more quickly than he would like, he can donate these excess distributions to charity while he is still living, and beat the income tax by means of a charitable deduction.

Pitfall: charitable pledges and other debts

A charitable pledge which remains unfulfilled at death may, depending on the facts and applicable state law, constitute a debt enforceable against the estate. See, *e.g.*, *Robinson v. Nutt*, 185 Mass. 345, 70 N.E. 198 (1904) (unpaid written charitable subscription enforced as a debt against the estate due to charity's reliance), and discussion in *Congregation Kadimah Toras-Moshe v. DeLeo*, 405 Mass. 365 (1989), affirming the principle that a written pledge is enforceable if there is consideration or reliance, although holding that the oral pledge in this particular case was not enforceable.

When an income item is assigned to a charity by an estate in payment of an enforceable charitable pledge, the estate realizes income. See *John T. Harrington Estate*, 2 TCM 540, Dec. 13,405(M) (1943), transfer of appreciated securities by an estate to a charity in fulfillment of pledges was treated as a sale or exchange. The pledges had been deducted as debts on the estate tax return.

If retirement benefits are made payable to a charity at death in fulfillment of an enforceable pledge, or to any other creditor in payment of a debt, the IRS might treat this as generating taxable income *to the estate*. Although generally retirement benefits and other "IRD" are taxed to the person who "receives" them (in this case the charity) (see Chapter 2), the IRS could say that the estate "received" the IRD from the decedent, because the estate's debt was cancelled by the benefits' passing to the charity. See Reg. s. 1.691(a)-2(a)(1).

Funding charitable gifts with plan benefits during life

How wonderful it would be if P could, upon retirement, transfer all his retirement plans to a CRT, reserving the income for himself and his spouse for life, never paying income tax on the "principal," and even getting an income tax charitable deduction for the value of his remainder gift. The author has seen this strategy recommended in print more than once, but it seems unlikely to work. For one thing, true "qualified plan" benefits are completely non-assignable (with limited exceptions for divorce and tax liens). S. 401(a)(13). Thus, this "strategy" cannot work with qualified plan benefits.

How about IRAs? An individual retirement account is not *per se* non-assignable. One type of assignment is prohibited by the Code: if an IRA is pledged as security for a loan, it ceases to be an IRA and is treated as being distributed to the participant. S. 408(e)(4). The fact that one particular type of assignment is dealt with, and "punished," in s. 408 implies that *other* assignments do *not* result in loss of IRA status. However, the IRS has two other arrows in its quiver with which to shoot down purported assignments of IRAs.

If P assigns his IRA to a CRT or other charity, and takes back an annuity or income interest, the IRS might say there is a "prohibited transaction" under s. 4975 -- either a use of plan assets for the benefit of a disqualified person (s. 4975(c)(1)(D)) (other than a mere distribution in accordance with the terms of the IRA, which would of course be exempt, s. 4975(d)(12)), or a "receipt of consideration" in connection with plan assets. A prohibited transaction causes loss of IRA status and the IRA is treated as if it were entirely distributed to P on the first day of the taxable year. S. 408(e)(2).

What if P assigns the IRA to a charity and does not take back an annuity or income interest? All he wants is a charitable deduction for the value of the IRA, without having to pay income tax on that value. It seems reaching to say that getting an income tax charitable deduction is a "use of plan assets for personal benefit," and therefore is a prohibited transaction -- but the IRS might say that.

Alternatively, the IRS might simply treat this, or any other purported lifetime transfer of an IRA not specifically covered by the statute, as an "assignment of income," not effective to shift the tax burden away from P. In its final regulations under s. 2056A (marital deduction for assets left to a non-citizen spouse), the IRS did address the subject of IRA assignments. These regs. confirm that an IRA is "assignable," but state that the assignment of an IRA to any assignee other than a 100% "grantor trust" under sections 671 *et seq.* would cause the assignor to be taxed immediately on the full value of the IRA. Reg. s. 20.2056A, preamble, s. E. For further discussion of these regulations, see Chapter 4.

It is strange that there is no statute, regulation, case or ruling specifically dealing with the consequences of assigning an IRA to charity, either with or without receiving an income or annuity interest in return. Despite the unlikelihood of success, it does seem that someone should try it -- with a small IRA -- and see if it works.

Who Are the "Beneficiaries" of a Trust?

Introduction

In many instances under the minimum distribution rules of s. 401(a)(9) it is necessary to determine who are the "beneficiaries" of a trust. For example, in determining whether all trust beneficiaries are "individuals" for purposes of the proposed regulations "trust rules" (see Chapter 1), can we disregard vested or contingent remainder interests? What rights must a spouse have as beneficiary of a trust to be considered the "designated beneficiary" (DB) when that trust is named as beneficiary of retirement benefits?

Unfortunately, the proposed regulations give very little guidance on these questions, and letter rulings on the subject are not all consistent.

Disregarding "contingent" beneficiaries

In determining who are the "beneficiaries" of a trust,

both for purposes of determining whether all beneficiaries are individuals, and for purposes of determining which of them has the shortest life expectancy, the proposed regs. say to disregard any beneficiary whose "entitlement to an employee's benefit is contingent on the death of a prior beneficiary." Prop. reg. D-5(b), E-5(e)(1). Unfortunately, the exact meaning of this provision, and its application in a number of common situations, are unclear.

For example, suppose a trust names the decedent's child as beneficiary. The trustee is given discretion to use income and principal for the child's support, education, and welfare. The trust is to terminate, with all remaining assets being distributed to the child outright, when the child reaches age thirty. If the child dies before age thirty, the Red Cross receives the trust property. In determining whether all trust beneficiaries are individuals, you presumably can disregard the Red Cross, because its interest does not take effect unless the other beneficiary (the child) dies before age 30.

But what if the trust is not to be distributed outright to the child until age 80 rather than age 30? Or age 90? Or age 110? At some point, the charity's interest presumably ceases to be "contingent" and becomes more like a vested remainder with a slight likelihood of being divested.

Are remaindermen beneficiaries?

It is not clear at this time how the rule applies to a life estate followed by a remainder interest. Suppose the trust is to pay all income to child for life, and on child's death the principal goes to the Red Cross. One school of thought is that the reg. means you can simply ignore all remainder beneficiaries, that is to say, you can ignore any beneficiary who receives no benefits until the death of a prior beneficiary.

The other school of thought holds that "contingent"

means "dependent on something which may not occur." In a CRT, the charity's interest is *postponed* until the death of the income beneficiary(ies), but is not, strictly speaking, *contingent* on their deaths (unless you postulate that the income beneficiary may never die). The principal author of the proposed regulations, Marjorie Hoffman, is apparently of this view, which gives it considerable weight.

Thus some commentators have concluded that, under the proposed regs., although this result may not be intentional and "should be changed," if a CRT is named as beneficiary of retirement plan death benefits, the participant "has no DB," and must accordingly, at his RBD, withdraw his benefits over a period not exceeding his own LE; he cannot use the joint LE of himself and the income beneficiary of the CRT. Any benefits paid to a trust of this type would have to be paid out within five years after the date of death of a participant who died before his RBD. See Shumaker and Riley article cited in the Bibliography. See, *e.g.*, Ltr. Rul. 9322005 (2/24/93) (marital trust to a spouse for life, remainder to children; spouse *and children* regarded as beneficiaries).

When is a "trust for the spouse" the same as "the spouse?"

Theoretically, if retirement benefits are payable to a trust, and the spouse is the "beneficiary" of that trust, and the participant dies before age 70½, s. 401(a)(9) will apply as if the spouse herself were the DB. Prop. reg. s. 1.401(a)(9)-1, E-5. The trust would then have the right to defer commencement of benefits until the year the deceased participant would have reached age 70½ (see Chapter 3).

Unfortunately, it is not clear what rights the spouse would have to have in order to be considered the "beneficiary" of the trust. Is it enough that she has the right to all of the income for life, and no principal can be distributed to anyone other than her (the requirements for the marital deduction)?

Although the proposed regulations are not as clear as they could be on this subject, it appears that, if S is not the *sole* beneficiary of the trust, then the trust is not entitled to the benefit of s. 401(a)(9)(B)(iv), postponing distributions until P would have reached age 70½. Rather, the trust will be stuck with s. 401(a)(9)(B)(iii), distributions commencing within one year after the date of the P's death over the life expectancy of the oldest trust beneficiary. See Prop. reg. E-5(a)(1), last sentence, and H-2(b), second to last sentence.

If the IRS regards remainder beneficiaries as "beneficiaries" for this purpose, even if they have no rights until the death of the spouse, then it will not be possible to have a trust of which the spouse is the sole beneficiary, unless all principal and income of the trust are to be distributed to her at some point within her life expectancy, or she has the right to withdraw all principal and income from the trust. Such provisions would rarely be included in a trust, since, if those provisions are to be included, the decedent might as well leave the money to the spouse outright.

(But see Chapter 4, "Retirement Benefits and the Non-Citizen Spouse." A QDOT (qualified domestic trust) with these terms might well be established for a *non-citizen* spouse, where the purpose of establishing the trust is purely to protect the marital deduction and provide for collection of the deferred estate tax, and there is not necessarily any intention to restrict the surviving spouse's access to the principal. S should also be regarded as the "sole" beneficiary of an "estate trust," an obscure and rarely-used type of marital trust; estate trusts are discussed in the "Alternative 2" section of Chapter 4.)

It is not clear whether the IRS regards remainder beneficiaries as "beneficiaries" for this purpose. Compare Ltr. Rul. 9322005 (2/24/93) (marital trust to spouse for life, remainder to children; spouse *and children* were regarded as "beneficiaries") with Ltr. Rul. 9442032 (7/27/94), in which P died, leaving his benefits payable to a trust. S was the life income beneficiary of the trust. The principal would pass to P's issue on S's death. S's only right was to income, plus principal if needed for support. The IRS ruled that S was the "designated beneficiary" for purposes of s. 401(a)(9) and, because she was the spouse, distributions could be made under s. 401(a)(9)(B)(iv).

Probate Issues

In some states, "custodial" IRAs and 403(b) accounts are treated as probate assets subject to the requirements applicable to wills, so that the mere filing of a "designation of beneficiary" form, lacking the formalities of a will, is not sufficient to pass the asset to the beneficiary. In Massachusetts, this problem has been overcome by M. G. L. ch. 167D, s. 30, which gives effect to the designation of a beneficiary under IRAs and other retirement plans, if proper under the plan, "notwithstanding any purported testamentary disposition allowed by statute, by operation of law or otherwise to the contrary."

Under Age 59½ -- Excise Tax on Premature Distributions

A client under age 59½ may be interested in starting withdrawals from his retirement plans. The obstacle is the 10% excise tax on premature distributions imposed by s. 72 (t). If the under-age-59½ client wants to take money out of his plans, but does not want to pay the 10% tax, he has limited options:

1.   If he has large medical expenses, he can withdraw money up to the amount of his *deductible* medical

expenses for the year. This option applies only to employer-sponsored retirement plans, not IRAs. S. 72(t)(2)(B).

2.   He can withdraw money from an employer's plan (but not from any "individual retirement plan") after age 55, if he "separates from the service" of the employer. See the "Lump Sum Distributions: The Requirements" section of Chapter 2 for discussion of meaning of this term.

3.   He can begin a program of annual (or more frequent) withdrawals from the plan in substantially equal periodic amounts over his life expectancy, and continue the program for at least five years or at least until age 59½, whichever occurs later. This exception is not available for distributions from 401(a) qualified plans unless there has been a "separation from service."

The liberalized rollover rules introduced by UCA '92, combined with exception no. 3, have produced greatly expanded flexibility for penalty-free pre-age 59½ withdrawal programs. With the help of a professional actuary, an employee can do a partial rollover from a profit sharing plan to an IRA, then set up a program of installment payouts from the IRA in compliance with exception no. 3. A detailed discussion of this useful planning device is beyond the scope of this book.

Planning for Disability

Designating a beneficiary for disability benefits

A popular estate planning treatise, *Loving Trust* by Robert A. Esperti *et al.* (1994) urges the reader to name his revocable living trust as beneficiary of any disability benefits under his retirement plans. Ideally, retirement plan documents would be written so as to permit direct payment of lifetime benefits (disability and retirement) to a revocable living trust. However, such provisions are rarely encountered.

S. 401(a)(13) prohibits "assignment" of qualified retirement plan benefits. Regulations provide that a voluntary, revocable assignment is not an "assignment" for purposes of 401(a)(13). A voluntary revocable assignment would be ideal for transferring lifetime benefits to a revocable trust.

S. 72(p)(1)(B) treats all "assignments" of plan benefits as loans from the plan, apparently taxable as distributions, and neither s. 72(p) nor regulations thereunder suggest an exception for a voluntary revocable assignment of benefits. However, an "assignment" to a revocable living trust should not be treated as an assignment for purposes of s. 72(p) because the participant and his revocable living trust are essentially treated as "one person" for income tax purposes under the grantor trust rules (ss. 671-677).

Power of attorney

The client's power of attorney should at a minimum enable the power holder to receive benefit checks and endorse them. It can go further and give the holder the power to make elections as to the form and timing of benefits (subject to the rights of client's spouse) but this would necessarily involve the attorney in making choices between the client and the beneficiary of death benefits under the plan. Giving the power to designate a beneficiary of plan death benefits gives even greater responsibility to the power holder. See form 8.1 in Appendix B.

Summary of Planning Principles

1.   For a client who wishes to make charitable gifts upon his death, retirement benefits are often the best asset to use to fulfill those gifts.

2.   Despite the tax advantages of funding charitable bequests with retirement benefits, such gifts have some pitfalls and complications, particularly once the client reaches age 70½, or if the benefits flow through a trust, or if part of the benefits will pass to individual beneficiaries, or if the charitable gift is in fulfillment of a lifetime "pledge."

3.   It is prudent to assume for planning purposes that remainder beneficiaries are considered "beneficiaries" of a trust for purposes of the "minimum distribution rules" trust requirements (all "beneficiaries" must be individuals, and use life expectancy of the oldest "beneficiary").

4.   Execute beneficiary designations with the formalities of a will if required by applicable state law; and be sure subsequent wills or codicils do not revoke or contradict the designation.

5.   Consider disposition of the client's benefits in case of disability, and be sure the power of attorney (and "living trust," if any) are properly set up to deal with these benefits.

10

Case Studies

The Ables: When There Is No Other Asset Available to Fund the Credit Shelter Trust
(A Non-Excise Tax Case)

The facts

Allen and Alice Able are both age 66. Both are retired. They are living on Social Security, Allen's pension from Big Corp. and investment income. Their assets are:

Ables	Husband	Wife
House		250,000
Mutual Funds		350,000
Life Insurance	100,000	
IRA	500,000	
Subtotals	600,000	600,000
Total family assets for estate planning purposes: $1.2 million		

Allen's Big Corp. pension is not listed as an asset for estate planning purposes because it ends on the death of the surviving spouse. Therefore it will not be subject to estate taxes and it is not an asset the Ables can pass to their child, Abigail. Right now Allen and Alice do not need to make any withdrawals from the IRA for their living expenses. They would like to preserve the IRA as a nest egg and let it continue to build up as long as possible, with the goal of leaving it to their child.

Allen Able wants to take advantage of the tax saving ideas he has read about in several books on estate planning. He states his goals as follows:

1.   Allen's primary goal is to provide for Alice Able's financial security, support and comfort.

2.   He also wants to take advantage of his federal estate tax $600,000 "exemption" or "credit shelter," so that neither spouse's estate will exceed the $600,000 limit, and the Ables' child will have no estate taxes to pay.

3.   Finally, Allen wants to maximize the income tax deferral potential of his IRA by causing it to be paid out to the Ables' child over her life expectancy.

The bad news for Allen is: your estate plan can achieve any two of your goals, but cannot achieve all three.

Scenario 1: How to maximize income tax deferral and eliminate estate taxes

Allen can best achieve his tax saving goals by naming his daughter, Abigail, directly, as designated beneficiary (DB) of his IRA. That way, when he dies, the benefits will not be subject to estate tax in his estate (because the total passing to the child will be less than the $600,000 credit shelter amount). The benefits are also kept out of Alice's estate because they passed directly to daughter Abigail at Allen's death.

Income tax deferral is maximized for reasons explained in Chapter 1: after Allen's death, the child can withdraw the benefits over her life expectancy, which is longer than Alice's life expectancy since Abigail is 27 years younger than Alice.

This approach will also provide maximum income tax

deferral during Allen's life. When Allen reaches his required beginning date (RBD), if Abigail is named as his DB, Allen can withdraw from the plan over the joint life expectancy (LE) of Abigail and Allen (as limited by the MDIB rule). In contrast, if Allen names wife Alice (or a trust of which she is the oldest beneficiary) as his DB, their joint life expectancy at Allen's RBD will be only 19.8 years, and Allen will be forced to make withdrawals more quickly.

Clearly, naming the child as his DB is the most tax effective course for Allen. Unfortunately, this choice utterly fails to achieve Allen's primary goal -- to provide for Alice.

Scenario 2: How to provide for Alice and achieve some income tax deferral

The best way to achieve the goal of providing for Alice is to name her personally as the DB. If she survives Allen, she can roll the benefits over to an IRA in her own name, then withdraw as much as she wants or needs to every year. She will be required to withdraw something each year from her rollover IRA once she reaches her RBD; assuming she names daughter Abigail as her DB, her minimum required distributions (MRD) will be calculated based on the joint LE of herself and Abigail, as limited by the MDIB rule. When she dies, the remaining balance will be distributed to Abigail over the remainder of the joint LE of Alice and Abigail. Thus the deferral period for much of the benefits will be shorter than if Abigail had been named directly as Allen's DB, but is still very generous.

If Alice dies before Allen and before Allen's RBD, Abigail, the contingent beneficiary, will become Allen's "DB" and the results will be the same as under scenario 1.

What if Allen passes his RBD, having Alice as his DB, and then Alice dies after Allen's RBD but before Allen? Then all possibility of deferring income taxation of these benefits over the LE of daughter Abigail is lost. The payout of the benefits will have to be completed over no longer than the joint LE of Allen and Alice.

Thus, under scenario 2, the family gets the following result:

- Best financial protection for Alice.
- Income tax deferral will not be as favorable as under scenario 1; it will be "not bad" if Alice survives Allen but "very limited" if Alice predeceases Allen after his RBD.
- The estate tax result is terrible. The entire IRA will be included in Alice's estate. Adding this to her existing assets of $600,000 will generate a big estate tax bill.

Scenario 3: How to eliminate estate taxes and still protect Alice

Another approach is to name a credit shelter trust as beneficiary. This would achieve the estate tax goal, since the trust would keep the benefits out of Alice's taxable estate.

Alice can be the life beneficiary of the credit shelter trust, so the retirement benefits will be available for her if she needs them, and the goal of "protecting Alice's financial security" is achieved. However, her financial security is not as well protected as it would be if the benefits were paid to her personally because of the income tax effects of this form of disposition. The negative income tax effects are:

1.   To the extent benefits are paid to the credit shelter trust as "principal," they will be taxed at the trust's income tax rate, which is probably going to be higher than Alice's. See "Income in Respect of a Decedent" section of Chapter 2.

2.   Benefits will have to be distributed, beginning within one year after Allen's death, over Alice's LE only, since she is the oldest beneficiary of the trust. This will produce a much more rapid distribution of the benefits than would be required if the benefits were payable to Alice personally, and she rolled them over to an IRA and began withdrawing over the joint LE of Alice and Abigail (as limited by the MDIB rule).

The shorter deferral period and higher income tax rate will mean less money available for Alice during her life than if benefits were paid to her personally.

Estate tax savings of credit shelter trust

The estate tax savings from funding a credit shelter trust with Allen's IRA will not be as great as they would be if Allen had non-IRD assets with which to fund his credit shelter trust. If we assume that the $500,000 in the IRA will eventually be distributed to the credit shelter trust at an income tax cost of about 40%, or $200,000, the net that is truly being preserved from estate taxes is only $300,000 (the after-tax value of the IRA), which produces estate tax savings of only $100,000 to $150,000. If Allen had a $500,000 "regular" asset with which to fund his credit shelter trust, the estate tax savings would be more like $200,000 to $250,000.

Higher income taxes on benefits paid to trust

The following calculations are based on 1994 federal income tax rates.

After Allen's death, Alice will be in the 31% marginal federal income tax bracket, even if she withdraws $35,000 a year or so from Allen's IRA. The trust will be in the 36% or 39.6% bracket for annual income over $5,500/$7,500.

If the benefits were payable to Alice *personally*, the total income tax on the IRA would be:

31% X 500,000 = $155,000.

The amount ultimately passing to daughter Abigail from the IRA would be:

500,000 gross amount of IRA
-155,000 31% income tax
345,000 net from IRA to Alice
-131,550 estate tax at Alice's death
$213,450 net to child

If the benefits are paid to the credit shelter trust over, say, 17 years, the income tax would be, approximately:

5,500 X 17 X .31 =   28,985
2,000 X 17 X .36 =   12,240
372,500 X .396 =   147,510
                     $188,735

...but there would be no estate tax.

Net to the child: $500,000 minus $188,735 = $311,265

Thus the credit shelter plan is better for the next generation; because of the estate tax savings, the remainder beneficiaries of the credit shelter trust end up with $311,000, versus only $213,450 if the benefits had been paid to Alice during her life. But the credit shelter plan is worse for Alice because the net benefit from the IRA after income taxes, which is what she has to live on, is only $311,000, whereas if the benefits were paid to her personally she would realize $345,000.

How to name credit shelter trust as beneficiary

Based on the above analysis, the Ables decide to go ahead and use Allen's IRA to fund his credit shelter trust. The next question is to how to do this. The credit shelter trust must be named as beneficiary of the IRA in a manner that complies with the proposed regulation trust rules (see Chapter 1) so that Alice, as the oldest beneficiary of the credit shelter trust, will be recognized as a DB. Also, we want the credit shelter trust to receive as much of the IRA as is needed to fully fund the credit shelter amount, without overfunding it.

Although right now Allen's IRA is only $500,000, and thus can be expected to be entirely used to fund the credit shelter trust, it is still growing in value and the Ables are not drawing down any benefits. If it is growing at 8% a year, it will be well over $600,000 by the time Allen reaches age 70½. We want this estate plan to be workable even if his IRA goes over $600,000. To the extent the IRA produces any excess over what is needed to fund the credit shelter trust, we want that paid to Alice individually, so she can roll it over to her IRA, thus getting both the marital deduction and further income tax deferral. We do *not* want the excess to go into a marital deduction trust, with its unfortunate income tax consequences. (See Chapter 3.)

This is not a simple problem that can be readily solved with boilerplate estate planning provisions. What is needed is a funding formula for the credit shelter trust, with a matching custom drafted beneficiary designation, so that the IRA beneficiary designation directs that a fractional portion of the IRA benefits are distributed directly to the credit shelter trust (called the "Family Trust" in the forms in this book). The fractional portion of the IRA to be paid to the Family Trust is whatever is needed to use up the credit shelter amount. The balance of the IRA is paid to the surviving spouse individually. See form 3.1 in Appendix B. Mr. Able could also use form 3.2

or 3.6, which take different approaches to this problem.

Note that the approach used for the Ables will not work for all clients. For example, if the participant's benefits are substantial enough to be subject to the 15% tax on excess accumulations, then using them to fund the credit shelter trust will trigger this tax. See the *Eaton* case study.

Looking ahead to the RBD

Another vital point: if Mr. Able's trust is revocable, this carefully drafted estate plan will not work for its intended purpose after Mr. Able's required beginning date. Solutions for this problem are suggested in Chapter 1.

The Bensons: A Second Marriage: Using Plan Benefits to Fund a Marital Trust at the RBD

The facts

Bob Benson turned 70½ in 1996. By April 1, 1997, he must begin taking out benefits from his IRA. Under the terms of his prenuptial agreement with Betty, she is entitled to sole ownership of the home on Bob's death. Bob wants his life insurance to go to his children upon his death; the IRA he would like to leave in a QTIP trust for Betty, so she will receive all income of it for life, but the principal (minus income taxes) will be retained in trust to pass eventually to his children.

Bensons	Husband	Wife	Joint
Home			500,000
Cash	150,000	150,000	
IRAs	900,000	10,000	
Insurance	150,000		
Stocks & Bonds		200,000	
Subtotals	1,200,000	360,000	500,000
Total family assets for estate planning purposes: $2,060,000			

How does he accomplish this?

Naming a QTIP trust as beneficiary

Bob has specified that he wants Betty to receive the income from the entire IRA. One way to accomplish this is to create one single QTIP trust to be the beneficiary of Bob's IRA. The trust will be a simple QTIP trust, providing all income to Betty for life, with any principal remaining at her death to be distributed to Bob's then living issue.

The trust will contain all required marital deduction provisions, including those which are a safety valve to comply with the IRS's requirement for "QTIPing" retirement plan benefits (see Chapter 3), namely a requirement that, if the trust is the beneficiary of any retirement plan, then, during Betty's life, the trustee must withdraw from the plan, each year, and distribute to Betty, at least all income of the IRA for that particular year. The trustee will also withdraw, and retain in the trust as principal, such additional amounts as may be required by the minimum distribution rules, or as may be determined in the discretion of the trustee. To comply with Rev. Rul. 89-89, the IRA beneficiary designation will *also* contain marital deduction

deduction provisions, namely, the requirement that all income earned by the IRA after Bob's death must be distributed to the trustee of the QTIP trust.

Because the part of Bob's estate going to his children totals less than $600,000, Bob's executor will probably not elect the federal marital deduction for the entire QTIP trust. The executor will need to make only a partial (fractional) QTIP election to eliminate the estate tax on Bob's estate. Some of the QTIP trust will therefore in effect become Bob's "credit shelter trust." Thus, a portion of the assets remaining in the trust at Betty's death will be included in her estate (whatever proportion the QTIP election was made for), and the balance will not be included in her estate, under s. 2044.

Bob uses form 3.5 in Appendix B.

Variation: If Bob wants to maximize income tax deferral

Because not all of the IRA needs to be qualified for the marital deduction, there would be another way to handle this estate plan *if* Bob Benson specified that he wanted to obtain maximum income tax deferral for the IRA income after his death. That way would be: to have a formula in the IRA beneficiary designation, or in the trust which is named as beneficiary of the IRA, so that part of the IRA would be paid to the QTIP trust (as much as was necessary to eliminate the federal estate taxes) and part would be paid to a credit shelter trust (the balance needed to soak up Bob's remaining federal credit shelter amount). See form 3.3 in Appendix B. With a fractional formula making this division, and two separate trusts as beneficiaries of the benefits, the credit shelter trust could get the benefit of some additional income tax deferral during Betty's life, since it would not be required to comply with the marital deduction rule of withdrawing all of the income from its share of the IRA every year.

While this approach might be better tax planning, it is not what Bob wants, since Bob wants Betty to receive all of the IRA income. Thus in this particular case there is no need to complicate the estate plan by having the IRA divided up between two separate trusts on Bob's death, with all the necessary separate accounting that that entails. Credit shelter benefits can still be preserved (if not maximized) by making a fractional QTIP election.

Using a trust beneficiary as "DB"

Bob Benson is now reaching his RBD. Thus, it is extremely important to comply with the trust rules since we want the trust beneficiaries to be his "designated beneficiary." See Chapter 1. If we do not comply with the trust rules, then, when Bob reaches his RBD, he will have to withdraw from his IRA over only his own life expectancy (15.3 or 16 years), and will not be able to use his and Betty's joint life expectancy to measure the payouts. Thus, Bob must make sure that, no later than his RBD, the trust named as beneficiary of the IRA becomes irrevocable (see form 7.1), and does not have any non-individual or non-ascertainable beneficiaries (see forms 7.2 and 7.3), and that a copy of it is given to the IRA provider.

Because Bob wants the benefits paid to a trust and not to Betty individually, Betty will not have the option of a rollover on Bob's death. Thus, once Bob dies, distribution of the IRA will have to be made over the balance of Betty's life expectancy (or over the balance of Bob's and Betty's joint life expectancy if he dies after his RBD). There will be no possibility of extending it over the life expectancies of his children since that possibility would only be obtainable through a spousal rollover (or by naming the children directly as Bob's DB).

Impact of trust income tax rates

Eventually, because of the minimum distribution rules, the QTIP trustee will be required to withdraw some principal from the IRA, not just income. Unlike the IRA *income* (which is paid out to the QTIP trust, and then immediately distributed to Betty), the IRA *principal* will be retained in the QTIP trust and thus taxed at *trust* rates. The trust will be in the 39.6% bracket for its taxable income over $7,650 per year (1995 rates), whereas Betty will probably be in only the 31% bracket. See Chapter 2. The only way to avoid the high trust income tax rates would be to distribute all or most of the "principal" to Betty as soon as it is received by the QTIP trust.

This poses a dilemma for Bob. He doesn't want his survivors to pay unnecessarily high income taxes on the IRA benefits, but he also wants to preserve as much of the principal of the IRA as possible for his children. Because Bob wants to protect the principal for his children, he must accept a higher income tax cost as the price of this protection. Income taxes would probably be lower if he allowed the principal to be distributed to Betty, but then this principal would be lost altogether to his children.

Other solutions are available in other situations. Someone who was leaving his IRA to a QTIP trust only because he did not want his spouse to have control of the entire amount at once (due to fears of the spouse's spending or investing proclivities) might provide that the trust would distribute outright to the spouse each year the *greater* of (1) the income for the year or (2) the minimum required distribution for that year. Another variation would be to permit discretionary principal distributions, and suggest that the trustee distribute enough principal to minimize the combined income taxes paid by the spouse and the trust.

Attorney Cavalho: The Rollover Decision

The facts

Attorney Chester Cavalho started his practice as a sole practitioner in 1955. In 1968 he adopted a Keogh profit sharing plan and contributed to it annually through 1977. His total contribution over the years was $50,000. In 1978, he joined a larger firm, a professional corporation with its own pension and profit sharing plans. The Keogh plan was "frozen." Now, in 1994, he is 65 and wants to retire. His plan balances are:

Keogh	400,000
Corp. Pension	200,000
Corp. PSP	500,000
Total	1,100,000

He has never taken any distribution from any plan. Should he roll everything over to an IRA? Cash in some plans and roll others? Chester figures that, for the next five years, he and his wife probably will be in the 36% marginal income tax bracket (joint filers with taxable income in excess of $140,000) and after that (based on present tax law) they would drop down to the 31% bracket.

Chester is tempted to roll over all his plans to an IRA, to gain continued income tax deferral. On the other hand, the possibility of cashing out one or more of the plans and using "lump sum distribution" (LSD) treatment is also intriguing. See the "Lump Sum Distributions" sections of Chapter 2 to understand the following discussion.

What would be the tax on various LSDs?

First, Chester looks at what his tax would be under various lump sum options. Before any detailed analysis, it appears that he could take a s. 402(d) LSD from any one or two of his plans, or from all three collectively. Because he was born before 1936, he is entitled to use either five or 10 year averaging for any LSD. Which method is more favorable depends on the size of the LSD (see Table in Appendix A).

If he takes the smallest plan (the $200,000 corporate pension plan) as a lump sum distribution, 10 year forward averaging would produce the lowest tax, namely, $35,822 (18% of the distribution). This compares favorably with his normal tax rate of 31% to 36%.

For the next largest plan, the $400,000 Keogh plan, he is entitled to use (in addition to either five or 10 year averaging) the 20% capital gains tax method for a fractional portion of the plan, representing his participation before 1974. The pre-1974 participation fraction (capital gains portion) would depend on the year of the LSD. As of 1994, it would be approximately six (representing the years 1968-1974) divided by 26 (representing the years 1968-1994), times $400,000, or $92,308. 20% of this would be $18,462; add to this the 10 year forward averaging tax on the ordinary income portion ($370,692), which would be approximately $67,752, and he would have a total tax of $86,214, or only 22% of the total.

If he were to cash in the $500,000 profit sharing plan, the tax on that under the five year forward averaging method would be about $133,000 or approximately 27%.

Finally, if he cashed in all three plans in one year he would have a total distribution of $1.1 million. Some of this would be eligible for the 20% capital gains treatment, but the total tax would still be approximately $400,000 or more, which, at a 38% rate, is not at all attractive.

Aggregation issue

Before deciding whether he wants to take a LSD from any of these plans, he would have to resolve the question whether his profit sharing Keogh plan is required to be aggregated with his corporate profit sharing plan. If he cannot find a satisfactory answer to that question from an ERISA lawyer, and does not want to pay for a private letter ruling, he could limit himself to taking a LSD from the pension plan only, where the aggregation problem is not raised, since there is no other pension plan maintained by either employer.

Other benefits of LSD

Cashing out one of the plans using LSD treatment would provide a benefit in addition to a low tax rate on that particular distribution. The distribution (provided it is less than $750,000) would be exempt from the 15% excise tax. See Chapter 5. Right now, Chester's benefits total $1.1 million, which (at current interest rates) is not enough to create a pressing 15% excise tax problem. However, if he does not draw on the plan benefits for a number of additional years, this conclusion could change. Withdrawing one of the plans now would reduce the likelihood of future 15% excise tax problems.

Having said all this, it is not easy to determine whether Chester should cash in a plan now. It would be nice to have money outside the retirement plans available for gifting, or funding a credit shelter trust, or just for emergencies, so if he does not have substantial assets outside of his plans, this should be considered. On the other hand, if he already has substantial assets outside his retirement plans, continued tax-deferred growth inside the plans is also attractive.

If he does decide to cash in one plan and roll over the others, he should not do the rollovers in the same year as the cashout. S. 402(d) treatment, if elected, must be elected for all distributions received in the same year that qualify for it.

Chester should also consult the "Rollover Checklist" in Appendix C before making a final decision.

The Dingells: A Young Family; Life Insurance in the Retirement Plan

The facts

Dingells	Husband	Wife
Home		400,000
Profit Sharing Plan:		
Side Fund	200,000	
Life Insurance	300,000	
Summer House	200,000	
Liquid Investments	200,000	200,000
Subtotals	900,000	600,000
Total family assets for estate planning purposes: $1,500,000		

Dave and Diana Dingell are in their mid-40s. They want a basic credit shelter/marital trust tax saving estate plan. Their children are too young to manage money. Who should be named as beneficiary of Dave's profit sharing benefits?

The solution

A "pure vanilla" situation could be defined this way: both spouses have at least $600,000 of assets, not counting retirement benefits, which can be used to fund the credit shelter trust; nothing dictates that the marital deduction share must go into a QTIP; the spouses do not want to leave assets to their children until both spouses are deceased; and all children are adults and capable of handling money and are to share the estate equally. In a pure vanilla situation, you can simply name the surviving spouse as beneficiary of all retirement benefits, with the children (or their issue) as contingent beneficiary. See form 1.1 in Appendix B.

The Dingells are vanilla with a twist. Dave Dingell's profit sharing plan contains a $300,000 life insurance policy as well as an investment "side fund." The pure death benefit portion of life insurance is not subject to income taxes in the hands of the beneficiary. See Chapter 6. That makes it different from all other retirement benefits: it is not IRD (see Chapter 2), so there is no need to try to defer income taxes on that money. It is not eligible for a spousal rollover; non-taxable distributions cannot be rolled over.

Dave needs the insurance in his profit sharing plan to fund his credit shelter trust, but he wants the rest of the profit sharing plan (the part that is subject to income tax) to be paid to his wife so that she can roll it over to her own IRA and defer the income tax. Accordingly, we have to split the benefit at Dave's death, between the part that is partly or wholly free of income tax (the life insurance, which is going to be used to fund the credit shelter trust), and everything else, which is going to be paid to Diana. Form 3.8 or 3.9 in Appendix B could be used to accomplish this.

Another important factor in the Dingells' situation is that their children are too young to manage money. Thus, if the Dingells both die, the money must be left in trust, rather than outright to the children. The Dingells want to be sure the trustee can withdraw the benefits over the life expectancy of the children if the plan permits it. Thus, Dave needs to name a trust for the children as his contingent beneficiary, and comply with the minimum distribution "trust rules" (see Chapter 1).

The Eatons: Pension Millionaires With Few Other Assets

The facts

Eatons	Husband	Wife
Home	350,000	
IRAs		3,000,000
Liquid investments		250,000
Subtotals	350,000	3,250,000
Total family assets for estate planning purposes: $3,600,000.		

Ed and Emily Eaton are in their mid-60s and are retired. Emily's substantial IRA is a rollover from her self-directed account in her former employer's plan, which was generously funded by the employer and invested very successfully by Emily. Each year, the Eatons have been withdrawing $80,000 from the IRA. They pay income taxes on this amount, and spend the rest. The plan is growing faster than they are withdrawing it. None of the IRA is "grandfathered" from the 15% excise tax. (See Chapter 5.)

Their estate planning goals are: to have the entire estate benefit the surviving spouse for life; defer all estate taxes until the second death; and take advantage of both spouses' $600,000 federal estate tax "exemptions" ("credit shelter amount") to reduce estate taxes for their children.

Their concerns:

(a)   Should Emily withdraw at least $150,000 a year?

More than $150,000 a year?

(b)   Who should be named as beneficiary of the IRA? Should some of these benefits be used at death to fund a credit shelter trust?

Emily is $350,000 short of having $600,000 worth of non-IRA assets in her own name. This means she must either withdraw money from the IRA to make sure she is up to the credit shelter amount; or make part of her IRA payable to the credit shelter trust at her death, to bring it up to $600,000; or give up on having a fully funded credit shelter trust.

To understand the following discussion, first read Chapter 5.

Triggering 15% "excess accumulations" tax at Emily's death

The main drawback of using the IRA to fund Emily's credit shelter trust is that it will make Emily's estate subject to the 15% tax on the "excess plan accumulations." If Emily were to die in the immediate future at age 63, the "threshold amount" for this excise tax would be (based on an IRS interest rate of 6.0% and an annual annuity of $150,000) $1,483,560. The excess over this amount, approximately $1,500,000, would be subject to the 15% excise tax. The resulting tax of $225,000 would be payable at Emily's death.

This tax can be deferred until Ed's death -- but *only* if 100% of the benefits are made payable to him personally. Having the benefits paid to a trust for his benefit would not qualify. Thus if any part of the IRA (while it is still in the IRA) is used to fund Emily's credit shelter trust at her death, the result would be an excise tax of $225,000 on Emily's death that otherwise could have been deferred until Ed's death.

This excise tax is deductible for purposes of the

"regular" estate tax. However, the "benefits" of that tax deduction are not realized until the surviving spouse's death, regardless of when the excise tax is paid, because the estate taxes are not paid until then.

To raise the money to pay this tax at Emily's death, Ed would have to liquidate other assets or cash in some of the IRA. Cashing in some of the IRA would generate income taxes. He would have to take out about $375,000 from the IRA in order to get enough money to pay the income tax on the withdrawal itself as well as the $225,000 excise tax.

Advantage of paying 15% excise tax at Emily's death

If Emily makes her entire IRA payable to Ed as beneficiary, he can make a 4980A(d)(5) election and not pay any 15% excise tax on her death. Furthermore, if he rolls over the benefits to his own IRA, he will not have to pay any income taxes at her death (other than on whatever he withdraws from the IRA to live on). He will also not have to pay any federal estate taxes on her death because of the unlimited marital deduction.

While this seems ideal (payment of zero taxes at the first spouse's death), it does have a downside: from then on, Ed will continue to be forever subject to the $150,000 per year limit on withdrawals from the IRA (just as Emily is now) (although this number will be indexed for inflation).

Furthermore, at Ed's subsequent death, the 15% excise tax will be due on whatever is left in the plan (in excess of his "threshold amount"). The 15% excise tax at the death of Ed could be substantially higher than the $225,000 tax that would be payable if the tax were paid at Emily's death if she died now. There are two reasons for this: first, if Ed is withdrawing only the "threshold amount" each year (the legal limit without paying an excise tax), he may well not be withdrawing money as fast as the plan is growing. This will cause the plan to keep growing internally so that the amount in there at his death will be substantially more than what is in there at Emily's death.

Second, the excise tax at death is based on the excess of the plan balance over a certain "threshold amount." The threshold is, the value of a hypothetical annuity equal to the annual "threshold" limit as of the date of death, for a person the age of the decedent, if purchased immediately before his death. The older the individual is at death, the lower is the value of this hypothetical annuity, because the life expectancy is shorter. As mentioned above, the at-death threshold amount for a person age 63 (assuming a 6% "s. 7520 rate") is $1,483,560, so that only amounts over $1,483,560 are subject to the 15% excise tax. For a person age 80, the threshold amount drops to $853,785.

In other words, if Emily died at age 63, leaving 100% of the IRA to Ed, Ed would have the option of paying the 15% excise tax on the difference between $3 million and Emily's "threshold amount" (approximately $1.5 million) resulting in a $225,000 tax. Paying the tax at that point would get it over with once and for all. His subsequent withdrawals from the plan would be free of the 15% excise tax regardless of size.

If he elects *not* to pay the tax on Emily's death, and then dies at age 80, the threshold amount at his death will be only $853,785. Even if the plan balance has not grown at all, the 15% excise tax would be applied to an "excess" accumulation of $2.1 million, resulting in a tax of $322,000. The tax would be even higher if the plan has grown above $3 million.

Other drawbacks of using IRA to fund credit shelter trust

If the entire IRA is payable to Ed personally, then he can set it up so that, at his death, payments will come out over the life expectancy of the children. In other words, although some part of it would have to be withdrawn shortly after the death of the surviving spouse to pay estate taxes, the balance could be left in the IRA, being paid out gradually over the life expectancy of the oldest child. If part of Emily's IRA is made payable to the credit shelter trust, on the other hand, that part must be paid out over *Ed's* life expectancy only, assuming he is the oldest beneficiary of the trust. This part could not be "flipped" into the mode of a longer payout over the life expectancy of the children.

Other benefits of using IRA to fund credit shelter trust

By making $350,000 of the IRA payable to the credit shelter trust (which, when added to $250,000 of other assets in Emily's name, will make up her $600,000 credit shelter trust), Emily will achieve an estate tax savings for the children on the subsequent death of Ed. The amount of estate taxes saved will be approximately as follows: $350,000 IRA payable to the credit shelter trust, minus income taxes (assumed rate 40%) of $140,000, leaves $210,000 which is kept out of Ed's estate. This saves approximately $100,000 of estate taxes for the children. This estate tax savings must be weighed against the acceleration of the 15% excise tax and some acceleration of income taxes.

Emily may decide to make the IRA payable to Ed solely, giving him the option to keep it (and defer the 15% tax) or to disclaim part of it, so it would go directly to the children or to a credit shelter trust as contingent beneficiary, to save estate tax. See form 3.6, Appendix B. This puts a certain amount of pressure on Ed at Emily's death to make a decision within nine months following her death whether to disclaim some of the benefits. See Chapter 8.

Should Emily withdraw sufficient money now to fund her credit shelter trust?

Another alternative is for Emily to withdraw (and pay income tax on) substantial amounts from the plan now, so she will have sufficient assets outside of her IRA to fund a credit shelter trust. The advantage of this would be that she could use her federal estate tax exemption of $600,000 without making IRA benefits payable to the credit shelter trust, and therefore without forcing an acceleration of the 15% excise tax.

The drawback of this proposal, of course, is paying the income taxes on any such withdrawals (and possibly excise taxes as well). Emily needs $350,000 to fully fund a credit shelter trust. In order to get $350,000 of cash after taxes, she would have to withdraw approximately $580,000 from the IRA, assuming that she is in the 40% income tax bracket. Even if the withdrawal could be staged over a couple of years, so that she stayed within the 36% bracket, she would still have to withdraw $547,000 from the plan in order to have $350,000 left after taxes.

She would also have to pay excise taxes of 15% on everything over $150,000 withdrawn in one year. If Emily had made the grandfather election (see Chapter 5) for the August 1986 value of the IRA ($1.8 million), then she could make the $580,000 withdrawal and just pay the income taxes. She could liquidate 20% of the IRA in order to generate $350,000 after taxes which would be her "estate" to fund the credit shelter trust (along with the other $250,000 she already has).

If the grandfather election had been made in a case like this, the individual would have more options. She could take out larger-than-$150,000 amounts for a few years without paying excise taxes. Or, she could take out a large lump sum without paying excise taxes. Not many people choose to exercise the large lump sum option; even people who have a large grandfather balance are not usually willing to pay the substantial *income* taxes involved in order to draw their grandfather balance out of the plan. This reluctance is usually supported by actuarial projections that show that the economic value of the continued income tax deferral outweighs the drawback of possibly increased 15% excise taxes in the future. See the *Sherman and Herman Levine* case study.

Should Emily withdraw $150,000 a year?

The Eatons' IRA constitutes a vastly disproportionate share of the estate. The government allows them to take out up to $150,000 a year without paying the 15% excise tax. Taking out this much would not put them into the highest income tax bracket. Even if they take out as much as $150,000 a year, the account is still growing faster than they are depleting it. In other words, the "penalty" of taking out the full permitted threshold is not very great.

By taking out the "threshold" amount each year, they are achieving the advantage of relatively increasing the non-IRA portion of their balance sheet. While IRAs are wonderful and tax deferral is wonderful, there are some major advantages to having *non*-IRA assets also, such as:

    (a)   Increased funds available for use in case of any unforeseen needs. If they have a need for a lump sum for some reason (buying a house, or an extraordinary medical expense), and all of their money is tied up in the IRA, then withdrawing the needed funds all at once from the IRA may trigger higher income taxes and/or subject them to 15% excise taxes. The larger the emergency fund outside the IRA the better.

    (b)   They would have cash available to make $10,000

per year "annual exclusion" gifts to their children. This is the best way available to reduce future estate taxes.

(c)   They would have more assets available to fund a credit shelter trust as previously discussed.

(d)   They would have a smaller portion   of their assets held hostage to the government's ever-changing rules and regulations on retirement plans.

Thus, Emily should consider taking out the "threshold amount" each year even if the Eatons don't need it to live on. If they take it out as early in the year as possible the income it generates will help increase the non-IRA side of their balance sheet.

Should the contingent beneficiary be the children or the trust?

If Ed predeceases Emily, it might be best to have the three children named as beneficiaries, rather than Emily's revocable trust. If the three children are named as contingent beneficiaries, they can withdraw the IRA over the life expectancy of the oldest child if Emily dies before her RBD. If something were to happen to Ed and Emily in the immediate future, this life expectancy period would be over 50 years.

The children would have to withdraw some money from the IRA in order to pay the estate taxes on Emily's estate. However, even if they withdrew 100% of the estate tax money from the IRA, there should still be $1.1 million left in the IRA. This could then be withdrawn by the children over 50 years.

If the children are unhappy with a joint commingled investment fund, they can probably divide up the IRA into separate ones, one for each child; this has been permitted by the IRS in a letter ruling. Withdrawals may still have to come out of each account over the life expectancy of the oldest child, but each child could pursue his own investment objectives. Also, one child could take out more than his required minimum if he wanted to, without altering the other children's distribution schemes.

If the benefits are payable to a trust, the same result could be achieved, *i.e.*, the payments could come out over the life expectancy of the oldest child. However, the IRS imposes elaborate requirements when retirement benefits are paid to a trust. See Chapter 1. Slipping up on these requirements means loss of the option of spreading out the payout over the life expectancy of the beneficiary. Since the Eatons' estate plan calls for the estate to be distributed to the children outright anyway, there is no need to place a trust between the IRA and the children.

If a child predeceases Ed and Emily, the Eatons would want the children of the deceased child to take his share. Emily can specify that any payments going to a grandchild under the age of 21 would be paid to a custodian under the Uniform Transfers to Minors Act for that grandchild. In the unlikely and tragic event that one of the Eatons' children predeceases them, the situation can be reevaluated at that time. If all the children survive Ed and Emily, then each child can arrange (in the event such child dies before complete distribution of his share) for his share of the IRA to go to a trust for his children, if the IRA provider permits this.

Forms 1.1, 1.2 and 2.2 in Appendix B illustrate the suggestions in the two preceding paragraphs. Note, however, that some IRA providers balk at allowing a beneficiary to name a "successor beneficiary" for his share of the benefits. If a very long payout period, with numerous beneficiaries and potential contingent beneficiaries, is contemplated, a trust may be the best choice to receive and pass out the benefits.

The Fallons: Pension Millionaires with Lots of Other Assets; Planning after the RBD (Married Couple); Generation Skipping; Naming Multiple Beneficiaries

The facts

In addition to income generated by their balance sheet assets, Fred Fallon receives several life annuities (nonqualified) from his former employers, totalling $180,000 per year, and Felicia Fallon receives income for life from a $3 million trust established by her grandmother.

Fallons	Husband	Wife	Joint
Home			1,200,000
Tangibles			300,000
IRA	2,300,000		
Liquid Investments	1,000,000	1,000,000	
Subtotals	3,300,000	1,000,000	1,500,000
Total family assets for estate planning purposes: $5,800,000			

Their children are already well provided for through their own earnings, prior gifts and family trusts. The Fallons would like to steer the IRA to a long term trust for their grandchildren.

Fred is age 72, past his "required beginning date" (RBD); and is taking distributions from his IRA in installments over the joint life expectancy of himself and Felicia, who is age 69, with both life expectancies recalculated annually.

It's too late to change Fred's "DB"

Because Fred is past his RBD, it is too late to change to a new "designated beneficiary" (DB) for his IRA with a longer life expectancy. To be more precise, Fred can change the beneficiary of his IRA, that is to say he can change the name of the person or persons who will receive the IRA balance on his death, and could name his grandchildren instead of Felicia; but making that change at this point, after his "RBD," would not be effective to lengthen the payout period for distributions either during his life or after his death. See Chapter 1.

On Fred's RBD, his DB was Felicia (and still is). Thus, the "slowest" he can withdraw benefits from his IRA is over the joint life expectancy of himself and Felicia.

Recalculation of life expectancy

Another decision which becomes irrevocable on the RBD is the decision whether to recalculate the LE of the participant and/or spouse annually. The IRS, in its proposed regulations, takes the position that any election made becomes irrevocable as of the first payment. See Chapter 1.

Recalculation is, in one sense, desirable in that it stretches out the distribution of benefits from the IRA if the client lives beyond his "life expectancy." However, there is a downside to recalculation. As each spouse dies, then his or her life expectancy becomes zero in the year following death. If Fred and Felicia both die, then the entire $2.3 million IRA will have to be cashed in by the end of the calendar year following their deaths.

There is only one escape hatch: If Fred dies first, Felicia can roll over the IRA to her own IRA (or elect to treat Fred's IRA as her own) and start a whole new payout period based on the LE of herself and a new DB. See Chapter 3. Thus, this rollover (or election) by Felicia at Fred's death is crucial to obtaining a long term payout.

How do we assure Felicia "rolls over" Fred's IRA?

Felicia is now designated as Fred's beneficiary. This is as it should be. If Fred dies before Felicia, all of the benefits are paid to her. She then rolls them over to her own IRA.

However, it is important that she do this as soon as possible after Fred's death. If they die simultaneously, or if Felicia dies shortly after Fred but before completing the rollover, her executor probably cannot do the rollover for her (see Chapter 3). Is there any way to assure that the payout period desired on Felicia's death is attainable, even if Felicia dies simultaneously with or shortly after Fred? The only hope for accomplishing this would be for Fred's IRA to be treated as *Felicia's own* IRA *immediately* upon the death of Fred, with a beneficiary designation by Felicia, naming the children or grandchildren, that would immediately kick in in that case.

In order to have the best shot at getting this treatment the Fallons could take the following steps:

(1)   Name Felicia as beneficiary (this is already the case); and include a provision that in case of simultaneous death she is presumed to survive Fred.

(2)   Include a provision that if Felicia survives Fred, or if she is deemed to survive Fred, she elects to treat the IRA as her own IRA, names the children or grandchildren as her DB, and elects to have benefits distributed according to the result that would be desired in that case (discussed below).

(3)   Finally, have this beneficiary designation

co-signed by Felicia *now* (even though Fred is still living).

There is no guarantee whatsoever that the IRS will recognize Felicia's election to treat Fred's IRA as her own IRA if she makes this election before Fred has even died. Accordingly, it is still vital, if Fred predeceases, for Felicia to actually do the rollover as soon as possible after Fred's death. But if she doesn't get around to it, having her sign this "pre-death election" may possibly succeed. It is worth trying. See Form 4.1 in Appendix B.

Once Felicia survives Fred, what beneficiary designation is desirable for Felicia's (formerly Fred's) IRA?

After Fred's demise, and once Felicia has transferred the IRA into her own IRA, the clients would like the IRA, if possible, to be paid out at Felicia's demise to a trust for their grandchildren. The trust would be able to withdraw the money from the IRA over the life expectancy of the oldest grandchild, which should be in excess of 60 years.

The problem is the limit on what can be left to grandchildren, under the generation skipping transfer ("GST") tax. Each individual can leave up to $1 million in the form of a GST free of this tax; but amounts over that would be subject to the GST tax. The GST tax is equal to the highest estate tax rate, currently 55%.

Because the Fallons do not wish to incur GST tax, they decide upon the following disposition of the IRA on Felicia's demise: $1 million to a long-term generation skipping trust for the grandchildren, designed to take advantage of Felicia's $1 million GST exemption and to defer distributions from the IRA over the grandchildrens' long life expectancy; and the balance to the Fallons' children.

However, there are further complications:

Need to divide the IRA before Fred's death

When more than one person is named as beneficiary of a retirement benefit, the life expectancy of the oldest individual in the group will be treated as the measuring life. See Chapter 1. Thus, for example, if Felicia had an IRA, and she named a grandchildren's trust as partial beneficiary and the children as partial beneficiary, the *children* are the oldest members of the entire group. The oldest child's life expectancy would have to be used as the measuring period for all payouts, *even the payouts to the grandchildren's trust*. Thus, if the Fallons want the grandchildren to receive their share (or the grandchildren's trust to receive its share) over the life expectancy of the *grandchildren*, Felicia must make the grandchildren (or their trust) the sole beneficiary of her rollover IRA.

[There is an exception to this rule, under the proposed regulations, if the IRA has "separate accounts" maintained within it. See Chapter 1. The author has never seen this actually implemented; if there are to be "separate accounts" within one IRA, with different assets in each and different accountings for each, the client might as well have two IRAs. Many IRA custodians will not be able to handle it any other way.]

So in order for the desired distribution of Felicia's rollover IRA to be attained at Felicia's demise, of $1 million to the grandchildren's trust and the rest to the children, the IRA would have to be divided up into two separate IRAs, one of approximately $1 million and the other with all of the rest of the money. To increase the likelihood that this occurs even if Felicia dies simultaneously with Fred, the division into two separate IRAs would have to occur before *Fred's* death.

Accordingly, the Fallons take the following steps:

(a)   Fred's IRA would be divided into two totally separate IRAs now. One account would contain approximately $1 million. The other would contain all the rest of the money.

(b)   Felicia would be designated as the beneficiary on each of these new IRAs. Both IRAs would contain the elaborate provisions described above whereby, in case of simultaneous death, Felicia is deemed to survive Fred, and she elects to treat the IRA as her own. See form 4.1 in Appendix B.

(c)   Then, on the $1 million earmarked "generation skipping" IRA, the beneficiary designation would say that, if Felicia survives Fred, or is deemed to survive him, the beneficiary of the IRA would be, up to the first $1 million, the "Fallon Grandchildren's Trust" with any excess over $1 million being distributed to the grandchildren outright; or else 100% to the "Fallon Grandchildren's Trust."

(d)   On the "children's" IRA, the children would be named as Felicia's DBs.

Beneficiary designation for the "grandchildren" IRA

As noted above, the plan is to set up a separate $1 million IRA which, if Felicia survives Fred, would be funneled into a trust for the grandchildren. It is anticipated that Felicia's $1 million GST exemption would be allocated to this trust. (See discussion below about whether this is the best use of the GST exemption.)

But since Fred's IRA is still growing with investment income, and going up and down as Fred takes out required minimum distributions each year, what happens if the IRA is *more* than $1 million at the relevant time (Felicia's death)? The answer is, the excess over $1 million should *also* be paid to the grandchildren's trust but with the trust being required to keep such excess segregated from the first $1 million; or alternatively, and more simply, the excess should simply be distributed outright to the grandchildren. That excess over $1 million will be subject to GST tax but there is no avoiding that. Here is why.

If some beneficiary *other* than the grandchildren (or their trust) is named as the beneficiary of the excess over $1 million, the Fallons would be right back where they started, having multiple beneficiaries for that IRA. If the "excess" beneficiaries have a shorter life expectancy than the grandchildren, the *entire IRA* would be subject to minimum distribution rules based on the life expectancy of some person older than the grandchildren.

Is it desirable to use the $1 million GST exemption on retirement benefits?

There are mixed views among estate planners on this subject.

One school of thought focuses on the fact that retirement plan benefits are subject to income taxes. Therefore, when the client leaves the grandchildren $1 million of retirement benefits, the beneficiaries will realize only $600,000 to $700,000, ultimately, from this asset, not the full $1 million. Leaving them some other asset worth $1 million, on which the client had already paid the income taxes, would make better use of the GST exemption.

The other school of thought holds that retirement benefits are the *best* assets to leave to grandchildren, because of the tremendous value that can be achieved by tax-deferred investing over the grandchildren's long life expectancy.

What if Felicia predeceases Fred?

If Felicia predeceases Fred, the planner faces a different problem. Because both spouses' life expectancies are being recalculated annually, the minimum distributions increase substantially after Felicia's death (because they will then be based on Fred's life alone, not joint lives); and on Fred's ultimate demise 100% of the account would have to be paid out to the beneficiaries within a year after his death.

In this situation, the Fallons agree that a charitable remainder trust for the life benefit of their children is the most desirable beneficiary. The benefits would have to be distributed within a year after Fred's death; however, they can be distributed to the charitable remainder trust without any income tax, because a charitable remainder trust is tax-exempt. See Chapter 9. The children would receive a life income from the *entire* IRA, undepleted by income taxes (although the 15% excise tax would have to be paid) (and of course the children would pay income tax on the income distributions to them from the CRUT). See Chapters 2 and 9.

The Gregorios: A Childless Couple

The facts

Ginny Gregorio is age 59. George is age 69 and considering retiring. They have no children. While there are several nieces, nephews, friends and charities they would like to benefit, their primary estate planning concern is the financial security of the surviving spouse.

They want to know the best way to dispose of George's IRA at his death for maximum benefit to Ginny. The options they are comparing:

(a)   Name Ginny as sole beneficiary.

(b)   Name a charitable remainder unitrust as beneficiary with Ginny as life beneficiary of the CRUT.

Gregorios	Husband	Wife	Joint
Home - no mortgage			400,000
IRA	1,000,000		
Summer Home		200,000	
Liquid Investments	200,000	200,000	
Subtotals	1,200,000	400,000	400,000
Total family assets for estate planning purposes: $2,000,000			

Naming a charitable remainder trust as beneficiary

The Gregorios' ideal disposition of the IRA would be, if George dies first, for Ginny to live on the income of the IRA for her entire life. The obstacle to that result is the minimum distribution rules (see Chapter 1). Under the minimum distribution rules, at some point (in her 80s) Ginny would have to start withdrawing principal from the IRA. These principal withdrawals would be subject to income tax, and thereafter the principal fund available to generate income for Ginny would be diminished.

Probably the Gregorios will have the IRA made payable to Ginny solely, on the theory that she can protect herself from minimum distribution rule requirements by withdrawing less than all of the income in the early years. The principal will then build up over the years, so that by the time she starts being forced to take out larger distributions in her 80s, the fund will be large enough so that she can annuitize it without any loss of income. Furthermore, they plan to have her elect to recalculate her life expectancy so that the IRA will last for her entire lifetime (or at least until she is 110).

If she can live on the minimum distributions in the early years (which would be less than all of the income), this might work to produce a steady after-tax income for her entire lifetime. She probably would not have 15% excise taxes to worry about, because there would probably be little or no excise tax due at George's death. She could pay whatever small excise tax was due at George's death and thereafter be forever free of the $150,000 a year limit. See Chapter 5.

Another advantage of naming her as the sole beneficiary is that she would have unlimited access to the principal of the IRA if she needed it for any reason. Of course, taking out the principal would generate additional income taxes for her and cause more rapid depletion of the principal, which would jeopardize her future financial security.

The alternative of a charitable remainder unitrust (CRUT) may be attractive for a childless couple. George could make the IRA payable to a CRUT of which Ginny was the sole life beneficiary. There are a number of ways to structure the payout from a CRUT. Two of these are mentioned in the *Widow Heinrich* case study, which are ways designed to achieve the objectives in that particular case. A third approach, which might be attractive to the Gregorios, would be to set the payout rate much higher than the anticipated income, but include a "net income limitation" in the CRUT.

For example, George could provide that the CRUT would pay out to Ginny every year, for her entire lifetime, 26% of the value of the trust at the beginning of the taxable year, or the net income of the trust for that taxable year, whichever was less. Barring runaway inflation, this formula would effectively mean that Ginny would receive all of the income of the $1 million IRA for her lifetime but no principal.

This payout formula would reduce the estate tax

charitable deduction in George's estate to just about zero for the CRUT; but we do not care about that because *Ginny's* entire interest in the CRUT qualifies for the marital deduction under s. 2056(b)(8) because she is the sole life beneficiary. Thus, there will be no estate tax on this asset at George's death because the income interest qualifies for the marital deduction and the remainder interest qualifies for the charitable deduction.

The advantage of naming a charitable remainder trust would be that Ginny would have the life income of this fund, and the principal would never be diminished by income taxes. She could be sole trustee of the CRUT, and have the right to change the charitable remainder beneficiary, so there would be a great deal of control. Obviously, the drawback is that she would have no access to the principal, regardless of the emergency.

This option is not attractive, usually, to couples with children, since the principal is taken away entirely from the family. If George and Ginny had children, theoretically George could name a charitable remainder trust with Ginny and then his children as consecutive life beneficiaries. However this does not really work very well, because, if the spouse is not the *sole* noncharitable beneficiary, the spouse's interest ceases to be eligible for the marital deduction. Thus George's estate would have to pay estate taxes on the value of the spouse's and the children's interests.

If the Gregorios cannot make up their minds which course of action is best, another possibility is to split the IRA, making part of it payable to Ginny outright and part payable to a CRUT. Ginny could roll over the part of the IRA that is payable to her to her own IRA (see Chapter 3). This way Ginny would have principal available for an emergency from the rollover IRA, but also the life income from a trust that would never be subject to income tax on its principal, and whose principal could not be reached by her creditors.

Another alternative: George could make the entire benefit payable to Ginny but "disclaimable" to a CRUT, so Ginny could decide which course was best at George's death, and how much the CRUT should receive. The Gregorios will probably choose this alternative once George reaches his RBD, so that he can use the joint life expectancy of himself and Ginny to measure payouts during his life. See Chapter 9.

The Widow Heinrich: Planning after the RBD

The facts

Helga Heinrich is a widow, age 75. Her assets are:

IRA	400,000
House	300,000
Cash	100,000
Total	$800,000

Mrs. Heinrich is withdrawing benefits over her life expectancy recalculated annually. She named her revocable trust as beneficiary of her IRA. The trust was named as her beneficiary on her RBD.

She thought that on her death her two adult children, Heidi and Hans, could withdraw their shares of the IRA, through the revocable trust, over their life expectancy. She was shocked to find out, from an article in the New York Times, that they would not be able to do this. They would be required to withdraw the entire IRA within one year after her death!

Application of minimum distribution rules

The first issue is whether Mrs. Heinrich had a "DB" as of her RBD. Under the IRS's proposed regulations (see Chapter 1) she did not; her beneficiary was a *revocable* trust. In order to be able to "look though" a trust and treat the trust beneficiaries as her "DB," she would have had to use an *irrevocable* trust, according to the proposed regulations.

This means that Helga had "no DB" on her RBD, and payments must come out over her life expectancy. Her RBD is past, so it is too late to add a DB at this point and begin to use the combined life expectancy of Helga and the DB. Furthermore, since she elected to recalculate her life expectancy annually, and that election was irrevocable, all payments will have to come out no later than the end of the calendar year following the year of her death.

To emphasize: Because she had no DB on her RBD, and because she made the irrevocable election to have her life expectancy recalculated annually, *all benefits* must come out no later than the calendar year after her death, and there is no way to change this result at this point. Her beneficiaries will not even get the benefit of the "five year rule," let alone the use of their life expectancy as a measuring payout period.

Ways to soften the blow

If Helga should pass away early in the calendar year, Hans and Heidi could spread the distributions out over two years: the year in which death occurred, and the following year. However, if Helga dies very late in the year, there might not be enough time in that year for Hans and Heidi to pull some money out of the plan and thus they might be stuck with one balloon payment in the year following the year of death. A distribution of $200,000 to each of them would put them both into the highest tax bracket so that a substantial portion of the money would be taxed at 39.6%. There would be some estate tax deduction available as an offset (see "Income in Respect of a Decedent," Chapter 2), but this is really not much consolation.

The only way to soften the blow would be to make the benefits payable to a charitable remainder unitrust for Hans's and Heidi's joint lives, and the life of the survivor. The CRUT could be structured in one of two ways.

One way would be to view the CRUT as a way to eliminate income taxes on the benefit, and simply enable Hans and Heidi to have a life income based on the entire amount of the IRA. Under this approach, Mrs. Heinrich would make the IRA payable to a CRUT which provided a payout rate to Hans and Heidi designed to approximate the anticipated income of the trust, such as 6, 7, or 8%. This way they would have a steady income from the trust for life, or possibly an income that would gradually increase with inflation, if the CRUT's investments grew in value faster than the payout rate.

The other approach would be to use the CRUT as a method of *deferring* income taxes on the benefit rather than *eliminating* them. Under this approach, Mrs. Heinrich would set the unitrust payout rate substantially higher than the anticipated income of the trust. For example, she might set it at 15%. With the payout rate exceeding the income actually being earned by the trust, the principal of the trust would gradually decline. As the principal was distributed out gradually over the years to the children, it would all be subject to income tax to them based on the unique accounting rules applicable to CRUTs (see s. 664 *et seq.*). However, at least the tax would be spread out over a number of years and not all paid at once.

Dr. Vincent Valdez: Whether to Stop Funding a Large Retirement Plan

The facts

Vincent Valdez is a 55 year-old widowed doctor. Highly allergic to both taxes and malpractice claims, he has stashed money in his retirement plans to the maximum extent allowed by law. The combined balance of his pension and profit sharing plans is now $1.3 million. Vincent's current marginal income tax bracket for earned income is 43.6% (39.6% federal income tax (FIT); plus 2.9% Medicare tax, half of which is deductible, so the effective rate of the Medicare tax is 2.3258%; plus 2.8% state income tax (SIT), deductible for FIT purposes, so the effective SIT rate is 1.6912%.

He has substantial other assets, and so does not need any money from his retirement plans to fund living expenses. He is in the 55% estate tax bracket.

Upon retirement at age 70, he plans to move to Florida. In retirement, his income tax bracket will be only the 36% FIT rate, with no SIT or Medicare tax. Is it tax-effective for Vincent to continue contributing $30,000 per year to his retirement plan? Obviously, by making further contributions, he is increasing his future 15% excise tax problem. The alternative is to pay the $30,000 to himself as additional taxable salary.

Review of alternative scenarios

The answer depends on *what Vincent would do with the money* if it is paid to him as additional salary rather than being contributed to the pension plan. If we assume Vincent lives to his normal life expectancy of age 85, then investing these dollars on a tax-deferred basis *inside* the pension plan produces a better result for Vincent and his family than non-tax-deferred investing *outside* the pension plan. The following discussion assumes an 8% pre-tax return on all investments (both inside and outside the plan), 3% per year COLAs in the 15% excise tax "threshold," and an 8.6% "s. 7520 rate" (see Chapter 5).

Scenario A: If Vincent keeps contributing to the plan for the next 15 years, withdraws only the minimum required distribution amount beginning at age 70½, and reinvests all distributions, then, after his death in 2025, if the family cashes out the plan at that time, the family will have, net of all income, estate and excise taxes, $3,434,670...despite paying over $866,000 of excise taxes.

Scenario B: In contrast, if he doesn't contribute to the plan, but pays himself the $30,000 as taxable salary, he will be left with $16,920 a year after-tax to invest. If he invests $16,920 per year for 15 years in 8% bonds, his after-tax yield is 4.72% in his pre-retirement years and 4.83% thereafter. If he accumulates this after-tax yield, then, after his death in 2025, the family will net $3,208,219. The 15% excise tax paid by the family will be less than under scenario no. 1: only $625,342 instead of $866,000....but the net to the family is also less. $226,451 less to be exact.

Scenario C: What if Vincent takes the $30,000 as salary and invests the after-tax proceeds ($16,920) in a purely capital gain asset (growth not taxed currently, stepped up basis at death) instead of bonds? The family is then better off than under either scenario A or scenario B...they net $3,537,600. However, this result is due entirely to the favorable income tax treatment of unrealized capital gain and has nothing to do with excise taxes.

Scenario D: Another way Vincent's family can do much better than having the money contributed to a retirement plan is: *if*

Vincent will use the after-tax salary payments to fund annual exclusion gifts to his children, grandchildren, etc; and *if* there is no other asset available for this purpose, so that if the money is contributed to the retirement plan there will be no annual exclusion gift program; then this use of the money is more tax-effective than contributing it to a retirement plan. Under this scenario, the family ends up with $3,607,182, which is more than under any other scenario, even if the donees invest the money in currently taxable investments.

But this savings comes from avoiding some estate taxes on Vincent's death; it has nothing to do with the 15% excise tax.

At death:	Contribute to Plan:	Don't contribute,	Don't contribute,	Don't contribute,
	A. contrib to plan	B. Bonds o/s plan	C. cap gain o/s plan	D. give to kids
In plan	7,167,736	5,907,498	5,907,498	5,907,498
Outside plan	4,139,356	4,211,066	4,943,016	4,211,066
Total	11,307,092	10,118,564	10,850,514	10,118,564
Net to Family	3,434,670	3,208,219	3,537,597	**3,607,182**

Note: Although columns B and D show the same asset values "In the plan" and "Outside the plan," the difference is that, due to lifetime gifts, much of the column "D" value is also "outside the estate." Lower estate taxes produce the higher "Net to Family."

Also note: although scenarios C and D show a higher "net to family" after 30 years than would be achieved with continued plan contributions (scenario A), remember all these scenarios assume the retirement plan is entirely cashed out in the 30th year. In fact, there would probably be another 20 to 30 years of potential income tax deferral available, based on the life expectancies of Vincent's children as his DBs. It is possible, if this additional potential deferral is taken into account, that continued plan contributions under scenario A would produce better results than even scenarios C and D.

Conclusion

Always contribute the maximum to your tax-deferred retirement plan unless you have a better, more tax-effective use for the money--such as another tax-favored investment (*e.g.*, capital gain property), or giving the money away to reduce future estate taxes. The 15% excise tax is not a reason not to contribute to a retirement plan when long-term income tax deferral inside the plan is available. If the alternative is to pay high current taxes and invest in a non-tax-favored investment, the family will be better off paying higher 15% excise taxes, because they will still net more after tax. Other factors--such as the cost of contributing to a retirement plan (if you have to cover other employees for example), and your income tax bracket on current earned income--are more significant in making the decision whether to contribute.

Sherman and Herman Levine: Planning When Death is Imminent

The facts

Sherman and Herman Levine are twin brothers, age 78. Each has a $1.8 million IRA. Each elected in 1988 to "grandfather" his 8/1/86 plan balances from application of the 15% excise tax (see Chapter 5). Each now has $1 million of his grandfather balance remaining. Each wants to leave his IRA to his 53 year-old daughter. Both brothers are in failing health, unlikely to live more than a year or two.

All family members are in the 39.6% income tax bracket. Each brother has $2 million of assets outside his IRA.

The two brothers made different elections on their "required beginning date" (RBD). Sherman named his daughter Pearl as his "designated beneficiary," and elected to withdraw his benefits in instalments over their joint life expectancy (subject, during his life, to the restrictions of the MDIB rule). Herman named his estate as his beneficiary; even though his daughter Ruby is the sole beneficiary of his estate he was deemed to have had "no designated beneficiary" as of his RBD, and is withdrawing his benefits over his life expectancy only. Both brothers elected to have their life expectancies recalculated annually. (See Chapter 1.)

If a 78 year-old dies in 1995, his "threshold amount" for application of the 15% excise tax on "excess retirement accumulations" is (assuming an 8.6% 7520 rate) $815,500--or his remaining grandfather balance if greater. Thus, if either brother dies in 1995 his "threshold" will be his remaining grandfather balance ($1 million) since that is greater than $815,500. The estate would pay 15% excise tax on $800,000 (the plan balance, $1.8 million, minus the $1 million threshold). The excise tax would thus be $120,000. Since this tax is deductible for estate tax purposes, and each brother is in the 55% estate tax bracket, the true cost of the excise tax is only $54,000.

Should each brother draw down his $1 million grandfather balance now, while he is still alive? He can do so free of excise tax, since this withdrawal would be fully sheltered by the "grandfather" election. Then on his death the estate would be able to use the "regular" threshold of $815,500 to shelter the rest of the IRA, and pay NO excise tax, a savings of $54,000. This move clearly would save excise taxes--but would the family really net more? The following discussion assumes an

8% pre-tax return on all investments (both inside and outside the plan), 3% per year COLAs in the 15% excise tax "threshold," and an 8.6% "s. 7520 rate" (see Chapter 5).

Review of alternatives

If a brother dies with his IRA intact at $1.8 million, his daughter will use up almost all of the $2 million of non-IRA assets to pay the excise tax ($120,000) and estate tax ($1.84 million). The daughter will be left with a $1.8 million IRA and $40,000 of other assets--total $1.84 million.

For Pearl, Sherman's daughter, this would be a good deal. She could draw down the $1.8 million IRA gradually, over her remaining 29.7 year life expectancy. Even if she doesn't live that long, her child or other beneficiary is entitled to continue the withdrawal schedule established at Sherman's RBD, which is based on Pearl's life expectancy. She will get a tremendous benefit from three decades of income tax deferral. By the end of the 29.7 years, when the IRA has been entirely drawn down, she will have accumulated over $7 million.

For Ruby, on the other hand, Herman's daughter, it is not such a good deal. Because Herman was withdrawing from the IRA based only on his own life expectancy, recalculated annually, Ruby cannot continue to defer income tax on her inherited IRA. She must withdraw 100% of it by the end of the calendar year following Herman's death. After she pays income taxes on the $1.8 million IRA ($356,400, after taking into account the income tax deduction for estate taxes paid on this asset) (see Chapter 2), she is left with $0 in the IRA and $1,483,600 outside of the IRA. After 30 years, this will grow to $5.9 million, much less than the $7+ million Pearl has.

What if, instead of leaving the IRA intact, each brother withdraws his $1 million "grandfather" balance before death? Under this scenario, the brother would pay $396,000 of income taxes on his distribution, and be left with $604,000 from that distribution, plus his $2 million of other assets, plus $800,000 still in the IRA, at death (total $3,404,000). After paying estate taxes of $1,702,000 from the non-IRA assets, each daughter would be left with an $800,000 IRA and $902,000 of non-IRA assets, total $1,702,000. This is $138,000 LESS in absolute dollars than under scenario 1, but more of the inheritance is outside the IRA.

For Pearl, in 30 years, her gradual withdrawals from the $800,000 inherited IRA, plus the $902,000 non-IRA assets, will have grown to $6.5 million. This is $500,000 less than she would have had if her Dad had NOT withdrawn his grandfather balance before death.

For Ruby, who has to cash in the entire IRA within a year after her Dad's death, however, the fact that he saved her some excise taxes results in more in her pocket. She cashes in the $800,000, pays $158,400 of income taxes, and invests the net ($641,600) plus the $902,000 of non-IRA assets for 30 years. She ends up with $6,066,400--which is a little better than the $5.9 million she had under scenario 1. The difference is, approximately, the accumulated value of the $54,000 Herman saved by not paying any 15% excise tax.

Conclusion

If the participant has a very short life expectancy, and his retirement plan will be cashed out shortly after his death (whether because the minimum distribution rules require it, or because the money will be needed to pay estate taxes, or because the beneficiaries want to spend it, or for some other reason), consider withdrawing any "grandfathered" balance prior to death.

Appendix A
Tables

1. IRC s. 4980A indexed "threshold amounts" for application of 15% Excise Tax (see Chapter 5).

The indexed threshold amount under s. 4980A for each year since 1987 is:	
1987	112,500
1988	117,529
1989	122,580
1990	128,228
1991	136,204
1992	140,276
1993	144,551
1994	148,500
1995	150,000
1996	155,000

2.   MDIB Rule Divisor Table

See "Naming a Non-Spouse DB: The Incidental Benefit (MDIB) Rule" in Chapter 1. From IRS Publication 590.

Table for Determining Applicable Divisor for MDIB (Minimum Distribution Incidental Benefit)			
Age	**Applicable divisor**	**Age**	**Applicable divisor**
70	26.2	93	8.8
71	25.3	94	8.3
72	24.4	95	7.8
73	23.5	96	7.3
74	22.7	97	6.9
75	21.8	98	6.5
76	20.9	99	6.1
77	20.1	100	5.7
78	19.2	101	5.3
79	18.4	102	5.0
80	17.6	103	4.7
81	16.8	104	4.4
82	16.0	105	4.1
83	15.3	106	3.8
84	14.5	107	3.6
85	13.8	108	3.3
86	13.1	109	3.1
87	12.4	110	2.8
88	11.8	111	2.6
89	11.1	112	2.4
90	10.5	113	2.2
91	9.9	114	2.0
92	9.4	115 and older	1.8

3.   IRS "Table V" -- Single life expectancy.
       From IRS Publication 590.

Age	Divisor	Age	Divisor
35	47.3	73	13.9
36	46.4	74	13.2
37	45.4	75	12.5
38	44.4	76	11.9
39	43.5	77	11.2
40	42.5	78	10.6
41	41.5	79	10.0
42	40.6	80	9.5
43	39.6	81	8.9
44	38.7	82	8.4
45	37.7	83	7.9
46	36.8	84	7.4
47	35.9	85	6.9
48	34.9	86	6.5
49	34.0	87	6.1
50	33.1	88	5.7
51	32.2	89	5.3
52	31.3	90	5.0
53	30.4	91	4.7
54	29.5	92	4.4
55	28.6	93	4.1
56	27.7	94	3.9
57	26.8	95	3.7
58	25.9	96	3.4
59	25.0	97	3.2
60	24.2	98	3.0
61	23.3	99	2.8
62	22.5	100	2.7
63	21.6	101	2.5
64	20.8	102	2.3
65	20.0	103	2.1
66	19.2	104	1.9
67	18.4	105	1.8
68	17.6	106	1.6
69	16.8	107	1.4
70	16.0	108	1.3
71	15.3	109	1.1
72	14.6	110	1.0

4.   IRS "Table VI": Joint Life and Last Survivor Expectancy: Participant is Age 70 (or 71), Beneficiary is Age 35-74. From "Table II," IRS Publication 590.

AGES	70	71
35	47.5	47.5
36	46.6	46.6
37	45.7	45.6
38	44.7	44.7
39	43.8	43.8
40	42.9	42.8
41	41.9	41.9
42	41.0	41.0
43	40.1	40.1
44	39.2	39.1
45	38.3	38.2
46	37.4	37.3
47	36.5	36.5
48	35.7	35.6
49	34.8	34.7
50	34.0	33.9
51	33.1	33.0
52	32.3	32.2
53	31.5	31.4
54	30.7	30.5

AGES	70	71
55	29.9	29.7
56	29.1	29.0
57	28.4	28.2
58	27.6	27.5
59	26.9	26.7
60	26.2	26.0
61	25.6	25.3
62	24.9	24.7
63	24.3	24.0
64	23.7	23.4
65	23.1	22.8
66	22.5	22.2
67	22.0	21.7
68	21.5	21.2
69	21.1	20.7
70	20.6	20.2
71	20.2	19.8
72	19.8	19.4
73	19.4	19.0
74	19.1	18.6

5.   **Tax on various lump sum distributions.** This table
        shows the federal income tax that would be payable on
        various "lump sum distribution" amounts under the
        5YFA or 10YFA method. The 5YFA amounts are based
        on 1995 rates.

Distribution	"5 Year Tax Option"		"10 Year Tax Option"	
	Amount	Rate	Amount	Rate
100,000	15,000	15%	14,471	14%
200,000	40,823	20%	36,922	18%
300,000	69,340	23%	66,330	22%
400,000	100,340	25%	102,602	26%
500,000	131,340	26%	143,682	29%
600,000	162,853	27%	187,368	31%
700,000	198,853	28%	235,368	34%
800,000	234,853	29%	283,368	35%
900,000	270,853	30%	332,210	37%
1,000,000	306,853	31%	382,210	38%

Appendix B
Forms

Table of Contents

Introduction: Drafting Checklist for Beneficiary Designations

1. Simple Beneficiary Designation Form

    1.1   Spouse then children (or their issue)

2. More Complex Beneficiary Designation Forms -- Standard Introductory Provisions

    2.1   IRA
    2.2   Qualified Plan
    2.3   Alternative clause providing for disposition of benefits if beneficiary dies after participant

3. Nine Ways to Leave Benefits to the Marital and/or Credit Shelter Share

    3.1   Fractional split of benefits between surviving spouse and credit shelter trust
        (A) Beneficiary designation form
        (B) Related trust provisions
    3.2   Benefits payable to "pourover" trust, under which assets are divided between a marital share (paid to spouse outright) and a credit shelter trust by a fractional formula; benefits are allocated to marital share
        (A) Beneficiary designation form

(B) Related trust provisions

3.3 Benefits payable to "pourover" trust, under which assets are divided between a marital "QTIP" trust and a credit shelter trust by a fractional formula; drafter may choose to specify allocation of benefits to marital trust or credit shelter trust
(A) Beneficiary designation form
(B) Related trust provisions

3.4 Benefits payable to a marital trust which is part of a "pourover" trust with a pecuniary marital formula
(A) Beneficiary designation form
(B) Related trust provisions

3.5 Benefits payable to "One Big QTIP" trust -- trustee has authority to divide the trust
(A) Beneficiary designation form
(B) Related trust provisions

3.6 Benefits payable to spouse, "disclaimable" to credit shelter trust; different contingent beneficiary specified depending on whether spouse actually predeceases or merely disclaims

3.7 Benefits payable to credit shelter trust, "disclaimable" to spouse
(A) Beneficiary designation form
(B) Related trust provisions

3.8 Life insurance proceeds payable to credit shelter trust, all other benefits to spouse

3.9 Non-taxable portion of benefits payable to credit shelter trust, balance to spouse

4. Other Beneficiary Designation Forms

4.1 Designating spouse as primary beneficiary of IRA with presumption spouse survives, and election by spouse to treat the IRA as her own if she survives participant

4.2 Designating spouse as primary beneficiary; trust as contingent beneficiary if P dies before RBD, children as contingent beneficiaries if P dies on or after RBD

5. Miscellaneous Clauses for Beneficiary Designation Forms

5.1 Recognizing power of attorney

5.2 Allowing beneficiary to appoint investment manager

5.3 Surviving spouse's election to treat deceased spouse's IRA as surviving spouse's own IRA

6. Election Regarding Form of Benefits and Method of Determining Life Expectancy at Age 70½ (IRA)

6.1 Individual Retirement Account

7. Trust Provisions Dealing with Retirement Benefits

7.1 Trust administration during donor's life, including irrevocability provision

7.2 Insulating retirement assets from estate claims and charitable gifts

7.3 Excluding older adopted "issue"

7.4 Marital deduction saving language

8. Miscellaneous Forms

8.1 Power of attorney for retirement benefits

8.2 Tax clause in will

Introduction

This Appendix contains forms which the author has used in particular situations to achieve the dispositive and tax goals of particular clients. These forms can be used to provide ideas, or a starting point, for drafting forms for your clients and *their* particular situations.

In drafting forms to dispose of retirement benefits, consider the following points:

1.   Impress on the client that the "Designation of Beneficiary Form" is just as important a legal document as a will or trust. Often, more of the client's assets are controlled by this form than by his will. To draft or change a beneficiary designation form without consulting a lawyer could cost the client's estate and family thousands of dollars in taxes, lost deferral opportunities and increased settlement costs.

2.   Read the applicable sections of the "Account Agreement" establishing the client's individual retirement account, and refer to them specifically in the form if possible. In the case of a qualified retirement plan, read and refer to the applicable sections of the plan, if possible. In the case of a substantial benefit, try to read the actual plan document especially if the proposed disposition is in any way complex. In the case of a smaller benefit and/or a simple disposition, it may be sufficient to rely on the "Summary Plan Description" or the description of available benefit payout options in the employer-provided beneficiary designation form.

3.   There are certain issues in the disposition of death benefits which are quite likely to arise, yet may not be covered

at all in the IRA agreement or qualified plan documents. You should cover these in the beneficiary designation form:

A.   Who chooses the form of death benefits? Either the client-participant imposes a certain form of distribution or should specify that the beneficiary can choose it.

B.   Client-participant dies leaving the benefits to the primary beneficiary. On the participant's death, the primary beneficiary is entitled to the benefits, but does not withdraw them immediately. What happens to benefits that are still in the IRA (or plan) when the *primary beneficiary* dies? Will those remaining benefits then go to the person the client-participant originally named as *contingent* beneficiary? Will they pass to a new beneficiary designated by the primary beneficiary? Do they now belong to the primary beneficiary's estate?

C.   In the case of an individual retirement account, can the beneficiary transfer the benefits to another IRA still in the name of the decedent?

4.   Consider whether you wish to alter the applicable presumptions in case of simultaneous death (see Chapter 3).

5.   If the disposition is intended to qualify for the marital deduction, include language to that effect (see Chapter 3).

6.   Consider the extent to which you need to define any terms such as "issue *per stirpes*," or "income"; and/or specify which state's law shall be used to interpret terms you use in the form. It is highly likely that the retirement plan or IRA account agreement specifies that the law of the sponsor's state of incorporation will be used. Since that may well not be the state in which your client lives (or dies), there is a potential for

problems if the disposition depends on a definition which varies from state to state. Although you cannot change the governing law of the "plan," a statement that the language of the beneficiary designation will be interpreted according to the laws of a particular state should be accepted in the sense that it will lead to the correct determination of the client's intent. Of course, if intent is irrelevant on a particular question, this approach will not solve the problem.

7.   Follow the required formalities of execution. Most IRAs are, in essence, simply custodial accounts. As such, they may be considered "probate" assets of the participant's estate. Some states do not recognize a disposition of certain forms of retirement benefits unless executed with the formalities of a will. See Chapter 9.

8.   The choice of a contingent beneficiary should not be overlooked. For example:

A.   If benefits are being made payable to a trust, to take advantage of the client's unified credit while providing life benefits for the surviving spouse, consider naming the trust as primary beneficiary only if the spouse survives. Consider naming the children directly as contingent beneficiaries if the spouse does not survive, to avoid the complications of running benefits through a trust.

B.   For a client who has not yet reached his RBD, remember that the "contingent beneficiary" will become the "designated beneficiary" if the original primary beneficiary dies before the participant.

C.   Consider whether different contingent beneficiaries should be named depending on whether the primary beneficiary actually dies before the participant, or merely disclaims the benefits.

9.   Take into account the age of the client. In this Appendix, form 4.1 is useful primarily for a client who is past is RBD; form 4.2 is only for a client who has not yet reached his RBD. Otherwise, the beneficiary designation forms in sections 1, 2 and 3 are generally suitable for a client of any age. However, the effects of each form on the minimum required distributions of the client's benefits will be quite different depending on whether the form is signed before, at or after the client's RBD; see Chapter 1. When the client reaches his RBD, form 6.1 (or its QRP equivalent) must be filed with the plan IN ADDITION to the beneficiary designation form.

10.   Whenever a trust is named as beneficiary, review the proposed regulations' "trust rules" (see Chapter 1); these rules differ depending on whether the client has reached his RBD.

11.   If the participant dies before his RBD, and his beneficiary is his spouse, or a trust of which the spouse is the oldest beneficiary, it is advisable to specify that the spouse's life expectancy will not be recalculated annually (unless the beneficiary affirmatively elects otherwise prior to the first required distribution). If this is not specified, it is possible that a plan rule (or IRS rule) would create a presumption that the spouse's LE is to be redetermined annually, which could have disastrous effects if the spouse dies prematurely.

        This issue does not arise if the participant dies on or after his RBD, assuming he has made deliberate elections regarding the method of determining life expectancy, because P's elections at the RBD will also govern upon his later death. The issue also does not arise if the participant dies before December 31 of the year he turns age 70½ naming his spouse individually as beneficiary, and she *also* dies before December 31 of the year P would have reached age 70½, because then the "five year rule" is applied as if the spouse were the "participant," not as if the spouse were the "designated beneficiary."

1.   SIMPLE BENEFICIARY DESIGNATION FORM

Who might use this form: The simple beneficiary designation form may be suitable for a client who wants to leave benefits outright to his spouse if living, otherwise to his children equally (and issue of deceased children).   This client has sufficient non-retirement assets to fully fund his credit shelter trust (or for some reason does not want a credit shelter estate plan); and his children are all living, competent adults.

1.1   Simple Beneficiary Designation Form: Spouse, Then Children (or their Issue)

DESIGNATION OF BENEFICIARY

TO: [Name of IRA Provider or Plan Administrator]
FROM: [Name of Participant]
RE: Individual Retirement Account No._____
          [or Name of Plan]

1.   Pursuant to the [agreement establishing the above "Individual Retirement Account" or "Individual Retirement Trust"] [terms of the above plan], I hereby designate as my beneficiary, my spouse, [SPOUSE NAME], whose date of birth is [SPOUSE BIRTHDATE], to receive all benefits payable under the above [account] [plan] in the event of my death.

2.   If my spouse does not survive me, I designate as my beneficiaries, in equal shares, such of my children as shall survive me; provided, that if any of my children is not then living, but leaves issue then living, such issue shall take the share such deceased child would have taken if living, by right of representation.

My children are:

| | | Social |
| Name | Date of Birth | Security Number |

3.   If any beneficiary dies after becoming entitled to benefits, but before distribution to such beneficiary of all benefits to which such beneficiary is entitled, such beneficiary's remaining share of the benefits shall be distributed to such person, in such manner, as the beneficiary shall have indicated by written instructions to you, or, in the absence of such instructions, to such beneficiary's then living issue by right of representation, if any, otherwise to my then living issue by right of representation, if any, otherwise to such beneficiary's estate.

4.   Any benefits becoming distributable to a person under the age of twenty-one (21) years shall be distributed to such person's surviving parent, if any, otherwise to my oldest then living child, as custodian for such person under the Uniform Transfers to Minors Act. Such custodian shall be entitled to act for the minor in all respects with regard to the benefits.

5.   Each beneficiary may choose the form and timing of distribution of his or her benefits, subject to limits imposed by the [plan] [IRA Account Agreement] and applicable law.

6.   If my death occurs prior to April 1 of the year following the year in which I reach age 70½, then, unless the beneficiary makes a different election prior to the date of payment of the first "minimum required distribution" (under s. 401(a)(9) of the Code) after my death, the life expectancy of my spouse shall not be redetermined annually.

Signed this _____ day of _____, 199_.

_____
Signature of Participant

Witnesses: _____

_____

2.   MORE   COMPLEX   BENEFICIARY DESIGNATION   FORMS: STANDARD INTRODUCTORY PROVISIONS

Who should use this form: These introductory provisions are meant to be used with all beneficiary designation forms provided in Sections 3 and 4 of this Appendix. Form 2.1 is meant to be used with IRAs. Form 2.2 is for qualified plans. Although most of the subject matter in these sample "introductory provisions" is not dealt with at all in most IRA agreements and QRP documents, it is desirable nevertheless to make sure the IRA agreement or plan document does not contradict anything contained in this form before using it.

Other notes: Drafters may choose not to use all of these introductory provisions in every beneficiary designation form.

Paragraphs "A," "B," and "C," and "D" if minors may become beneficiaries, are the "probably indispensable" sections. The "Determination of Life Expectancy" section should be used only if the participant has not yet reached his RBD *and* the beneficiary is either the spouse or a trust of which she is the oldest beneficiary.

These introductory provisions, like all forms, should be modified as necessary for individual clients. Also, note that a particular IRA provider or QRP administrator may not be willing to accept some of these provisions, particularly C, F and G. See form 2.3 for an alternative version of paragraph "C."

2.1   Introductory Provisions: IRA

DESIGNATION OF BENEFICIARY

TO: _____

Name of Custodian or Trustee of IRA or IRT

FROM: _____

Name of Participant

RE: Account No. _____

I.   Introductory Provisions

    A.   Definitions

The following words, when used in this form and capitalized, shall have the meaning indicated in this Section.

"Account" means the "Individual Retirement Account" or "Individual Retirement Trust" referred to above, which is established and maintained under s. 408 of the Code.

"Administrator" means the IRA custodian or trustee named above, and its successors in that office.

"Beneficiary" means any person entitled to ownership of all or part of the Account as a result of my death (or as a result of the death of another Beneficiary).

"Code" means the Internal Revenue Code of 1986, as amended.

"Contingent Beneficiary" means the person(s) I have designated in this form to receive the Death Benefit if my Primary Beneficiary does not survive me (or disclaims the benefits).

"Death Benefit" means all amounts payable under the Account on account of my death.

The "Minimum Distribution Amount" is, in each year, the minimum amount required to be distributed from the Account in such year under section 408(a)(6) of the Code (and regulations thereunder).

"Primary Beneficiary" means the person or persons I have designated in this form to receive the Death Benefit in the event of my death.

"Successor Beneficiary" means a person entitled to receive the balance of another Beneficiary's benefits if such other Beneficiary dies before distribution of all of his or her share of the Death Benefit.

B.   Form of Benefit Payments after my Death

After my death, there must be distributed, in each calendar year, at least the Minimum Distribution Amount for such year; provided, that this sentence shall not be deemed to limit any Beneficiary's right to use the alternative method of compliance described in IRS Notice 88-38. Except as may be otherwise specifically provided herein, or in the agreement establishing the Account, or by applicable law, each Beneficiary shall be entitled to elect the form and timing of distribution of benefits payable to him or her.

C.   Death of Individual Beneficiary

No person shall have the discretion, after my death, to change my Beneficiaries. The Death Benefit shall be payable to the Primary (or Contingent) Beneficiary specified herein, whichever is applicable. However if an individual Primary or Contingent Beneficiary, having survived me, becomes entitled to ownership of all or part of the Account, but later dies prior to the complete distribution of such Beneficiary's share of the Account to him or her, the remaining balance of such Beneficiary's share of the Account shall belong to a Successor Beneficiary, who shall be:

(i)   such person or persons as such Beneficiary shall have indicated by written notice to the Administrator; or, if such Beneficiary shall have failed to give such written notice, or to the extent such written notice does not make effective disposition of all of such Beneficiary's share of the Account,

(ii)   such Beneficiary's issue surviving such Beneficiary, by right of representation; or, in default of such issue,

(iii)   my issue surviving such Beneficiary, by right of representation, or, in default of such issue,

(iv)   such Beneficiary's estate.

D.   Payments to Minors

If any Beneficiary becomes entitled to ownership of any part of the Account at a time when he or she is under the age of twenty-one (21) years, such ownership shall instead be vested in the name of such Beneficiary's surviving parent, if any, otherwise in the name of my oldest then living child if any, otherwise in the name of some other person selected by my Executor, as custodian for such Beneficiary under the Uniform Transfers to Minors Act of the state of my domicile at death, and such custodian shall have the power to act for such Beneficiary in all respects with regard to the Account.

E.   Governing Law

The interpretation of this beneficiary designation form shall be governed by the law of the State of
_____.

F.   Multiple Beneficiaries

If there are multiple Beneficiaries entitled to ownership of the Account simultaneously, they shall be entitled, to the maximum extent permitted by law, by joint written instructions to the Administrator, to have the Account divided into separate accounts corresponding to each Beneficiary's separate interest in the Account, as of or at any time after my death, and following such division the separate accounts shall be maintained as if each were an Account in my name payable solely to the applicable Beneficiary. Following such division, no Beneficiary shall have any further interest in or claim to any part of the account other than the separate Account representing his or her interest.

G.   Transferring Account

The Beneficiary shall have the right to have the Account (or, if the Account has been divided, such Beneficiary's share of the Account) transferred to a different Individual Retirement

Account or Individual Retirement Trust, still in my name, with the same or a different custodian or trustee, if such transfer is permitted by law.

H.   Determination of Spouse's Life Expectancy

If my death occurs prior to April 1 of the year following the year in which I reach age 70½, then, unless the Beneficiary makes a different election prior to the date of payment of the first "minimum required distribution" (under the Code) after my death, the life expectancy of my spouse shall not be redetermined annually.

2.2   Introductory Provisions -- Qualified Plan

DESIGNATION OF BENEFICIARY

TO: _____

Name of Trustee or Plan Administrator

FROM: _____

Name of Participant

RE: _____

Name of Retirement Plan

I.   Introductory Provisions

A.   Definitions

The following words, when used in this form and capitalized, shall have the meaning indicated in this Section.

"Administrator" means the Trustee or Plan Administrator named above, and its successors in such office.

"Beneficiary" means any person entitled to receive benefits under the Plan as a result of my death (or as a result of the death of another Beneficiary).

"Code" means the Internal Revenue Code of 1986, as amended.

"Contingent Beneficiary" means the person(s) I have designated in this form to receive the Death Benefit if my Primary Beneficiary does not survive me (or disclaims the benefits).

"Death Benefit" means all benefits payable under the Plan on account of my death.

The "Minimum Distribution Amount" is, in each year, the minimum amount of my benefits under the Plan that is required to be distributed from the Plan under s. 401(a)(9) of the Code (and regulations thereunder).

"Plan" means the qualified retirement plan or other retirement arrangement described at the beginning of this form.

"Primary Beneficiary" means the person designated in this form to receive benefits under the Plan on account of my death.

"Successor Beneficiary" means a person entitled to receive the balance of another Beneficiary's benefits if such other Beneficiary dies before distribution of all of his or her share of the Death Benefit.

B.   Form of Benefit Payments After My Death.

Except as may be otherwise specifically provided herein, in the Plan, or by applicable law, each Beneficiary shall be entitled to elect the form and timing of distribution of any benefits payable to such Beneficiary, provided that there must be distributed, in each calendar year, at least the Minimum Distribution Amount for such year.

C.   Death of Beneficiary.

No person shall have the discretion, after my death, to change my Beneficiaries. The Death Benefit shall be payable to the Primary (or Contingent) Beneficiary specified herein, whichever is applicable. However if an individual Primary or Contingent Beneficiary, having survived me, becomes entitled to benefits under the Plan, but later dies prior to the complete distribution of such benefits to him or her, such deceased Beneficiary's remaining benefits shall be payable to a Successor Beneficiary, who shall be:

(a)   such person or persons as such Beneficiary shall have indicated by written notice to the Administrator; or, if such Beneficiary failed to give such written notice, or to the extent such written notice does not make effective disposition of all of such Beneficiary's benefits under the Plan, then

(b)   such Beneficiary's issue surviving such Beneficiary, by right of representation; or, in default of such issue,

(c)   my issue surviving such Beneficiary, by right of representation, or, in default of such issue,

(d)   such Beneficiary's estate.

D.   Payments to Minors.

If any Beneficiary becomes entitled to benefits under the Plan at a time when he or she is under the age of twenty-one (21) years, such benefits shall be instead payable to such Beneficiary's surviving parent, if any, otherwise to my oldest then living child, if any, otherwise to some other person selected by my Executor, as custodian for such Beneficiary under the

Uniform Transfers to Minors Act, and such custodian shall have the power to act for such Beneficiary in all respects with regard to the benefits to which such Beneficiary is entitled.

E.   Governing Law

The interpretation of this beneficiary designation form shall be governed by the law of the State of

_____.

F.   Multiple Beneficiaries

If there are multiple Beneficiaries who are simultaneously entitled to the Death Benefit, they shall be entitled, to the maximum extent permitted by law, by joint written instructions to the Administrator, to have the Death Benefit divided into separate accounts corresponding to each Beneficiary's separate interest in the Death Benefit, as of or at any time after my death, and following such division the separate accounts shall be maintained as if each were a Death Benefit payable solely to the applicable Beneficiary. Following such division, no Beneficiary shall have any further interest in or claim to any part of the Death Benefit other than the separate account representing his or her interest.

G.   Determination of Spouse's Life Expectancy

If my death occurs prior to April 1 of the year following the year in which I reach age 70½, then, unless the Beneficiary makes a different election prior to the date of payment of the first "minimum required distribution" (under s. 401(a)(9) of the Code) after my death, the life expectancy of my spouse shall not be redetermined annually.

2.3   Alternative Clause Providing for Disposition of Benefits if Beneficiary Dies After Participant

Who should consider using this form: The preceding forms all allow the beneficiary to designate his or her *own* beneficiaries, if the beneficiary dies after becoming entitled to the benefits but before the benefits have been fully distributed. Some IRA agreements and QRPs do not allow the beneficiary to designate a further beneficiary. These plans may specifically provide that, if a beneficiary dies before withdrawing all of the benefits to which he/she is entitled, the remaining benefits pass to the beneficiary's estate. In this case, it is desirable to clarify up front that the beneficiary's executor is not required to cash out the remaining benefits, but can instead simply instruct the plan to pay the benefits directly to the proper beneficiary of the estate (*e.g.*, the residuary beneficiary).

Warning: A plan requirement that, if a beneficiary dies after becoming entitled to benefits but before withdrawing them, the remaining benefits must be paid to the beneficiary's estate, could cause a severe financial loss if (a) the participant's spouse is his designated beneficiary and (b) the participant dies before December 31 of his "age 70½ year," and (c) the spouse survives him but also dies before that date, without having withdrawn and "rolled over" the benefits. Under these circumstances, the "five year rule" is applied "as if the spouse were the participant," and all benefits must be paid out within five years after the spouse's death unless the benefits are payable to a "designated beneficiary" (DB). If the benefits are payable to the surviving spouse's estate, the surviving spouse "has no DB," and the five year rule will apply. For this reason, if representing a client who is under age 70½ and who wants to name his spouse as DB, it is highly desirable to place IRA accounts and other "movable" retirement plans with a provider who does not insist that, when a beneficiary dies after the participant, the beneficiary's remaining benefits must be paid to the beneficiary's estate.

"C.   Death of Individual Beneficiary

If any individual Beneficiary becomes entitled to all or part of the Death Benefit, but later dies prior to the complete distribution of his or her share of the Death Benefit, the remaining balance of such Beneficiary's share of the Death Benefit shall be an asset of such Beneficiary's estate and shall be paid to the executor, administrator or other personal representative of the Beneficiary's estate, or shall be paid directly to the beneficiaries of the estate, as such personal representative shall direct by written notice to the Administrator. The death of a Beneficiary shall not cause any acceleration of distribution of the Death Benefit except as such Beneficiary (or personal representative) may direct or as required by law."

3.   **NINE WAYS TO LEAVE BENEFITS TO THE MARITAL AND/OR CREDIT SHELTER SHARE**

Each of the following forms is a "beneficiary designation" designed to leave benefits to a marital or credit shelter share, or to split benefits between a marital and credit shelter share. These should be used with the appropriate "introductory provisions" (for IRA or QRP) in the section 2 of this Appendix. Related provisions to be included in the client's trust instrument, when applicable, follow the beneficiary designation form.

3.1   **Fractional Split of Benefits Between Surviving Spouse and Credit Shelter Trust**

Who would consider using this form: Client who needs to use some of the benefits to "fill up" a credit shelter trust, but wants to make sure that any benefits not needed to fill up the credit shelter trust will go directly to the spouse so the spouse can roll them over. See, *e.g., Allen Able* case study.

Drawbacks of this form: Some IRA providers and QRPs will not accept a beneficiary designation which contains a formula. In such cases, use form 3.2 instead.

Other notes: If the client has multiple retirement plans, this form will have to be modified so it is clear which plan or IRA is used first, second, third, etc. to fund the credit shelter trust; or else use form 3.2. This form contemplates a client who has only one plan.

3.1(A) Beneficiary Designation Form

I.   Introductory Provisions

[insert form 2.1 or form 2.2]

II.   Designation of Beneficiary

A.   Primary Beneficiary

If my spouse, [SPOUSE NAME] survives me, then I name both my spouse, individually, and [TRUSTEE NAME] as Trustee of the "Family Trust" created under Article _ of the [TRUST NAME] Trust, a copy of which is attached hereto, (hereinafter referred to as "my Trustee") as my Primary Beneficiaries. The Death Benefit shall be divided into two shares at my death, one for each of the respective Primary Beneficiaries, according to the following formula:

1.   The share to be allocated to the Family Trust shall be determined by multiplying the Death Benefit by a

fraction. The numerator shall be the "Credit Shelter Amount" (as defined below). The denominator shall be the value of the Death Benefit.

2.   The fractional share allocated to my spouse individually shall be [one] minus [the fraction determined under paragraph 1] times the value of the Death Benefit.

3.   The relative fractional shares of the Primary Beneficiaries shall be determined as of the date of my death. The fraction as so determined shall then be applied to the values of the Death Benefit on the date(s) of distribution to the Primary Beneficiaries.

4.   The "Credit Shelter Amount" means the maximum amount which, if it passed at my death to beneficiaries other than my spouse or charity, would not be subject to federal estate tax by virtue of any credits and exemptions available to my estate, reduced by all amounts includible in my estate which pass to the said Family Trust (or to any other beneficiary other than my spouse or charity) otherwise than under this instrument. In applying the foregoing formula: the credit for state death taxes shall be taken into account only to the extent its use does not increase the state death taxes otherwise payable on my estate; and property passing to a trust which qualifies for the federal estate tax marital deduction, or which would so qualify if my executor so elected, shall be deemed to have passed to my spouse.

5.   The Primary Beneficiaries, and not the Administrator, shall have sole responsibility for determining and applying the foregoing formula. The Administrator may rely absolutely, without further inquiry, on a certificate of my Trustee as to the amount payable to each Primary Beneficiary under the above formula, and shall have no liability to any person for any misapplication of said formula.

B.   Contingent Beneficiary

If my spouse does not survive me, the entire Death Benefit shall be paid to [here insert contingent beneficiary, such as "my issue surviving me by right of representation" or "the trustee of the said [TRUST NAME] Trust"] as Contingent Beneficiary.

3.1(B) Related Trust Provisions

These provisions would be included in the trust agreement that is named as Primary Beneficiary under form 3.1(A).

___.   Payments After My Death

Upon my death, the Trustee shall hold and administer all property of the Trust, including any amounts received or receivable then or later as a result of my death or otherwise, as follows:

.01   If my spouse does not survive me, the Trustee shall designate all of such property as the "Family Trust."

.02   If my spouse survives me, the Trustee shall divide the said property into two separate trust funds, to be designated the Marital Trust and the Family Trust.

.03   There shall first be allocated to each of the said respective trusts any asset (such as life insurance proceeds, retirement benefits or a bequest under my will) which, by its terms, is payable to that trust specifically. Any assets received by the Trustee that are not, by their terms, payable specifically to either the Marital Trust or the Family Trust shall be allocated between the two trusts pursuant to the following formula. If application of the formula results in assets being allocated to only one of the trusts instead of both, the Trustee shall allocate such assets only to that one.

.04   The Trustee shall determine the maximum amount which, if it passed under this provision to beneficiaries other than my spouse or charity, would not be subject to federal estate tax by virtue of any credits and exemptions available to my estate; provided, that: the credit for state death taxes shall be taken into account only to the extent its use does not increase the state death taxes otherwise payable on my estate; and property passing to a trust which qualifies for the federal estate tax marital deduction, or which would so qualify if my executor so elected, shall be deemed to have passed to my spouse. This amount is referred to as the "Remaining Credit Shelter Amount."

.05   The Trustee shall allocate assets having a value equal to the "Remaining Credit Shelter Amount" to the Family Trust and shall allocate all other assets to the Marital Trust. In valuing assets for purposes of funding the Family Trust, the Trustee shall value assets as of the date of distribution to the Family Trust.

.06   The Marital Trust shall be held and administered as provided in Article ___. The Family Trust shall be held and administered as provided in Article ___.

3.2   Benefits Payable to "Pourover" Trust, under Which Assets are Divided Between a Marital Share (Paid to Spouse Outright) and a Credit Shelter Trust by a Fractional Formula.   Benefits are Allocated to Marital Share.

Who would consider using this form: Client who expects to need to use some or all of his retirement benefits to "fill up" a credit shelter trust, and wants any benefits not needed for that purpose paid to the spouse outright so she can roll them over. This client could use form 3.1, but in some cases 3.1 is not feasible because the plan administrator will not accept "formula" beneficiary designations, or because the existence of multiple retirement plans makes drafting the formula too difficult. In such cases 3.2 is a more viable alternative.

Drawbacks of this form: Under this form and the related trust provision, the trustee is required to fund the marital share with retirement benefits to the maximum extent possible, and then is required to distribute the marital share outright to the spouse on her request. This approach is based on IRS private letter rulings, permitting the surviving spouse to roll over benefits which pass to her through a trust, if she has the unfettered right to withdraw the benefits. See Chapter 3. Since this IRS policy has so far appeared only in private letter rulings, there is no guarantee the IRS will continue to recognize such rollovers, although it appears *likely* (and correct under the Code) that such rollovers will be allowed.

Other notes: This form names only the trust as beneficiary, regardless of whether the spouse survives. If the entire trust is to be distributed to the participant's issue outright on the death of the surviving spouse, consider naming the trust as primary beneficiary only if the spouse survives, and naming the issue directly as beneficiaries if the spouse does not survive. See form 3.5 for an example of this approach.

3.2(A) Beneficiary Designation Form

I.   Introductory Provisions

             [insert form 2.1 or form 2.2]

II.   Designation of Beneficiary

        A.   <u>Primary Beneficiary</u>

I hereby designate as my Primary Beneficiary, to receive 100% of the Death Benefit in case of my death, [TRUSTEE NAME] (hereinafter "my Trustee"), as Trustee of the [TRUST NAME] Trust, under Agreement of Trust dated [TRUST DATE], a copy of which is attached hereto.

B.   Distribution of Benefits to Spouse

My Trustee is directed under the said Agreement of Trust to allocate the Death Benefit, pursuant to a formula, between my spouse and the "Family Trust" established under said Agreement of Trust. My Trustee is further directed under said Agreement of Trust, if so requested by my spouse, to cause the part of the Death Benefit so allocated to my spouse to be (i) distributed outright to my spouse or (ii) transferred directly to an "individual retirement account" in my spouse's name. Accordingly, if the Administrator is so instructed by my Trustee, the Administrator shall, with respect to the amount indicated by my Trustee, (i) distribute such amount outright to my spouse or (ii) transfer such amount directly to an "individual retirement account" in my spouse's name.

3.2(B) Related Trust Provisions

__.   Payments After My Death

Upon my death, the Trustee shall hold and administer all property of the Trust, including any amounts received or receivable then or later as a result of my death or otherwise, as follows:

.01   If my spouse does not survive me, the Trustee shall designate all of such property as the "Family Trust," to be held and administered as provided in Article __.

.02   If my spouse survives me, the Trustee shall divide the said property into two separate shares, to be designated respectively the Marital Share and the Family Trust. The two separate shares shall be funded pursuant to the following formula. If application of the formula results in assets being allocated to only one of the shares instead of both, the Trustee shall fund only such one.

.03   The Trustee shall allocate to the Marital Share a portion of the Remaining Trust Property determined by multiplying the Remaining Trust Property by a fraction. The numerator of the fraction shall be: the smallest amount necessary, if allowed as a marital deduction to eliminate the federal estate tax otherwise payable by reason of my death; reduced by the value of all other items included in my estate which qualify for the federal estate tax marital deduction and which pass or have passed to my spouse otherwise than under this provision. The denominator of the fraction is the value of the Remaining Trust Property. For purposes of this formula:

(i)   It shall be assumed with respect to property not passing under this trust that my Executor will elect to treat as "qualified terminable interest property" all property eligible for such treatment.

(ii)   The "values" of assets shall be their values as finally determined for purposes of the federal estate tax on my estate.

(iii)   The "Remaining Trust Property" means all property of this trust that is included in my federal gross estate, reduced by the amount of any debts, expenses of administration, specific and pecuniary bequests and death taxes payable out of such property.

(iv)   The federal estate tax credit for state death taxes shall be taken into account only to the extent its use does not increase the state death taxes otherwise payable on my estate.

.04   All property not allocated to the Marital Share pursuant to the preceding formula shall be designated as the Family Trust, and administered as provided in Article __.

.05   In selecting which assets shall be used to fund which share, the Trustee shall, to the maximum extent possible, allocate tax-favored retirement plans to the Marital Share and assets other than tax-favored retirement plans to the Family Trust. A "tax-favored retirement plan" means an individual retirement account (within the meaning of s. 408 of the Code), qualified retirement plan (within the meaning of s. 401(a) of the Code), "tax-sheltered annuity" (described in s. 403(b) of the Code) and similar plans, accounts and arrangements.

.06   The Marital Share shall be distributed to my spouse, outright and free of trusts. To the extent that all or part of any tax-favored retirement plan is allocated to the Marital Share pursuant to the foregoing provisions, the Trustee may (and shall, if requested to do so by my spouse) cause such plan (or part thereof) to be paid directly from such plan to my spouse as beneficiary, or transferred (if so requested by my spouse) directly from such plan into an individual retirement account in my spouse's name, without the intervening step of transferring it to this Trust.

3.3   All Benefits Payable to a "Pourover" Trust, Under Which Assets are Divided Between a Marital "QTIP" Trust and a Credit Shelter Trust by a Fractional Formula; Drafter May Choose to Specify Allocation of Benefits to Marital Trust or Credit Shelter Trust

Who should consider this form: A client who does not want any benefits paid to the spouse outright and whose pourover trust will be allocated between a "marital trust" and a "credit shelter trust" by a fractional formula. The related trust provisions contain two alternatives regarding funding these shares: one version requires benefits to be allocated to the marital share to the extent possible; the other requires benefits to be allocated to the credit shelter share to the extent possible. A third option is to omit both versions of paragraph .06 and allow the trustee to choose which assets to use to fund which share.

Drawbacks of this form: No spousal rollover is possible under this form. Also, if the credit shelter and marital shares have different beneficiaries, this form probably would not work to permit each separate trust to use its own beneficiaries' life expectancy to measure payout of its share of the benefits.

3.3(A) Beneficiary Designation Form

I.   Introductory Provisions

[insert form 2.1 or form 2.2]

II.   Designation of Beneficiary

A.   Primary Beneficiary

I hereby designate as my Primary Beneficiary, to receive 100% of the Death Benefit, [TRUSTEE NAME] (hereinafter "my Trustee"), as trustee of the [TRUST NAME] Trust, under Agreement of Trust dated [TRUST DATE], a copy of which is attached hereto.

B.   Division of Benefit

Under the terms of said Agreement of Trust, my Trustee is directed, if my spouse survives me, to divide the assets of said Trust into two separate trusts, to be designated the "Marital

Trust" and the "Family Trust." If so instructed by my Trustee, the Administrator shall divide the Death Benefit into two separate accounts, both still in my name, one payable solely to the Marital Trust as Beneficiary and the other payable solely to the Family Trust as Beneficiary; or, in accordance with such instructions, shall designate the entire Death Benefit as payable to one of said trusts. The Administrator shall have no responsibility to determine the correctness of my Trustee's instructions regarding such allocation, and shall have no liability whatsoever to any person for complying with my Trustee's said instructions. The beneficiaries of the Marital Trust and Family Trust shall look solely to my Trustee for enforcement of their rights under the said Trusts.

C.   Benefits Payable to Marital Trust

With regard to any portion of the Death Benefit so allocated to the Marital Trust, there must be distributed to the Marital Trust in each year, beginning with the year of my death, from the Marital Trust's portion of the Death Benefit, at least the net income of the Marital Trust's portion of the Death Benefit for such year accrued after my death. My Trustee, and not the Administrator, shall have sole responsibility for determination of the amount of such income, and directing the distribution of such income to the Marital Trust.

3.3(B) Related Trust Provisions

___.   Payments Upon My Death

Upon my death, the Trustee shall hold and administer all property of the Trust, including any amounts received or receivable then or later as a result of my death or otherwise, as follows:

[here, copy sections .01 through .04 from form 3.2(B), but change "Marital Share" to "Marital Trust", and add:]

.05   The Marital Trust shall be held and administered as provided in Article ___.

[Use one or the other of the following optional funding provisions, or neither, but not both]

[optional funding provision: alternative 1].

.06   Any death benefit under any "qualified retirement plan," individual retirement account or similar tax-favored retirement arrangement that is payable to this Trust shall be allocated to the Marital Trust to the maximum extent possible within the limits of the preceding formula.

[optional funding provision: alternative 2].

.06   Any death benefit under any "qualified retirement plan," individual retirement account or similar tax-favored retirement arrangement that is payable to this Trust shall be allocated to the Family Trust to the maximum extent possible within the limits of the preceding formula.

[here insert form 7.4, or otherwise take steps to qualify for marital deduction; see Chapter 3.]

3.4   Benefits Payable to a Marital Trust Which Is Part of a "Pourover" Trust with a Pecuniary Marital Formula

Who should consider using this form: A client who wants to use a pecuniary marital formula for his marital/credit shelter share division because it is easier to administer; who wants his retirement benefits paid to a marital trust, and not outright to his spouse; and whose retirement benefits will probably not be needed to fund the credit shelter share. By making the benefits payable directly to the Marital Trust, the client avoids having any kind of formula applied to the benefits, avoids the complexity of transferring the retirement benefits from a "funding" trust into a Marital or Family Trust, and avoids having to use a fractional formula for any assets.

The preferred simplicity of administration which comes from using a pecuniary formula does not have to be sacrificed just because part of the trust will consist of retirement benefits. Under this form, the retirement benefits do not go through the pecuniary funding formula; the benefits bypass the formula and go straight into the Marital Trust.

Drawbacks: If the retirement benefits turn out to be a greater amount than is required to eliminate estate taxes, then this form would overfund the marital share. That problem can be solved easily post mortem by a fractional QTIP election, or, less easily, by a disclaimer by the marital trust. Also, no spousal rollover is possible under this form.

Other ideas: Another approach for this client would be to use a pecuniary *credit shelter* formula, and make the retirement benefits payable directly to the (residuary) marital trust. Form 3.1 can be adapted for this purpose.

3.4(A) Beneficiary Designation Form

I.   Introductory Provisions

[insert form 2.1 or form 2.2]

II.   Designation of Beneficiary

A.   Primary Beneficiary

I hereby designate as my Primary Beneficiary, to receive 100% of the Death Benefit, [TRUSTEE NAME], as trustee of the [MARITAL TRUST NAME] Marital Trust, established under Agreement of Trust dated [TRUST DATE], a copy of which is attached hereto.

B.   Form of Distribution of Benefits

After my death, there shall be distributed to the Beneficiary, in each year, so long as my spouse is living, whichever of the following amounts is the greatest:

(a)   the net income of the Death Benefit for such year;

(b)   the Minimum Distribution Amount for such year; or

(c)   such amount as the Beneficiary shall direct by written instructions to the Administrator.

The Beneficiary, and not the Administrator, shall have sole responsibility for complying with these instructions as to the Form of Distribution of Benefits.

3.4(B) Related Trust Provisions

___.   Payments After My Death

Upon my death, the Trustee shall hold and administer all property of the Trust, including any amounts received or receivable then or later as a result of my death or otherwise, as follows:

.01   If my spouse does not survive me, the Trustee shall designate all such property as the "Family Trust" to be held and administered as provided in Article ___.

.02   If my spouse survives me, the Trustee shall divide the said property into two separate trust funds, to be designated the Marital Trust and the Family Trust, pursuant to the following formula. If application of the formula results in assets being allocated to only one of the trusts instead of both, the Trustee shall fund only such one.

(a)   The Trustee shall allocate to the Marital Trust all benefits payable under any "qualified retirement plan," "individual retirement account" or other similar retirement plan, annuity or arrangement, as well as any assets which are payable by the terms of my will, beneficiary designation form or otherwise directly to the Marital Trust.

(b)   The Trustee shall allocate to the Marital Trust such additional amount, if any, as is necessary to bring the total value of the Marital Trust up to the Optimum Federal Marital Amount. This gift to the Marital Trust shall be funded only with assets or the proceeds of assets which qualify for the federal estate tax marital deduction.

(c)   The Marital Trust shall be held and administered as provided in Article ___

(d)   The "Optimum Federal Marital Amount" means the smallest amount which, if it passed to my spouse in a manner qualifying for the federal estate tax marital deduction, would eliminate the federal estate tax on my estate (or minimize such tax, if it is not possible to eliminate it), reduced by the value of any property passing to my spouse otherwise than under this trust to the extent such property qualifies for the federal estate tax marital deduction (or would so qualify if my Executor so elected). In computing the Optimum Federal Marital Amount, the federal estate tax credit for state death taxes shall be taken into account only to the extent its use does not increase the state death taxes otherwise payable on my estate.

(e)   All property not allocated to the Marital Trust pursuant to the preceding provisions (or, if no property is allocable to the Marital Trust pursuant to preceding provisions, then all property of the Trust) shall be designated as the Family Trust, to be held and administered as provided in Article ____.

[here insert form 7.4, or otherwise take steps to qualify for marital deduction; see Chapter 3.]

3.5   Benefits Payable to "One Big QTIP" Trust -- Trustee Has Authority to Divide the Trust

Who would use this form: The client who wants all income of his benefits paid to his spouse for life, but wants principal remaining at the spouse's death to pass to beneficiaries selected by client. This form is especially appropriate if the client has used much or all of his federal estate tax exemption for other assets. See the *Bob Benson* case study. This form leaves all the benefits to "one big QTIP trust," with the trustee having discretion to either make a fractional QTIP election, or divide the trust into two separate trusts at the client's death, with the QTIP election being made for only one of them, whichever seems best at the time.

Drawbacks: See discussion in the *Benson* case study.

Warning: The trust form 3.5(B) allows the trustee to divide the trust into two or more separate trusts. Such a discretionary "division" of a trust will not be recognized for purposes of allocating the decedent's generation skipping transfer (GST) tax exemption unless GST regulations are complied with. The form also does not include all language which may be necessary to qualify the trust for the marital deduction.

3.5(A) Beneficiary Designation Form

A.   Primary Beneficiary

I hereby designate as my primary Beneficiary, to receive 100% of the Death Benefit, if my spouse survives me, [TRUSTEE NAME], as Trustee of the [TRUST NAME] Trust under Agreement of Trust dated [TRUST DATE], a copy of which is attached hereto. The beneficiary of said trust, within the meaning of the Proposed Treasury Regulations, is my spouse, [SPOUSE NAME].

B.   Form of Distribution of Benefits

After my death, there shall be distributed to the Beneficiary, in each year, so long as my spouse is living, whichever of the following amounts is the greatest:

(a)   the net income of the Death Benefit for such year;

(b)   the Minimum Distribution Amount for such year; or

(c)   such amount as the Beneficiary shall direct by written instructions to the Administrator.

The Beneficiary, and not the Administrator, shall have sole responsibility for complying with these instructions as to the Form of Distribution of Benefits.

C.   Contingent Beneficiary

I hereby designate as my Contingent Beneficiary, to receive 100% of the Death Benefit if my spouse does not survive me, my issue surviving me, by right of representation.

3.5(B) Related Trust Provisions

___.   Payments After My Death

Upon my death, the Trustee shall hold and administer all property of the Trust, including any amounts received or receivable then or later as a result of my death or otherwise, as follows:

.01   If my spouse does not survive me, the Trustee shall designate all of such property as the "Family Trust," to be held and administered as provided in Article __.

.02   If my spouse survives me, the Trustee shall pay to my spouse the net income from the date of my death, at least quarter annually, for life.

.03   If this Trust is the beneficiary of death benefits under any "individual retirement account," "qualified retirement plan," or similar tax deferred retirement arrangement or annuity (the "Plan") the Trustee must withdraw from the Plan, in each calendar year, and deposit in this trust fund, at least whichever of the following amounts is the greater:

(a)   the Plan's net income for such year; or

(b)   the "minimum distribution amount" which is required to be withdrawn from such Plan under Section 401(a)(9) of the Code or other Code provisions or applicable law.

This paragraph .03 shall not be deemed to limit the Trustee's power and right to withdraw from the Plan in any year more than the greater of the said two amounts.

.04   Upon the death of my spouse, the Trustee shall pay the undistributed income (if any) to my spouse's estate, and the principal, as it may then exist, shall be held, administered and distributed on the terms provided for property of the Family Trust under Article __.

.__   Division of the Trust

The Trustee in its discretion may divide the trust into two or more separate shares, each such separate share to be administered as a separate trust on all the same terms provided herein for the undivided trust fund. I anticipate that the Trustee will exercise its discretion under this Article for reasons of administrative convenience, or in order to recognize different characteristics the separate shares or trusts will have for purposes of certain taxes.

3.6   Benefits Payable to Spouse, "Disclaimable" to Credit Shelter Trust; Different Contingent Beneficiary Specified Depending on Whether Spouse Actually Predeceases or Merely Disclaims

Who would consider using this form: A client who does not have sufficient non-retirement plan assets to fully fund a credit shelter trust, but wants nevertheless to leave the benefits to his spouse and allow the spouse to make the ultimate decision whether to (a) keep the benefits and roll them over to an IRA or (b) disclaim some or all of the benefits and allow them to flow to the credit shelter trust. See, *e.g.,* the *Eatons* case study.

Drawbacks: See Chapter 8.

3.6   Beneficiary Designation Form

I.   Introductory Provisions

[insert form 2.1 or form 2.2]

II.   Designation of Beneficiary

A.   <u>Primary Beneficiary</u>

I hereby designate as my Primary Beneficiary, to receive 100% of the Death Benefit, my spouse, [SPOUSE NAME], if my spouse survives me.

B.   <u>Contingent Beneficiary in Case of Disclaimer</u>

If my spouse survives me, but disclaims the Death Benefit (or part of it), I hereby designate as my Contingent Beneficiary, to receive the part of the Death Benefit so disclaimed, [TRUSTEE NAME], as Trustee of the [TRUST NAME] Trust, under agreement dated [TRUST DATE], a copy of which is attached hereto.

C.   <u>Contingent Beneficiary in Case of Death</u>

If my spouse does not survive me, I hereby designate as my Contingent Beneficiary, to receive 100% of the Death Benefit, my issue surviving me, by right of representation.

3.7   Benefits Payable to Credit Shelter Trust, "Disclaimable" to Spouse

Who would consider using this form: A client who does not have sufficient non-retirement assets to fund a credit shelter trust, and expects to use his retirement benefits for that purpose, but wants to leave the door open for a spousal rollover because he thinks that (a) there might possibly be sufficient other assets to fund the credit shelter trust by the time he dies so the retirement benefits won't be needed after all or (b) even if there are not sufficient other assets to fund the credit shelter trust when he dies the rollover might appear at that time likely to produce a better overall tax and financial picture for his beneficiaries. This client does not want to make the benefits payable to the spouse and disclaimable to the credit shelter trust because (a) he doesn't believe the spouse is capable of handling the decision, or can be relied upon to make the right decision or (b) only the children, not the spouse, are beneficiaries of the credit shelter trust and he does not want to risk having them be stuck with using the spouse's life expectancy if she disclaims (see Chapter 8).

Drawbacks of using this form: Do not use this form without first thoroughly investigating applicable state law on disclaimers by fiduciaries.

3.7(A) Beneficiary Designation Form

I.   Introductory Provisions

[insert form 2.1 or form 2.2]

II.   Designation of Beneficiary

A.   Primary Beneficiary

I hereby designate as my Primary Beneficiary, to receive 100% of the Death Benefit [TRUSTEE NAME] (hereinafter "my Trustee"), as Trustee of the [TRUST NAME] Trust, under Agreement of Trust dated [TRUST DATE], a copy of which is attached hereto.

B.   Alternative Primary Beneficiary

If and to the extent that my Trustee disclaims any of the Death Benefit, I name as my Primary Beneficiary, for the

portion so disclaimed, my spouse, [SPOUSE NAME], if my
spouse survives me.

3.7(B) Related Trust Provisions

.__   Disclaimers by Trustee

.01   The Trustee shall have the power and authority,
without the approval of any court, and without the consent of
any beneficiary, to disclaim (refuse to accept) any property or
interest in property that is payable to the trust by gift, devise,
inheritance, bequest or otherwise, if the Trustee, in its
discretion, determines that such disclaimer is in the best interest
of beneficiaries of this Trust or will otherwise help achieve the
objectives of this Trust.

.02   In exercising its discretion under this Article, the
Trustee shall be entitled to presume that any benefit conferred
on an individual is likewise a benefit to the descendants of that
individual, unless the trustee has been presented with clear and
convincing evidence to the contrary, and shall bear in mind my
objective of minimizing taxes for my family as a whole.

3.8   Life Insurance Proceeds Payable to Credit Shelter Trust, All Other Benefits to Spouse

Who would consider using this form: Any client who
holds life insurance inside his qualified retirement plan, and
wants the insurance proceeds payable to a trust (*e.g.,* to "fill up"
a credit shelter trust), but wants the surviving spouse to be able
to roll over the non-insurance portion of the benefits. See the
Dingells case study.

Warning: A client whose plan-held insurance is held in
a "subtrust" (see Chapter 6) cannot designate the beneficiary for
the policy.

3.8   Beneficiary Designation Form

I.   Introductory Provisions

[insert form 2.2]

II.   Designation of Beneficiary

A.   <u>Primary Beneficiary</u>

If my spouse, [SPOUSE NAME], survives me, the Death Benefit shall be distributed to the following Primary Beneficiaries:

1.   Any amount payable under any contract of life insurance on my life shall be paid to [TRUSTEE NAME], as Trustee of the [TRUST NAME] Trust, under Agreement of Trust dated [TRUST DATE], a copy of which is attached hereto.

2.   The balance of the Death Benefit shall be paid to my spouse.

B.   <u>Contingent Beneficiary</u>

If my spouse does not survive me (or to the extent my spouse disclaims any benefits otherwise distributable to my spouse under section A above), I direct that 100% of the Death Benefit (or the amount disclaimed as the case may be) shall be paid to [TRUSTEE NAME], as Trustee of the "Family Trust" of the said [TRUST NAME] Trust.

3.9 Non-Taxable Portion of Benefits Payable to Credit Shelter Trust, Balance to Spouse

Who would consider using this form: This is a more aggressive version of form 3.8, which attempts to leave all "rollable" benefits to the spouse, and all non-income-taxable distributions to a trust.

Warning: It is not known whether the IRS would recognize this allocation. The IRS might require apportionment of the taxable and non-taxable portions of the distributions between the two beneficiaries.

3.9 Beneficiary Designation Form

I.   Introductory Provisions

[insert form 2.2]

II.   Designation of Beneficiary

A.   <u>Primary Beneficiary</u>

If my spouse, [SPOUSE NAME], survives me, the Death Benefit shall be distributed to the following Primary Beneficiaries:

1.   The excess of any amount payable by reason of my death under any contract of life insurance on my life over the cash surrender value of such contract immediately prior to my death; plus any amount which is not subject to income tax by virtue of the "$5,000 death benefit exclusion" of s. 101(b) of the Code; plus any amount which represents the return of my non-deductible contributions to the Plan or other "basis" or "investment in the contract," shall be paid to [TRUSTEE

NAME], as Trustee of the [TRUST NAME] Trust under Agreement of Trust dated [TRUST DATE], a copy of which is attached hereto.

   2.   All other benefits payable under the Plan in the event of my death shall be paid to my spouse.

4.   OTHER BENEFICIARY DESIGNATION FORMS

4.1   Designating Spouse as Primary Beneficiary of IRA with Presumption Spouse Survives, and Election by Spouse to Treat the IRA as Her Own If She Survives Participant

   Who might consider this form: A participant who is past his RBD, and who wants to take all possible steps to allow his spouse, if she survives him, to elect to treat the IRA as her own IRA and name a new DB. See the *Fallon* case study.
   Drawbacks of this form: It is not yet known whether the IRS will recognize a spousal election executed prior to the original participant's death, or a presumption of survivorship in case of simultaneous death.

4.1(A) Designation of Beneficiary by Participant

I.   Introductory Provisions

               [insert form 2.1]

II.   Designation of Beneficiary

   A.   <u>Primary Beneficiary</u>

I hereby designate as my Primary Beneficiary my spouse, [SPOUSE NAME], if my spouse survives me. If my said spouse and I die simultaneously or under such circumstances that it is difficult to determine which of us survived the other, my spouse shall be deemed to have survived me.

B.   Contingent Beneficiary

I hereby designate as my Contingent Beneficiary, if my said spouse does not survive me, [TRUSTEE NAME], as Trustee of the [TRUST NAME] Charitable Remainder Trust, under Agreement of Trust dated [TRUST DATE].

4.1(B) Election and Designation of Beneficiary by Spouse

1.   I, [SPOUSE NAME], spouse of the above named participant, hereby elect, in the event that I survive or am deemed to have survived my said spouse, to treat the Account as my own individual retirement arrangement. Accordingly, if I survive my said spouse, or am deemed to have survived my said spouse, I hereby designate as my Primary Beneficiary, to receive 100% of the Account in the event of my death, my issue surviving me, by right of representation.

2.   I elect, as the form of payment of benefits to me, installments commencing no later than my required beginning date, over the joint life expectancy of myself and my oldest Beneficiary who is living on my required beginning date, subject to the requirements of the incidental benefit rule. My life expectancy shall not be recalculated annually.

Signed this _____ day of _____, 19__.

_____

[SPOUSE NAME]

4.2 Designating Spouse as Primary Beneficiary; Trust as Contingent Beneficiary If P Dies Before RBD, Children as Contingent Beneficiaries If P Dies on or after RBD.

Who would use this form: A client who is many years younger than age 70½, and who is leaving his benefits to his spouse if living; otherwise to his revocable living trust, which will hold the funds in trust for his young children. Although this 30, 40 or 50 year-old client will probably redo his estate plan many times before his "required beginning date," the planner is concerned that the client may not do so. If the client's spouse predeceases the client, the trust for the children becomes the "primary beneficiary"; and if the client reaches age 70½ still having a revocable trust as his beneficiary, he will have "no DB" and will have to withdraw benefits over only his own life expectancy. This problem could be solved by making the trust automatically irrevocable at age 70½ (see form 7.1), but some planners prefer not to use that approach. Under this form, the problem is solved by naming the children directly as (currently, contingent) beneficiaries once the participant reaches age 70½; the theory is that by that time the children will be old enough to receive the money directly. See discussion in Chapter 1.

4.2 Beneficiary Designation Form

I.   Introductory Provisions

[insert form 2.1 or 2.2]

II.   Dispositive Provisions

    A.   <u>Primary Beneficiary</u>

    I hereby designate as my Primary Beneficiary, to receive 100% of the Death Benefit, my spouse, [SPOUSE NAME], if my spouse survives me.

    B.   <u>Contingent Beneficiary</u>

    If my spouse does not survive me, I hereby designate as my Contingent Beneficiary, to receive 100% of the Death Benefit:

    1.   If my death occurs on or after my Required Beginning Date, my children surviving me, in equal shares; provided, that if any child of mine does not survive me, but leaves issue surviving me, such issue shall take the share such deceased child would have taken if living, by right of representation.

    2.   If my death occurs before my Required Beginning Date, [TRUSTEE NAME], as Trustee of the [TRUST NAME] Trust, under Agreement of Trust dated [TRUST DATE], a copy of which is attached hereto.

    3.   My "Required Beginning Date" is April 1 of the year following the year I reach age 70½.

5.   MISCELLANEOUS   CLAUSES   FOR BENEFICIARY DESIGNATION FORMS

5.1   Recognizing Power of Attorney

[alternative 1 -- limited to a particular power of attorney]

By separate instrument dated this date, a copy of which is attached hereto, I have authorized [NAME] as my agent to exercise on my behalf any and all rights I have or may have with respect to the [Account] [Plan]. I hereby direct the Administrator to comply with any instructions issued to it on my behalf by my said agent.

[alternative 2 - more general]

I direct the Administrator to comply with any and all instructions issued to it on my behalf by my duly appointed legal guardian, conservator or other personal representative, or, whether or not such a representative has been appointed, by my agent acting under a power of attorney executed by me which grants the authority the agent seeks to exercise.

5.2   Allowing   Beneficiary   to   Appoint   Investment Manager

The Beneficiary may designate an Investment Manager for the Account. Upon receipt of written authorization from the Beneficiary, and until receiving notice that such authorization is revoked, the Administrator shall comply with investment instructions of the Investment Manager in accordance with the Beneficiary's authorization.

5.3 Surviving Spouse's Election to Treat Deceased Spouse's IRA as Surviving Spouse's Own IRA

I hereby elect to treat my entire interest in my deceased spouse's individual retirement account described above as my own individual retirement account, pursuant to Proposed Treasury Regulation 1.408-8, Q&A 4(b). The result of such election, as provided in said proposed regulation, is that I shall be considered the individual for whose benefit the said account is maintained.

6. ELECTION REGARDING FORM OF BENEFITS AND METHOD OF DETERMINING LIFE EXPECTANCY AT AGE 70½

6.1 Individual Retirement Account

Note: This form can be adapted for use with a QRP.

To: _____
Name of Trustee or Custodian

From: _____
Name of Participant

Re: Individual Retirement Account No._____

Participant's Required Beginning Date: _____

A.   <u>Recital; Method of Determining Life Expectancy</u>

I am the owner of the above-entitled individual retirement account. Under s. 401(a)(9) of the Internal Revenue

Code, I am required to withdraw benefits from the account, beginning no later than my "Required Beginning Date," in installments over the joint life expectancy of myself and my Designated Beneficiary. Under Proposed Treasury Regulations, I am required to elect irrevocably the method of determining my "life expectancy," and (if my Designated Beneficiary is my spouse) the life expectancy of my Designated Beneficiary. I hereby elect as follows:

My life expectancy:

    _____   shall be redetermined annually

    _____   shall not be redetermined annually ("term certain" or "fixed term" method).

If my Designated Beneficiary is my spouse, the life expectancy of my Designated Beneficiary:

    _____   not applicable -- spouse is not designated beneficiary

    _____   shall be redetermined annually

    _____   shall not be redetermined annually ("term certain" or "fixed term" method).

B.   Form of Benefit Payments During My Lifetime

I elect as the form of payment of my benefits the following. There shall be distributed to me, in each calendar year, beginning with the year in which I reach age 70½, the Minimum Distribution Amount, except as follows:

1.   I reserve the right to request and receive, at any time, distribution of any amount greater than the Minimum Distribution Amount.

2.   The Minimum Distribution Amount for the year in which I reach age 70½ may be paid in January, February or March of the following year.

3.   I reserve the right to use the alternative method to satisfy the requirements for minimum distributions specified in IRS Notice 88-38, 1988-1 C.B. 524.

C.   Definition of Minimum Distribution Amount

In each calendar year, beginning with the year I reach age 70½, the Minimum Distribution Amount shall be the minimum amount required to be distributed for such year under section 401(a)(9) of the Code (and regulations thereunder) based on my election to take my benefits in annual installments over the joint life expectancy of myself and my Designated Beneficiary.

Signed this ___ day of _____, 19___.

_____
Signature of Participant

Witness: _____

Receipt of the above election form is hereby acknowledged this ___ day of _____, 19___.

_____

Name of Custodian or Trustee

By:_____
Authorized Representative

7.   TRUST   PROVISIONS   DEALING   WITH RETIREMENT BENEFITS

7.1   Trust   Administration   During   Donor's   Life, Including Irrevocability Provision

.__   Administration During my Life.

.01   The Trustee shall distribute to me such amounts of the principal or income of the trust (including all thereof) as I may request from time to time, or (if I am legally incapacitated) as my guardian, conservator or other legal representative may request on my behalf.

[alternative 1 -- trust is signed before age 70½, becomes automatically irrevocable at RBD]

.02   I reserve the right to amend or revoke this trust by one or more written and acknowledged instruments delivered to the Trustee, subject to the following restrictions:

(a)   No amendment shall be effective unless and until assented to by the Trustee.

(b)   I shall have no power to amend or revoke this Trust after March 31 of the year following the year in which I reach age 70½.

[alternative 2 -- trust is signed at or after age 70½]

.02   This trust shall be irrevocable, and I shall have no right to revoke or amend the same.

7.2   Insulating Retirement Assets From Estate Claims and Charitable Gifts

Notwithstanding any other provision hereof, and except as provided in this paragraph, the Trustee may not distribute to or for the benefit of my estate, any charity or any other non-individual beneficiary any benefits payable to this trust under any qualified retirement plan, individual retirement account or other retirement arrangement subject to the "minimum distribution rules" of s. 401(a)(9) of the Code, or other comparable provisions of law. It is my intent that all such retirement benefits be distributed to or held for only individual beneficiaries, within the meaning of s. 401(a)(9) and applicable regulations. Accordingly I direct that such benefits may not be used or applied for payment of my debts, taxes and other claims against my "estate" except to the minimum extent that would be required under applicable state or federal law in the absence of any specific provision on the subject in my will or this trust. This paragraph shall not apply to any charitable bequest which is specifically directed to be funded with retirement benefits by other provisions of this instrument.

7.3   Excluding Older Adopted "Issue"

Notwithstanding any other provision hereof or of state law, the class of my "issue" shall not include an individual who is my "issue" by virtue of legal adoption if such individual (i) was so adopted after my Required Beginning Date or my death, whichever occurs first and (ii) is older than the oldest beneficiary of this trust who was a living member of said class on the earlier of said dates. My "Required Beginning Date," for purposes of this paragraph, means April 1 of the year following the year in which I reach age 70½, or, if later, the date on which this trust is first named as a beneficiary of any retirement plan, benefit or arrangement subject to the "minimum distribution rules" of s. 401(a)(9) of the Code.

7.4   Marital Deduction Saving Language

If any marital trust created by this instrument becomes the beneficiary of death benefits under any "individual retirement account," "qualified retirement plan," or similar tax-deferred retirement arrangement or annuity (the "Plan") the Trustee must withdraw from the Marital Trust's share of the Plan, in each calendar year, and deposit in the Marital Trust, at least whichever of the following amounts is the greatest:

A.   the net income of the Marital Trust's share of such Plan for such year; or
B.   the "minimum distribution amount" which is required to be withdrawn from such share under Section 401(a)(9) of the Code or other comparable Code provisions or applicable law; or
[optional]
C.   Such greater amount as my spouse shall request by written notice to the Trustee.

This paragraph shall not be deemed to limit the Trustee's power and right to withdraw from the Marital Trust's share of the Plan in any year more than the greatest of the said amounts.

8.   MISCELLANEOUS FORMS

8.1   Power of Attorney for Retirement Benefits

My Agent shall have the power to establish one or more "individual retirement accounts" or other retirement plans or arrangements in my name.

In connection with any pension, profit sharing or stock bonus plan, individual retirement arrangement, s. 403(b) annuity or account, s. 457 plan, or any other retirement plan, arrangement or annuity in which I am a participant or of which I am a beneficiary (whether established by my Agent or otherwise) (each of which is hereinafter referred to as "such Plan"), my Agent shall have the following powers, in addition to all other applicable powers granted by this instrument:

1.   To make contributions (including "rollover" contributions) or cause contributions to be made to such Plan with my funds or otherwise on my behalf.

2.   To receive and endorse checks or other distributions to me from such Plan, or to arrange for the direct deposit of the same in any account in my name or in the name of [any revocable "living" trust established by me.] [or, name of specific trust].

3.   To elect a form of payment of benefits from such Plan, to withdraw benefits from such Plan, to make contributions to such Plan and to make, exercise, waive or consent to any and all elections and/or options that I may have

regarding the contributions to, investments or administration, of, or distribution or form of benefits under, such Plan.

4.   To designate one or more beneficiaries or contingent beneficiaries for any benefits payable under such Plan on account of my death, and to change any such prior designation of beneficiary made by me or by my Agent; provided, however, that my Agent shall have no power to designate my Agent directly or indirectly as a beneficiary or contingent beneficiary to receive a greater share or proportion of any such benefits than my Agent would have otherwise received unless such change is consented to by all other beneficiaries who would have received the benefits but for the proposed change.   This limitation shall not apply to any designation of my Agent as beneficiary in a fiduciary capacity, with no beneficial interest.

8.2   Tax Clause in Will

Any tax on "excess retirement accumulations" imposed on my estate under Section 4980A of the Internal Revenue Code shall be borne by the recipient of the retirement benefits included in the measure of such tax.   If more than one beneficiary received such benefits, the tax under section 4980A shall be apportioned among them in proportion to the relative amounts of benefits included in the measure of such tax payable to each such beneficiary.

Appendix C
Checklists

1. Checklist For Meeting With Client

Here is a list of information the estate planner needs to gather regarding retirement benefits when meeting with a client. This checklist will help determine what options are available for taking (or deferring) distributions from the client's retirement plans. The information provided here will establish the minimums the client must withdraw (to avoid penalties) and the maximum period of tax deferral available. While this information may be helpful in determining which benefits should be tapped first to fulfill the client's living needs, this checklist is not aimed at providing information for "financial planning," defined as determining the best investment mix and withdrawal schedule to provide a desired level of retirement income.

Today's date: _____

I. Client Information

A. Client: Name: _____
   Date of Birth: _____
   Current Age: _____
   Year the client turns 70½: _____
   Age on birthday in the "70½ year": _____
   Required beginning date: _____

B. Spouse: Name:_____
   Date of Birth: _____
   Current Age: _____
   Age on birthday that occurs
   in client's "70½ year": _____

C. Names and birthdates of children (or other intended beneficiaries):

D. If client is a surviving spouse, with benefits inherited from a deceased spouse, did client make s. 4980A(d)(5) election to defer 15% excise tax? _____ (Obtain a copy of 706 filed for deceased spouse to verify.)

II. Plan Information: Qualified Plans

For EACH qualified plan, obtain the following information:

A. Name of plan: _____

B. Sponsoring employer: _____

C. Type: _____ Profit sharing
          _____ ESOP
          _____ 401(k)
          _____ Plain old profit sharing

          _____ Pension
          _____ Money purchase
          _____ Defined benefit

          _____ Stock bonus

          _____ Other: _____

          _____ Type of plan not determined

D. Value of Benefits

   Total value as of _____: $_____

Amount of after-tax contributions or other "basis" or "investment in the contract" included in above, if any: $_____

Does the plan contain any life insurance? _____

If yes, insurance company name: _____

Policy No.: _____

Face amount of policy: $_____

Cash Value: $_____

E. Lump sum distribution (LSD) eligibility (if client is "participant")

1. If answer to any of the following is "NO," the client is not currently eligible for LSD treatment:

(a) Is client over 59½? _____

(b) Has client been a participant in the plan for five or more full calendar years prior to current year? _____

(c) Is it true that client has elected LSD treatment for no other plan in any other taxable year? _____

(d) Is it true that client has taken no distributions from any of the aggregated plans (see q. 2) since the most recent to occur of the following events: reaching age 59½; separation from service (common law employees only); disability (self-employeds)? _____

2. All employer plans of the same type must be aggregated to determine whether there has been a distribution of the employee's entire balance. List here plans which must be aggregated:

3. Was client born before 1936? _____ If yes, client is eligible for 10YFA (as well as 5YFA, which everyone over 59½ is eligible for).

4. Was client a participant in this plan before 1974? _____ If no, skip this question. If yes, determine:

(a) _____ Calendar <u>years</u> prior to 1974 during any part of which the client was an active participant in this plan (a whole number)

(b) _____ Calendar <u>months</u> after 1974 during any part of which client was an "active participant" in this plan

(c) _____ Portion eligible for 20% cap gains treatment:

$$c = (a) \text{ divided by } (a + b/12)$$

III. <u>Plan Information: Individual Retirement Accounts</u>

For each IRA:

A. Name of account: _____

B. _____ Custodian or _____ Trustee:

_____

C. Account No.: _____

D. Surviving spouses only:

What type of contributions does this account contain?

1. _____ This was deceased spouse's IRA; it has been changed to an IRA in name of spouse; or, this IRA contains benefits spouse inherited and "rolled over" from another IRA or other retirement plan belonging to deceased spouse.

2. _____ This IRA contains surviving spouse's own contributions (either contributions made on surviving spouse's behalf by deceased spouse during deceased spouse's lifetime, or surviving spouse's own $2,000/year contributions, or rollover of benefits from a qualified plan belonging to surviving spouse).

3. _____ This IRA contains both #1 and #2-type contributions. (Note: this result is bad if the surviving spouse did not make a 4980A(d)(5) election.)

E. Participants other than surviving spouses:

What type of contributions does this account contain?

_____ Rollover contribution from a qualified plan only

_____ Non-rollover contributions (up to $2,000/year)

_____ Both types

F. IRA balance as of _____: $_____

This includes $_____ of non-deductible contributions (attach IRS form 8606 for most recent year).

IV. Plan Information: 403(b) Plans

For each 403(b) plan:

A. Name of account: _____

B. Name of _____ Custodian or _____ Trustee:

_____

C. Account No.: _____

D. This annuity (or mutual fund custodial account) is funded by:

_____ Employer contributions other than salary reduction

_____ Salary reduction agreement

E. Plan value as of _____: $_____

Remaining 12/31/86 balance: $_____

V. Plan Information: for all IRAs, QRPs and 403(b) plans:

A. Benefit forms offered: death prior to RBD (cross out or skip if client is past RBD).

_____ Lump sum

If yes: Is this option permitted for spouse?_____

For other individual beneficiaries? _____

For trusts? _____

_____ Installments over LE of beneficiary

If yes: Is this option permitted for spouse? _____

For other individual beneficiaries? _____

For trusts? _____

_____ Other installment options (describe):

_____ Annuity options (describe):

B. Benefit forms offered: at RBD:

_____ Lump sum (suitable for rollover)

_____ Installments payments over:

_____ LE of participant?

_____ Joint LE of participant and spouse?

_____ Joint LE of participant and other individual?

_____ Joint LE of participant and trust beneficiary?

C. If installments over LE are permitted, is redetermination of
LE:

_____ Mandatory

_____ Not permitted

_____ Participant can choose

D. Documents needed from client (check if received):

Plan description or account agreement _____

Current beneficiary designation _____

VI. "Grandfathering" information

A. 15% excise tax

Did client have more than $562,500 of benefits in all plans
as of 8/1/86? _____ If yes, did client elect to "grandfather"
these benefits from 15% excise tax? _____ If yes, obtain a
copy of the form 5329 on which the election was made, and all
5329s filed since and complete the following:

1. Election was made on form 5329 filed with return for (check
one): _____1987 _____1988

2. The original grandfather balance was: $_____

3. The recovery method elected was:

_____ Attained age [very rare]

_____ Discretionary [most chose this method]

4. If the discretionary method was elected, has client ever elected to accelerate recovery? _____ If yes, in what year? _____

5. The client's remaining grandfather balance as of the beginning of the current year was: $_____

B. TEFRA 242(b) designation

1. Did the client file a designation, before January 1, 1984, regarding the timing of distribution of his plan benefits? _____ If yes, obtain a copy of the election(s) filed, and determine:

2. Did election meet requirements of Notice 83-22? _____

3. Has client done anything which would invalidate the election? _____

4. What "catch-up" required minimum distributions would be required if the election were revoked today? $_____

C. TRA '86 s. 1121(d)(d)-(5), as amended by TAMRA

1. Was the client born after 6/30/17? _____

2. Is the client a 5% owner of the employer (plan sponsor), or has client ever been a 5% owner at any time during a plan year ending on or after the calendar year (19___) in which he/she reached age 66½? _____

3. Is the client retired? _____

If the answer to ALL THREE of these questions is "NO" then the client is grandfathered from the minimum distribution rules until actual retirement.

D. Estate tax exclusion

1. Did client "separate from service" prior to 1983? _____ After 1982 but prior to 1985? _____

2. Has client changed the "form of benefit payments" since separating from service? _____

If the answer to either part of #1 is "yes" and if the answer to #2 is "no," client's benefits are eligible for total or partial federal estate tax exclusion.

VII. If client is already past his/her RBD:

For each plan and IRA:

A. Determine RBD.

B. Obtain: Copy of beneficiary designation in effect on the RBD. If there have been any changes since the RBD (e.g., benefits transferred from a plan to an IRA, or from one IRA to anther IRA; or beneficiary designation changes); obtain, in addition, copies of all beneficiary designations in effect since the RBD.

C. Based on the beneficiary designation and plan terms in effect on the RBD, what method of determination of life expectancy was irrevocably elected then?

Client's life expectancy: _____ Redetermined annually

_____ Not redetermined (term certain)

Spouse's life expectancy
(if spouse was DB):   _____ Redetermined annually

_____ Not redetermined (term certain)

D.   Determine whether required minimum distributions have been taken. Make this determination separately for (i) each qualified plan, (ii) each 403(b) plan and (iii) all IRAs collectively.

1	2	3	4
Year Client Turned	**Plan Balance on 12/31 of Preceding Year**	**Minimum Distribution for Year**	**Distributions Actually Taken**
70½ (19)	$	$ (a)	$ (a)
71½ (19)	$	$	$
72½ (19)	$	$	$
73½ (19)	$	$	$
Etc.			

Notes: (a) Distribution for 70½ year can be taken any time prior to 4/1 of following year.

2. Rollover Checklist

For most retirees, taking money out of an employer-sponsored ("qualified") retirement plan, and rolling over the distribution to an IRA, is an attractive way to increase their investment control, and the distribution flexibility, of their retirement benefits. However, the move from qualified plan to IRA (or, in the case of a surviving spouse dealing with inherited benefits, the change from a plan in the decedent's name to an IRA in the spouse's name) should not be made without a careful review of many factors, great and small, which may affect the desirability of such a step. It is unfortunate when benefits are transferred for one particular good reason (such as the ability to self-direct investments), and it is later discovered that, due to other factors not considered, the change has been disadvantageous.

This checklist presents factors to consider when deciding whether to take money out of a "qualified retirement plan" (such as a Keogh, money purchase pension, profit sharing, defined benefit pension or 401(k) plan) and "roll it over" to an IRA. The factors may differ depending on whether the client is a --

- PE: Participating employee who earned the benefits but does not own the employer business or control the administration of the plan.

- SS: Surviving spouse, dealing with a plan benefit or IRA inherited from a deceased spouse. Several of the factors, such as 2(L), 3(E), 4(B) and 4(C), apply regardless of whether the inherited benefit is in an IRA or a qualified plan.

- SBO: Small business owner, for whom the question is not solely whether to transfer the benefits to another type of plan but whether to terminate the qualified plan altogether. This checklist addresses only the issues facing the SBO whose plan covers no other employees. A plan which covers other employees besides the SBO involves many additional factors not considered here.

The checklist assumes that the plan participant is not losing any vesting or accrual of benefits by transferring out of the qualified plan, or has decided to forego available further vesting and accrual; and does not address whether there should be a termination of employment at a particular time.

Not all subjects mentioned in the checklist are discussed in the text. When a checklist item is discussed at greater length in the text, a cross-reference is provided.

Finally, this checklist does not cover the requirements for a valid rollover -- only the question of whether a rollover is advantageous.

1.   Consider the loss of the ability to receive a "lump sum distribution" (LSD).

PE, SS, SBO: A distribution of all benefits from a qualified plan within one taxable year may qualify for special treatment as a LSD under Code s. 402(d). See Chapter 2. IRA distributions are never eligible for LSD treatment. Once benefits come out of a qualified plan and into an IRA, this favorable treatment is lost -- although if the rollover IRA is kept separate from other IRAs, it can possibly be restored later by rolling back to another qualified plan (see 4(A), below).

Use IRS form 4972 as a checklist to see whether the contemplated distribution meets the numerous requirements for this special treatment. If it does not, skip this Part 1. If it does, then consider the following points:

A.   A LSD qualifies for one or more of three special methods of tax calculation known as "ten year forward averaging" (10YFA), "five year forward averaging" (5YFA) and "capital gains." See Chapter 2. For small LSDs, these methods can produce an income tax rate as low as 14%. This may compare favorably with the taxpayer's normal rate (up to 39.6%). It may be advantageous to pay tax now on the LSD, at this special low rate, and invest the net after-tax distribution outside of any retirement plan, rather than defer the taxation by rolling over to an IRA and pay a much higher tax on it later.

B.   A LSD is subject to a separate "threshold" for determining the 15% excise tax under Code s. 4980A. See Chapter 5.   While the normal threshold is $150,000/year (meaning that distributions in excess of $150,000 will be subject to the 15% excise tax), a taxpayer can receive a LSD of up to $750,000 free of the excise tax -- in addition to receiving $150,000 free of the tax, in the same year, from other plans, if he wants to. Once the LSD is rolled into an IRA, the possibility of receiving a large one-time LSD free of excise tax is lost.

C.   If the distribution qualifies for LSD treatment, but you decide you want to roll it over anyway, do not do the rollover in the same taxable year that you take a LSD from a DIFFERENT plan that you do NOT roll over. In order for your LSD from the OTHER plan to get the special tax treatments allowed for LSDs, the special LSD treatment must be elected for all distributions in the same year that qualify for it. Thus, rolling over the LSD from ONE plan would make the LSD from the OTHER plan ineligible for 10YFA, 5YFA, etc.

2. Consider the other advantages of a qualified plan that you may be giving up:

In addition to the special LSD treatment available for some qualified plan distributions, qualified plans offer certain features that IRAs do not. (Sometimes these advantages can be restored by rolling back to a qualified plan; see 4(A), below.)

A. **Creditor protection.** PE, SS, SBO: Both qualified plans and IRAs can offer some protection from creditors, and neither is completely invulnerable. Generally speaking, however, qualified plans are more protected than IRAs.

B. **Loans.** PE, SBO: Qualified plans often permit plan participants to take loans from the plan. IRAs cannot do this.

C. **Investment alternatives.** SBOs: IRAs cannot invest in "collectibles." Also, due to the requirement of having an institutional trustee or custodian, IRAs are effectively limited to investing in assets the institution is willing to hold -- which may not include partnerships, venture investments or other non-publicly traded or offbeat investments you would like to hold.

PE, SS: A large, employer-run plan may offer professional investment management superior to, and cheaper than, what you can provide through a self-directed IRA.

D. **Choice of trustee.** SBO: Although you can be trustee of your own business's plan, you cannot be trustee or custodian of your IRA. However, except for the issue of investment alternatives (C, above), this is rarely a significant factor, since a "self-directed IRA" can be easily obtained with no trustee's fee and a nominal custodial fee.

E.   **Life Insurance.** PE, SBO: An IRA cannot hold life insurance. Thus, any existing policies must be cancelled, distributed or purchased from the qualified plan before the plan benefits are "rolled" to an IRA. See Chapter 6. Cancellation may involve loss of needed benefits. Distribution requires payment of income tax on the policy's value, and loss of the potential for further income tax deferral on this value. Purchase of the policy for its cash value may be costly. On the bright side, distribution or purchase of the policy allows the participant to transfer the policy to an irrevocable trust, removing it from his taxable estate, which may be better for the family in the long run than leaving it in the plan indefinitely.

F.   **Distribution Options.** PE, SS, SBO: A QRP may offer annuity alternatives that are effectively subsidized by the plan. For example, the plan's "joint and survivor annuity" option may offer a married couple who are in good health a better value than the supposedly "equal value" lump sum distribution. Alternatively, actuarial factors (especially changing interest rates) may radically change the amount of your "lump sum distribution" from a defined benefit pension plan over a few months. If the plan offers subsidized annuities, and there are substantial dollars involved, consider hiring a professional actuary to evaluate the alternatives offered by the plan before opting for a lump sum.

G.   **State tax issues.** PE, SS, SBO: Certain states exempt from income tax all pensions paid by defined benefit plans; this exemption would cease to apply to benefits that had been rolled over to an IRA. It is essential to carefully review the tax laws of the taxpayer's state of domicile (and of the state taxpayer plans to retire in) before changing the status of retirement benefits.

H.   **Contribution limits.** SBO: The maximum IRA contribution of $2,000/year (or 15% of income, maximum $22,500, for a SEP-IRA) is less than the maximum qualified plan contribution, which is 25% of income, maximum $30,000 (or, potentially, much more for a defined benefit plan).

I.   **After tax contributions.** PE, SBO: An employee's after-tax contributions to a plan cannot be rolled over to an IRA. Thus, terminating participation in the plan will require distribution of the after-tax contribution account and loss of further tax deferral on the earnings from this amount.

J.   **TEFRA 242(b) election.** Rolling from a qualified plan to an IRA automatically terminates any TEFRA 242(b) election in effect for the plan. Such termination causes acceleration of any previously postponed required "minimum distributions." See Chapter 7.

K.   **Distributions before age 59½, PE, SBO:** Generally, distributions before reaching age 59½ are subject to a 10% penalty. See Chapter 9. There are exceptions for disabled participants and for distributions taken (from an IRA; or, after separation from service from a QRP) in annual installments over the recipient's life expectancy. Two additional exceptions exist for qualified plans: distributions made at or after age 55, and after termination of employment; and distributions for certain medical expenses. By rolling to an IRA, you lose the availability of these exceptions, and if you want to take a distribution before age 59½, will be limited to disability or installment distributions.

L.   **Distributions before age 59½, SS:** Distributions of death benefits are exempt from the 10% penalty for "premature distributions," regardless of the decedent's or beneficiary's age.

However, once the death benefits are placed in an IRA in the SS's own name, the SS becomes the "participant," and if the SS is under 59½, he/she will not be able to withdraw any benefits prior to attaining that age without paying the 10% penalty (or qualifying for the hardship or installment exception). Thus, the SS who is under age 59½ when the first spouse dies should only "roll over" amounts that will not be needed before age 59½.

M. **Loss of federal estate tax exclusion for grandfathered individuals.** An employee who separated from service prior to 1985 and has not since changed the form of distribution of his benefits may be entitled to have all or part of his remaining benefits excluded from his federal gross estate. See Chapter 7. This favorable tax treatment will be lost for benefits rolled to an IRA.

3. **Consider the advantages an IRA has over a qualified plan.**

A. **Investment alternatives.** PE, SS: The self-directed IRA offers more control of, and alternatives for, investment than the typical employer plan. This feature is attractive if you have the knowledge, skill and time to manage your own investments or to select and supervise an investment manager. This is not a factor for the SBO who can control his own plan's investments in much the same manner as an IRA.

B. **Administrative costs.** SBO: An IRA does not have to file the annual form 5500, and in general has minimal to non-existent administrative expenses, compared to a qualified plan which costs at least hundreds of dollars a year to administer, and can cost much more.

C. **Distribution options, PE:** To achieve maximum income tax deferral, the most desirable distribution option is usually (at age 70½), "installments over the joint life expectancy of the participant and designated beneficiary (DB)" or (in case of death prior to age 70½) "installments over the life expectancy of the DB." See Chapter 1. These options are often not offered at all by employer-maintained plans, or, if offered, are limited to only certain beneficiaries such as the spouse. Although some IRAs have similar undesirable limitations on distribution options, most self-directed IRAs offered by major mutual funds, brokerage firms and banks provide all distribution options permitted by the tax laws.

D. **Distribution options, SBO:** Although the SBO can draft his plan to provide every desired distribution option, as a practical matter, once the SBO dies or retires, the "employer" ceases to exist. Continuation of the plan may require careful (expensive) legal maneuvering or be legally impossible. Since surviving beneficiaries (with the sole exception of the spouse) cannot "roll over" inherited plan benefits to an IRA, it may be wise to get the plan terminated, and the benefits transferred to an IRA, before death. The survivors can maintain an IRA after the owner's death.

E. **Distribution options, SS:** By rolling over the deceased spouse's benefits to an IRA in her own name, the SS can achieve maximum income tax deferral by naming her own DB. Then, upon her subsequent death (or attaining age 70½) the benefits can be distributed over the DB's life expectancy (or the joint life expectancy of the SS and DB). See Chapter 1. In contrast, if the SS leaves the benefits in the decedent's plan, then the benefits will have to be distributed over only the SS's life expectancy (the only exception to this being, if the decedent died before reaching 70½, and the SS *also* dies before the decedent would have reached age 70½, the life expectancy of the contingent beneficiary, if there is one, can be used). See Chapter 3.

F.   **State tax law issues.** PE, SS, SBO: See 2(G) above.

G.   **Freedom from REA requirements.** PE, SBO: The spouse of a qualified plan participant has an automatic legal right under the Retirement Equity Act of 1984 to receive part of the participant's death benefits and (in the case of a pension plan) retirement benefits. See Chapters 3 and 8. These rights can be eliminated by transferring the benefits to an IRA (since IRAs are not subject to REA) although, in the case of all pension plans and some profit sharing plans, the distribution of a lump sum to the participant will require the spouse's consent.

4.   What IRA you will put the distribution into?

A.   SBO, PE: If the distribution is coming from a qualified plan, it can eventually be returned to a qualified plan, and regain some or all of the advantages of qualified plan benefits listed at 1 and 2 above, if the distribution is kept in a separate "rollover" IRA, and is not commingled with other ("contributory") IRAs.

B.   SS: If the SS did not make the election under s. 4980A(d)(5), the SS should not under any circumstances combine distributions from the deceased spouse's plans and IRAs with the SS's own IRAs. Commingling the two types would cause the deceased spouse's benefits to be added to the SS's benefits for purposes of computing the 15% excise tax. If the deceased spouse's benefits are maintained separately, they will be exempt from the 15% excise tax since the tax was assessed at the deceased spouse's death. See Chapter 5.

C. PE, SS, SBO: If you are over age 70½ when you receive the distribution, do not roll it into an IRA without first making sure that the beneficiary designation of the IRA is what you want it to be. Since you are over 70½, you must withdraw the benefits over the joint life expectancy of yourself and your designated beneficiary (DB). A SS can create a new IRA to receive the new distribution, with a new DB, and use the joint life expectancy of the SS and new DB to measure distributions. SBOs and PEs who receive an eligible rollover distribution after 70½ generally (*i.e.*, unless exempted by a grandfather rule) will have already established a maximum payout period for the benefits, but could inadvertently shorten it by rolling the benefits to an IRA with the "wrong" DB. See Chapters 1 and 3.

5. Other things to remember.

A. If you cannot decide what to do, and want to think about it for a while, do NOT in the meantime take a partial distribution from the qualified plan to *(e.g.)* pay for living expenses while you consider the question of what to do with the rest of the benefits. A partial distribution may permanently end eligibility for favorable LSD treatment later. See Chapter 2.

B. Finally, when the time comes to take the distribution, do it as a "direct rollover" from the plan trustee directly to the IRA, rather than as a distribution to the participant (or SS) followed by a rollover. A distribution will be subject to the 20% withholding tax even though it is going to be entirely rolled over.

3. Checklist of Required Distribution Results After RBD ("Permutations")

The following list of "permutations" describes every possible scenario there could be for a participant who (i) lives past his required beginning date (RBD) and (ii) does not change his designated beneficiary (DB) after the RBD. To understand the checklist, read Chapter 1.

To use this list, first determine who was the participant's "DB" ON the RBD. Then determine whether the participant had elected, as of his RBD, to redetermine life expectancy annually for himself, his spouse, both or neither. Then find the "permutation" in the list below that matches what you have found. This list will then tell you what will be required by way of minimum distributions after the first death and after the second death. Use this as a quick refresher when confronted with post-RBD distribution questions.

Please note: when this list states who was the "beneficiary" or "DB," it is referring to the beneficiary named ON THE RBD. That is the critical date. The fact that the person who was named as beneficiary on the RBD later dies HAS NO EFFECT on the question of "who is the DB." The DB is determined on the RBD.

Similarly, if a particular person is named as the participant's beneficiary but then dies BEFORE the participant's RBD, that person is not the "DB." In that case, the contingent beneficiary would in effect become the primary beneficiary, and therefore the contingent beneficiary would be the "DB."

Note also: Unfortunately, if the participant has changed his "DB" one or more times after the RBD, this list will not help you. Changing beneficiaries after the RBD introduces even more permutations, discussed in Chapter 1.

In the following list, "LE" stands for "life expectancy." For the exact method of computing the distributions referred to, see "How to Compute Installments" in Chapter 1.

1.   Spouse is beneficiary, spouse dies first

At his RBD, John names his wife, Mary, as his beneficiary, and the children as contingent beneficiaries. Mary later dies, and

. . . both spouses' LEs were being recalculated annually. In the year after her death, Mary's LE goes to zero. John continues withdrawing over his own LE only, recalculated annually. When he later dies, the children will have to withdraw all benefits within one year after his death.

. . . Mary's LE was being recalculated, John's was not. Mary's LE goes to zero in the year after her death. John continues withdrawing over his own LE only. In the final year of his LE (at age 86), he withdraws the remaining balance. If he dies before age 86, the children will continue to withdraw over the balance of John's original LE (*i.e.*, until he would have reached age 86).

. . . Mary's LE was not being recalculated, John's was. Mary's death has no impact on the withdrawal schedule. Mary expires but her LE lives on. John continues to withdraw over their joint LEs, with his being recalculated annually. When John dies, his LE goes to zero in the following year, but the children can withdraw over the remaining balance of Mary's LE, if any. If John's death occurs after Mary's LE had already expired, the children must withdraw all remaining benefits within one year after John's death.

. . . neither spouse's LE was recalculated. Mary's death has no impact on the withdrawal schedule. John keeps on withdrawing over their "term certain" joint LE. John's death also has no impact on the withdrawal schedule. Either John (if he lives that long) or the children (if he doesn't) will withdraw

the final installment in the last year of the "joint LE" that was originally established on his RBD.

2.   <u>Spouse is beneficiary, participant dies first</u>

At his RBD, John names his wife, Mary, as his beneficiary, and the children as contingent beneficiaries. John dies before Mary, and . . .

. . . *both spouses' LEs were being recalculated.* John's LE goes to zero in the year following his death. Mary can continue withdrawing over just her own LE, redetermined annually; or, better yet, she can roll over John's benefits to her own IRA, name a new beneficiary, and start withdrawing (once she reaches age 70½, or right away if she is already over 70½) over the joint LE of herself and her new beneficiary. If Mary dies without having rolled over the benefits, the children will have to withdraw all benefits within one year after Mary's death.

. . . *Mary's LE was being recalculated, John's was not.* Mary can continue to withdraw over the joint LE of both spouses, *just as if John had not died*; or she can roll over the benefits to her own IRA. If she dies without having rolled over the benefits, her LE goes to zero in the year following her death; the children can continue to withdraw over the remaining balance of John's LE, or, if his LE has already expired, they must withdraw 100% of the benefits within one year after Mary's death.

. . . *John's LE was being recalculated, Mary's was not.* John's LE goes to zero. Mary can continue to withdraw over just her own LE; or she can roll over the benefits to her own IRA. If Mary dies without having rolled over the benefits, the children can continue to withdraw John's benefits over Mary's remaining LE.

. . . *neither spouse's LE was being recalculated.* Mary can continue to withdraw benefits over the remaining joint LE of John and Mary, just as if John had not died; or, she can roll over the benefits. If she dies without having rolled over the benefits, the children can continue to withdraw the benefits over the balance of the joint LE of John and Mary.

3.   Non-Spouse Beneficiary

When the designated beneficiary is not the spouse, there are fewer possible permutations, because the rollover option is not available and because the non-spouse beneficiary's LE cannot be recalculated.

At his RBD, Parent named Child as his "designated beneficiary," and started withdrawing over the joint LE of Parent and Child, as limited by the MDIB rule.

A.   *Parent dies first, and . . .*

. . . *Parent's LE was being recalculated.*   Parent's LE goes to zero. Child can withdraw the remaining benefits over the remaining period of Child's actual LE, as it existed on Parent's RBD, but without the limitations of the MDIB rule. Child cannot roll over the benefits or recalculate his LE. If Child dies before the end of his LE period (whether he dies before or after Parent), the next beneficiaries can continue to withdraw over the remaining balance of Child's LE (still without application of the MDIB rule).

. . . *Parent's LE was not being recalculated.*   Child can continue to withdraw over the remaining joint LE of Parent and Child, but without the limitations of the MDIB rule. If Child dies before the joint LE has ended, the next beneficiaries can continue to withdraw over the balance of this joint LE period.

B.   *The Non-Spouse Beneficiary Dies First, and...*

. . . *Parent's LE was being recalculated.* Child's death has no impact on the withdrawals.   Parent continues to withdraw over the remaining joint LE of Parent and Child, as limited by the MDIB rule, and continues to recalculate his own LE. When Parent dies, his LE goes to zero, but the MDIB rule also disappears.   The next beneficiaries can withdraw the remaining benefits over the remaining term of Child's actual LE, as it existed on Parent's RBD.   Note that even if there is no "contingent beneficiary," and the benefits become payable to Parent's estate, the *estate* can continue to withdraw the benefits over the balance of Child's original LE, because Child was the DB on the RBD.

. . . *Parent's LE was not being recalculated.* Child's death has no impact. Parent continues to withdraw over the remaining joint LE of Parent and Child, as limited by the MDIB rule. After Parent dies, the next beneficiaries can continue to withdraw over the balance of the joint LE of Parent and Child, as it existed on Parent's RBD, without the limitation of the MDIB rule.

4.   When There is No Designated Beneficiary

Richard had no "designated beneficiary" on his RBD. He is accordingly withdrawing benefits over only his own LE. Richard dies and . . .

. . . *his LE was being recalculated annually.* All benefits must be withdrawn by December 31 of the year following his death.

. . . *his LE was not being recalculated.* His death has no impact. The beneficiary of his benefits can continue to withdraw over the remaining balance of Richard's LE.

Appendix D
Software Available

<u>Pension and Excise Tax Planner</u>

Available from: Brentmark Software, Inc.
P.O. Box 4205
Winter Park, FL 32793-4205
1-800-879-6665

Price: $349. Demo disk is free.

Compares, side by side, up to four alternative strategies for distributing benefits at client's required beginning date, such as lump sum distribution (in a year you designate), minimum distributions under s. 401(a)(9), "threshold" distributions (*i.e.* the maximum annual amount not subject to 15% excise tax) or a custom distribution schedule entered by you. You input birth dates and plan balance; the client's income tax rates and rate of return (both of which you can vary year by year and from one scenario to another); and the client's estate tax bracket. You can determine whether the participant and/or spouse will recalculate life expectancies, what year the first spouse will die, and whether the participant or the beneficiary will die first.

The resulting reports show, year by year, for up to 60 years from today, what is distributed, what is left inside the plan, and how much is built up in the participant's "personal account," consisting of the accumulated after tax distributions from the plan, and the accumulated after tax earnings thereon. The program also prints out the annual distribution fraction denominator for every year.

The program compares the scenarios using a "net to family" figure each year. This figure assumes that all plan benefits are cashed out upon the death of the surviving spouse.

I use this program extensively, and with some tinkering can get it to do most things I want it to do, if not all. It is menu driven and very easy to learn and use. Though the DOS interface is a little clunky, it will be especially easy for users of Leimberg & LeClair's "Numbercruncher" software because it is very similar.

Drawbacks: Does not allow user to specify different income tax rates for plan distributions and other income. This may be corrected in next release. Also, it does not produce a self explanatory graphically attractive printout which can be readily understood by clients.

Steve Leimberg's Pension and Excise Tax Calculator

This is the same program sold by Brentmark, above. Leimberg sells it under license from Brentmark. To purchase from Leimberg, write to:

Steve Leimberg
P.O. Box 610
Bryn Mawr, PA 19010
Phone: (215) 527-5216
Fax: (215) 527-5226

Price is: $349.

The National Underwriter Co. "Tax Facts Calculator"

This program calculates the various taxes (income, estate, gift, excise), one at a time, based on inputs for your specific query. It does not do a "spreadsheet" type comparison. Similarly, it will calculate the required minimum distribution for a particular year if you feed in all the inputs, but will not generate a schedule of projected future distributions as Brentmark's does.

This program may be handy for certain specific inquiries -- for example if you fill in the inputs for a proposed "lump sum distribution," it will calculate the "ordinary income and capital gain" portions, and print out the taxes due under all available alternatives -- ordinary income, capital gains, 5YFA, 10YFA, etc., so you can immediately see which is the lowest.

Also, it calculates the taxable portion of a distribution from an IRA to which the participant has made non-deductible contributions.

It appears to consider numerous elaborate alternatives for tax sheltered annuities.

The same product also contains many other tax calculations -- regular income, estate and gift -- and contains various annuity tables; the Brentmark program in contrast, does only pension distribution projections.

May be purchased from:

The National Underwriter Co.
Customer Service Dept. #2-NM
505 Gest Street
Cincinnati, OH 45203-1716
1-800-543-0874

Bibliography

General Notes

In this Bibliography, citations to <u>Estate Planning</u> refer to the magazine of that name published by Warren Gorham & Lamont, 31 St. James Ave., Boston, MA 02116-4112.

"TMP" refers to the "Tax Management Portfolio" series published by the Bureau of National Affairs, Inc., 1231 25th St., N.W., Washington, D.C. 20037.

"CCH" stands for Commerce Clearing House, Inc., 4025 W. Peterson Ave., Chicago, IL 60646-6085.

<u>ACTEC Notes</u> magazine is published by the American College of Trust and Estate Counsel, 3415 South Sepulveda Boulevard, Suite 460, Los Angeles, CA 90034

Introduction: Books and Other Resources

Stephen J. Krass, *The Pension Answer Book*, 10th edition (Panel Publishers 1995). Question and answer format. Far and away the best handy desktop reference work on pension topics I have encountered. Most of the 30 chapters deal with "employer" issues such as the design, funding and qualification of retirement plans, but several chapters provide good material on distributions. Available for $118 from:

> Panel Publishers
> PO Box 990
> Frederick, MD 21705-9727
> (800) 638-8437

A Professional's Guide to the IRA Distribution Rules, by Seymour Goldberg, CPA, (100 pages, softbound, Foundation for Accounting Education, 1994). In 277 questions and answers, the author carefully guides the reader through the tax rules applicable to IRA distributions: pre-59½, inherited IRAs, minimum distribution rules, excess distributions, etc. Citations are provided for some but not all questions. Indexed by section of the code and regulations. May be purchased from:

Foundation for Accounting Education
Attn: Self-Study Department
530 Fifth Avenue, 5th Floor
New York, NY 10036
(212) 719-8300, ext. 373

Another resource of interest is *Distributions from IRAs and Qualified Plans: Maximizing Benefits: the Short Course*, by Bruce J. Temkin, MSPA, EA. Two 90-minute audiotapes plus outline. Explains the financial implications of the distribution requirements applicable to retirement benefits. Available from:

The College for Financial Planning
4695 South Monaco Street
Denver, CO 80237-3403
(303) 220-4800

Chapter 1:   Minimum Distribution Rules

For discussion of withholding rules applicable to plan distributions, see Frederick J. Benjamin, Jr., *Qualified Plans: Taxation of Distributions*, TMP 370-2d.

Chapter 2:   Income Tax Matters

For more information about IRD, see Alan S. Acker, *Income in Respect of a Decedent*, TMP 32-3d.

For a more thorough discussion of lump sum distributions, see Frederick J. Benjamin, Jr., *Qualified Plans: Taxation of Distributions*, TMP 370-2d (1992).

For further information on cases defining "separation from service," and determining whether a distribution is "on account of" such a separation, a good place to start is the 1995 CCH *Standard Federal Tax Reporter*, ¶ 18,207.

Chapter 3:   Marital Matters

For more discussion of the spouse's options, see Frederick Kuhn, "Retirement Plan Benefits: What are the Spouse's Options?" Estate Planning (10/92, p. 276).

For more information on spousal waivers under REA, see Lynn Wintriss, Esq. "Practice Tips: Waiver of Rights Under the Retirement Equity Act and Premarital Agreements," 19 ACTEC Notes, no. 2, Fall 1993.

Additional information about the QJSA and QPSA requirements may be found in the *Analysis of Federal Taxes: Income* (Research Institute of America, New York, NY, 1995), Vol. 7, sections H-8600 *et seq.* See also the *Employment Coordinator* (Thomson Publishing/Clark Boardman Callaghan), ¶ B-24,120.

Chapter 4:   Retirement Benefits and the Non-Citizen Spouse

The material in this chapter assumes a basic familiarity with the requirements of the marital deduction when the surviving spouse is not a U.S. citizen. For details, see CCH *Federal Estate and Gift Tax Reporter*, ¶ 7650 *et seq.*

Chapter 5:   The 15% Excise Tax

The interest rates published monthly by the IRS can be most easily obtained either from the Daily Tax Report published by BNA or the Leimberg & LeClair (phone (610) 525-6957) "FaxNet Newsletter" which provides these rates (along with other interest rates and indicators) to subscribers by fax monthly.

Chapter 6:   Life Insurance in the Retirement Plan

For an excellent discussion of life insurance in the retirement plan, see Beverly R. Budin, Esq., *Life Insurance*, TMP 111-4th (1987), p. A-45 *et seq.*

For a discussion of the income tax treatment of life insurance held in a retirement plan, see *Federal Tax Coordinator 2d*, Research Institute of America, New York, NY (1993), Vol. 12A, ¶ H-10500.

For a general, if incomplete, discussion of life insurance in qualified plans, see CCH *Pension Plan Guide*, Vol. 1, ¶ 3808 *et seq.* ¶ 4540 discusses "prohibited transactions."

For description of the limits on plan-owned insurance, see Krass, *The Pension Answer Book*, Q 14:4.

Other sources consulted include: "Life Insurance in Qualified Plans," Tracie K. Henderson, CPA, The Tax Adviser (6/93, p. 378).

Regarding "subtrusts," see: "The Qualified Plan as an Estate Planning Tool," by Andrew J. Fair, Esq., booklet distributed by Guardian Life Insurance Co. Of America, 201 Park Ave. South, New York, NY 10003; "Estate Tax on Life Insurance Held in Qualified Plans," by Mervin M. Wilf, Esq., in Retirement Plan Trio seminar 6/22/95, materials published by ALI-ABA, 4025 Chestnut St., Philadelphia, PA 19104-3099 (Publ. No. Q239); "IRS opens the way toward favorable estate and income tax treatment of plan distributions," by Kenneth C. Eliasberg, Esq., Estate Planning (7/83, p. 208); "Subtrusts and Reversionary Interests: A Review of Current Options," by I. Meyer Pincus, L.L.B., Journal of the American Society of CLU & ChFC (9/92, p. 64); "Excluding Qualified Plan Insured Incidental Death Benefits from the Participant's Gross Estate; Minority and Non-Stockholders," by Jonathan Davis, Esq., The Estates, Gifts and Trusts Journal (9-10/83, p.4); "Excluding Defined Benefit Plan

Insured Death Benefits from the Gross Estate -- Sole and Majority Shareholders," by Jonathan Davis, Esq., <u>Tax Management Compensation Planning Journal</u> (5/84, p. 123).

Chapter 7:   The Grandfather Rules

Chapter 8:   Disclaimers

See, generally, on disclaimers, the CCH *Federal Estate and Gift Tax Reporter* or the RIA *Federal Tax Coordinator 2d.*

Mary Wenig, Esq., *Disclaimers* (TMP 848), discusses disclaimers of community property at pp. A-43, A-45.

Chapter 9:   Special Topics

Charitable dispositions:

Roger L. Shumaker, Esq., and Michael G. Riley, Esq., "Strategies for Transferring Retirement Plan Death Benefits to Charity," 19 ACTEC Notes, no. 3, p. 162 (1993), and follow-up comments published in 20 ACTEC Notes, p. 22 (1994). Compares the economic effects of various ways of funding a $1 million charitable gift from a $4 million estate, including the use of retirement benefits.

Louis A. Mezzullo, Esq., "Using an IRA for Charitable Giving," March/April 1995 <u>Probate & Property</u>, the Journal of the ABA Section of Real Property, Probate and Trust Law, p. 41.

Zoe M. Hicks, Esq., "Charitable Remainder Trust may be more Advantageous than a Qualified Plan," <u>Estate Planning</u> (5-6/90, p. 158). This is not about estate planning for plan benefits, but rather about using a CRUT *instead of* a qualified plan as an accumulation/payout vehicle for retirement.

Jonathan G. Blattmachr, Esq., "Income in Respect of a Decedent," 12 <u>Probate Notes</u> 47 (1986). This excellent article discusses numerous strategies for reducing taxes on retirement benefits and other IRD, including charitable dispositions.

For the rules of charitable remainder trusts, read *The Harvard Manual on Tax Aspects of Charitable Giving (1992)*, by David M. Donaldson, Esq. and Carolyn M. Osteen, Esq. of Ropes and Gray, Boston, available from the Harvard University Office of Planned Giving (suggested donation of approximately $60), Cambridge, MA 02138.

REA, creditors' rights:

For an excellent discussion of the spousal consent requirements of REA, and of the status of retirement benefits as against claims of creditors, see Alson R. Martin, P.A., "Income and Estate Planning for Individuals with Qualified Retirement Plans and IRAs," in <u>How to Determine the Capital Necessary to Retire</u>, seminar materials published by ALI-ABA, 4025 Chestnut Street, Philadelphia, PA 19104-3099, 10/28/93, pages 107 to 114 and pages 116 to 122.

Glossary

This book assumes the reader is familiar with estate planning concepts and retirement plan terminology. The purpose of this Glossary is to provide brief definitions of terms in these specialized fields to accommodate readers who do not have expertise in both fields.

Bypass Trust. See "Credit Shelter Trust."

Charitable Remainder Trust. A trust which lasts for either a term of years or the life or lives of specified individuals. The term (or life) beneficiary(ies) are individuals and the remainder beneficiary is a charity (or several charities). Because of abuses of these so-called "split-interest trusts," Congress in 1969 amended the Code so that only certain types of rigidly defined charitable remainder trusts receive favorable tax treatment. These are, primarily, "charitable remainder annuity trusts" (under which the non-charitable beneficiary receives a fixed dollar amount every year) or "charitable remainder unitrusts" (under which the non-charitable beneficiary receives a fixed percentage of the value of the trust's assets each year). As used in this book, "charitable remainder trust" means a charitable remainder annuity trust or charitable remainder unitrust which complies with all of the detailed requirements of s. 664.

A "charitable remainder trust" pays no income tax (although the beneficiary may be subject to income tax on distributions from the trust). Also, the person who funds the trust receives either an estate tax deduction (if the transfer occurs at death) or an income and gift tax deduction (for lifetime transfers) for the value of the charitable remainder interest. For more information about this kind of trust, see the Bibliography under Chapter 9.

Credit Shelter Trust. The Code allows each person a tax credit of $192,400 which may be applied to gift or estate taxes owed by that person. To the extent the credit is not "used up" by lifetime transfers, it is available to shelter the person's estate from estate taxes. Because it may be applied to either gift or estate taxes, it is referred to as a "unified" credit.

A credit of $192,400 happens to be exactly equal to the estate tax on a taxable estate of $600,000. Accordingly, the effect of the credit is that each person can transfer up to $600,000 free of gift or estate taxes to his children, or any other beneficiary who is not the person's spouse or a charity. (Unlimited amounts may be transferred tax-free to the spouse and charitable beneficiaries.)

Basic tax-oriented estate planning for a husband and wife involves making sure that each spouse takes full advantage of his or her $600,000 "exemption." This is most commonly done by making sure that the first spouse to die leaves the first $600,000 of his or her estate either to the children directly, or (more popularly) to a trust. The surviving spouse may be a beneficiary of this trust, but does not have sufficient control over it to make it includable in the surviving spouse's estate. Thus, this $600,000 trust escapes estate tax at both deaths: it is not taxed in the first spouse's estate because it was sheltered by the decedent's unified credit; it is not taxed in the surviving spouse's estate because he or she does not own it.

Because these trusts take advantage of the fact that the first $600,000 of the first spouse's estate is "sheltered" by the "unified credit," it is usually referred to as a "credit shelter trust." It is sometimes also called a "bypass trust" because, even though the surviving spouse may be a beneficiary of the trust, it "bypasses" the surviving spouse's taxable estate and goes directly to the next generation tax-free.

403(b) plans. These plans (also called "tax-sheltered annuities"), are available only to tax-exempt employers.

As far as the employ*er* is concerned, these plans are quite different from qualified retirement plans in many respects, but these differences need not concern the estate planner. As far as the employ*ee* is concerned, these plans function similarly to any other qualified retirement plan in that the employee is not taxed currently on the contributions to the plan, or on the earnings inside the plan, but is taxed as distributions are made to him. However, there are some differences.

One difference from the employ*ee*'s perspective is that the plan assets will be solely in the name of the employee, like an IRA; once the employer has made its contribution, the employer generally has no further involvement. Another difference is that 403(b) money can be invested in only two types of investments: annuity contracts purchased by the employer and issued in the name of the employee; and "regulated investment companies" (mutual funds) that are held by a bank (or other approved institution) as custodian for the employee.

The main differences between 403(b) plans and other plans from a tax planning perspective are:

1.   A 403(b) plan distribution is never eligible for treatment as a "lump sum distribution" under s. 402(d). See Chapter 2.

2.   The minimum distribution rules apply differently. See Chapter 7, "The Grandfathers."

Generation Skipping Transfer (GST) Tax. The estate tax applies to all assets transferred by a decedent at death. The decedent's estate pays estate taxes, and then distributes whatever is left to the beneficiaries of the estate -- typically, to the decedent's children. In the normal course of events, the children themselves die some decades later and the same assets are taxed again before being passed along to the children's own children.

To avoid having assets be subject to estate taxes in every generation, a grandparent might leave assets directly to grandchildren (to "skip" the estate taxes at the child's generation level), or to a trust which would benefit the children's generation for their lifetimes but not be included in the children's estates. (Generally speaking, a trust is not includable in the estate of someone who is merely a life beneficiary of that trust.)

Generation skipping trusts are an important and valid way to reduce the estate tax burden on a family. Perceiving these as a tax-avoidance device, Congress enacted the Generation Skipping Transfer Tax. This extremely elaborate tax essentially allows each person to transfer up to $1 million in the form of "generation skipping transfers," but imposes a 55% tax on generation skipping transfers that exceed that limit.

Grantor Trust. Generally speaking, a trust is a separate taxpayer. It files its own tax returns and pays income tax on its income at special trust rates. (The only exception is that income distributed to the beneficiaries of the trust will normally be taxed at the beneficiary's rate rather than the trust's rate.)

However, in certain cases, the Code ignores the trust as a taxable entity and treats the income and deductions as belonging directly to the "grantor" (the person who contributed the money to the trust). The most obvious example is a "revocable living trust," under which the grantor can take the assets back any time he wants to. The Code just ignores the trust during the grantor's life and treats its income and deductions as belonging directly to the grantor. There are many less obvious examples, and quite a number of complicated rules under ss. 671-678, under which part or all of a trust's income may be taxable directly to the grantor (or even in some cases a beneficiary or a trustee).

Keogh plan. Also called "H.R.10 plans," these are simply qualified retirement plans adopted by self-employed persons. The term "Keogh plan" never appears in the Code; the name comes from the Congressman who sponsored legislation allowing the self employed to have retirement plans. At one time, the Code made numerous distinctions between Keogh plans which covered "owner-employees" (sole proprietors and 10% partners) and QRPs adopted by corporations (or other QRPs which covered only "common-law employees"). While TEFRA '82 ended most differences, a few distinctions still remain, particularly in the areas of plan loans (not covered in this book) and lump sum distributions (see Chapter 2).

Marital deduction. An unlimited estate tax deduction is allowed for property left by the decedent to his surviving spouse. To qualify for this "marital deduction," the property must be left to the spouse either outright or in certain particular forms of trust, one of which is called a "QTIP" trust. See Chapters 3 and 4.

Pecuniary bequest. A bequest or gift of a specific sum of money. A typical pecuniary bequest: "I bequeath the sum of $10,000 to my son." A pecuniary gift may be in the form of a formula which produces a specific dollar amount, such as: "The Trustee shall set aside, as a separate trust to be known as the Marital Trust, an amount of money or other property equal in value to the smallest amount necessary, if taken as a marital deduction, to eliminate the federal estate tax on my estate."

QTIP. A "qualified terminable interest property" trust is a special kind of trust that qualifies for the marital deduction. See Chapter 3.

Tax-sheltered Annuity. See "403(b) Plans."

Index

403(b) plan
Grandfather rules, 230
Incidental benefit rule, 231
Lump sum distributions, 84
Minimum distribution rules, 226, 230
Normal retirement age, 234
Planning considerations, 235, 237
Regulations, 230
Required beginning date, 235
Spousal rights, 136
4980A(d)(5) election
And spousal rollover, 109, 190, 194
Benefits paid to estate or trust, 192
By executor, 193
Case study, 302
Definition of de minimis, 191
Estate tax return, 189
In general, 188
Life insurance, 192
Marital trust, 191
Planning considerations, 189, 199
Regulations, 191
Requirements for, 190
Rollover of "grandfathered" amount, 190
Tax clause in will, 196
5% owners
Minimum distribution rules, 225
691(c) deduction
And "2% floor", 82
As an itemized deduction, 82
Charitable remainder trust, 81
Instalment and annuity payouts, 79
Lump sum distributions, 84
Adjusted gross income
Lump sum distributions, 93
Adoption
Minimum distribution rules, 21
After-tax contributions
15% excise tax and, 176, 181
Age 59½
10% tax on distributions, 279

Lump sum distributions, 85, 86
Rollover by spouse under, 270
Age 70½
Before 1988, 228, 230
Both spouses die before, 112, 133
Death after, one year rule, 36
Death before, 11, 270, 277
Divorce after, 46
Grandfather rules, 228
History, 224
Marriage after, 46
Minimum required distributions, 26
Rollover at, 101
Vs. actual retirement, 229
Vs. required beginning date, 47
Age 70½ year
Distribution for, 49
Age 75
403(b) plans, 234
Vs. actual retirement, 238
Annuity tables
Excess accumulations, 186, 187
Minimum distribution rules, 49
Assignment
Of benefits to living trust, 281
Of IRA , 274
At least as rapidly rule
History, 225
Basis in retirement plan
After-tax contributions, 66
Life insurance and, 204
No stepped up basis, 65
Pecuniary bequest funded with IRD, 76
Beneficiary designation
And "separate accounts" rule, 269
Changing after RBD, 43
Differing based on age at death, 33
Life insurance, 193, 221
Naming designated beneficiary, 13

Simultaneous death clause, 133, 135
Statute of Wills, 279
Bequest(s)
Funding with IRD, 72
Borrowing
On life insurance, 220
Capital gain
Lump sum distributions, 96, 99
Charitable remainder trust
And 691(c) deduction, 81
As beneficiary, in general, 265, 267
Case study, 316, 320
Funding with benefits during life, 273
Non-citizen spouse, 171
Planning considerations, 322
Charity
15% excise tax and, 196
As beneficiary of trust, 270
As beneficiary, in general, 265
As one of several beneficiaries, 18, 63, 267
As remainder beneficiary, 22, 276
IRD paid to, 70
Planning considerations, 269, 270, 272, 282
Pledges, 272
Cleanup strategies
4980A(d)(5) election, 191
Benefits paid to estate or trust, 118
Death before RBD, 24
Non-individual beneficiary, 19
Pecuniary bequest funded with IRD, 74
Spousal rollover , 106
Trust rules, 23, 322
Contingent beneficiary
Case study, 307
Importance of, 114
In case of disclaimer, 245
Cost of living adjustments
Excise tax threshold, 175
For 15% excise tax

"grandfathers", 182
Credit shelter trust
403(b) plans, 236
Case study, 284, 300, 304
Funding by disclaimer, 243, 245
Funding with insurance in plan, 221
Funding with IRD, 67, 102, 104, 129
Income tax on benefits paid to, 67
Minimum required distributions, 61
Non-citizen spouse, 170
Death benefits
15% excise tax and, 176, 189
Age 59½ requirement, 86
Five years participation requirement, 92
Lump sum distributions, 86
Paid to charity, 265
Rollover of, 100
Spousal rights, 136
Spousal rollover , 108
Death, as of the date of
And "separate accounts" rule, 268
Defined, 16
Trust rules, 22
Deduction
For estate tax on IRD, 78
Designated beneficiary
At RBD, 26
Benefits paid to charity, 271
Changing after RBD, 43, 310
Death after RBD, 43
Defined, 13
Disclaimers and, 255
Effect of elections, 48
Effect of having "no DB", 34, 43, 268, 321, 327
History, 225
How to compute life expectancy, 58
Importance of designated beneficiary, 62

Importance of, death before RBD, 12

More than one, pitfalls of , 17

Multiple beneficiaries, 59, 63, 313

Non-spouse as; MDIB rule, 39

Recalculating LE--how to compute, 59

Spouse as, when benefits paid to QTIP trust, 279

Trust as beneficiary (death before RBD), 20

Disability

Lump sum distributions, 85

Planning considerations, 280, 282

Disclaimer(s)

After RBD, 258

By fiduciaries, 246

Case study, 304, 320

Defined, 241

Drawbacks of, 246

ERISA aspects, 248

If charity is beneficiary, 272

Impact of REA, 250

Impact on "designated beneficiary", 255

Requirements of, 246

To enable spousal rollover, 244

To fund credit shelter, 243, 254

Uses of, 74, 243, 245

Distributable net income

And pecuniary formula bequest, 76

Described, 67

Paid to charity, 70

Divorce

After RBD, 46

Employee contributions

Lump sum distributions, 87

ERISA

Fiduciary rules, 201

Prohibited transaction, 207

Purchase from plan, 213

Estate

4980A(d)(5) election, 192

As beneficiary at RBD, 34

As beneficiary, case study, 327

As beneficiary: 5 year rule, 14, 24

As beneficiary: rollover, 116

Estate tax

And income tax, QDOT, 145, 160

Deduction for excess accumulations tax, 197

Estate tax exclusion for retirement benefits, 238

Income tax deduction for, 77

Life insurance and, 222

On life insurance, 217

Estate tax return

15% excise tax and, 186, 195

4980A(d)(5) election, 189

Estate trust

And minimum distribution rules, 152, 278

Non-citizen spouse, 151

Excess accumulations

Age, 186

Annuity tables, 186

Case study, 303, 327

Estate tax deduction for, 197

Excise tax threshold, 185

Grandfather rule, 194

How to compute, 193

In general, 174, 185

Interest rate, 187

Life insurance, 188, 192

No 691(c) deduction, 197

Option to defer 15% excise tax, 188

Planning considerations, 197

Excess distributions

Amounts excluded, 176

Defined, 175

In general, 174

Excise tax, 15%

4980A(d)(5) election, 189

691(c) deduction and, 77, 78

And alternate payee, 176

Attained age method, 184

Case study, 300, 323, 326

Charitable deduction, 196

Computation grandfather amount, 181

Cost of living adjustments, 175, 182

Death benefits, 176

Discretionary method, 183

Double exemption, 182

Estate tax return, 186, 195

Excess accumulations, 185

Grandfather rule, 179

How to compute, 187

In general, 174

Life insurance, 188, 214, 219

Lump sum distributions, 95, 176

Marital deduction, 196

Planning considerations, 184, 195, 197

Rollover of "grandfathered" amount, 190

Spouse's option to defer, 188, 190

Triple exemption, 194

Unified credit and, 196

Who pays, 195

Five year forward averaging
15% excise tax and, 178

For 15% excise tax "grandfathers", 184

How to calculate, 95

Five year rule
Deadline for distribution, 16

Defined, 11

Exceptions, 11

Simultaneous deaths of spouses, 133

Vs. life expectancy method, 12

Fractional bequest
And "separate accounts" rule, 268

Generation skipping
Case study, 312, 313, 315

Gift tax
Spousal waiver and, 252

Grandfather rules
10 year averaging, 96

15% excise tax and, 179, 305

403(b) plans, 230

Acceleration of recovery, 183

Attained age method, 184

Capital gain for LSD, 96

Computation grandfather amount, 183

Discretionary method, 183

Estate tax exclusion for retirement benefits, 238

Excess accumulations, 194

In general, 223

Lump sum distributions, 85, 87, 99, 182

Minimum distribution rules, 223

Planning considerations, 184, 185, 229, 240, 327

Rollover by non-spouse beneficiary, 240

Rollover of "grandfathered" amount, 182, 190

TEFRA 242(b) designation, 226

Grantor trust rules
And general power marital trust, 150

And QTIP-QDOT, 147

Disability, 281

IRA assigned to QDOT, 163

Non-citizen spouse, 148

Hardship distributions
Advantages of, 173

From QDOT, 139, 144

Incidental benefit rule
403(b) plans, 231

History, 233, 234

Life insurance and, 201, 205, 209

Planning considerations, 238

TEFRA 242(b) designation, 226

Income
Spousal rollover, 130

Trust accounting, 158

Income in respect of a decedent
Assignment of, 71, 73

Deduction for estate taxes on, 76, 79

Fractional bequest of, 71
General, 65
Paid to charity, 70, 81
Paid to trust or estate, 66, 68
Retirement benefits as, 65
Income tax
Benefits paid to charity, 265
Benefits paid to QTIP trust, 132, 294
Charitable remainder trust, 81
Deferral, by spousal rollover, 105
Deferral, marital trust, 129, 131
Deferral, multiple IRAs, 61
General, 65
Non-citizen spouse, 144
On fulfilment of charitable pledge, 273
On life insurance, 202
On life insurance proceeds, 209
On principal paid to trust, 150
Second to die insurance, 220
Income tax deferral
QDOT-IRA, 156
Installment payout
Effect on 691(c) deduction, 79
IRA
Assignment, 163
Assignment to charity, 274
Election to treat decedent's IRA as spouse's IRA, 113
Inherited, 112
Lump sum distributions, 84
Minimum distribution rules, 113
Multiple plans or IRAs, 59
Spousal rights, 136
Transfers between IRAs after RBD, 61
IRD, deduction for estate tax
Non-citizen spouse, 147, 170
Keogh plans
Lump sum distributions, 84
Minimum distribution rules, 224
Key employee
Minimum distribution rules, 224
Life expectancy
Participant and spouse, 119

Life expectancy method
At RBD, 26
Case study, 328
Financial value of, 12
Fixed term method, 35
How it works, 14
How to compute, 48
If charity is beneficiary, 271
Joint, how to compute, 53
Participant and spouse, 28
Recalculation election, 27, 35
Life insurance, 201
4980A(d)(5) election, 192
At retirement, 204
Basis in, 204
Beneficiary designation, 193
Case study, 298
Estate tax issues, 210
Excess accumulations, 188
Funding credit shelter trust with, 221
Income tax, beneficiary, 209
Income tax, employee, 202, 205
No rollover of, 108, 205
Prohibited transaction, 207
Purchase from plan, 207
Reasons to buy in plan, 216
Sale of policy at retirement, 212
Second to die insurance, 217
Subtrust, 211
To reduce 15% tax, 216
Living trust
Charity as beneficiary of, 270
Disability, 281
Must be irrevocable at 70½ , 30
Planning considerations, 270
Lump sum distributions, 83
"Participation" defined, 91
10 year averaging, 96
15% excise tax and, 95, 176, 182
5 year averaging, 95
Age 59½ requirement, 86
Aggregation of employers, 91
Aggregation of plans, 91
Benefits of, 93

Case study, 295
Definition, 87
Disability, 85
Double exemption, 182
Effect of prior rollover, 92, 108
Effect on itemized deductions, 94
Exclusion from AGI, 94
Five years participation
    requirement, 91
For 15% excise tax
    "grandfathers", 182
Grandfather rules, 85, 96
Planning considerations, 178
Plans eligible, 84
Reason for, 85
Regulations, 83
Rollover disqualifying, 93
Self-employed, 85
Marital deduction
15% excise tax and, 196
Benefits paid to QTIP trust, 122,
    124, 291
Estate trust, 151
Income distribution requirement,
    128
Non-citizen spouse, 138
Regulations, 127
Trusts that qualify for, 143
Marital trust
4980A(d)(5) election, 191
Contrast rollover, 131
Determining "beneficiaries" of
    trust, 278
Funding with IRD, 102
Income distribution requirement,
    125
Minimum distribution rules, 121,
    131, 133, 277
Minimum required distribution,
    128
Pecuniary formula pitfall, 74
QDOT, 149
Marriage
After RBD, 46
Second, case study, 290
MDIB rule

Contrast "at least as rapidly"
    rule, 40
Contrast incidental benefit rule ,
    232
Disappearance at P's death, 40
How to compute, 39, 56
In general, 39
Planning considerations, 42
Year of death, 57
Minimum distribution rules
403(b) plans, 230
And "separate accounts" rule,
    18, 268
At RBD, 26
Benefits paid to QTIP trust, 293
Benefits paid to trust, 19, 278
Death after RBD, one year rule,
    36
Determining "beneficiaries" of
    trust, 275
Disclaimers and, 256
Effect of spousal rollover, 105
Estate as beneficiary at the
    RBD, 34
Estate trust, 152
Grandfather rules, 223, 229
History, 224
Importance of designated
    beneficiary, 13
IRAs, 113
Life expectancy payout, 14
Marital trust, 131
Marital trust vs. spouse
    individually, 277
MDIB rule, 39
Multiple beneficiaries, 16, 270
Multiple plans or IRAs, 59
Non-citizen spouse, 161
P.S. 58 cost and, 220
Penalty for failure to comply, 9
Planning considerations, 10, 62
Purpose, 9
Recalculation election, 35
Regulations , 10
Spousal rollover, 194
Surviving spouse, 119

Trust as beneficiary (at RBD), 29, 246
Trust beneficiary as (death before RBD), 19
Using single life expectancy despite having a DB, 48
Minimum required distribution
403(b) plans, 235
Account balance, 50
Age 70½ year, 49, 101
Deadline for taking, 15
Death before RBD, how to compute, 58
Effect on rollovers, 101
Fixed term method, 2 lives, 53
Fixed term method, one life, 49
How to compute, 49
Marital trust, 128
MDIB rule, how to compute, 56
Multiple plans or IRAs, 59
No rollover of, 100, 110
Recalculating LE--how to compute, 51
Split method, how to compute, 55
Vs. 15% excise "threshold", 51
Withdrawing more than, 15, 49, 306, 327
Year of death, 57, 58, 110
Non-assignable property
Inherited by alien spouse, 140
Non-citizen spouse
Deduction for estate tax on IRD, 147
Non-assignable assets, 166
Non-spouse beneficiary
Planning considerations, 42
Rollover by, 240
Non-taxable distributions
No rollover of, 100, 108
Normal retirement age
403(b) plans, 234
Notice 88-38
Multiple plans or IRAs, 59
Planning considerations, 60
One year rule
Death after RBD, 36, 55

P.S. 58 cost
10% penalty and, 220
After retirement, 209
Explained, 203
Income tax, employee, 203
Minimum distributions and, 220
Second to die insurance, 203
Participation, year of
Lump sum distributions, 98
What constitutes, 91, 97, 98
Pecuniary bequest or formula
And "separate accounts" rule, 18, 268
And IRD, 102
Pitfall of funding with IRD, 74, 132
Penalty on premature distributions
P.S. 58 cost and, 220
Penalty tax, 50%
Waiver of, 10
Plan provisions
Designating beneficiary, 14
Limiting payout options, 48
Recalculation election, 59
Power of attorney
Planning considerations, 281
Premature distributions
10% tax on distributions, 279
Spousal rollover, 109
Probate issues
In general, 279
Prohibited transaction
Purchase from plan, 213
QDOT
Created by surviving spouse, 143
Definition, 141
How it works, 139
IRA combined with, 153
Non-taxable distributions, 144
Postponing MRD to P's age 70½, 278
Significance of, 138
Tax on death of spouse, 160
QDOT-IRA

Advantages of, 155
Choice of trustee, 154, 162
QDRO
15% excise tax and, 176
Grandfather rule, 181
QJSA, 251
QPSA, 251
QTIP
As beneficiary, 291
Election, 128
Marital deduction for benefits paid
to, 122, 124
Minimum distribution rules, 279
QTIP trust, 129
Spousal rollover , 118
Recalculation of life expectancy
Advantages, 35
Benefits paid to charity, 272
Benefits paid to trust, 134
Case study, 309, 321
Compared with fixed term, 35
Drawbacks, 35
Effect of death, 54
Effect of having "no DB", 327
Election at RBD, 27, 35
History, 225
How to compute, 51, 54
How to make the election, 38
Non-spouse beneficiary, 41
Planning considerations, 36, 41
Split method, explained, 37, 55
Regulations
403(b) plans, 230
4980A(d)(5) election, 191
Marital deduction, 127
Minimum distribution rules, 10,
113, 268
Remainder beneficiary
Minimum distribution rules, 276,
282
Required beginning date
403(b) plans, 235
Benefits paid to charity, 271
Changing DB after, 43
Death before, 270
Defined, 10, 26

Divorce after, 46
Importance of, 62
Living until vs. death before, 26
Marriage after, 46
Planning choices after, 44, 309,
320
Planning considerations, 27
Recalculation election, 38
Spousal rollover after, 116
Transfers between IRAs after
RBD, 61
Vs. age 70½ , 47
Retirement Equity Act
Described, 251
Disclaimers and, 250
In general, 136
Plans affected, 251
Spousal waiver, gift tax, 252
Rollout
And 3 year rule, 212
Income tax, employee, 205
Of insurance at retirement, 204
Rollover
15% excise tax and, 179
After age 70½ , 115
Benefit paid to estate, 116
Benefits paid to trust, 117
By non-spouse beneficiary, 240
By spouse's executor, 114, 135
Case study, 295
Deadline for making, 111
Death benefits, 100
Disclaimer to enable, 244
Effect on lump sum distribution
treatment, 92, 93
For 15% excise tax
"grandfathers", 182
In general, 100
In post mortem planning, 106
Life insurance and, 205
Minimum required distribution,
101, 110
Non-taxable distributions, 100
Of trust income, 161
Partial distribution, 109
Plans eligible, 100

Pre age 59½ , 280
Regulations, 100
Series of substantially equal
    payments, 100, 108
Spousal, 105, 130
Spousal, after P's RBD, 44, 311
Spousal, and 15% excise tax, 190,
    194
Spousal, to QDOT-IRA, 153
Spouse under age 59½ , 269
To another IRA in name of
    decedent, 109, 114
Vs. deferring distributions to
    decedent's age 70½ , 120
Vs. election to treat decedent's
    IRA as spouse's, 112
Ruling, getting IRS, 25
Second-to-die insurance
15% excise tax and, 219
Self-employed
Lump sum distributions, 85
Separation from service
10% tax on distributions, 280
Estate tax exclusion for retirement
    benefits, 239
Lump sum distributions, 85
Simultaneous death
4980A(d)(5) election, 193
After age 70½ , 135
Planning considerations, 132, 311
Slayer statute, 249
Spouse
As beneficiary, advantages, 104,
    285
As DB at age 70½ , 28
Election to treat decedent's IRA
    as spouse's IRA, 112
Marital trust vs. spouse
    individually, 277
New, after RBD, 46
Non-citizen, 138
Option to defer 15% excise tax,
    188
Postponing MRD to P's age 70½,
    277
Spouse under age 59½, 269

Vs. marital trust, as beneficiary,
    122
Statute of Wills
Vs. IRA beneficiary designation
    , 279
Subtrust
Estate tax issues, 222
Holding life insurance, 211
TAMRA '88
Grandfather rules, 229
Tax clause in will
15% excise tax and, 196
Tax Reform Act of 1984
Estate tax exclusion for
    retirement benefits, 238
Minimum distribution rules,
    225
Tax Reform Act of 1986
403(b) plans, 230
Estate tax exclusion for
    retirement benefits, 238
Grandfather rules, 229, 238
Minimum distribution rules,
    226
TEFRA
Estate tax exclusion for
    retirement benefits, 238
Minimum distribution rules,
    224
Planning considerations, 228
TEFRA 242(b) designation,
    226
Ten year forward averaging
How to calculate, 96
Term insurance
Income tax, employee, 202
Threshold amount
Effect of interest rate changes,
    187
Excess accumulations, 185, 194
Excess distributions tax, 175
For 15% excise tax
    "grandfathers", 180
Lump sum distributions, 176
Transfer for value
Purchase from plan, 212

Trust accounting
   "Principal" as taxable income, 68
   Charitable remainder trust, 81
   Principal, 167
   QDOT-IRA, 159
**Trust rules, minimum
       distribution**
   At RBD, 29
   Beneficiaries must be individuals,
       270, 271
   Benefits of, 23
   Case study, 320
   Charitable remainder, 22
   Death before RBD, 20
   Definition of beneficiary, 275
   Must be irrevocable at 70½, 27
   Planning considerations, 23, 31
   Purpose, 34
Trust, marital deduction
   Types of, 142
Trust(s)

   As DB at age 70½, 29, 320
   Definition of beneficiary, 275
   Income tax rates of, 66, 102
   Irrevocability requirement, 27,
       31, 246
   Minimum distribution rules, 19
   Must be irrevocable at 70 ½, 29
   Naming as beneficiary after
       RBD, 46
   Rollover of benefits paid to, 117
   Who are beneficiaries of, 21
Trustee, choice of
   QDOT-IRA, 154
UCA 1992
   Effect on rollovers, 100, 280
Unified credit
   15% excise tax and, 196
Will(s)
   Vs. IRA beneficiary
       designation, 279